A BARK BUT
NO BITE

INEQUALITY AND THE 2014
NEW ZEALAND GENERAL ELECTION

JACK VOWLES, HILDE COFFÉ
AND JENNIFER CURTIN

Australian
National
University

PRESS

ANU PRESS

Published by ANU Press
The Australian National University
Acton ACT 2601, Australia
Email: anupress@anu.edu.au
This title is also available online at press.anu.edu.au

National Library of Australia Cataloguing-in-Publication entry

Creator: Vowles, Jack, 1950- author.

Title: A bark but no bite : inequality and the 2014 New Zealand
             general election / Jack Vowles, Hilde Coffé,
             Jennifer Curtin.

ISBN: 9781760461355 (paperback) 9781760461362 (ebook)

Subjects: New Zealand. Parliament--Elections, 2014.
             Elections--New Zealand.
             New Zealand--Politics and government--21st century.

Other Creators/Contributors:
             Coffé, Hilde, author.
             Curtin, Jennifer C, author.

Cover design and layout by ANU Press

Contents

List of figures

List of tables

List of acronyms

CEO	chief executive officer
CNN	Cable News Network
COMPASS	Centre of Methods and Policy Application in the Social Sciences
ETS	Emissions Trading Scheme
GCSB	Government Communications Security Bureau
GFC	global financial crisis
GST	goods and services tax
HSBC	Hong Kong and Shanghai Banking Corporation
IMF	International Monetary Fund
MBIE	Ministry of Business, Innovation and Employment
MMP	Mixed Member Proportional
MP	Member of Parliament
N	Number of respondents
NZES	New Zealand Election Study
OECD	Organisation of Economic Co-operation and Development
OIA	Official Information Act
SFO	Serious Fraud Office
SIS	Security Intelligence Service
SWIID	Standardized World Income Inequality Database
TVNZ	Television New Zealand
UK	United Kingdom
US	United States

Preface and acknowledgements

This book has a dual purpose: to provide an account of the 2014 general election in New Zealand, and to inquire into the implications of social and economic inequality as a matter of political party contest in that country. We chose the latter as a theme both because of its importance nationally and internationally, and because it posed a puzzle. Adapting a metaphor from a famous Sherlock Holmes story, during the 2014 election campaign, inequality was a dog that barked but did not bite. On the basis of well-known assumptions, its salience in the campaign should have benefited the centre-left, but did not. In a nutshell, this was our starting point.

This book is a collaboration by three authors, all principal researchers of the 2014 New Zealand Election Study (NZES). We want to gratefully acknowledge the contributions of others, both financial and in kind. Our funding came from three main sources: Victoria University of Wellington, the New Zealand Electoral Commission and the University of Auckland. We particularly thank Robert Peden, Anastasia Turnbull, Kristina Temmel and Robert Marsh of the Electoral Commission. Working with them all has been a pleasure. More particular thanks go to Gerald Cotterell and Martin von Randow at the University of Auckland's Centre of Methods and Policy Application in the Social Sciences (COMPASS). COMPASS was responsible for administering the NZES fieldwork and did so smoothly and efficiently. The COMPASS commitment to the NZES is much appreciated, and invaluable. Gerry Cotterell was another principal researcher, and his NZES-related research is the subject of a separate Marsden Fund project. Ann Sullivan, Lindsey MacDonald and Brian Easton read sections of the manuscript. Within Victoria University, Sam Bigwood helped us with tidying up the manuscript, the figures, the tables and the references. Simon Hay was a meticulous copyeditor, vigilantly detecting errors everyone else had missed and helpfully pointing out how we might better clarify otherwise cryptic or confusing sentences.

Frank Bongiorno, the chair of the ANU Press Social Sciences Editorial Board, guided us smoothly through the review process. We also thank the two reviewers and the members of the ANU Press Social Sciences Board, who together gave us some extremely helpful comments and suggestions for improvement that indicated their deep engagement with the manuscript. The authors remain responsible for any remaining flaws in this book, but are most grateful to those who helped us improve it. Finally, we thank the 2,835 randomly selected people who answered and returned our questionnaire. Our gratitude for their participation is enormous. Without them, this book could not have been written.

Jack Vowles
Hilde Coffé
Jennnifer Curtin

1

The 2014 New Zealand election in perspective

The central theme of this book is how and why social and economic inequality affected the campaign and the outcome of the 2014 general election in New Zealand. Discourse about inequality before and during the campaign posed a puzzle that is our main focus of inquiry: according to the assumptions of many observers, the discussion should have benefited the centre-left, but did not. While the distribution of wealth and income is not a new theme in New Zealand politics, and while differences between social groups have always been at the root of party choice in New Zealand, this may well have been the first election since the 1940s in which social and economic equality, expressed as a principle, was seen to play such an explicit role. Yet it had so few apparent consequences.

This is the puzzle central to our book. As explained in Chapter 3, an important strand of theory in political economy suggests that increasing levels of inequality, if real, should push more people to the left in their party choices, since left-wing parties are expected to do more than others to redistribute income and wealth. But some argue to the contrary in the form of a disempowerment hypothesis: that increasing inequality may instead suppress political engagement among those who are most adversely affected. Inequality is a lively topic in political science, particularly in the United States, where levels of inequality are among the highest in the developed world (Bartels 2008, 2016; Schlozman, Verba and Brady 2012). Indeed, the American Political Science Association commissioned a special report on the matter in 2001 (Task Force on Inequality and American Democracy 2004). Theories and current debates within political science frame much of our inquiry. In particular, we consider one influential brand of theory that 'solves' the puzzle because it assumes ordinary people think little about 'issues' and respond more in their political behaviour by way of their emotions, group loyalties and perceptions about government competence. While this 'solution' is partly correct, we argue that it is not entirely so.

Because inequality 'barked but did not bite' at the 2014 election, we describe it not as 'an inequality election', but instead as an 'unequal election'. The election was 'unequal' for three reasons. First, and most of all, like many other post-industrial democracies, in 2014 New Zealand was a more unequal society than it had been 30 years earlier, and debate was emerging about what could and should be done about it. Second, the election itself was unequal in the sense that the centre-right National Party was by far the largest party in votes cast and seats won, and had a further advantage by having much more money than its rivals to spend on its campaign and its activities in general. Third, the election was unequal since despite discussions about declining class voting in most post-industrialised societies, economic inequalities continued to underpin the social foundations of voting choices between the parties. These economic inequalities and their associated patterns of vote choice are also crosscut and intensified by social inequalities between women and men and between ethnic groups, most notably between indigenous Māori and the European or Pākehā majority.[1]

This chapter begins our inquiries. It first describes the historical context, the election results and the government that formed as a result, the flows of the votes between the 2011 and 2014 elections, and party policy positions. Next, it explores the issues voters considered most salient in the 2014 election. We are particularly interested in knowing how important the issue of inequality was to voters, and which parties they considered best able to address it.

Reviewing the results

The 2014 General Election in New Zealand was the country's seventh election under the Mixed Member Proportional (MMP) electoral system, and resulted in a third consecutive victory for the New Zealand National Party. The result was not unexpected. The National Party has been the

---

1   Pākehā is the Māori name for New Zealanders of European descent.

country's most successful political party since 1949, and has never held office for less than three consecutive parliamentary terms. Indeed, prior to 1972, its two experiences of government were underpinned by four successful elections in a row.

On the morning after the 2014 election, national media were proclaiming National's win as a triumphant and historically significant 'landslide'. Several commentators considered the 2014 result remarkable, in part because National's share of the vote increased marginally on election night and the party increased its share of parliamentary seats—although as it turned out, only by one. After the initial count, it appeared the election had broken three records. First, on election night figures National had won 61 seats; sufficient seats to govern alone, a rare event in any proportional representation system. This would have been a new experience in New Zealand's history of MMP. Even Germany has only experienced a single party majority government once, in 1957, and MMP has been that country's electoral system since 1949. Second, National had apparently increased its vote share, unusual for an incumbent government gaining its third term of office. Third, the centre-left Labour Party's vote share was the lowest since 1922.

Neither of the first two 'records' stood up more than a few days. On election night, it looked as if the National Party's winning vote share would be 48 per cent; larger than its vote shares in 2008 and 2011. This would have been the first time that a third-term government had increased its margin in almost 90 years. As can be seen from Table 1.1, at the final count including special votes, National's party vote was 47 per cent, 0.3 per cent less than in 2011, but 3 per cent more than when it first won government in 2008.[2] Its seat count fell to 60, one seat short of an absolute majority.[3]

---

2   Special votes are those cast outside the electorate in which a person is enrolled, and include votes from overseas. These votes are sent to the electorate of enrolment for counting, delaying the final count for several days.
3   New Zealand's MMP electoral system is a 'compensatory' form of the mixed member type. In 2014, there were 71 electorate seats and 50 list seats. The party vote is used to calculate the seat allocations per party, on which basis list seats are allocated to 'top up' each party's seats to that number. There is a threshold for parliamentary representation that can be crossed in two ways: either by gaining 5 per cent or more of the party vote, or by winning one or more electorate seats. In 2014, an extra list seat was added because Peter Dunne won an electorate seat and therefore crossed the threshold, but his party, United Future, failed to win enough party votes to justify even one seat on the basis of party vote. In this situation of 'overhang', the number of list seats can be augmented for the purpose of adjustment. There were also overhang seats in 2005, 2008 and 2011 elections, in these cases adjusting for the Māori Party's electorate seats. The 'normal' size of the House of Representatives is 120.

The third record did stand, and was sobering for those on the left. The Labour Party's vote share dropped to 25 per cent. Even when Helen Clark's Labour-led government was defeated in 2008 after three terms in office, its vote had been 9 percentage points higher. In the end, Labour's count of electorate seats increased from 22 in 2011 to 27 in 2014, but Labour's number of list seats more than halved: from 12 in 2011 to five in 2014.

Table 1.1: The party and electorate votes, New Zealand elections, 2008–2014

	2008		2011		2014	
	% Vote	Seats	% Vote	Seats	% Vote	Seats
National Party (total seats)		58		59		60
Party Vote (list seats)	44.9	17	47.3	17	47.0	19
Electorate Vote (seats)	46.6	41	47.3	42	46.1	41
Labour Party (total seats)		43		34		32
Party Vote (list seats)	34.0	22	27.5	12	25.1	5
Electorate Vote (seats)	35.2	21	35.1	22	34.1	27
Green Party (total seats)		9		14		14
Party Vote (list seats)	6.7	9	11.1	14	10.7	14
Electorate Vote (seats)	5.6	0	7.2	0	7.1	0
NZ First Party (total seats)		0		8		11
Party Vote (list seats)	4.1	0	6.6	8	8.7	11
Electorate Vote (seats)	1.7	0	1.8	0	3.1	0
Conservative (total seats)	-	-		0		0
Party Vote (list seats)			2.7	0	4.0	0
Electorate Vote (seats)			2.4	0	3.5	0
MANA/Internet-MANA[1]	-	-		1		0
Party Vote (list seats)			1.1	0	1.4	0
Electorate Vote (seats)			1.4	1	1.7	0
Māori Party (total seats)		5		3		2
Party Vote (list seats)	2.4	0	1.4	0	1.3	1
Electorate Vote (seats)	3.3	5	1.8	3	1.8	1
ACT (total seats)[2]		5		1		1
Party Vote (list seats)	3.7	4	1.1	0	0.7	0
Electorate Vote (seats)	3.0	1	1.4	1	1.2	1
United Future (total seats)		1		1		1
Party Vote (list seats)	0.9	0	0.6	0	0.2	0
Electorate Vote (seats)	1.1	1	0.9	1	0.6	1

	2008		2011		2014	
	% Vote	Seats	% Vote	Seats	% Vote	Seats
Jim Anderton's Progressive		1	-	-	-	-
Party Vote (list seats)	0.9	0				
Electorate Vote (seats)	1.1	1				
Others (total seats)		0		0		0
Party Vote (list seats)	2.8	0	0.7	0	0.9	0
Electorate Vote (seats)	2.1	0	0.2	0	0.9	0
Total		122		121		121

Note: Full results can be found on the New Zealand Electoral Commission's results pages for the 2008, 2011, and 2014 elections (Electoral Commission 2008, 2011, 2014a). Seat shares for the ACT, Māori, United Future, MANA, and Jim Anderton's Progressive parties come from their capture of at least one electorate seat, allowing them to cross the threshold for representation under MMP without the 5 per cent otherwise required in the party vote. In 2008, New Zealand First failed to cross the threshold by either means.

[1] MANA alone in 2011. In 2014, MANA formed an electoral alliance with the Internet Party for the party vote, with the two parties running individually in some electorate seats.

[2] ACT began as the Association of Consumers and Taxpayers, it derives it current name from this original party.

The Green Party retained the 14 list seats it had won in 2011, but made no gains. The populist New Zealand First Party increased its number of list seats: from eight in 2011 to 11 in 2014. Of the small parties, the Māori Party lost one seat, leaving only two representatives in parliament (one list and one electorate MP). Neo-liberal ACT and centre-liberal United Future each won one electorate seat, both of which they had held in 2011. Neither the Conservative Party nor the left-wing Internet-MANA alliance crossed the threshold for representation, failing to attain 5 per cent of the party vote and not winning an electorate seat.

However, the presence of Internet-MANA did matter to the campaign and to the results. Contesting extradition to the United States for alleged intellectual property theft, German internet entrepreneur Kim Dotcom had helped to create and fund the Internet Party. The party campaigned against breaches of privacy and civil liberties and against mass surveillance, and sought to mobilise the young. It formed an alliance with the MANA Movement that championed left-leaning policies on Māori self-determination, poverty reduction, wage equality and tertiary education reform. Although the policies had some support, this two-party alliance was unable to disentangle itself from Dotcom. Many voters appeared nervous about his political motives and National played to these fears, relentlessly suggesting that Internet-MANA could create havoc if it held pivotal seats backing a centre-left coalition.

As with all elections, the 2014 electoral contest exhibited other unique features. The campaign was disrupted by the publication of the book *Dirty Politics* (Hager 2014), which alleged that ministers and officials serving the National government were engaged in apparently dirty tactics. Labelled by the US-based broadcaster CNN as describing a South Pacific 'House of Cards', the book made headlines for two weeks of the campaign and was a potential disaster for the National-led government (Hume 2014). The furore that resulted drew attention away from policy and issue debates for two weeks. But, for the most part, it was campaign business more or less as usual. There was a continued focus on the economy, understandable in the wake of the global financial crisis (GFC); however, as we shall see later in this chapter, traditional concerns like health and education moved into the background. Instead, the issue of inequality emerged to apparently replace them.

Government formation took place smoothly in the days after the election. Government party composition remained the same as that after the previous two elections in 2008 and 2011. Formally, the government can be classified as of minority single-party status, as it has a Cabinet entirely composed of National Party MPs. The government's parliamentary majority on matters of confidence and supply is secured by agreements with the ACT, United Future and Māori parties. United Future MP Peter Dunne and Māori Party leader Te Ururoa Flavell were appointed to ministerial positions outside Cabinet, and ACT MP David Seymour as a Parliamentary Under-Secretary.

Despite the over-excited commentary of some media personalities on election night, the 2014 election was no 'landslide'. From the official party vote data displayed in Table 1.1, one can calculate aggregate net vote shifts: they were just under 6 per cent between the parties in 2014 and 2011, the smallest since 1963, and the third smallest since 1908 (Vowles 2014b: 34).[4] Of course, the changes in vote shares recorded in the official results conceal considerable movement among individuals, and examination of shifts at the individual level uncovers much more information about the movements of votes between the 2011 and 2014 elections. Indeed, much of our later analysis attempts to separate out the behaviour of those who stayed with the same parties, and those who shifted their votes.

---

4   One simply calculates the differences between each party's vote share in 2014 and 2011, adds them together, and divides by two.

Table 1.2: Flow of the party votes, 2011–2014 (total percentages)

2011 Vote	2014 Vote								
	No Vote	Labour	National	Green	NZ First	Māori Party	Conservative	Other	Total
No Vote	12.6	2.7	5.1	1.5	2.8	0.2	0.5	0.4	25.9
Labour	2.7	12.5	1.5	1.7	1.3	0.1	0.4	0.3	20.4
National	5.5	0.6	26.6	0.7	0.7	0.2	0.7	0.2	35.1
Green	0.5	2.0	0.9	3.8	0.8	0.0	0.2	0.1	8.2
NZ First	0.7	1.1	0.5	0.1	2.2	0.1	0.2	0.1	4.9
Māori	0.2	0.1	0.2	0.0	0.1	0.3	0.0	0.0	0.9
Conservative	0.5	0.0	0.4	0.1	0.2	0.0	0.7	0.2	2.0
Other	0.6	0.4	0.7	0.3	0.1	0.3	0.1	0.5	2.8
Total	23.3	19.2	36.0	8.2	8.0	0.9	2.7	1.8	100.0

Notes: Percentages are of the total. N=1,313. Cell and marginal percentages do not add up exactly to 100 due to rounding.

Source: New Zealand Election Study 2014. The data is weighted to conform with voting and non-voting patterns in 2011 and 2014.

We draw this information from the New Zealand Election Study (NZES), which is our main source of data for this book. As explained in more detail later in this chapter, the NZES is based on a random sample of eligible voters, taken from the electoral rolls. Part of the NZES sample goes back to people who responded at the previous election, and merges the responses at time t (the election in question) and $t - 1$ (the election before). This means that we can construct a panel containing responses from both elections—in this case, 2011 and 2014. The NZES also asks people in 2014 how they voted in 2011, but there is a great deal of evidence that too many people misremember their previous behaviour. Using data from the panel avoids this recall error problem. NZES data is also validated: whether respondents voted or not was checked against official data at each election, further reducing error.

Table 1.2 lays out how votes flowed between the two elections among NZES panel respondents. It is important to note that numbers of respondents in many of the cells in the table are very small, so any inferences we might draw from those cells or even from combinations of cells must be cautious at best. Shaded cells indicate the voters who made the same voting choice in both elections. Of the entire electorate (those enrolled to vote), 46 per cent remained true to their previous party. Of those who did vote in 2014, 39 per cent made a different choice than they did in 2011. That could include a shift from not voting in 2011 to voting in 2014. This individual-level volatility is very similar to that of 2008 and 2011, but much lower than that of 2005 and 2002; the latter two elections being marked by the highest levels of individual-level vote shifts in New Zealand elections since 1935. The individual-level volatility does indicate considerable 'churning': people moved between parties, but many offset each other by going in opposite directions.

The results of the election were not unexpected. National Party prime minister John Key had experienced exceptionally high leadership ratings in polls in the six years leading up to the 2014 election. In July 2014, according to one Digipoll survey, his popularity stood at 73 per cent (Curia 2014). His ratings remained resilient despite the publication of *Dirty Politics*, even when the fallout from that book indirectly claimed the scalp of cabinet minister Judith Collins three weeks before the election. Indeed, Key's rating a week before the election, at 61 per cent, was still almost 45 points ahead of his closest rival, Labour's David Cunliffe

(James 2015). By contrast, Labour had endured several leadership challenges in the years since Clark retired, with limited electoral success; indeed, after each change, the party's polling mostly got worse. As in most parliamentary elections around the world, the pulling power of effective leadership is very important.

Alongside this, Key has presided over a long period of relatively slow but steady economic growth as New Zealand recovered from the effects of the GFC. While theories of voting that highlight economic factors may no longer have the same explanatory capacity as once thought, the National government had overseen an economy in which 'middle New Zealand' felt comfortable. In the first quarter of 2009, the annual growth rate reached a record low of −3.4 per cent, but the economy emerged from this trough to reach 3.9 per cent in the second quarter of 2014. A week before the election, New Zealand's biggest circulation daily newspaper, the *New Zealand Herald*, published a survey of corporate chief executive officers (CEOs): the 'Mood of the Boardroom'. It revealed that 97 per cent of the 114 CEOs questioned supported a National government (*New Zealand Herald* 2014). Housing affordability and increasing inequality might have played on some voters' minds, but many observers and commentators find it puzzling that these problems did not dent National's claim to be the party of good economic management. In John Key's own words, the National Party had 'hugged the centre ground' (Foley 2014). Key's government had done its utmost to appeal to the median voter—the person in the middle if all voters were to be lined up from left to right.

The distribution of voters along this left–right continuum is therefore the next port of call for analysis. As the left is traditionally identified with efforts to reduce inequality, and the right tends to resist them, this returns us to the main theme of this book. Since 1990, the NZES has asked survey respondents to position themselves and the political parties on the left–right scale with most left at 0 and most right at 10. This way of estimating people's ideological positions can be criticised, as it is a very general measure and not everyone thinks in this left–right way. But many do, and assign themselves accordingly.

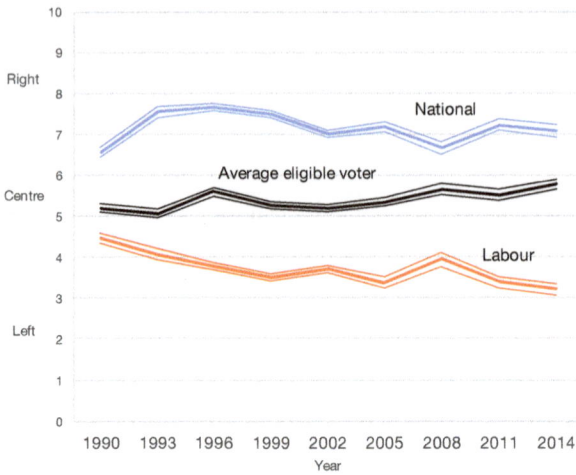

Figure 1.1: Eligible voters and their ratings of the National and Labour parties on the left–right scale, 1990–2014

Note: Average ratings with 95 per cent confidence intervals.

Source: New Zealand Election Study 1990, 1993, 1996, 1999, 2002, 2005, 2008, 2011, 2014.

A time series since 1990 shows distinct trends among those able and willing to rate themselves and the parties on a left–right continuum. The starting point of 1990 represents an unusual election, a moment when the National Party presented itself as closer to the centre than it turned out to be once it took office, after Labour had moved significantly to the right in its social and economic policies during the 1980s. In 1993 and 1996, National was placed above 7.7 on the left–right scale. By 2008, according to the NZES respondents, the party had moved closer to the centre at 6.7. Meanwhile, NZES respondents have perceived the Labour Party to have moved steadily to the left, except for temporary minor rightward shifts in 2002 and 2008. Respondents themselves have moved to the right, from an average of 5.1 in 1990 on the scale to nearly 5.9 in 2014. Respondent evaluations reflect general impressions rather than intense study of party promises and policies, but such impressions are important. Content analysis of party promises also confirms Labour's shift to the left post-1990, although National's movement to the centre is not so apparent (Gibbons 2011: 53). As in all figures drawing on NZES data, we show 95 per cent confidence intervals.[5]

---

5   This means that for every 20 samples we might have hypothetically drawn for our survey, we would expect 19 of them to produce estimates within those intervals. Where confidence intervals between estimates of interest overlap, we can be less certain of our findings even though the estimates themselves are different. Small overlaps may still be reported as statistically significant in the tables from which they are derived in the Appendix to this book, in which case we cannot entirely dismiss the evidence and our interpretation becomes a matter of judgement.

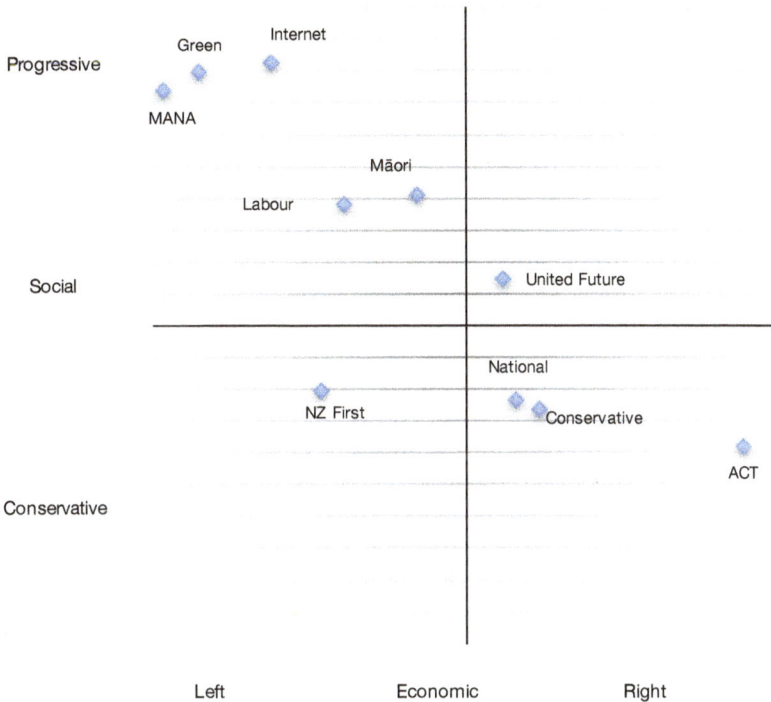

Figure 1.2: Party positions, New Zealand general election of 2014

Source: Vote Compass New Zealand 2014, Lees-Marshment et al. 2015.

Thanks are due to Clifton van der Linden for his agreement to use this data. Left–right issues were the rich–poor gap, the value of government spending, trickle-down economics, increasing the gap of New Zealand superannuation, the amount of the minimum wage, the private role in health care, free doctor visits for children, more or less for welfare recipients, business tax, tax on the wealthy, a capital gains tax, education (three questions) and housing policy (two questions). Progressive–Conservative issues were funding the Department of Conservation, fracking, the Christchurch rebuild, corporal punishment, sentences for crime, immigration, foreign ownership of farmland, the Treaty of Waitangi, Māori self-determination, support for the Māori language, the age threshold for alcohol purchase, legalisation of marijuana, and abortion.

Figure 1.2 plots the relative positions of the political parties, calibrated by a team of political scientists and research assistants who worked on Vote Compass (a 'Voting Advice Application' sponsored by Television New Zealand's *One News* during the election campaign). Party responses were coded from the various parties' policy statements, and parties were also given an opportunity to respond and ask for corrections if they wished. Thirty issue areas were defined, and chosen so that they made up a two-dimensional policy space reflecting economic left and right, and 'progressive/liberal' and 'conservative' positions (for a detailed description of the methodology and results see Lees-Marshment et al. 2015).

People using the site answered the same questions as the parties, and were informed how closely their positions aligned with those of the various parties. The placing of the various parties on these two dimensions should come as little surprise to most. The most unexpected result of the calibration was the position of New Zealand First—slightly to the left of Labour on the economic left–right dimension—but few commented at the time. The two dimensions correlate to some extent; there is clustering to the left-liberal side, and to the conservative right. New Zealand First is the most obvious outlier, positioned on the conservative left. Later chapters will explore the positioning of these parties and their voters in more depth.

As we shall explain further in Chapter 3, the left–right ideological dimension is a crucial tool in our analysis and one that is recognised by many people, if not all. But it is an obvious simplification of a much more complex pattern of preferences and opinions. The most obvious way to address this problem is to identify a second dimension that also has resonance in public opinions and preferences. We choose to call it authoritarian–libertarian, but it has been described variously as progressive–conservative or materialist–postmaterialist. Its theoretical basis and surrounding literature will be explained further in Chapter 3, but we introduce it here to map the party positions as background to the voter left–right positions introduced above. As later chapters will explain, political differences across this second dimension tend to crosscut the left–right dimension, and can reduce the salience of questions of equality and inequality in political debate.

Issue salience

We now turn back to the voters, to inquire into what lies beneath voters' policy positions, and which issues voters considered the most salient, thereby paying particular attention to inequality and its associated dimensions. Asked for the single most important issue in the 2014 General Election, in an open-ended question, NZES respondents were classified as presented in Figure 1.3.

Interpreting their responses, we found respondents pitched overwhelmingly for the economy (at 18 per cent). The second most salient issue was a broad category of 'governance', chosen by 11 per cent. According to our coding of 2014 NZES respondents, directly expressed as a general principle, inequality was the third most important issue of the 2014 election, chosen by just over 7 per cent. But other responses also addressed inequality and poverty more indirectly, particularly under 'housing' and 'children and family', under which child poverty was classified. Adding all these together, inequality in principle and practice moves into second place.

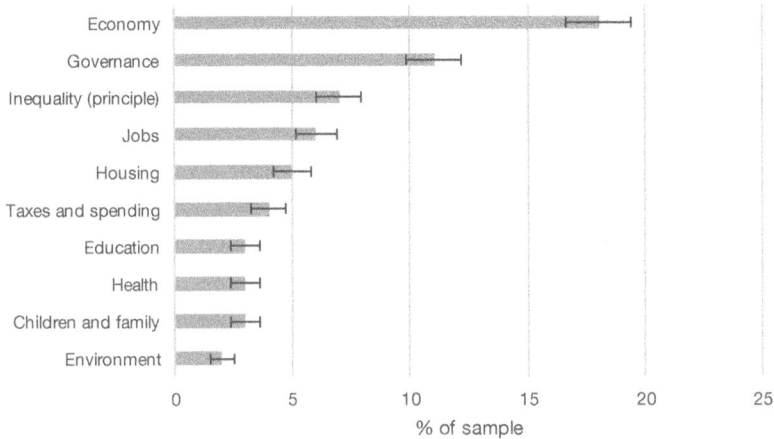

Figure 1.3: Issue most important in 2014 election as reported by respondents

Notes: The question was: 'What do you feel was the single most important issue in the 2014 Election?' Responses were open-ended, and coded into 24 categories. The categories presented in Figure 1.3 are those that were mentioned by at least 2 per cent of the respondents. The categories falling below 2 per cent and therefore not presented in Figure 1.3 were cost of living, law and order, foreign ownership, the political system, superannuation and the elderly, social programs/welfare, moral and social issues, immigration, Māori issues, the Christchurch earthquake, civil liberties, privatisation, media, and international. Twenty-one per cent of the respondents did not respond to the question, and 4 per cent could not name an issue or named more than one.

Source: New Zealand Election Study 2014.

Health and education have traditionally rivalled the economy as matters of concern to New Zealand voters (Vowles 2004a). As can be seen from Figure 1.3, in 2014 health and education were each named as most salient by only 3 per cent. In 2002, when asked in a similar open-ended format for 'the most important issue facing New Zealand in the last three years', very few mentioned any concerns tapping into inequality in either specific or general terms (Vowles 2004a: 43). We can see that the salience of health and education has significantly decreased in New Zealand politics over the last 10 years. A decrease in salience can also be observed for the economy, as almost 30 per cent responding to the 2008

NZES named the economy as the most important issue. At the height of the GFC this was as expected. We also observe that the issues associated with the progressive–conservative or libertarian–authoritarian dimension had relatively low salience in 2014.

There has been much recent discussion about inequality in New Zealand (e.g. Bertram 2014; Boston 2013; Rashbrooke 2013; Statistics New Zealand 2016a), and attention to inequality seems stronger among New Zealanders in 2014 compared with previous election campaigns. In more depth, Figure 1.4 compares the importance of the issue of inequality over time. It relies on various waves of the NZES and is based on counts of the use of the words 'inequality', 'poverty', the 'rich and poor' or 'income and/or wealth distribution' when respondents were asked open-ended questions asking what issue they found most important. Where more than one of these words appeared in a response, it was only counted as one.

Figure 1.4 shows a large increase in the use of words associated with inequality in 2014, from less than 1 per cent of the respondents mentioning inequality-related issues in 2008 to 11 per cent of the respondents referring to it in 2014. Unfortunately, this question was not asked in 2011.

People may be concerned about inequality, but what they would like to see done about it matters most. Analysis of social policy opinions in New Zealand over the period since 1990 shows that preferences for generous government spending on health and education have remained relatively high, but preferences for more expenditure on unemployment and welfare benefits have been in decline (Humpage 2014). Cuts to welfare benefits in the early 1990s were one of the contributing causes of the increase in inequality (see Chapter 2). More recent governments have sought to further reduce those expenditures, most recently by moving beneficiaries and unemployed people back into work as soon as possible. But it seems that some New Zealanders have begun to worry about aspects of this. Following how these preferences have changed over time indicates that people appear to be happy to continue to support government expenditure where provision is universal; everyone benefits from public health and education systems at some time in their lives—in the case of education, first as children, and then as parents.

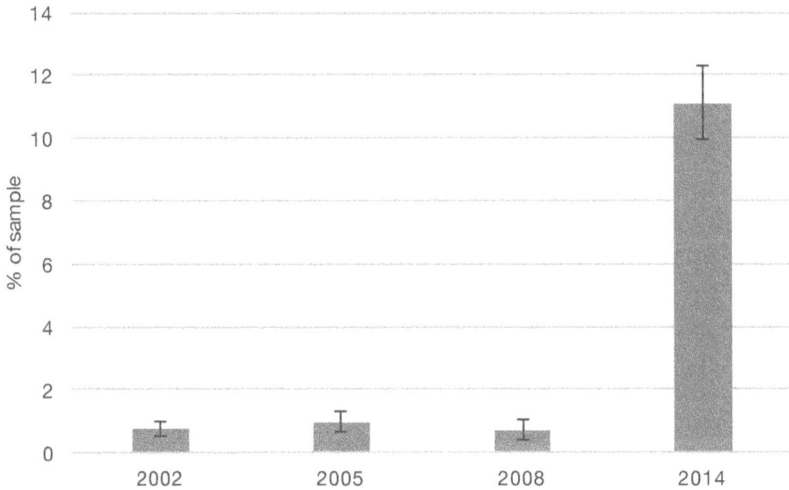

Figure 1.4: Percentage of respondents directly referring to inequality, poverty, rich and poor, or wealth distribution

Note: The questions were: 2002, 2005: 'What do you think has been the most important issue facing New Zealand over the last three years?'; 2008: 'What do you think is the most important political problem facing New Zealand today?'; 2014: 'What do you feel was the single most important issue in the 2014 election?'

Where provision is targeted, New Zealanders have become more reluctant to support it. Not everyone expects to go on a benefit or to be unemployed. Yet, since 2008 and the GFC, more people have become exposed to job insecurity. Over the longer term, changes in social structure and in the labour market have increased the proportion of people exposed to economic risks. More people are in insecure jobs. Union coverage is now relatively low in New Zealand, particularly in the private sector. In 2014, the time was ripe for increased concern about inequality, insecurity and poverty.

The issue of inequality in the public debate

The issue of economic inequality began to emerge on the public agenda before the 2011 election. Prime minister John Key was attacked by then Labour leader Phil Goff for using a new Ministry of Social Development report to claim that income inequality had not widened but had 'actually fallen in recent years' (Vance 2011). The ministry's report stated that income inequality peaked in the early 2000s, then fell from 2004 till 2007; largely because of the Working for Families policy introduced under Labour, which provides tax credits for low- and middle-income families with children where a parent is in work. Criticism was directed at the prime minister because the report did not cover the government's NZ$2.5 billion yearly tax cuts given to the top 10 per cent of earners in 2010. Moreover, child poverty rates were high, and there was an over-representation of indigenous Māori and minority Pasifika children living in poor families (Vance 2011; Collins 2011; Trevett 2011a).

The discussion that followed in parliament and in the communications media led some commentators to believe that a focus on class politics and economic inequality was the new hot issue (Edwards 2010, 2011). But the left gained little at the 2011 election, and by April 2014 commentators were once again lamenting Labour's alleged inability to focus firmly on the needs of working-class voters, with a particular focus on men (Armstrong 2014a; Edwards 2014a; Hubbard 2014). There was some momentum gained on the issue of inequality in early May 2014, because of the impending government Budget. *The Spirit Level* (Wilkinson and Pickett 2009), a bestselling book published internationally and examining social inequality, had received some attention in New Zealand. Its authors arrived in New Zealand in the same week as the Budget to give a series of lectures on why more equal societies do best (Bradbury 2014a). The Budget contained a NZ$500 million package for families and children, including raising tax credits for those on low and middle incomes, expanding paid parental leave and removing doctors' and prescription charges for children under 13. Journalists and political commentators largely agreed that National had 'won' the early battle on who would or could do more to combat inequality.

By contrast, the commentators deemed that Labour was unable to develop policy solutions that would resonate with its core constituencies. Economist Matt Nolan (2014) argued that the policy solutions of both the Greens and Labour were too focused on those who already had money, or were just platitudes. National used the budget to dispel concerns over inequality; two weeks later it appeared to have worked, with two major TV opinion polls revealing a significant 'Budget bounce' and 73 per cent of respondents favouring National's 'families' package' (Bennett 2014; Gower 2014a).

Inequality continued to feature in public debate throughout May and June, underpinned by more books on inequality published in New Zealand and elsewhere. TV3's weekly political program *The Nation* dedicated nearly an entire show to this topic, while academic and commentator Bryce Edwards conducted a one-hour 'Vote Chat' interview with *Inequality: A New Zealand crisis* author Max Rashbrooke. Commentators were also engaging with Thomas Piketty's bestseller, *Capital in the twenty-first century*, with Patrick Smellie's in-depth *Listener* feature (2014; see also Ferguson 2014; McLauchlan 2014a). Academics gave the debate momentum with Victoria University hosting a free one-day conference on 19 June on 'Inequality: Causes and consequences', followed by the launch of Jonathan Boston and Simon Chapple's book *Child poverty in New Zealand*.

Opinion polls also highlighted the influence the inequality debate might have on the election outcome. A report on inequality from the market research company UMR (2014) found that 50 per cent of the public were 'very concerned' about 'growing inequality', 37 per cent were 'somewhat concerned', and only 13 were 'not concerned at all'. Alongside this, 71 per cent believed that the gap between the rich and poor was widening, and 78 per cent believed that the effects of this gap were bad for New Zealand. During the election campaign, Vote Compass found a similar result: 17 per cent of its 300,000 participants placed 'inequality/affordability' almost equal with the economy as the most salient election issue (Lees-Marshment et al. 2015: 120).

Perhaps because no issue can retain its prominence for long given the fast news and public attention cycles, discussion of inequality waned during the campaign. Reports were infrequent, or canvassed only by internet bloggers on the left, while the opposition parties did not appear to be championing the issue to any significant extent. Ten days out from the election, there was once again a flurry of media focus. The Leaders Debate on TV3 spent eight minutes on the topic. Labour leader David Cunliffe made a 'dramatic heartfelt promise' to make addressing poverty his priority as prime minister (Newshub 2014a; Edwards 2014b). By this time, polls were suggesting the inequality gap was a key election issue. According to pollster Roy Morgan, in 2011, only 4 per cent of voters saw inequality as the biggest issue facing New Zealand, but 18 per cent did so in 2014 (cited in Collins 2014). Similarly, Vote Compass reported that '67 per cent say the Government should be doing more to reduce the gap between rich and poor' (Television New Zealand 2014), and should do more to address child poverty. Only 19 per cent of its respondents felt that National was doing enough on this issue.

Even some business leaders were admitting 'growing disquiet about the rising inequality of wealth and income' (*New Zealand Herald* 2014). There also appeared to be recognition across party lines that higher wages and tax reform were part of the answer to poverty and inequality. The difference between the left and the right was over how to achieve this. Labour and the Greens were promoting an increase in the minimum wage and a capital gains tax, while National focused primarily on tax cuts. Polls suggested both options were popular: 69 per cent wanted the minimum wage raised (Colmar Brunton 2014) but were ambivalent about higher taxes (Collins 2014).

Parties' ability to handle salient issues

If inequality had become a much more salient issue since 2008, many would have expected a shift to the left, traditionally assumed to pay more attention to inequality, and have more support for policies aimed at reducing social inequality. Over the last three elections in New Zealand, there has, however, been no such change. Combining the National and ACT party votes, support for the right and centre-right has remained stable at about 48 per cent. Indeed, the advent of the Conservative Party grew the right vote, although not its seats, to nearly 52 per cent in 2014. The left, by contrast, has shrunk. As can be seen from Table 1.1, adding Labour, the Greens and MANA (in 2008 and 2011) and Internet-MANA (in 2014), the result is 37 per cent in 2014, down from 42 per cent in 2008. The tendency to assume that when inequality is salient people will move to the left, will only hold true if voters believe that left-wing parties are best able to deal with the problem. The 2014 NZES asked respondents which party they thought was best able to deal with the issue they found most important.

Table 1.3 shows that 79 per cent of those who found the economy to be the most salient issue chose National as the party best to handle it, compared with 11 per cent for Labour. Of those who identified governance as the most important issue, 63 per cent found qualities of good governance in National, but only 5 per cent in Labour. The left held the advantage regarding inequality as a principle: 42 per cent of those considering inequality the most important issue chose Labour as the party best qualified to deal with the problem, and 21 per cent the Greens. Despite the apparent success of the 2014 Budget, 30 per cent identified Labour as the party best handling problems associated with children and family, compared with 23 per cent for National. National did 'win' the battle with regard to housing, preferred by 38 per cent of those who named the issue, as against Labour's 33 per cent.

Table 1.3: Party best at dealing with the issue by those finding it to be the single most important

Percentages by Row	None	Labour	National	Green	NZ First	N
Economy	3	11	79	2	2	520
Jobs	9	31	41	0	7	156
Taxes/Government Spending	9	12	59	2	4	103
Governance	9	5	63	7	4	298
Inequality (Principle)	12	42	8	21	4	205
Housing	11	33	38	2	1	131
Children and Family	8	30	23	19	4	91
Health	4	30	38	3	4	82
Education	3	35	37	6	0	89
Environment	7	0	3	87	0	56

Note: The question was: 'Thinking about the single most important issue in the 2014 election that you wrote above, which party do you think would be best at dealing with it?'

Whereas those who found inequality important saw Labour as the party best able to handle it, many also perceived National to be the best party to handle some of the key issues closely related to poverty and inequality, such as housing. And while the issue of inequality had come to the fore in the public debate, and while its salience had grown in the electorate, the state of the economy and governance were still the primary concerns of voters. On those matters, National was evaluated significantly more positively than Labour.

The remainder of this book examines to what extent, how and why the issue of inequality affected party choice and political behaviour in the 2014 New Zealand General Election. As noted above, its main source is the 2014 NZES, a dataset made up of responses from 2,835 people whose names were randomly selected from the electoral rolls and who either returned questionnaires sent to them in the post or completed the survey online. Of these, 1,419 had responded to the 2011 NZES, making it possible to compare their responses between the two elections. The remaining 1,462 responded for the first time in 2014. Further details can be found in supplementary materials for this book on the NZES website (www.nzes.org), where the full questionnaire used in 2014 is available for inspection. Those enrolled in the Māori electorates were oversampled, with 547 responses.

As there is a tendency for some people who did not vote to report that they voted, whether or not respondents voted or not was checked from the master rolls, and the data corrected when required. For most analysis, the dataset is weighed by gender, age, education, vote shares and turnout. The response rate for those sampled for the first time in 2014 was 33 per cent, and for those who participated in 2011 it was 63 per cent of the earlier sample. The sample is as representative of those who were able to vote in 2014 as is possible. But we cannot exclude some bias toward those who are more interested in politics than average. Indeed, even after validation, the proportion of non-voters in the unweighted sample is much less than that reported in the official data. To address this problem in some analysis, we are able to use data from both respondents and non-respondents, removing non-response bias entirely. Data from earlier versions of the NZES are also used, as are published polling and other data, both from New Zealand and elsewhere.

Chapter 2 begins our study by outlining the dimensions of inequality in New Zealand. It discusses inequality as a concept, and the important role that the pursuit of equality has played in New Zealand history. Moving up to the present, it traces the development of greater inequality in New Zealand in the 1980s and 1990s, and some of the explanations of the process. It places New Zealand in an international context, and discusses regulatory, tax and benefit changes that contributed to increasing inequality. It also introduces the two other sources of inequality that crosscut the economic dimension: gender and ethnic inequalities, the latter in particular affecting the indigenous Māori population.

Chapter 3 introduces the theoretical models on which we rely, and explains how these help frame and guide our analysis, drawing out their implications for inequality in relation to voting behaviour. The economic or rational choice theory of electoral behaviour assumes that voters are rational, and therefore people vote for the party that promises to most benefit them. This provides the foundation of what one might call the naïve theory, purporting to explain how people experiencing inequality would respond electorally: they should vote for the left. By contrast, the social-psychological model acknowledges that human beings are social animals with habits and loyalties, and we follow the example of others in making our choices. Our families, opinion leaders, political commentators and even political parties give us cues about what to do and think. We also discuss further the second attitudinal continuum that underlies the New Zealand party system: the authoritarian–libertarian dimension. Political disagreements around the attitudes bound up in this dimension can sometimes distract attention from traditional left–right or distributional issues affecting income inequality.

In Chapter 4, we begin the analysis of the NZES data. Applying the theoretical models described in Chapter 3, this chapter outlines the social foundations of voting choices in New Zealand in 2014, and addresses some of the competing explanations of the election result. We explore how social group location affects vote choice and left–right positions. Because one feature of increasing inequality has been a reduction in income security for many people, we bring in voters' own perceptions of security or insecurity, and their aspirations. We investigate the extent of inequality between the parties, particularly in their funding.

Chapter 5 turns our attention to the election winner, the National Party. We show how the National Party won the 2014 election because of perceptions that it was competent and well led; the economy mattered, but as part of a wider package of perceptions associated with competence and leadership.

Chapter 6 moves the focus to Labour. Why did the party fail to mobilise concern about inequality as an election issue? To address this, we explore the range of positional issues around priorities for government expenditure to address inequality and other issues, and the distribution of public attitudes around tax and social policy in particular. We also assess claims made by internal and external critics of the party: Labour focused too much on 'identity politics', promised too much and those promises failed to cohere into a convincing narrative.

In Chapter 7, we turn to the Green Party. The Green Party came to the 2014 election with promises to address inequality, but these were secondary to its tax proposals that would have shifted business taxes toward paying for the costs of pollution. During the campaign, Greens were sidelined by Labour's failure to acknowledge them as a likely coalition partner and coordinate with them accordingly. Yet the Green Party would have been a crucial component of any centre-left government alternative. We discuss the advice of commentators that the Green Party should move to the right, reducing its commitment to the reduction of inequality, and instead focus on environmental issues.

In Chapter 8, we note that aside from the mainstream National Party, the 2014 election had three other conservative parties in contention: New Zealand First, the most significant conservative party with centre-left stances on some economic issues, but populist and socially conservative; the ACT Party, leaning to the right on both dimensions; and the Conservative Party, particularly strong on socially conservative issues. As we shall see, New Zealand First voters do tend to lean to the left on inequality issues. As another party potentially needed to form an alternative government to one led by the National Party, New Zealand First and its voters lie in a pivotal position.

In Chapter 9, we explore the gender dimensions of inequality. Since the end of the nineteenth century, New Zealand has been presented as a leader in the field of gender equality. But major gender differences in opportunities and income still exist. This chapter addresses the gender dimension of inequality and assesses the extent to which there is a gender gap in attitudes and vote choice in light of the gender disparities in economic and political life. We also examine changes in descriptive representation, women in Cabinet and parliament, and whether voters view gender quotas for parliamentary representation as a gender equality mechanism.

Chapter 10 addresses the main ethnic dimension of inequality, examining electoral politics and opinion among Māori, New Zealand's indigenous minority. In 2014, there were seven dedicated electorate seats for Māori who wished to vote in them. Traditionally, Māori have tended to vote Labour; however, in 2005, for the second time in recent years, Labour lost much of the Māori vote, and most of the Māori seats, to the Māori Party. By 2014, all but one Māori electorate had returned to Labour. Labour's tide had apparently come back in among Māori, while going out among the rest of the electorate. The chapter questions this interpretation, and traces the decline and fall of the vote for independent Māori parties, the shifts in Māori preferences, and analyses where Māori issue and candidate preferences differ from the rest. We find some evidence that inequality is beginning to have effects between Māori, and is no longer simply a gap between Māori and the Pākehā majority. The Māori Party forms another potential pivot in the party system, and while currently aligned with National is by no means committed permanently.

Chapter 11 notes the small recovery in voter turnout in the 2014 election, and puts this into the context of developments since 1996. It examines the development of an age gap in turnout, but finds that the evidence for an increasing income or resource gap is less apparent. Those who are young on low incomes and with few assets do tend to be less likely to vote than others, perhaps making politicians less attentive to their needs. We address arguments about reforms that might raise turnout: compulsory voting, automatic registration and online voting. The chapter expands the focus on participation toward wider indicators of engagement, use of the internet, media exposure and campaign mobilisation.

Chapter 12 pulls the threads together, identifying the extent to which attitudes toward inequality, aspirations and perceptions of security or insecurity made a difference to the election outcome. Connecting its findings back to the earlier theoretical discussions, it draws out the likely implications for the future politics of inequality in New Zealand.

2

The fall and rise of inequality in New Zealand

Discussion of social and economic inequality in political debate is not unique to New Zealand; concerns about inequality have re-entered politics around the world. In many countries, inequality in incomes and wealth has increased. Technological change, globalisation and the conscious policy decisions of government elites are the explanations usually assigned (Pakulski 2005; Wilkinson and Pickett 2009; Piketty 2013). Before turning to the theoretical and empirical dimensions of our study, this chapter outlines the philosophical context, and unpacks the ideas and realities of economic inequality in New Zealand with reference to comparable countries. It also reviews inequalities experienced by women and by Māori, New Zealand's indigenous population.

Inequality in philosophy and New Zealand politics

The concepts of equality and inequality are complex and contested. It is only since the eighteenth century that the idea that all human beings deserve equal respect and dignity has been widely accepted (Vlastos 1962; Kymlicka 1990: 5). If one accepts equality of respect and therefore dignity, one should also accept equality of opportunity: the idea that everybody should have an equal chance of making their way in the world, and should be able to develop their potential however they wish. Acceptance of equality of respect and opportunity has been delayed until more recently for women and many minority ethnic groups. Arising from these dimensions of the concept, group-based demands for equal rights, equal voice and equal access to political and economic power raise the stakes still further.

Equality is not the same as identity, which is the mathematical sense of equality. Numerically, an 'equals' sign means 'the same as'. Outside mathematics, a judgement of equality presumes a difference between whatever is being compared (Westen 1990). The idea of absolute social and economic equality is therefore self-contradictory: human beings cannot all be the same, living in entirely identical situations. Even in a communist society, Marx (1875) thought that income should be distributed according to people's needs, which are often different.[1] Dealing with inequality is about dealing with differences that are acknowledged, justified on grounds of fairness and rationality, and treated with respect. The existence of difference, including entrenched inequalities, may mean that the pursuit of greater social equality may require treating some groups of people more favourably than others, if only on a temporary basis.

Our main focus in this book is on economic inequality. On the economic dimension, there are obvious differences between income and wealth inequality. Wealth is a result of the accumulation of previous income, some of which may be inherited within a family. It forms a 'stock' of assets that may be used to generate day-to-day income by way of interest, rents or dividends from stocks and shares. Income is a 'flow'. Most people's income derives from a wage or a salary. Those on higher incomes may be able to save, and thus accumulate assets and wealth. Those on lower incomes find it more difficult, and may need to have their incomes supplemented by the state. In our analysis of inequality in New Zealand, we distinguish between income and wealth, the latter in the form of asset ownership.

Most economists used to argue that greater inequality leads to a wealthier society. In his influential theory of justice, John Rawls (1971) argues that economic inequality can be justified if the benefits of increasing wealth make the poor better off than they would have been had society remained equal and wealth not increased. After 30 years' experience of policies based on that assumption, it is now sharply contested, even among economists

---

1   Under communism, the principle would be 'from each according to their ability, to each according to their need'; again, a degree of inequality justified by circumstances.

(IMF 2014; Ostry et al. 2014). Within many countries, increased wealth has gone to the wealthy. The poor and even the not-so-poor are doing worse, or just holding on (Milanovic 2016). Too high a level of inequality in outcomes inevitably harms social mobility and equality of opportunity. Some try to minimise the importance of seeking more equality in outcomes while endorsing equality of opportunity. But where outcomes are greatly unequal, there can be little or no equality of opportunity.

Inequality in New Zealand politics

Consistent with John Rawls' ideas, Tony Blair and 'New Labour' in Britain argued that increased inequality that helps generate wealth can be welcomed as long as the rich pay their taxes and the poor get an appreciable share (Mandelson, quoted in Brown 2012; Blair, quoted in Lansley 2006: 24). Even earlier, when the New Zealand Labour Party reviewed its principles in the late 1970s, it also seemed to adopt this interpretation of Rawlsian philosophy (Vowles 1987). As Labour prime minister David Lange put it in 1986, 'social democrats must accept the existence of economic inequality because it is the engine that drives the economy' (Lange 1986).

Lange's statement was a departure from a long tradition. From its beginnings as an outpost of the British Empire, New Zealand has had an egalitarian tradition, shared in part by its neighbour, Australia. New Zealand was a leader in the achievement of full representative democracy, giving voting rights to Māori as early as 1867, and to women in 1893. Late nineteenth- and early twentieth-century reforms pursued in New Zealand and Australia were underpinned by a rich tradition of egalitarian liberal ideas that overlapped with the principles of the emerging Labour movement. This combination produced a brand of politics whereby moderate Labour activists and unionists aligned themselves with the governing Liberal Party. Together they pioneered a set of policies that reflected early colonial values of equal opportunity for all and the desire for social, moral and racial harmony (Belich 2001: 853; Sawer 2003; Sinclair 1967). The early Liberals imagined themselves as able to represent labour, farmers and entrepreneurs, prompting legislative change on four fronts: land, labour, welfare and women's rights (Belich 2001: 22–23, 42–44; Curtin 2015; Lyon 1982; Vowles 1982).

After the Liberals fell from power in 1912, the egalitarian torch was taken up by the Labour Party; established in 1916 with a leadership of socialists and former syndicalists. Labour's radical aspirations moderated rapidly during the 1920s. In office from 1935 until 1949, the First Labour Government established one of the world's first welfare states. Labour's *Social Security Act 1938* was underpinned by the principle that every New Zealander had a right to a reasonable standard of living, and that this was best ensured through universal welfare benefits. Universalism eliminated the humiliation of receiving charity and brought together the needy and the middle classes into a 'new welfare society' (Belich 2001: 262). The increased wages and salaries of low- and middle-income earners benefited businesses and manufacturing, as did improved pensions. This collective response was viewed as enabling individual advancement, and reinforcing traditional and popular understandings of equality of opportunity and respect in New Zealand. Over the next 40 years, governments did little to modify the relevant policy settings, reinforcing the notion that sharing wealth and prosperity across society was desirable (Chapman 1981).

Equality of respect and equality of opportunity were strongly held values among the European settlers who arrived in New Zealand and Australia in the nineteenth century. Many were 'aspirational', seeking to improve their lives and those of their families. But faced with successive recessions as the new colonies struggled to find overseas markets and products to sell in them, a concern for security emerged early. The isolation and small size of the Australasian colonies also meant that the state took on more economic responsibilities than in most other countries. People adopted a 'utilitarian' attitude that the state could and would provide any necessary collective goods; in particular, pensions and aid for the poor (Gascoigne 2002). As American scholar Leslie Lipson wrote in the 1940s, if any sculptured allegory were to be placed at the approaches of a major New Zealand harbour, it would not be a statue of liberty but instead a statue of equality (Lipson 1948: 8). Lipson identified in New Zealanders a hatred of privilege, passion for social justice and a desire to eradicate poverty. Notions of egalitarianism in New Zealand were not about the absence of class but the absence of extreme class distinction, class oppression and conflict, and elite rule. While much has changed since the late 1940s, it is still argued that the related theme of fairness remains part of the values many people associate with being a New Zealander (Hackett-Fischer 2012).

Inequality realities: Economic and social

For our purposes, the relevant dimensions of inequality are equality of respect, equality of opportunity and the reduction of differences in outcomes that make equality of opportunity difficult if not impossible to achieve. Equality of respect matters because it is challenged by discourses implying that many seeking social assistance are 'undeserving'. It is a moral judgement that weakens if not denies people's equal rights as human beings, and is often made without any direct knowledge of their circumstances. In practice, the three dimensions of inequality we discuss are inter-related, and extend into gender and ethnic differences as well as those between classes or groups defined by their income or wealth. Of these dimensions, economic inequality as measured in incomes and wealth is usually the most significant.

Traditionally, the reduction of income inequality has taken place through progressive taxation, tax credits for the working poor, universal services and income transfers to categories of people, which may take universal form in the case of pensions or targeted payments to those in particular need, such as the unemployed or disabled. Taxes on wealth or capital have also been used, but much less so now than in the past. Two related goals of redistributive social policies are often identified: the first to generally promote equality of opportunity, such as in the provision of state education; and the second to protect against risk in the form of unemployment benefits, universal health services and income support for those who find themselves in bad circumstances through no fault of their own.

Despite their turn to the market in the 1980s, most countries with advanced capitalist economies continue to redistribute income by progressive tax systems, albeit less progressive than in the past. Most countries continue to provide benefits or transfers to designated groups, most, but not all, because they are in need by way of inadequate market incomes. There remains significant variation in the extent to which various countries redistribute incomes.

Figure 2.1 provides a bar chart that displays three indicators of income inequality across nine countries in 2008, the year immediately before the main effects of the global financial crisis (GFC) took hold. The Gini index is a summary measure of income inequality. In a country scoring 0 on this index, all incomes would be equal. A score of 100 would indicate that all income would be concentrated among a very small elite. In the black bar for each country, the net disposable income Gini index summarises the income distribution after taxes have been taken off and benefits added to people's incomes. The countries are ordered based on this index from the most equal on the left to the least equal on the right. In this data, the most equal country in the figure is Denmark, which scores 24.2. The most unequal is the United States, scoring 37.8. The grey bar for each country, the next in line, indicates the *market Gini index*: the income distribution before taxes and benefits. The third bar for each country shows a country's *level of redistribution* through taxes and benefits: it reflects the main role that government plays in promoting greater equality. It is calculated as the difference between the market and net Gini figures, divided by the market Gini, multiplied by 100 to produce a percentage.

Figure 2.1 reveals that New Zealand was ranked quite closely with Canada and Australia on the three measures, with the net disposable income Gini index of New Zealand being 33, Canada 32 and Australia 34. Market inequalities are in a similar range, with New Zealand at 45.5, and Australia and Canada respectively scoring 46.8 and 43.8. On the redistribution measure, New Zealand scores in between Canada and Australia with a score of 27.5. Australia redistributes a little more, at 28.2; Canada a little less at 26.7.[2]

Other countries stand out for various reasons. The UK has the highest level of market inequality, but its net Gini disposable income index is only just above the other three 'British world' countries to its left (Australia, New Zealand and Canada). The United States has a very high level of market inequality, and the lowest level of redistribution. Its net Gini index is the highest of all Organisation for Economic Co-operation and Development (OECD) countries included in Figure 2.1. Levels of redistribution are highest in the four continental European countries. Greater redistribution is primarily responsible for their lower levels of net inequality.

---

2   It should be noted that estimates of Gini coefficients tend to differ between sources, either because of different data sources or different assumptions underpinning their analysis. For the most part, the different sources are consistent in their broad patterns and in what can be deduced from them.

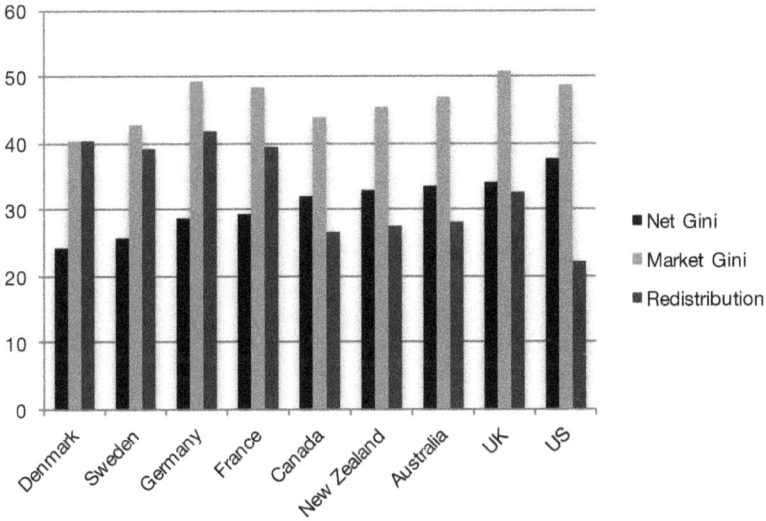

Figure 2.1: Net disposable income Gini, market Gini and difference between net and market Gini (redistribution) in nine countries, 2008
Source: OECD 2016.

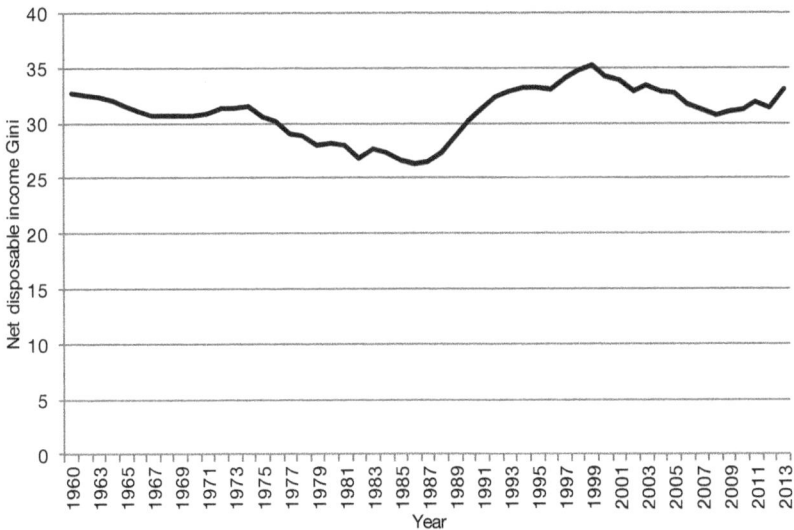

Figure 2.2: The net Gini index for New Zealand, 1960–2013
Sources: SWIID 2016; OECD 2016; Perry 2014.

Figure 2.2 shows the net disposable income Gini index in New Zealand, tracked back to 1960. The early data are less robust than later data, and thus need to be treated with caution (Easton 2013; Perry 2014). Because most data series tend to start in the 1980s, people have tended to assume that New Zealand was a more equal country in the 1950s and 1960s than it actually was. Contrary to what many people believe, New Zealand's income equality in that period was probably no better than in other Western democracies. If the Standardized World Income Inequality Database (SWIID 2016) estimates are correct, income inequality in New Zealand was about the same in the early 1960s as in 2014.[3] Ironically, given the policy traditions associated with New Zealand's major parties, the drop to the lowest level of income inequality took place under the National Government of Robert Muldoon (1975–1984), and the steepest increase took place under Labour (1984–1990).

If there was a strong perception of egalitarianism in the 1950s and 1960s, perhaps it is more to do with what may have underpinned an observation that Keith Sinclair made in his *A History of New Zealand* (1959: 276): 'New Zealand must be more nearly classless, however, than any other society in the world. Some people are richer than others, but wealth carries no great prestige and no prerogative of leadership'. Many might now doubt that the last part of Sinclair's statement applied in New Zealand under John Key's leadership, with a multimillionaire prime minister and a 'celebrity culture' prevalent throughout the various communications media. However, as we will explore in greater depth in Chapter 5, much of John Key's popularity was based on an 'ordinary bloke' image.

How one sees these numbers will depend on one's values and preferences. On the one hand, one can claim that current levels of inequality are nothing new or unusual. On the other hand, one can argue that New Zealand is a richer and more prosperous country than in the early 1960s. The benefits of that growth appear to be have been mostly taken by those on higher incomes.

---

3   Brian Easton warns that household data can only be imperfectly estimated before 1985; while personal income data exists from earlier periods, it cannot be easily translated given changes in households over time. It should also be noted that increasing levels of women's labour force participation may have been partly responsible for decreasing household income inequality up to the 1980s (Easton 2013).

Policy paths to inequality

The narrative of New Zealand's path to a less egalitarian society identifies the key events as the election of the Fourth Labour Government in 1984 and the subsequent economic and social policy reforms given the name 'Rogernomics'—named for their principal architect, Labour minister of finance Roger Douglas. These developments were underpinned by a combination of technological change and global influences, and shaped by public policy. Britain's accession to the European Economic Community (now the European Union) brought an end to New Zealand's neo-colonial position as Britain's outlying farm. The need to sell New Zealand's exports elsewhere in a context of high levels of protectionism in those markets meant that New Zealand had to become more economically competitive to survive. Large increases in the price of oil between 1974 and the late 1980s added to the pressure for change, contributing to historically low terms of trade—the balance between the prices of New Zealand exports and imports (Rankin 2014). The demise of wool as a major export earner in the 1960s compounded the problems. Economic reforms were necessary, if not overdue. However, many actors could see opportunities for their personal or collective enrichment, and were able to capture much of the necessary process of reform for their own benefit, justifying their actions with an ideology of extreme market-led individualism.

Public policy played a major role in spreading out the income structure. The biggest increase in inequality was the result of widening market incomes, but tax and benefit changes also played a major role (Aziz et al. 2012). A flat income tax system was avoided only by Labour prime minister David Lange (1984–1989), who single-handedly vetoed the change in defiance of constitutional convention, breaking his alliance with Roger Douglas and throwing the government into the disunity that led it its defeat in 1990. New Zealand did move to a flatter but not entirely flat system of income tax.

Most systems of income tax are progressive or graduated into steps. The lowest step is taxed at the lowest rate, reflecting the low incomes of those who fall below it. The steps above are taxed at progressively higher rates, reflecting the greater ability of those on high incomes to pay more; however, they only pay the higher rate for their income above each step. Tax rates above these steps are therefore described as 'marginal' tax rates. Figure 2.3 summarises the changes that took place in the top marginal income tax rate and corporate tax. It also shows the introduction of the goods and services tax (GST) under Labour in the 1980s, and further changes since. The top marginal rate of income tax has been reduced, as well as the number of steps—now currently at four. The rate of tax a person pays overall is based on the accumulation of the marginal rates applied up to their income level. As to be expected, those on the highest incomes have done best out of these tax changes. For those on and above the highest marginal rate, the average rate of tax was just under 49 per cent in 1983–84. In 2014, it was 28.5 per cent (Rankin 2014). Corporate tax also came down and the value-added GST was introduced at 10 per cent, increasing to 12.5 and later 15 per cent. As an expenditure tax, the GST is 'regressive'; that is, people on low incomes tend to pay more GST as a proportion of their incomes than people on higher incomes who have more cash to save or invest.

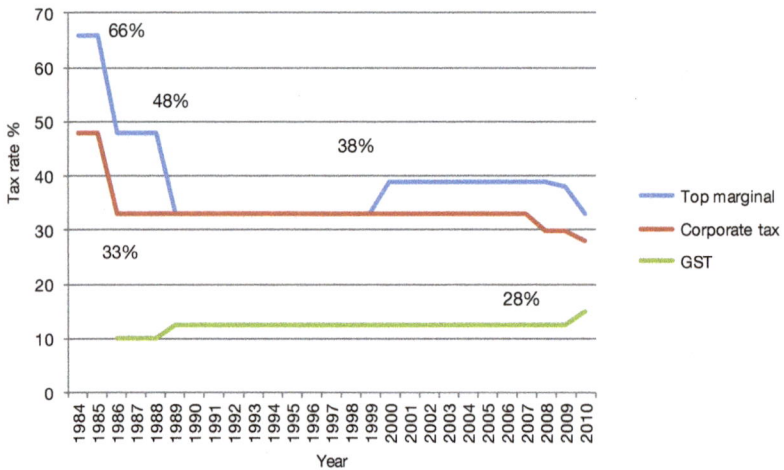

Figure 2.3: Tax changes, 1984–2010
Note: GST=goods and services tax.
Source: Rankin 2014.

In tandem with the 1980s changes in income tax, other advantages for those on higher incomes and to companies were reduced. Many tax loopholes for businesses and high-income individuals were abolished and a fringe benefits tax introduced. Welfare benefits for family and child support became more closely targeted, as was housing provision for those on low incomes. New Zealand Superannuation, established by the Muldoon National Government, remained as a universal pension after strong opposition emerged to means-testing by way of a high-income surcharge applied for two years before being dropped. But the age of eligibility was shifted from 60 to 65 during the 1990s. Targeting of social assistance required closer integration of the tax and benefit systems. In 2005, the Labour-led government introduced the Working for Families package that consolidated and expanded previous provisions for low- and middle-income family support. Fully available only to those in the labour market, it is one of the reasons why income inequality in New Zealand has not significantly increased since the mid-1990s, despite the GFC (Perry 2014: 92).

Tax and benefits are not the only means by which inequality may be addressed. New Zealand continues to provide public services that are state-funded and universally available to all citizens and permanent residents, most notably in the domains of health and education. Medical care is not immediately free at the point of access, although fees are subsidised for those on low incomes and for children. Care in public hospitals is free, although often subject to waiting lists unless the need for treatment is urgent. Injuries from personal accidents are covered by a unique Accident Compensation scheme funded by levies from employers and employees and run by a government-owned corporation. Primary and secondary education are theoretically free, but in practice schools solicit donations and parents face pressure to contribute. The state continues to fund about 70 per cent of the effective fees for tertiary education and operates a student loan scheme for which no interest is liable while studying, so long as graduates subsequently remain in New Zealand.

These universal services are often criticised as open to capture by those on higher incomes, but the potential market costs of those services would fall most heavily on those on low incomes. Universally available public services provide a counterweight to the regressive nature of the GST. Because they are more valuable for those on low incomes, they offset the GST's otherwise regressive effects (Aziz et al. 2012: 36). As will be shown in subsequent chapters, the universal nature of these services means they retain high levels of public support for government funding. The same applies to New Zealand Superannuation, also available universally. However, public support for benefits to those on low incomes and those not in work is much lower and has decreased over time (Humpage 2015).

The interaction of the tax and transfer systems means that when transfers are offset against income tax liabilities, the bottom 40 per cent of households pay no net income tax, receiving more from government than they pay for. A paper authored by Treasury economists adds in the effects of the GST and the use of health and education services across income groups, calculating 'final income' on that basis. It indicates that in 2010 it was only people in the top four income deciles who paid more for government services and benefits that they received from them (Aziz et al. 2012). While this data does not include the effects of the rise in the GST to 15 per cent, it confirms that the New Zealand state continues to redistribute income quite significantly, although as noted above not as generously as do many European governments.

Market incomes and pre-distribution

Increased inequality in market incomes was the main source of the increase in disposable income inequality in New Zealand in the 1980s and 1990. Immediately prior to the public policy changes of the 1980s, New Zealand had one of the most highly regulated economies in the western world. Attempting to cope with a cascade of economic problems, the government was directly controlling wages, prices and interest rates. The farming industry was highly subsidised, international capital movements restricted and imports were subject to a wide range of controls and tariffs. The market revolution in the second half of the 1980s swept most of this away.

The Fourth Labour Government began the process of economic and financial deregulation. National continued it in the early 1990s with additional reforms to social policy provision. It delegated the day-to-day control of monetary policy and the responsibility for setting interest rates to the Reserve Bank. It maintained inflation within a range defined by government as the only objective, leaving out growth and, most significantly, unemployment, from the objectives (Nagel 1998).

A remaining element of the regulatory toolkit is the minimum wage. In 1946, the minimum wage was as high as 83 per cent of the average ordinary time weekly earnings, although in terms of real incomes wage rates at that time were significantly lower than they are today. By the early 1980s, the minimum wage had fallen to 30 per cent of that average. The Fourth Labour Government (1984–1990) left office at the beginning of the 1990s, having raised the minimum wage to 50 per cent of average weekly earnings, but it fell again during the 1990s to a low of 42 per cent (Hyman 2002). In 2014, the minimum wage stood at 49 per cent of ordinary time weekly earnings, and was raised marginally further to 52 per cent after a review (MBIE 2014). While the minimum wage was being paid to only 2.7 per cent of employees in 2014, it acts as a floor above which other wages may rise and is, of course, paid to the poorest and most vulnerable employees.

A campaign for a minimum wage was also a feature of the 2014 election. The Labour Party campaigned to raise the minimum wage to 56 per cent of average earnings. Relative to wages and salaries, New Zealand's minimum wage is one of the highest in the world, but this reflects New Zealand's relatively low wage and salary structure. But it is unlikely that a significant increase in the minimum wage could greatly affect inequality in New Zealand, particularly as some of its effect would be absorbed by a lower uptake of tax credits and targeted benefits.

The rise in inequality in advanced capitalist democracies has been accompanied by a decline in the influence of trade unions and their decreasing membership. Trade unions provide a countervailing power to employers in the labour market. Strong trade unions usually generate higher wages than would be the case in their absence for members and non-members alike, at least for those in the same industry or workplace.

The position of trade unions in New Zealand society has been transformed over the past half century. At the turn of the twentieth century, trade unions were in the vanguard of the campaign for a more equal society, and the most effective instrument for achieving that goal within the broader framework of New Zealand liberalism (Belich 2001: 853; Sawer 2003; Sinclair 1967). The main vehicle for this accomplishment was the *Industrial Conciliation and Arbitration Act 1894*. It gave legal recognition to trade unions that wished to register, and established a system of compulsory arbitration for those unions, with appeals to an Arbitration Court. Strikes against Arbitration Court decisions were not permitted. For this reason, stronger socialist or syndicalist-led unions such as the Miners and Watersiders remained outside the system in its early years and sought their economic and political goals through strike actions that were ultimately unsuccessful.

As it developed, the Arbitration Court came to regulate the minimum wage and make binding wage awards across industries. A similar system developed in Australia and, under this form of state regulation, levels of union membership in Australia and New Zealand were among the highest in the world in the early twentieth century (Castles 1985). High levels of union membership in New Zealand were further underpinned by the First Labour Government that legislated for compulsory union membership and a 40-hour working week in 1936.

Consensus around the Arbitration system began to break down in the 1970s as economic pressures began to mount. Some employers wanted an end to compulsory unionism and the stronger unions wanted to engage in free collective bargaining. The Muldoon-led National Government legislated for voluntary unionism in 1983, but this was overturned by the following Labour Government, led by David Lange. Despite its zeal in pursuing market-led reform, beyond marginal changes to improve the efficiency of collective bargaining, the government did not extend the process into the labour market.

National's *Employment Contracts Act 1991* opened a new chapter in New Zealand's industrial relations. Compulsory unionism was abolished and unions no longer had a legal status other than of voluntary associations. The Act provided no duty on the part of employers to bargain and no responsibility to do so in good faith. The Employment Court did have the power to act if employment contracts were deemed to be 'harsh or oppressive'. Provisions in the Act were designed to push employment contracts to a workplace rather than across multiple employers in an industry, and encourage individual rather than collective employment agreements (Hince and Vranken 1991). Not without reason, the Act was described as 'an Employers' Charter' (Anderson 1991).

In office once more from 1999, Labour sought to redress the balance through the passage of the *Employment Relations Act 2000*. The Act reinstated recognition of trade unions and removed the most obvious hindrances in the way of collective bargaining and later re-established a 'good faith' provision. Once re-elected in 2008, National again began to shift the balance back toward employers. The government enacted a 90-day trial period whereby employers could dismiss newly hired workers without reason. Prior to the 2014 election, the National Government was seeking to water down the good faith provision by no longer requiring a collective agreement to be reached. As we shall see, National's position on workers' rights appeared to do little harm to its campaign efforts.

Figure 2.4 indicates the decline in union membership since the passage of the Employment Contracts Act. Since 2000, union membership as a proportion of wage and salary earners has remained relatively stable.

Under the Labour-led government of 1999 to 2008, union membership rose in tandem with growth in the labour force. Since 2008, with National in power, the trend has become choppier, ending with two falls in 2013 and 2014 that may or may not be precursors to further long-term decline. Weak unions in a context of reduced rights to collective bargaining and grievance procedures are almost certainly associated with lower wages than would otherwise be the case (for US evidence of the effects of union decline see Jacobs and Myers 2014).

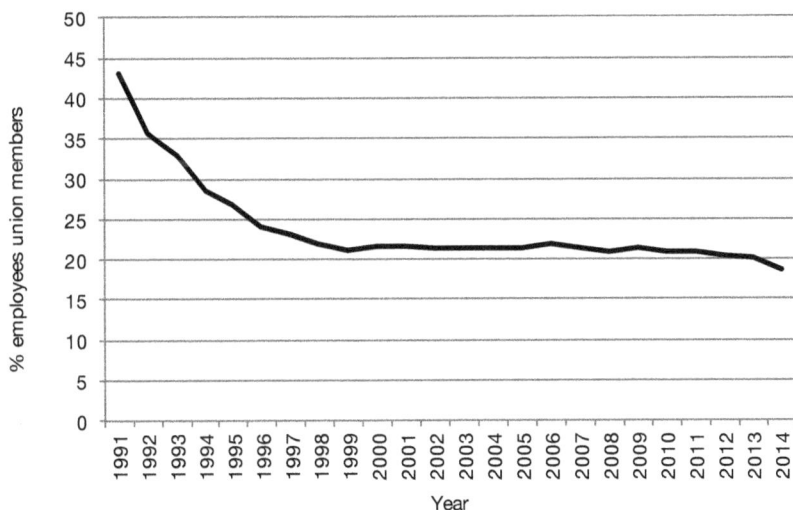

Figure 2.4: Union membership in New Zealand (percentage of wage and salary earners)
Sources: May, Walsh and Otto 2003; New Zealand Companies Office 2006, 2009, 2014.

Wealth inequality

While most of the inequality debate worldwide has been about income, wealth is arguably more important than income because it is associated with the entrenchment of inequality across generations. Short-term wealth inequality is associated with life-cycle, with most people acquiring more wealth and assets as they grow older. But wealth is often transmitted from generation to generation. Table 2.1 presents data about the distribution of income and wealth in Australia and New Zealand.

As can be seen from Table 2.1, the ratio of household wealth from the top to the bottom is 'off the scale', in that the bottom quintile of wealth holders in New Zealand apparently have no significant wealth to hold. The top quintile of wealth holders, by contrast, own 59 per cent of wealth. In Australia, the bottom quintile owns 1 per cent whereas the top quintile holds 61 per cent. When looking at the distribution of income, Table 2.1 reveals that in both Australia and New Zealand, the bottom quintile of income holders owns 8 per cent of the income, whereas the top quintile holds 40.

Table 2.1: Percentage shares of income and wealth by respective quintiles

		Q1 (low)	Q2	Q3	Q4	Q5 (high)	Share ratio, Q5:Q1
% Household income	Australia	8	13	17	23	40	5
	NZ	8	13	17	23	40	5
% Household wealth	Australia	1	5	12	21	61	61
	NZ	0	5	12	24	59	

Note: Because the wealth share of the bottom quintile in New Zealand is not statistically distinguishable from zero, no share ratio can be calculated.

Source: Perry 2015: 6.

Some earlier New Zealand wealth data comes from 2004–05. It indicated that the top 10 per cent of wealth holders then had about 50 per cent of the total wealth, making for a 'Wealth Gini' of 69, double that of income. In terms of international comparisons, New Zealand and Australia lie in the middle of the OECD countries for which data is available. Wealth in New Zealand is more concentrated than in the UK, where 45 per cent of the total wealth is held by the top 10 per cent. The United States has the highest wealth concentration: 71 per cent of the total wealth is held by the top 10 per cent (Perry 2015: 181).

Many will be surprised that wealth inequality is higher in New Zealand than in the UK, as the UK is often believed to be a society with a much more entrenched economic and social elite. Unlike the UK, New Zealand lacks taxes on wealth, either by way of death duties or capital gains. One of the main sources of wealth in New Zealand is the appreciation of the value of land for housing and agriculture that can be captured by those lucky or prescient enough to own such land in the right place and at the right time. In the decade of 1910–20, land tax made up 15 per cent of New Zealand's tax revenues. Land and property tax no longer exists in New Zealand, except to fund local and regional government in the form of rates. There have been proposals to reintroduce a more comprehensive and effective land tax in recent tax reviews, but governments have had little taste for the idea. A land tax would keep land prices lower over the longer-term as land would become a less attractive form of investment.

Estate and death duties also contributed to government tax revenues and helped to reduce wealth inequality under the Liberals in the early twentieth century. Over subsequent decades, under National Party governments, death duties became progressively lower in real terms and became increasingly subject to high levels of avoidance, and were finally abolished in 1993. A final residue of gift duties was removed in 2011 (Littlewood 2012; McAlister et al. 2012). Only one way remains in which wealth and assets may be prevented from being passed from the old to the younger generations of a family: where old people require intensive care in a retirement home, their assets are tested and used to fund the cost until exhausted. This taxing of assets is based on luck rather than fairness.

Differences in wealth have become more apparent in New Zealand because of increasing house prices, making it increasingly difficult for younger people on modest incomes to buy their own homes. Instead, favourable tax treatment for investors has led to increased demand for residential property to rent, one of the drivers of increasing prices. The absence of a capital gains tax in New Zealand and the ability to offset expenses and losses against other income makes owning rental property very attractive to New Zealanders who can afford to enter this market. High levels of immigration and a shortfall in housing construction further put pressure on prices, particularly in Auckland, New Zealand's largest city. Added to the poor quality of much rental accommodation, concern about housing underpinned much of the inequality debate in 2014. As we shall discuss in Chapter 5, Labour and the Greens both promised a capital gains tax if they were to form a government.

Women's equality

Paying attention to gender introduces further dimensions to an analysis of equality. Equality of respect and opportunity took longer to establish for women than men. Because of discrimination limiting their political and social rights, women have demanded equality of voice and equal rights to live their lives freely, extending the coverage and vocabulary of the concept. Equality of voice implies voting rights, rights to stand for national office and efforts to secure more proportionate representation between women and men in positions of power in government and in other institutions, both public and private. Equality of rights means freedom from discrimination, protection from male domination and, for many, women's right to control their own bodies, including the choice to abort an unwanted foetus. Of course, inequality for women also has an economic dimension. Most data on income and wealth inequality are collected on a household basis. In terms of personal income and wealth, and within households, gender inequality is also well documented and well known, and a significant gender pay gap persists.

New Zealand was home to one of the world's earliest and most successful feminist movements, and achieved female suffrage under the Liberal Government in 1893. Feminism has a strong presence in New Zealand. Feminists have been most active within the Labour and Green Parties. The Green Party ensures equal male and female representation among its MPs. Labour has failed to reach that target and there are divisive debates within the party about the priority and means of securing that goal. Some see pressing for more women in parliament as a distraction from Labour's primary purposes of pressing for equality across all dimensions— an excessive focus on 'identity politics'.

Post-suffrage, various women's organisations took up concerns about the status of women. Franchise Leagues morphed into Women's Political Leagues and the National Council of Women was established. Members and leaders of these organisations used their influence to lobby parliamentarians. Prime minister Seddon attributed many of the reforms initiated by his Liberal Government to the pressure brought to bear on his government by women. In 1928, the President of the National Council of Women listed 44 pieces of legislation on which she claimed the organised effort of women had had a decisive influence (Page 1996).

The *Family Allowance Act 1926* instituted a means-tested benefit that was applied for by the breadwinning husband but paid to the wife. The measure had wide political support and it helped to unravel the sole focus on the man in New Zealand's family wage breadwinner model (Nolan 2000: 139–41). The family allowance might not have promoted women's wage work, or equal pay as workers, but it gave many women for the first time an income and a taste of economic independence. In 1946, the First Labour Government removed the means test, paying to all mothers a fixed amount per child, initially under the age of 16, and eventually under the age of 18 (Nolan 2000). In 1985, the Fourth Labour Government moved family income support back into the means-tested targeted model and, despite considerable resistance from women, the fixed family benefit was abolished by National in 1991 (Curtin and Sawer 1996).

The principle of equal pay for women was finally recognised in legislation in 1960; first applied to the public sector, and extended to the private sector in 1972. Equality for women moved back into a more prominent position in the 1970s in the context of the 'second wave' of feminism. Feminists demanded social policy reforms around childcare, health and reproductive rights, and sexual violence, and Labour Party feminists were influential in ensuring the descriptive and substantive representation of women became a priority for the party (Curtin 2008).

By the 1980s, feminism in New Zealand had three main strands: an 'equal rights' agenda that focused on remaining forms of discrimination; a political agenda to increase the representation of women in politics; and an economic agenda that began with the traditional issue of equal pay with a stronger underlying objective of greater economic independence. Meanwhile, more women were moving into the labour market, and New Zealand trade unions were becoming more responsive to the interests of women workers.

More effective promotion of human rights in New Zealand began with the formation of the Human Rights Commission in 1977 under a National Government. In the 1980s, the Labour Government established a Ministry for Women's Affairs (now the Ministry for Women). Common Law understandings of rights were given statutory recognition and extended to gender in the *Human Rights Act 1990*, and further developed in the *Human Rights Act 1993*. The Equal Pay Act was not legally understood to apply to equal pay for different work of equal value across different industries. In 1990, a Labour Government passed the Employment Equity Act to legislate for that principle. It was repealed by the National Party when it returned to office in that same year. But in response to union sponsored court action, a Court of Appeal decision in 2015 reinterpreted the Equal Pay Act as applicable to 'different work of equal value'.

Under the Fifth Labour Government (1999–2008), women's economic independence became a central platform. With this came an explicit recognition by Labour that women were permanent labour market participants, and that economic conditions often required them to work, and many were choosing to work. The government also recognised that the market alone was unable to sufficiently support working mothers. The boosting of child care support, paid parental leave, benefits for working families and welfare to work policies were core parts of Labour's agenda (Curtin 2015; Curtin and Devere 2006). The current National Government has recognised the importance of women's labour market participation by extending paid parental leave and retaining benefits for working families. It has been less generous with sole parents who are primarily women, targeting them explicitly in their 2011 campaign for re-election (Curtin 2014).

In the most recent World Economic Forum global gender gap index, New Zealand scored 10th overall (with Australia 36th). But New Zealand ranks 30th for 'economic participation and opportunity', much closer to Australia's ranking of 32nd. The lower overall ranking of Australia is largely due to women's 'political empowerment', where Australia stands at 61st and New Zealand at 15th (World Economic Forum 2015). In 2014, the New Zealand Ministry for Women reported that the gender pay gap stood at 9.9 per cent. In 2015, the gap had increased slightly to 11.8 per cent (Ministry for Women 2016). Over the long term, the trend is positive as the gap was 16.3 per cent in 1998. Women still remain significantly under-represented in the highest-paid professions and over-represented among those on low wages. There are few women chief executives in either the public or private sectors. Women remain under-represented in parliament and the executive. On the same assumptions we apply to economic groups, women should be more likely to vote for the left or centre-left. In Chapter 4 and Chapter 9 we test this expectation, and in the latter chapter broaden the discussion to other gender questions.

Māori, indigenous rights, the treaty and equality

There are many parallels between arguments for ethnic minority rights and those for women. Equality of respect directly challenges racist attitudes to which such minorities are often vulnerable. Equality of voice demands political representation, and equality of rights demands equal treatment that may sometimes require taking account of differences by targeting affirmative action policies toward ethnic groups.

Questions of equality and inequality can be particularly challenging when they concern differences between ethnic groups, particularly where an ethnic group claims indigenous status.

In discussions prior to the signing of the Treaty of Waitangi on 6 February 1840 by representatives of the British Crown and various Māori chiefs, there was agreement that Britain could set up a government over the increasing numbers of new settlers arriving in the country. The Māori text of the Treaty, now accepted as the most authoritative version, did assign 'complete government forever' to the British Crown in Article One, but also guaranteed that Māori chiefs would retain their existing authority in Article Two (Kawharu 1989).[4] This left ambiguous the authority that the government would have over Māori. The British Crown went on to declare sovereignty over New Zealand on the basis of an English translation of the Treaty. In Article Two, the Treaty also promised that the British Crown would protect Māori, their property and valued possessions. Article Three promised that Māori would have the rights of British subjects (Orange 2011). Article Three can therefore be interpreted as an equality principle.

The promises made in Articles Two and Three of the Treaty were soon ignored, and disputes between land-hungry settlers, the colonial government and Māori tribes led to war, most intensely in the 1860s. Māori lost land in a combination of confiscation, conflict among themselves, fraud and sales. With little resistance to imported disease, and demoralised by defeat, the Māori population dropped to a low point at the turn of the twentieth century, and then began to recover. Recognition of injustices began to emerge under the Liberals in the beginning of the twentieth century. But pressure on Māori to sell land and attempts to suppress Māori language and culture on assumptions of racial 'assimilation' continued well into the late twentieth century. In the 1930s, the First Labour Government moved to begin to honour Article Three of the Treaty by removing discriminatory provisions that prevented Māori from accessing welfare benefits. Māori subsequently benefited from the formation of the New Zealand welfare state and the expansion of state housing for those on low incomes, cementing a tradition of Māori support for Labour that has continued, albeit with recent interruptions.

---

4   The English translation of the Māori version that is most cited is that of Hugh Kawharu, and can be found at: www.nzhistory.net.nz/files/documents/treaty-kawharau-footnotes.pdf.

A new generation of urban Māori spearheaded a Māori cultural and political renaissance in the 1970s, beginning with renewed protests about land alienation. Responding to this pressure, the Third Labour Government (1972–1975) set up the Waitangi Tribunal to address current disputes about Treaty issues. In 1985, the Fourth Labour Government gave the Waitangi Tribunal the power to review past actions back to the signing of the Treaty, and inserted compliance with the principles of the Treaty into some legislation. Waitangi Tribunal decisions are recommendations only, but governments are obliged to address them by subsequent negotiation. Over the years, significant resources have flowed to Māori iwi (tribes) as the result of the recognition of the previous failures of past governments to meet their Treaty obligations to protect Māori. A new 'Māori economy' has developed, spreading more income and wealth toward Māori than in the past, but also increasing inequality between Māori. Māori retain a hierarchical culture in which status and birth count for more than among European or Pākehā New Zealanders (Metge 1967). More to the point, Treaty of Waitangi settlements are made with iwi, but many Māori in urban areas have lost sufficient knowledge of their descent to be included. Devolution of social assistance to Māori providers is one of the ways in which some of these problems are being addressed.

The need to address problems of inequality with respect to Māori sits uneasily with the values and attitudes of many Pākehā. Popular Pākehā ideas of equality tend not to be inclusive of Māori collectively, although Māori are fully accepted as individuals and fellow New Zealanders. While philosophical principles of equality can be brought to bear to justify unequally treating groups of people so that they can become more equal, such arguments have often been difficult to sell in everyday politics. Māori claims are also based on a claim that the government should restore rights of property and self-determination that have been wrongly denied.

While many understand this logic, others, as former National leader Don Brash (2004) put it, fear that New Zealand has been developing 'two sets of laws, and two standards of citizenship'. Brash fuelled this fear in the months before the 2005 election. During Labour's third term in office, in response to criticism, its policy to 'close the gaps' between Māori and non-Māori was reframed to remove any reference to ethnic identity. To be explained further in Chapter 10, the Clark Government's foreshore and seabed legislation was a breach of Māori rights and led to the establishment of the Māori Party—the most successful attempt by Māori to establish an independent presence in parliamentary politics and government. The Māori Party has worked in alliance with the National Government since 2008. However, the question of equality for Māori is still one of the most difficult issues for New Zealanders to address in the early twenty-first century. Significant socio-economic gaps remain between the Māori and Pākehā population, with the Māori population having lower average formal qualifications and incomes, and higher rates of unemployment compared with the Pākehā population (Statistics New Zealand 2014a, 2014b, 2016b).

Conclusion

New Zealand's political history reveals an early commitment to egalitarian liberalism, although it fell very short in the treatment of Māori and women. Chartist, Fabian, socialist and radical liberal ideas informed many of the economic and social policies implemented in the nineteenth and early twentieth centuries. Some of these policies became entrenched over time, acceptable to political parties on the left and the right. But this great consensus began to unravel in the 1970s. Income and wealth differences increased in tandem with greater recognition of the gender and ethnic dimensions of inequality. There were various reasons: increased market inequalities, changes in the role of the state in taxing and spending, and changes in the nature and regulation of the labour market that weakened the power of trade unions to bargain collectively. In very recent times, inequality has become more prominent in the public debate, with varying responses from the political parties and with the current National Government often tending to address legal inequalities rather than the substantive inequalities that require budgetary commitments or state regulation in the market (Chappell and Curtin 2013).

A strong common thread runs through the various narratives and analyses in this chapter: the importance of party politics and party policies in shaping the fall and rise of inequality in New Zealand. Government policies have both offset and fostered social and economic inequality, and thus this study of inequality in the context of an election is timely and relevant.

3

Electoral behaviour and inequality

Having outlined the broad parameters of the 2014 election and examined the recent increase of social and economic inequality in New Zealand, our next step is to establish why and how inequalities might be connected to vote choice. To this end, this chapter introduces the main theoretical models that inform our empirical analyses, and how they may assist in addressing our research question.

The models we identify are intrinsic to the understanding of electoral politics and resonate with both political discourse and practice in New Zealand and elsewhere. For example, in September 2016, New Zealand Labour leader Andrew Little rejected the advice of former Labour prime minister Helen Clark (1999–2008) that parties on the left must 'command the centre ground' in politics, describing it as a 'pretty hollow view'. Instead, he proposed that Labour should build 'a coalition of constituencies' (Sachdeva 2016). Clark's understanding of politics is of an ideological contest between left and right. National Party prime minister John Key has made similar statements about 'hugging the centre'. Andrew Little apparently sees politics as about constructing a coalition of social groups that can be persuaded to favour his party.

Clark's position is based on the assumption that people's policy preferences across an ideological dimension from left to right are shaped by their relative economic positions in society. To win, a party or coalition of parties must capture the support of the people in the centre: the median voters. The theory presents a rational calculus of voting: each voter compares the expected utility (or value to them) of having party A in government with the expected utility of having party B in government. The utility differential determines the voters' party choice. Those in a lower socio-economic position who would gain most from redistribution of incomes are expected to support left-wing parties that pledge to tax the rich and transfer income to those who are poor. Those in higher socio-economic positions will vote for parties that say they will allow those with wealth and higher incomes to keep them. Those in the centre weigh up which party, left or right, will be closer to their interests. Parties of the left and right will therefore tend to moderate their ideological appeals to try to capture the votes of those in the centre. This model puts inequality between individuals and families in a capitalist democracy at the heart of its assumptions.

In contrast to this economic model, the social psychological model focuses on psychological affinities and identities. Defenders of this model argue that politics is fundamentally about identities that construct group affinities, not about ideologies (Achen and Bartels 2016); very close to Little's idea of a 'coalition of constituencies'. A group affinity—party identification—is said to be the main factor behind the behaviour of voters. The central role of partisanship is presented through the so-called funnel of causality, which presents a chain of events that contributes to the voters' eventual party choice. It distinguishes factors that generate the basic conflicts of interest within society, such as economic structure, historical patterns and social divisions, from proximate factors that more directly influence people's party choices: issues, candidates, election campaigns, the influence of friends and the media (Dalton 2014). As we discuss in more detail below, these models provide us with different ways of understanding the relationship between social and economic inequality and voting behaviour.

The economic model

Anthony Downs' book *An Economic Theory of Democracy* (1957) applied the theoretical tools of economics to electoral behaviour. Voters were assumed to be instrumentally rational and self-interested. People vote in order to maximise their 'utility', defined as whatever they might want. In practice, though, Downs assumed that most voters wanted to increase their incomes, and would therefore vote for parties and politicians that promised to do so.

Downs started from the idea that voter preferences and party positions fall across the left–right dimension. Those on the left prefer government to redistribute income and use various other means to ensure the social security and wellbeing of all members of a society—they take a position favouring equality. By contrast, those on the right prefer a limited role for government. They want to protect private property and allow a free market to generate wealth and deliver income accordingly to those who work for it. They thus take a position likely to generate inequality, accept a degree of inequality and resist more than minimum efforts to reduce it.

To win an election in a two-party system, a party must attract the vote of the median voter; that is, the person in the middle if all voters stood in a line from left to right. The job of the two major political parties is to convince those people that hug the centre to shift one way or the other. Their best strategy for doing so is to present party policies that are attractive to the median voter. In a multi-party system, the logic is a little different— particularly for smaller parties closer to the left or right extremes. But if there are two larger parties competing to lead a government, it is expected that the median voter remains their main target. A party staying close to the median voter should have a good chance of being elected and re-elected, and large office-seeking parties will therefore tend to stay close to the centre (Adams 2012; Meyer 2013).

Several commentators have asserted that the National Party under the leadership of John Key has been extremely successful at winning median voters. National is thought to have been pragmatic by some, or an opportunistic office-seeker by others (Hooton 2016; Hosking 2014a; Nagel 2012). But National resisted getting on the inequality bandwagon during the 2014 election, despite the salience of the issue during the campaign. Only one new initiative was promised of potential benefit to those on low incomes: an extension of free medical care to children up to 13 (from the age of six) and a small boost to early childhood education funding (National Party 2014a). Nevertheless, despite this lack of largesse, National has been identified (Nagel 2012) as mathematically closer than Labour to the median voter since 2008. As shown in Chapter 1 (Figure 1.1), this is confirmed by public perceptions of the two parties' positions. Only a few months after the 2014 election, National's centrism or alleged opportunism re-emerged, and the government announced that to reduce 'child material hardship' it would increase welfare benefits (New Zealand Government 2015). One can take this as another sign of Key's 'middle-of-the-road' strategy, potentially making the government less vulnerable to concern about inequality and poverty in the future. But this still does not entirely explain the failure of inequality to shift votes to the left at the 2014 election.

Early extensions of the Downs theory also fail to provide an explanation for this puzzle. A self-interested median voter should support redistribution of income in conditions of economic inequality where the average income tends to be higher than the median. Political parties aiming for median voter support, including those on the right, should adopt policies that reinforce this position (Meltzer and Richard 1981). This may have worked in the 1960s and 1970s. From the 1980s and 1990s onwards, growth in the size of government and the extent of social expenditure has flattened, with significant decreases in some countries. Political parties on the right have shifted further to the right on both economic and social policy, and parties on the left have tended to follow them. Inequality has increased, but median voters are not responding as the Meltzer-Richard (1981) extension of Downsian theory predicts.

One reason given for this apparent contradiction lies with increasing wealth through the ownership of assets, noted in Chapter 2. When house prices rise, this may increase the apparent wealth of those on median incomes and encourage them to borrow and spend more, and vote for parties of the right that support unregulated, free market wealth accumulation (Ansell 2014). It may be that many people think less in terms of their immediate interests and more in anticipation of what their incomes are likely to be over their lifetime. The prospect of upward mobility may dispose those on low incomes to vote for parties on the right because they anticipate higher incomes in future, and they may therefore behave like traditional right wing party voters (Alesina and La Ferrara 2005; Benabou and Ok 2001). Another way of defining those who see themselves as likely to be upwardly mobile is as 'aspirational' (Smith, Vromen and Cook 2006: 10–12; Simms and Warhurst 2005). Others may be more pessimistic about their economic futures and thus attracted to parties on the left. They may feel insecure economically and thus also be attracted to the left because the welfare states provide insurance against bad luck or unexpected adverse events such as job loss or illness (Iversen and Soskice 2001; Lupu and Pontusson 2011; Moene and Wallerstein 2001; Mughan 2007; Rehm 2016).

Another modification of Downs suggests that rather than voting for parties that are closest or most proximate to their position, people will vote according to the 'direction' of their position (for reviews and the various extensions of this literature see Adams 2001; Merrill and Grofman 1999). Consider a left–right dimension from 0 to 10, and a person who scores 5.1, just marginally to the right. If the left and right parties have positioned their policies at 4.5 and 6 respectively, the most proximate party to the person in question is the one on the left (a difference of 0.6). However marginally, that person is on the right, and might therefore vote for the right wing party directionally regardless of its more distant proximity (0.9) when compared with that of the left party. This means that large parties that are more extreme than the median voter can continue to attract moderate people on their side of the left–right dimension, even if those moderates might have policy preferences closer to the party on the other side.

There is another reason why moderate or median voters might vote for parties that are more right wing than themselves. Median voters may prefer a moderate redistribution that would benefit them but would resist high levels of redistribution that would require them to pay higher taxes. In two-party systems, the risk of a redistribution that might harm those on median incomes will dispose people in that situation to vote for the right. In a multi-party system, a significant centre party might be expected to defend the interests of middle-income voters and resist high levels of redistribution, thus capturing their votes. Thus coalitions of centre-left and centre parties may establish and defend systems of moderate redistribution (Iversen 2005; Iversen and Soskice 2006).

Downs' model assumes that the acquisition of information is one of the costs of voting. Most voters lack political knowledge, an assumption confirmed by empirical research (for example, Delli Carpini and Keeter 1996). When deciding to vote, people acquire information from trusted sources, such as people they know, as well as from the communications media or the political parties or candidates themselves (Lupia 1994; Lupia and McCubbins 1998; Page and Shapiro 1992; Popkin 1991). Once people select a political party they believe is close to their views, often on the basis of limited information, they may use it as a source of further information, reinforcing their likelihood of giving that party their vote. People may have party identifications, but they can be updated as a result of various events and new cues, and can change over the long term (Fiorina 1981).

Those with the least economic resources and with most to gain from a reduction in inequality are also known to be the least knowledgeable and informed about politics (Grönlund and Milner 2006). Consequently, they may be more likely than those who are well-informed to vote for a party that is not the closest to their own position. It may also be that these people choose not to vote at all (Brady, Verba and Schlozman 1995; Smets and van Ham 2013). In most countries, including New Zealand, turnout has declined over time, and the trend continues with only temporary upswings (Vowles 2010, 2014a, 2015a, forthcoming). Low turnout tends to be more prevalent amongst those on low incomes, without wealth or assets (Solt 2008), with lower levels of education and the young (Franklin 2004). The Downs model provides a clear explanation for these groups not voting: the costs of making an informed vote are higher, as they tend to have lower levels of political knowledge than those who are older, more educated and middle class. With increasing levels of inequality, the young, less educated and the poor tend to feel that government policy is tilted against them, and they have little confidence that their vote will make a difference or result in any sort of benefit (Griffin and Newman 2013; Mahler 2008). We can label this a 'disempowerment thesis' (see Chapter 11). Research in other countries shows that economic adversity may depress turnout when social protection is less generous. Where beneficiary incomes are increasingly means-tested and access to these becomes more stigmatised, those most affected may withdraw from politics, rather than holding government accountable (Pacek and Radcliff 1995; Radcliff 1992; Rosenstone 1982).

Some suggest that if more people of lower socio-economic status voted, this would affect election outcomes. In particular, left-leaning parties would benefit from higher turnout (for example, Fowler 2013; Mackerras and McAllister 1999). Others argue that those on low incomes would benefit from higher turnout because both left and right leaning governments would pay more attention to addressing their needs. When low-income voters fail to turn out, it becomes easier for governments to tolerate inequality (Boix 2003; Husted and Kenny 1997; Mueller and Stratmann 2003).

According to Downs, people vote according to the benefits they can expect from tax and social policies. Beginning with Donald Stokes (1963), critics have argued that people are more likely to vote according to a set of shared interests that they might have in common: a strong and growing economy, for example. Alternatively, people might vote according to their perceptions of the competence of the government and its leaders in delivering public services and handling matters of the day. The focus thus becomes not the issue itself but which party is most likely to deliver growth, good public services and stable government. This vein of theory has become known as the 'valence' or performance model of electoral choice (Clarke et al. 2011). Within a broad economic model of voting behaviour, this 'valence' or performance theory contrasts with Downs' 'positional' theory that is founded on his assumption that issue and ideological positions are based on different sets of economic interests that mostly fall across the left–right dimension.

Many others have taken up the idea that people might vote according to the economic performance of a country, returning governments to power under conditions of economic growth and dismissing them during a recession. While some have empirically confirmed models of retrospective economic voting (Fiorina 1981; Lewis-Beck and Stegmaier 2013), more generally, the findings have been mixed and contested. Clarity of government responsibility for the economy varies across countries because of cross-national differences in political institutions, and whether governments are made up of single parties or coalitions (Anderson 2007). It has been argued that voters use immediate past records of economic performance as an indicator of probable future performance. Expectations are therefore the driving force rather than wishes to reward or punish (Duch and Stevenson 2008). When voters are asked to rank election issues, they frequently identify 'management of the economy' as the most important issue driving their vote choice (Bean and McAllister 2012).

Despite the richness of research within the Downsian tradition, it has been subject to continual criticism (led most famously by Green and Shapiro 1994; see also Hug 2014; and, most recently, Achen and Bartels 2016). The criticism mainly targets the 'thin' assumptions on which Downs' theory is based: that people can be assumed to be rational, at least up to a point; that political competition can be usefully simplified in a simple one-dimensional model; and that people with low knowledge can be successfully 'cued' to behave politically in accord with their interests (Kaye 2015). In sum, the model is theoretically elegant, helps us to think about aspects of electoral politics clearly and has identified many useful lines of inquiry. It is a good place to start, but not a place where we can comfortably conclude our inquiries.

The social psychological model

A second theoretical model through which we can examine voting behaviour and the relevance of inequality to such behaviour is the social psychological model, recently given new impetus by its recasting into a revived 'realist' theory of democracy (Achen and Bartels 2016; also Lenz 2012). The antecedents of the social psychological model are a little older than those of its economic rival. The earliest election studies in the United States in the 1940s began with assumptions that voters were akin to consumers and parties sold themselves as products. This was an approach that Downs took up and developed more successfully later. But researchers found that voters were too strongly loyal to their parties to behave as consumers in a market should or would (Lazarsfeld, Berelson and Gaudet 1944). This led to a shift in emphasis and a turn to psychology and group theories of politics (Berelson, Lazarsfeld and McPhee 1954). This underpinned the development of the theory of party identification, most clearly articulated in *The American Voter* (Campbell et al. 1960). Partisanship came to be seen as a central explanation for voting behaviour, conceptualised as a psychological affinity with a political party.

The social psychological model begins with the sociological idea that political parties both respond to and shape social cleavages and identities that might reflect class, language, ethnicity or religion, depending on the society in question (Lipset and Rokkan 1967). As such differences often reflect social and economic inequalities, this vein of theory also has implications for our analysis. Around those social cleavages and identities, people develop loyalties to political parties that are constructed and reinforced by social networks such as churches, trade unions, families and the political parties themselves. People's apparent ideological and issue preferences are shaped for them by the discourses of the groups with which they identify. Individual preferences often shift to be consistent with group norms or changing party policies.

Such loyalties are not absolute and might be overcome temporarily by an effective or charismatic leader, attractive promises or a strong performance by another party. Votes may also change because of a shift away from a tired and exhausted incumbent government that has been in office for a long time. Yet, according to this model, the majority of people are expected to eventually default back to older loyalties; they have a 'homing' tendency. The social psychological model combines both sociological and psychological influences on voting into the so-called *funnel of causality* (Campbell et al. 1960). It distinguishes distant influences from more concrete, immediate and direct influences on voting behaviour (Dalton 2014). Partisanship and party identification are influenced by more distant factors, such as economic structure, social divisions, group identities and value orientations. Partisanship then influences issue opinions, candidate images and, both directly and indirectly, the actual voting act. This pattern of influence is itself influenced by various other factors, including campaign activity, media, friends and family, and economic and political conditions.

The central core of the social psychological model is its idea of party identification as rooted in loyalty and identity, and as possibly inherited through the family. It is emotional or 'affective' rather than rational or cognitive, as is the case in the Downsian economic model. However, the idea of party identifications as being stable over time has turned out to be the weakest claim of the psychological approach (Dalton and Wattenberg 2000; Dalton 2013). Voting choices from one election to the next have also become more volatile over time in many countries, including New Zealand, although perhaps not as consistently as some of the literature suggests (Dassonneville and Hooghe 2011; Mainwaring and Zoco 2007; Mair 2005; Vowles 2014b).

The continued strength of the psychological approach lies mainly in its claim that rationality does not provide sufficient explanation for political behaviour. Research into political psychology bears this out. For example, people are more affected by the prospect of loss than of gain and tend to be risk-averse (Kahneman and Tversky 1979). As a consequence, people may need to be more convinced to vote against a government than to vote in favour of it, providing a micro-level explanation for the old adage that 'governments lose elections, oppositions do not win them'. Perceived government failure or disruptive policy changes may generate fears of loss. If voters are considering voting against a government, a perception of a viable alternative that reduces fears of loss will increase their probability of doing so.

Daniel Kahneman (2011) tells us that human beings have two modes of response to stimuli: a 'fast' mode by which we respond rapidly by instinct or emotion; and a slower mode, where we think about consequences. Much political behaviour takes place in the fast mode, in which voters are likely to be influenced by a recent experience or interaction that primes their response. At another time, or in a different context with different cues or influences, they might behave, vote or express their opinions differently. This reinforces the early findings of Philip Converse (1964), who analysed panel surveys that included people who had been interviewed three times over two to three years, with many of the questions repeated. He found very little stability in opinions, except among the most politically knowledgeable. Of even greater interest, he found evidence of 'non-attitudes', with people expressing opinions when asked trick questions about nonexistent legislation. Developing this line of inquiry, John Zaller (1992) has shown how mass opinion often follows cues from political elites (see also Lenz 2012; McAllister and Bean 2006). This phenomenon is affected by political knowledge. Those with lower levels of political knowledge receive fewer cues than those with higher levels of knowledge, but the former are more likely to follow them.

As discussed earlier, exponents of the economic model also accept that most people have low knowledge about politics, but argue that the cues they receive shape their preferences in ways consistent with what their preferences would be if they were more knowledgeable. In other words, voters' preferences have an indirect rational foundation. But psychological research also finds that people are selective in the cues to which they respond, and people with higher levels of knowledge are not immune from bias. We can interpret many responses to questions about public opinion on the basis of 'they would say that, wouldn't they'. Even the most knowledgeable voters are prone to make choices that they may not normally make had they considered them further. Instead, they stay with pre-conceived ideas and assumptions and are prone to reject evidence that refutes them (Kuklinski et al. 2000; Kuklinski 2007; Lodge and Taber 2013; Nyhan and Reifler 2010).

People may therefore resist updating their party identification despite new information that challenges it. A strong emotional identification with a political leader may blind people to negative aspects of a president's or prime minister's leadership. Perceptions of an effective and likeable leader are more important than the economy and can play into a more general feeling that a government is competent. Perceptions of competent leadership almost certainly affect how people assess the performance of the economy and the government's responsibility for that performance. Even perceptions of the state of the economy can be affected by party choice, depending on circumstances (Chzhen, Evans and Pickup 2014; Evans and Andersen 2006; Evans and Pickup 2010; Pickup and Evans 2013). Where the economy is strong, people who vote for opposition parties may declare that the economy is weak, as we shall see in Chapter 4. There are very few if any simple one-way causal pathways between perceptions and behaviour.

This all begs the question of where voters get their information about the performance of their country's economy, as at least some of the sources of that information may be biased, and voters are often selective in their media consumption. In addition, governments in countries such as New Zealand can only have marginal effects on the performance of their economies, because of small size, global exposure to trade and investment and greater vulnerability to 'shocks'. Using cues generated by the communications media, rather than responding to absolute changes in the economy, people may compare their country's economic prospects to those of other countries that may be close trading partners or neighbours. For example, economic growth in New Zealand is frequently compared to or 'benchmarked' with economic growth in Australia, much as the strength of the dollar, tax and wage rates, and house prices relative to income are often compared. The role that the media plays in communicating these perceptions has been described as 'pre-benchmarking' (Kayser and Peress 2012). Achen and Bartels (2016) discuss the example of shark attacks on New Jersey beaches that adversely affected the local economy and later influenced voting in a presidential election. Droughts in American farming states can lead to the defeat of governors at the next state election. However, sometimes voters can evaluate the effectiveness of a government response to a shock, and in this case incumbent politicians can be reasonably held to account (Gasper and Reeves 2011). The impact of exogenous shocks can also work in reverse. In New Zealand, it has been suggested that the National Government was able to win key seats in Christchurch after the February 2011 earthquake in part because the government-funded recovery program helped both the local community and the national economy, demonstrating the government's apparent skills in economic and crisis management (Young 2011).

The timeframe within which judgements about economic performance are made is also considered important. British evidence indicates that people do not respond so much to moderate or small short-term shifts in the economy but acquire perceptions over longer periods or when an economic shock is particularly strong (Chzhen, Evans and Pickup 2014). But if voters' perceptions are based on short-term evaluations of strong shocks, they may be influenced by a temporary upswing or downturn that may not reflect a longer-term trend. In the United States, the evidence is different: while Democratic presidencies tend to be associated with better outcomes for people on lower and middle incomes, short-term economic upswings have coincided with crucial elections faced by Republican incumbents who have usually been re-elected (Bartels 2008).

The attribution of responsibility for a large 'shock' may be significantly misplaced. For instance, in Britain, the Labour Party was in government when the global financial crisis (GFC) of 2007 occurred. The Conservative Party, while in opposition between 1997 and 2010, had been if anything more strongly committed than the Labour Party to the 'light-handed regulation' of the financial sector that made the crisis possible. After the crisis hit, the Labour Government under Gordon Brown responded with an economic stimulus and avoided the deep economic downturn that many had feared. Brown played a large role in successfully arguing for a coordinated international stimulus. After Labour left office, the Conservative and Liberal Democrat Coalition's austerity policies almost led Britain back into recession, its recovery since has been sluggish, its government finances remain in deficit and its government debt high. Nonetheless, Labour has been widely blamed for the effects on the economy of the GFC (Cowley and Kavanagh 2015; O'Hara 2015).

By contrast, Australia's economy began to boom after 2003, not because of good economic management but because of China's insatiable demand for natural resources. Consequently, the Howard, Rudd and Gillard governments could ride out the worst of the GFC (Kelly 2014). Nonetheless, voters saw Labor as poor economic managers (Koukoulas 2016), and when Abbott's Liberal–National Coalition government came to power in 2013, it introduced policies of austerity. The latter did not lead to recession, but nor did they ameliorate Australia's economic downturn. Using this sort of evidence, Achen and Bartels (2016) have been able to make a strong case that much voter evaluation of governments is 'myopic' if not 'blind'. If these pessimistic findings hold true generally, voters who might benefit from or simply wish to see more redistributive government policies are unlikely to recognise and reward the politicians or the parties promoting them.

Positional politics in two dimensions

In Chapter 1, we introduced not just the traditional economic left–right ideological dimension, but also a second social dimension that partly cuts across it. Political conflicts around that second dimension may help to explain why preferences about equality or inequality, which might be expected to be shaped by the left–right dimension, may move in other directions. This dimension can be described as representing the 'new politics', as opposed to the 'old politics' of the left and right. The idea of the new politics emerged in political science and sociology in the late 1960s, when new divisions concerning cultural issues began to emerge in advanced western democracies. Based on the psychology of Abraham Maslow, Ronald Inglehart (1977, 1990) theorised the dimension as one of materialism versus post-materialism. Post-materialism is said to be found among people who have been born into recent generations in the developed democracies and brought up under conditions of material and physical security. Taking these conditions for granted, their political aspirations are said to become focused on enhancement of human freedom and creativity and the protection of the natural environment for aesthetic reasons. A significant literature has emerged, some of it developing the concept, but there has also been much criticism (for example, Davis and Davenport 1999; Duch and Taylor 1993). Subsequent developments also weaken the theory; material and physical security are not as fully assured in the developed democracies as may have been assumed in the 1970s when the theory emerged. Moreover, protection of the environment is not merely an aesthetic concern; for many, climate change is a serious problem that threatens physical and economic security in the present and the not-too-distant future.

Nonetheless, post-materialism has contributed to an analysis of politics in advanced democracies that moves beyond the left–right dimension of the 'old politics' (Dalton 1996; Poguntke 1987). In New Zealand and elsewhere, the political space is now generally modelled in two dimensions: the economic left–right dimension and the 'new politics' dimension, which can be taken to represent materialist versus post-materialist values; or, more simply, socially conservative against more liberal attitudes.

Indeed, a stronger theoretical basis for the second dimension may lie in orthodox psychology. The idea of a second dimension beyond left and right was anticipated in the 1950s by psychologist Hans Eysenck, and in his terms it was based on personality. It distinguished between the 'tough-minded' and the 'tender-minded' (Eysenck 1954). An even more influential strand of theory developed even earlier and came out of efforts to understand the appeal of Fascist and Nazi movements: the idea of the 'authoritarian personality' (Adorno et al. 1950). The concept of authoritarianism fell out of favour in subsequent decades, but in revised form has recently become popular again, particularly among political psychologists (Altemeyer 1988; Stenner 2005; Whitley 1999).

Indeed, materialist and post-materialist attitudes tend to correlate strongly with attitudes along a continuum from libertarian to authoritarian (Kitschelt 1994). This cleavage centres on questions of morality and freedom, and cross-cuts the traditional 'old politics' economic cleavage. It divides society according to levels of education, rather than economic class (Bornschier 2010; Flanagan and Lee 2003; Inglehart 1984; Houtman 2003; Van der Waal, Achterberg and Houtman 2007). Authoritarian attitudes can be enhanced by fear, by perceptions of insecurity and by experiences of rapid change that generate uncertainty. Authoritarians tend to be conformist and live structured and disciplined lifestyles. By contrast, libertarians tend to be critical and question orthodoxies, and to have lifestyles that are less structured and less anchored in ongoing commitments.

The rise of authoritarian populism in parts of Europe and more recently in the United States has placed the concept even more on the map (Lubbers, Gijsberts and Scheepers 2002; Mudde, 2007; Norris 2005; Rydgren 2007; Van den Berg and Coffé 2012; Van der Brug, Fennema and Tillie 2000). Some theorise this development is also associated with globalisation, a phenomenon that tends to threaten both material security and provoke cultural concerns associated with immigration (Kriesi et al. 2008). The two-dimensional structure of public opinion in New Zealand is not a new phenomenon and was comprehensively mapped after the 1993 and 2002 elections (Vowles et al. 1995: 100–21; Vowles 2004b). In this book, we operationalise the authoritarian/libertarian dimension, particularly in our discussions of the Green Party, New Zealand First and the Conservative Party.

The existence of these two cross-cutting dimensions to positional politics has significant political implications to be explored in later chapters. New politics issues include the rights of minorities or relatively powerless groups of various kinds: religious, ethnic and gendered, as already discussed in Chapter 2. They also include immigration, an increasingly sensitive topic in many countries.

New politics draws heavily on identities that can cut across the traditional debates between left and right that have obvious implications for social and economic inequality. So-called 'wedge politics' (Hillygus and Shields 2008) can mobilise cultural issues around race (Iyengar and McGrady 2007) and immigration (Newton 2008), detaching voters from their traditional loyalties and sidelining debates about the country's high levels of inequality. Frustrations borne out of the stagnation of low and middle incomes in the United States have been mobilised on a racial and cultural basis, as Donald Trump's election to US presidency bears out only too well. In Australia, refugees arriving by boat made control of the country's borders a highly salient political issue, driving a 'wedge' between the Labor Party and many of its traditional supporters (Jupp 2012, 2015; Ward 2002). In Britain, similar concerns about border control featured strongly in the successful 'Brexit' campaign; immigration policy divided the Opposition Labour Party internally, alienating it from many of its traditional working-class voters (Dennison and Goodwin 2015: 171).

In New Zealand, from the other side of that dimension, 'new politics' support briefly helped the Lange-Douglas Labour Government of the 1980s retain votes in 1987, particularly the popularity of the government's nuclear-free policies (Vowles 1990: McAllister and Vowles 1994). But in more recent years, critics have argued that Labour's apparent focus on 'identity politics' has placed another wedge between the party and its traditional voters (Maddison 2006), a wedge that has been exploited by Labour's opponents and may help explain its lack of electoral success in recent elections. Chapter 6 takes up these claims. New Zealand's geographic location relieves it of most of the problems of border control faced elsewhere. Immigrants tend to be accepted, but a high rate of influx in recent years has made immigration a potential wedge issue, potentially drawing some voters away from their previous loyalties. Chapter 8 takes up this issue in more depth.

Finally, it is worth observing that the underlying assumptions of the 'new politics' model are derived from psychology, but differ significantly from those of the social psychological or group theory. Just as the economic model assumes that people have 'interests' that are largely independent of the ways in which elites construct the political world, new politics theorists assume that people have underlying values that are derived from psychological dispositions relatively independent of elite influence. By contrast, the social psychological model is based on the assumption that interests and values are mostly constructed by a combination of group interactions and elite cues. In practice, most researchers in electoral politics accept that it is reasonable to entertain the possibility that some interests and values may be relatively independent of group and elite influences, while others may not—these are ultimately empirical questions.

Conclusion

The economic voting model starts from the idea that people are guided by self-interest and therefore vote for the party that promises to promote their interests. The main difficulty they face is the cost of information needed to make that calculation. In contrast to the cognitive approach of the economic voting model, the social psychological model is based on social group identities and, in particular, partisanship and party identification based on psychological affinities. Social group affinities can give cues to provide people with information that helps them make decisions, but there are no guarantees that these decisions will serve their interests. Partisanship and other group identities are also major sources of 'cognitive bias', the tendency of people to resist new information that challenges their ideas and assumptions. Even if people care about inequality, affecting themselves or others, they may not necessarily respond politically as one might expect. The 'new politics' or 'values' approach identifies a second dimension to positional politics that may also cut across debates about inequality, distracting voters and diverting their economic concerns into cultural channels.

This chapter has compared and contrasted the three approaches to thinking about voting choice, and we consider all three to be of value. Despite decades of criticism, the ideas of left and right continue to resonate in political discourse. They still stand for state-led redistribution of resources on the left and preferences for free markets on the right. In the wake of the GFC and the great recession, with increasing international concern about inequality, we can hardly say they are irrelevant. Neither can we ignore the existence of the new politics dimension that may channel voting behaviour in new directions. The normative ideal of a democratic citizen who listens, learns and participates, and whose preferences are fundamentally 'rational', is not one that we should lightly dismiss. Knowledge of political psychology alerts us to the limitations of that vision, and the way democratic ideals can be perverted, often at the hands of less than scrupulous elites.

4

The social foundations of voting behaviour and party funding

Having introduced the theoretical frameworks underpinning our analysis, we move on to an investigation of how people's party choices at the 2014 elections reflected their economic and social positions in society. Was their social and economic position reflected in their party preference for a left- or right-leaning party? And did it matter that some might have benefited economically from increased economic inequality by way of lower marginal tax rates on higher incomes, increased profits or higher salaries, as compared with others for whom economic inequality has generated lower salaries or benefits, less affordable houses and increased insecurity?

Focusing on the four main parties (Labour, National, New Zealand First and the Greens), we present baseline models for voting behaviour including the major socio-economic characteristics and identities expected to explain voting behaviour. We also investigate how owning assets like a house, business and stocks interact with income and how this relates to party voting and left–right position. Both income and wealth distributions are obvious indicators of inequality, but the interaction between them has only rarely been investigated in election studies, and may have significant political implications. Controlling for baseline social structure, we explore how aspirations for a more prosperous future or, alternatively, the fear of losing one's job or losing one's income relates to party choice and left–right position.

Our starting point and theoretical framework for these inquiries is that of self-interested voters who are nested in a social context—within their families and the wider community in which they live, and the groups to which they can be matched. Our argument is simple: interests and ideologies are constructed within networks associated with group identities, but they are not constructed out of nothing. Group identities and the ideological positions with which they become associated tend to have a footing in social structure, and can have a 'rational' basis. For example, all else being equal, we expect that it is more probable than not that someone on a benefit and in rental accommodation will have preferences for a lower rent and a higher benefit.

When exploring how voters' socio-economic position relates to their party choice, and thus the social foundations of the main political parties, we also look at the implications of these social foundations on the parties' campaigns and, in particular, the funds they have at their disposal.

The construction of interests

Individuals and families in New Zealand sustain themselves economically in a market economy in which there is a complex division of labour and a variety of ways to earn a living, including full or partial income support from the state. This division of labour determines the incomes people receive that in turn affects the assets they may or may not be able to accumulate. It slots some people into jobs that are relatively secure and well-paid, and others into jobs that may be less secure but where a balance of risk and opportunity may or may not lead to prosperity, depending on a combination of talent, skills and luck. These economic and social differences are the foundations upon which people may define their 'interests' or, in theoretical terms, their utility. The theory, as discussed in the previous chapter, tells us that people will choose a political party to vote for that will maximise their utility. For some, utility maximisation may dispose them to vote for a party to the right in favour of a free market that determines the distribution of wealth and income; for others it may be a vote for a party to the left that promises to intervene to correct the inequalities inevitably generated by the market.

Political scientists have traditionally followed through this line of inquiry by way of the analysis of class voting, most recently focusing on the extent to which class voting has declined (Clark and Lipset 2001; Evans 2000; Manza, Hout and Brooks 1995). Most work has been based on the Weberian concept of occupational status, with research influenced by Marx bringing in asset ownership (Wright 2009). People define themselves, or are defined, by classes that can be approached from two directions. The first direction distinguishes ownership from non-ownership of property, with property including 'the means of production'. The second distinguishes classes according to their 'status', defined by a hierarchy of occupations, structured by education, skills and the value attached to occupations by way of income and social status. There are numerous ways of defining and operationalising the concept of class. One of the most influential has been a three-way classification that distinguishes people who work in manual or service occupations, those who work in non-manual occupations and farmers.

Figure 4.1 displays the standard Alford Index of class voting for New Zealand since 1963, drawing on previous New Zealand election studies. It is calculated by subtracting the proportion of people in non-manual/non-service/farming households voting Labour from the proportion of people of manual/service households who also voted for that party (an index originating in Alford 1962).[1] From a low point in 2002, class voting has recovered to a level comparable to that in the early 1980s, although with one significant difference: the proportion of the population in manual/service households has somewhat declined, and is currently at about 34 per cent of the sample that can be classified, compared, for example, to about 42 per cent in 1987 (Vowles 2014b: 40).[2]

---

1   In multiple working adult households, we classify occupational class of the household by the occupation of the male in the household (the respondent his/herself, or the respondent's partner). This reflects the reality of gender pay inequity, which means that in most cases the occupation of the male is a better guide to the economic position of the household. The NZES does not ask for the gender of respondents' partners, but because most couples are made up of a male and female, this classification is the best reflection of the economic position of a male–female household that can be estimated from our data.

2   It is important to note that this estimate of class voting is 'relative'. If one focuses on 'absolute' class voting, for example, because of the large gap between the National and Labour party votes in 2011, National gained a slightly higher share of the votes from manual/service households than Labour; however, this was no higher than National's usual vote from this part of the electorate. But Labour's share of the working class vote had shrunk to an historically low level in tandem with its low level of overall support (Vowles 2014b: 40).

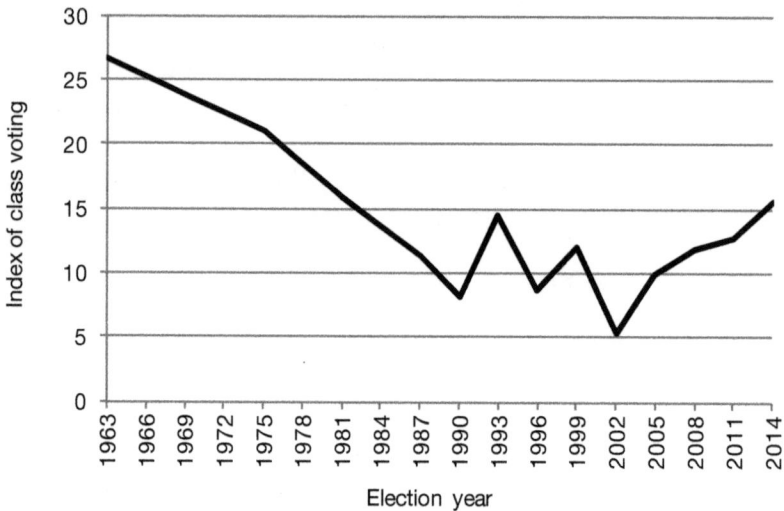

Figure 4.1: Class voting in New Zealand, 1963–2014

Note: The figure displays the difference between the proportion of manual/service households and the proportion of non-manual/service households voting for the Labour Party.

Source: Victoria University of Wellington Election Study 1963, 1975 (see Bean 1986); New Zealand Election Study 1987–2014.

Changes in technology and production have had deep effects on labour markets that go beyond a simple decline of the working class. Differences between those who work in the private sector, the public sector and the non-profit sector have become more significant. The growth of self-employment would potentially increase insecurity that might benefit the left; however, self-employment has traditionally been associated with voting for the right because of the business and individualistic values that often lie behind it. In fact, despite expectations to the contrary, household labour force and census data indicate that self-employment has not increased in New Zealand over the last 20 years or so.

The development of a more competitive society makes the accumulation of assets both more important and more difficult, particularly given the increasing unaffordability of house ownership for those on low incomes. The ownership of assets can be separated into two forms: low risk and high risk. The New Zealand Election Study (NZES) contains questions measuring ownership of low- and high-risk assets, with low-risk assets including two assets (a house to live in and some savings) and high-risk assets also including two assets (a business or business activity, and investment in stocks and shares). To simplify the inquiry, we can distinguish between no assets or perhaps only one asset and those with all four types of assets. Analysis of the scale indicates a high correlation between those who have high-risk assets and those with the highest scores. People with high-risk assets tend to have low-risk ones as well, whereas the majority of asset owners tend to only have low-risk assets. Both income and wealth are obvious indicators of inequality; we also include other variables that are expected to have effects on inequality and life chances such as gender and age. Age is important given there is a broad consensus that the current generation of young people are finding it significantly more difficult than earlier generations to establish secure careers and accumulate assets such as housing.

To get a more comprehensive understanding of inequality and party choice, we need to set class beside other social cleavages such as urban and rural differences, ethnicity, level of education and gender. Occupational class is not the only group focus of the formation of interests associated with work across the primary production, industrial and service sectors of the economy, not to mention public versus private sector employment. Analysis of New Zealand politics has tended to focus on the urban–rural and class cleavages, although these tend to overlap. Increasingly, New Zealand politics must also come to grips with the ethnic cleavage, not just between European-descended or Pākehā New Zealanders and Māori, but also incorporating other ethnic groups. Ethnic cleavages usually overlap with class cleavages, as in New Zealand, with Māori over-represented among those with low incomes and in lower status occupations. All these differences can be identified as affecting vote choices for parties of the left—particularly Labour, the party of equality, representing those on lower incomes—and the right—the National Party, the strongest support for which comes from the business community. We also need to consider the influence of political socialisation through the family.

Meanwhile gender, although a potent source of inequality, has not formed a consistent cleavage in New Zealand politics. In the 1960s and probably earlier, women were slightly more likely to vote for the right (Vowles 1993), while in the 1990s into the 2000s they were slightly more likely to vote for the left, particularly when Helen Clark led the Labour Party. Marginally, women are more likely to vote Green than men, and men have usually been more likely to vote New Zealand First or ACT (Coffé 2013b; Curtin 2014). We deepen our analysis of these patterns in Chapter 9.

Finally, education is another crucial variable shaping party choice. As new politics issues such as gender equality and the environment have become more salient and Green parties have developed, a cleavage has grown along levels of education. It divides the higher educated with generally libertarian attitudes and a tendency to vote for the left from the lower educated with more authoritarian attitudes and a greater likelihood to support right-wing, populist parties (for example, Bornschier 2010; Flanagan and Lee 2003; Inglehart 1984).

Table 4.1 lists the variables from our baseline multinomial multivariate model of the social and demographic correlates of inequality and voting choice; the various party choices and non-vote are unordered categories, so this is the appropriate approach. Vote National is the base category, and the others are non-vote, Labour, Green, New Zealand First, Conservative, and 'Other'. We include non-vote because it is an important element in overall voting choice, but the topic is left for deeper analysis in Chapter 11. The baseline model accounts for about 11 per cent of the variation in voting choices in 2014. The figures below display the significant results, estimated as predicted probabilities of voting for each of the three main parties (National, Labour and Green). The probabilities take account of the effects of all the other variables in the models. The full models are presented in Appendix, Tables 4.A1 and 4.A2.

Table 4.1: The social and demographic structural correlates of inequality and voting choice

Model 1: Baseline Model	
Occupation Household	No Occupation Reported
	Farming Household
	Non-Manual Household
	(Ref. Manual Household)
Sector of Employment	Self-Employed
	Public Sector
	(Ref. Private Sector)
Assets (0–4)	
Relative Income (1–5)	
On Benefit	Yes
	(Ref. No)
Education	Low
	(Ref. Middle)
	High (University)

Gender	Female
	(Ref. Male)
Age (18+)	
Ethnicity	Māori
	Asian
	Pasifika
	(Ref. European or other)
Living in Urban Area	Urban (100,000 plus inhabitants)
	(Ref. Not Urban)
Membership Union	Yes
	(Ref. No)
Church Attendance	Never–At least Once a Week (0–1)
Model 2: Addition of	
Interaction of Income x Assets	
National or Labour Parents at 14	

Notes: A range, for example (0–4), indicates that it is a continuous variable. Bracketed categories are the reference category in the analyses and means that it is the category to which an effect is estimated. For example: female against the reference category male. The wealth or assets index is made up of four questions: 'Do respondents own a home, house, or apartment; a business, property, a farm or livestock; stocks, shares or bonds; and any savings?' This generates a simple additive scale that ranges from zero (none of the above) to four (all of them). Low education is defined as those at level 2 or below (that is, a sixth form qualification). Ethnic identity is defined as the strongest where multiple identifications were reported. Relative income is based on the question: 'How do you think your household's income compares to that of the average person in New Zealand?', with response categories much lower, lower, about average, higher, much higher. This has a high correlation with the question asked on income itself, and has a higher response rate.

Figure 4.2 shows significant relationships between socio-demographic characteristics and voting National, net of the effects of all other variables in the model. Of the entire enrolled electorate, including non-voters, National's vote was just over 36 per cent. Various factors did not relate significantly to voting National after taking all other baseline model variables into account and are thus not presented in Figure 4.2, for example, there was no significant relationship between gender and choice to vote National or not, or for Asian ethnicity, church attendance, urban or rural location, education, economic sector and occupational group. While there is broad acceptance among political commentators that Asian voters tend to vote National more than average, NZES data suggests otherwise.

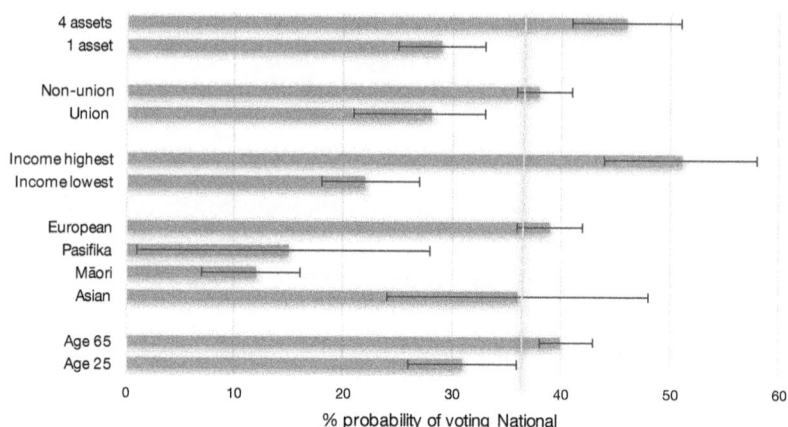

Figure 4.2: The social and demographic correlates of structural inequality and vote for the National Party

Source: Appendix, Table 4.A1. Grey vertical line indicates overall probability of National vote choice. Error bars are 95 per cent confidence intervals.

Focusing on the inequality-related measures, Figure 4.2 confirms that people who vote National are more likely to have much higher incomes than average, have accumulated more assets and are less likely to belong to a union. They are significantly more likely to be 65 and above, and more likely to be European and less likely to be of Māori or Pasifika ethnicity. Figure 4.2 thus confirms expectations: those voting National tend to be those who have benefited from, or at least those not adversely affected by, the increase in inequality in the 1980s and 1990s.

Turning to voting for Labour, Figure 4.3 shows that voting Labour is in many respects the other side of the coin of voting National. Gender, age, economic sector, urban–rural and receipt of benefits had no significant effects in the model. In our data, Asians were a little less likely to vote Labour than average, but not at a level of statistical significance. Māori were somewhat more likely than average to give their party vote to Labour, but the relationship is not strong and the confidence intervals overlap considerably (see Chapter 10 for more analysis). The model controls for occupation, income and assets, all of which are significant; as Māori are more likely to be on lower incomes, manual occupations and have relatively few assets, these characteristics may pick up the effect of being Māori. As expected, there is very likely a strong Pasifika element to the Labour vote, but the small size of that subsample means that the confidence intervals are very wide. Similarly, being on a benefit or not is 'soaked up' by income. Labour continues to draw on the manual and service classes, less on those in non-manual households, more on those on lower than average incomes, with few assets and in union households. Less traditionally, but not unprecedented since the 1980s, the university-educated are more likely to vote for Labour than average. Overall, though, according to these structural or socio-demographic indicators, Labour remains the party representing those who have lost rather than gained because of increased inequality.

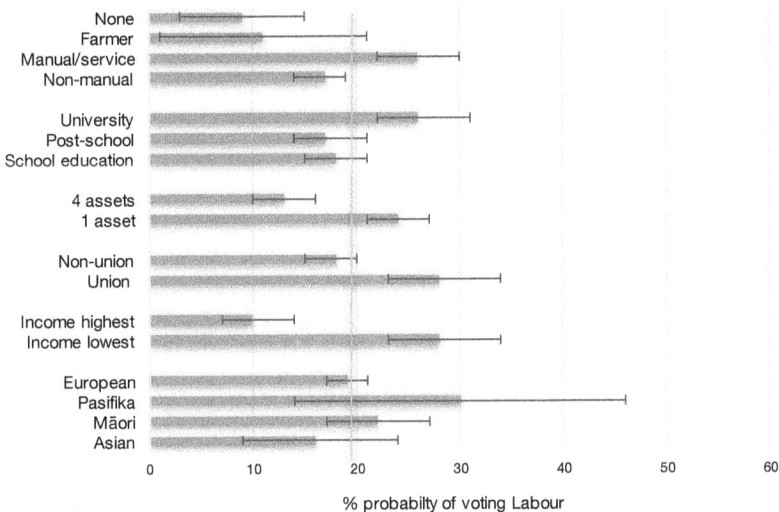

Figure 4.3: The social and demographic correlates of structural inequality and vote for the Labour Party

Source: As Figure 4.2.

Figure 4.4 shows probability estimates for those social and demographic variables that significantly affect Green voting. Green voters formed just over 8 per cent of the entire electorate. The Green Party appeals more to younger voters than the old. However, the Green Party appeals significantly less to ethnic minorities, and is particularly unattractive to the Asian community. Green Party voting choice is somewhat affected by lower than average income and asset ownership, although these differences fall within confidence intervals. As with Labour, voting Green is also associated with some social advantage as the university-educated are much more likely to vote for the Green Party than are other educational groups. The Greens are significantly less likely to appeal to people in farming households, not unexpected given the Green Party's strong policy positions on reducing rural environmental pollution. Green voters are more likely to live in a major urban area of over 100,000 in population, which means living in one of New Zealand's largest cities: Auckland, Christchurch, Wellington, Hamilton, Dunedin or Tauranga.

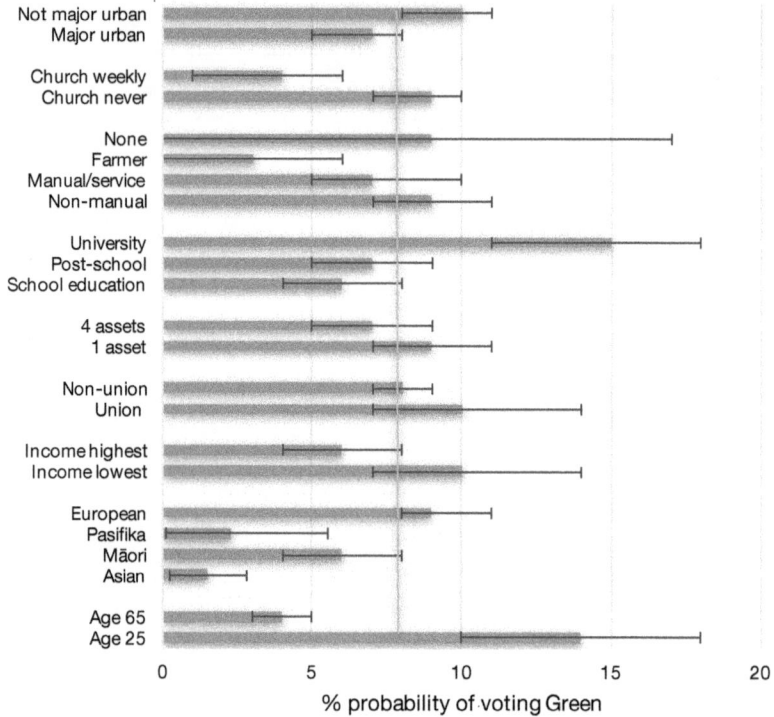

Figure 4.4: The social and demographic correlates of structural inequality and vote for the Green Party
Source: As Figure 4.2.

The New Zealand First vote was almost 7 per cent of the enrolled electorate, and only a scattering of socio-demographic factors were significant. For the party vote, New Zealand First retains a Māori appeal; Māori being 3 per cent more likely to vote New Zealand First than Europeans, although the difference is well within confidence intervals. Pasifika respondents also tend to be somewhat more likely than Europeans to vote for New Zealand First, but the confidence intervals are extremely wide, which do not allow us to draw firm conclusions. By contrast, Asians had a zero probability of voting for New Zealand First, not unexpected given New Zealand First's policy positions on immigration. People on lower incomes are also more likely to vote New Zealand First. Men were slightly more likely than women to vote for New Zealand First. Further analysis of the New Zealand First vote can be found in Chapter 8.

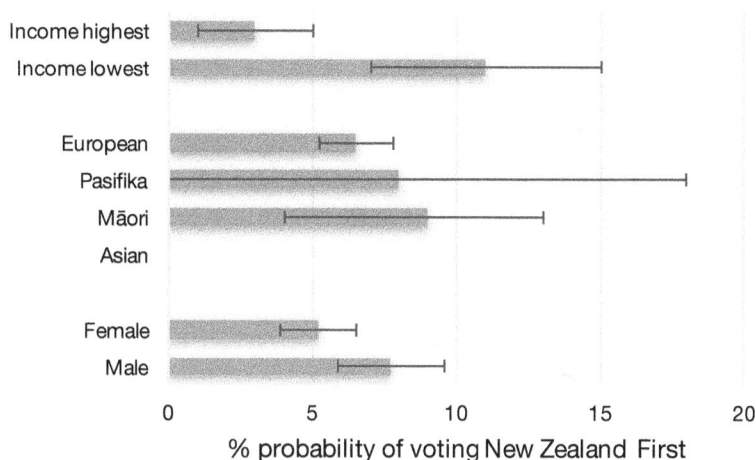

Figure 4.5: The social and demographic correlates of structural inequality and vote for the New Zealand First Party
Source: As Figure 4.2.

Parental partisanship, income and assets interactions

Having presented the baseline model for each of the main parties, we now move on to add an interaction between income and assets to the models and, in addition, parental partisanship. In the US, people's party choices still tend to be influenced by their parents' party choices; confirming findings from much earlier research that party choice is a habit passed down between generations (Jennings, Stoker and Bowers 2009). Parental partisanship is important because it can be a key source of identity, particularly if it is passed on from parents to children. In countries in which party identifications have declined over the last 20 or 30 years, as in New Zealand (Vowles 2014b: 46–47), we might expect to find less transmission of party identification from parents to children than in the past.

Within the sample, 16 per cent reported two parents who supported National when respondents were aged 14. Recollections of having two Labour parents were higher at 22 per cent. Five per cent reported divided parents, and 42 per cent reported no parental partisanship. Older respondents were slightly more likely to report parental partisanship. As one would expect, few respondents recalled parents supporting the Green Party or its forerunner (the Values Party) or New Zealand First, and the numbers were too small for statistical analysis.

As Figure 4.6 indicates, those for whom both parents voted National are significantly more likely to vote National, while respondents who recall both their parents being Labour voters are appreciably more likely to support Labour. Recollection of parental support for Labour also slightly increases the probability to vote both for the Green Party and for New Zealand First. We should be a little cautious about these findings since the likelihood of recalling parental partisanship is likely to be associated with current loyalties.

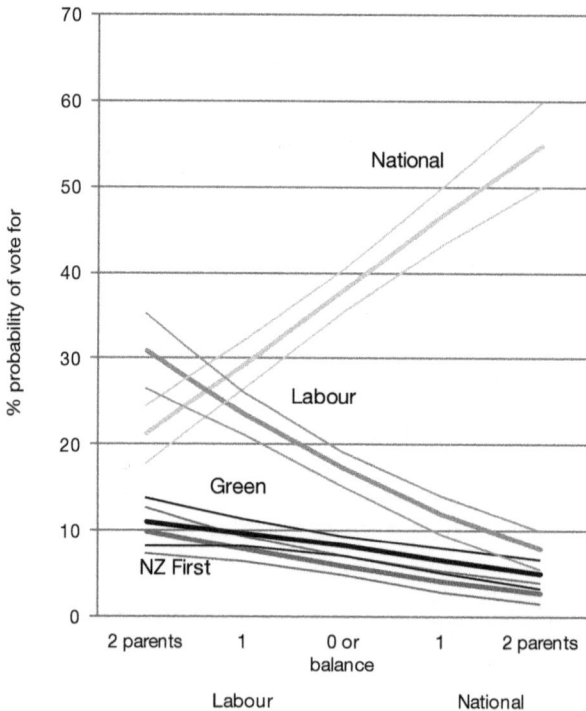

Figure 4.6: Parental partisanship and voting choice, 2014 election
Source: Appendix, Table 4.A2.

The purpose of our analysis of the interaction between income and assets is to explore how party choices are affected when one has high or low levels of one of the two, or both. Our focus also moves to perceptions of risk and (in)security, and the choices people make to protect themselves. One way to achieve security is to acquire an asset that may reduce the need for income; in particular, a home that is mortgage-free, and also some savings, while remaining confident that the state will provide a guaranteed pension in old age: a 'low-risk' strategy.

Other people, however, may choose to take risks, setting up their own businesses, borrowing money to invest in order to make more money, and accumulating other assets such as stocks and shares, the value of which could move down as well as up. This high-risk path can lead to wealth, but can also go wrong, sometimes seriously so. A successful high-risk strategy can make people so prosperous that their resources can cover all possible contingencies; for example, a business setback, loss of employment or the need for expensive hospital treatment. Those prepared to take the high-risk strategy are a minority. However, their values are individualistic; they believe in self-reliance and are likely to be opposed to government action to reduce inequality, possibly regardless of their current incomes. Analysis of the assets scale indicates that, as one would expect, those who own higher-risk assets are found at the top of the scale, as they tend to also own lower-risk assets as well. Hence, the assets scale can also be interpreted as estimating the propensity to take risks.

Those with no assets are unlikely to have the resources necessary to cover losing their jobs or suffering a serious blow to their health—they form about 7 per cent of the sample. Those with one asset make up about 20 per cent, those with two nearly 30 per cent, while 45 per cent have three or four. Those with limited assets will tend to look to the state to provide safety nets—for example, through income support for the unemployed and the sick, and a government-funded health service—and are likely to support a party that defends redistribution and an active welfare state, since private markets can rarely provide affordable comprehensive cover for all possible contingencies. The safety net itself also reduces inequality, as it prevents people from falling into deprived situations in which their ability to support themselves can go from bad to worse, from which they may find it hard to recover.

Funding services such as health and unemployment insurance requires taxation and, since the market incomes of the lowest paid do not leave much of a surplus after basic needs are met, that taxation must bear more heavily on those with higher incomes. If those with fewer low-risk assets are more favourably disposed to the idea of collective risk-pooling, we would expect them to be more willing to pay for it, even when their incomes increase, and we therefore expect them to vote for parties that pledge to fund social services regardless of their incomes. If they do not, the project of collective risk-pooling will lack the essential support of those with the incomes to pay for it by way of progressive taxation. We would likewise expect support for such services among those with high-risk assets to be low, regardless of their incomes.

Figure 4.7 shows the interaction between relative household income and the ownership of assets and how it relates to voting Labour, the party traditionally most in favour of redistribution of wealth. No significant effects were found on the probabilities of voting for parties other than Labour (see Appendix, Table 4.A2). Figure 4.7 shows, as expected, that those following the high-risk strategy and having accumulated all four asset types had a relatively low probability of voting for the Labour Party, regardless of their incomes. By contrast, among those with only one asset, those on lower than average incomes and only one asset have a significantly higher probability of voting Labour than those with one asset but a higher income. Those who saw themselves as on average incomes had a probability of voting Labour that more or less matched the party's overall vote. Among this income group as well as among the lower income groups, those with only one asset were significantly more likely to support Labour than those with all four assets. Those with higher than average incomes were least likely to vote Labour, irrespective of the number of assets they reported. A more sustainable and equality-enhancing pattern would have been to see those with fewer assets but higher incomes also voting Labour. Those who have accumulated fewer assets should be ideologically more disposed to collective risk-pooling and therefore to support redistribution and vote accordingly.[3] In 2014, they tended not to do so.

---

3   Plotting this figure for the Green vote finds a flatter line for low-risk voters across the income scale, indicating some high-income low-risk support for the left, but confidence intervals are too wide for significance. Modelling the Green and Labour votes together generates a pattern very similar to that of Labour alone, although the addition of low-income/high-asset Green voters makes the two slopes more parallel.

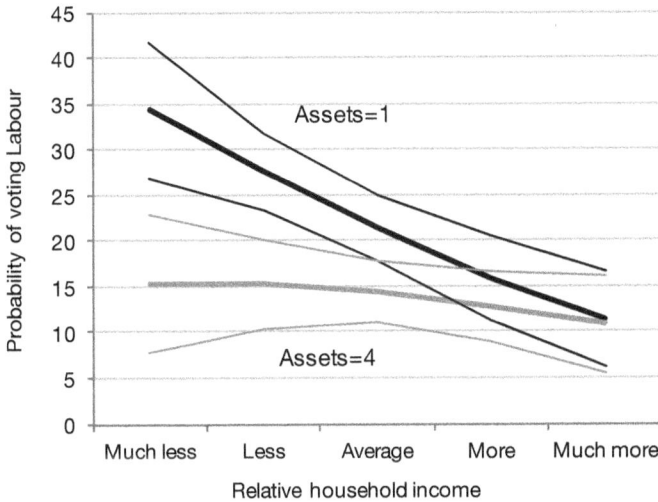

Figure 4.7: Income and assets interaction and Labour vote (with 95 per cent confidence intervals)
Source: Appendix, Table 4.A2.

Perceptions of insecurity

To move beyond a structural approach to voting behaviour, we need to investigate people's perceptions of their economic situation. The 2014 NZES contained several relevant questions, including how much people feel exposed to risks such as losing their jobs or incomes, their senses of security or insecurity and, from a positive angle, their aspirations for the future.

Figure 4.8 displays the responses to the relevant questions. Again, we see evidence of an overall satisfaction with New Zealand's economic performance. We also see evidence of cognitive bias, with a third of respondents believing, against most of the economic statistics, that the economy had got worse over the previous year. The economy question is one of the standard instruments of electoral research and is usually a good predictor of support or opposition to an incumbent government (Duch and Stevenson 2008). People who are positive about the economy are more likely to support the incumbent government. However, responses are invariably coloured by bias among those who have long-standing or even more immediate loyalties, and therefore need to be interpreted cautiously (Evans and Andersen 2006).

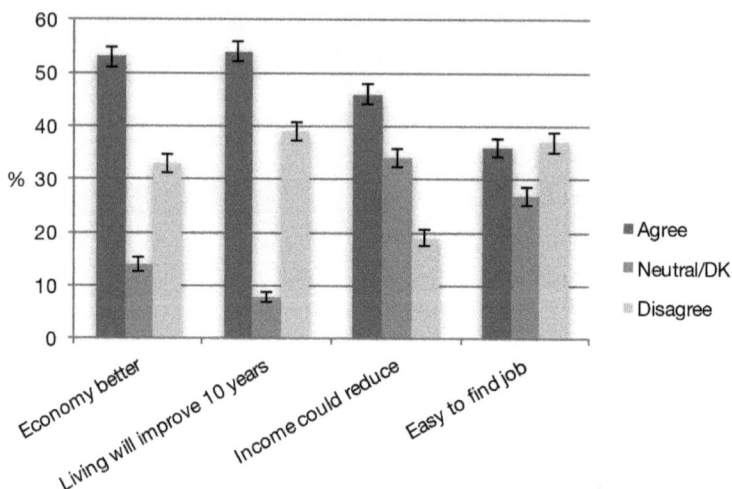

Figure 4.8: Perceptions of economic security or insecurity

Note: The questions were: 'If you (your partner) lost your/their job, how easy or difficult would it be to find another job within the next 12 months?' Coded to the respondent, or to their partner if the question did not apply to the respondent or was not answered. Five-point scale, very easy/easy into 'Agree' and difficult /very difficult categories into 'Disagree'; 'Over the next 10 years, how likely is it you will improve your standard of living?' Five-point scale, very likely/likely into 'Agree' and unlikely/very unlikely categories into 'Disagree'; 'How likely or unlikely do you think it is that your household's income could be severely reduced in the next 12 months?' Five-point scale, very likely/likely into 'Agree' and unlikely/very unlikely categories into 'Disagree'; 'Would you say that over the last 12 months the state of the New Zealand economy has got a lot better, got a little better, stayed the same, got a little worse, got a lot worse?' Agreement is with both better categories, disagreement both 'worse' categories. All 'don't know' responses or missing values are coded to the 0 mid-point.

Source: New Zealand Election Study 2014.

More evidence of optimism that is less likely to be contaminated by partisanship comes from the question that enquires if and to what extent people feel that their own standard of living will improve over the next 10 years. This question is also an estimate of 'aspirational' attitudes, which will be further discussed in Chapter 5.

As can be seen from Figure 4.8, 54 per cent believed that their standard of living would improve. However, nearly 40 per cent took the opposite position, although some of that may be discounted as it is likely to capture a number of older people approaching retirement. There remains some evidence of insecurity among a significant minority. One third of the respondents considered that it was likely their household income would reduce over the next year, and 37 per cent believed that if they or their partner lost their job it would be difficult to find another within the next year.

The questions introduced above were added to the baseline model, reported in full in Table 4.A3. Here we focus particularly on the two indicators of feelings of personal insecurity: the fear of income loss and the difficulty of finding another job.

In addition, we included perceptions of the economy over the last year in the models. This acts as a useful further control for potential partisan bias in answering the questions about income decline and job loss, as do expectations of a better standard of living in 10 years. Both associate strongly and positively with National vote choice.

Figures 4.9 and 4.10 present the predicted probabilities of voting for the main parties depending on the confidence people have in getting a new job and their fear of losing the job on which they depend for income, after controlling for all factors included in the baseline social structure model. The slopes are only presented for those parties where the perceptions relate significantly to supporting that party.

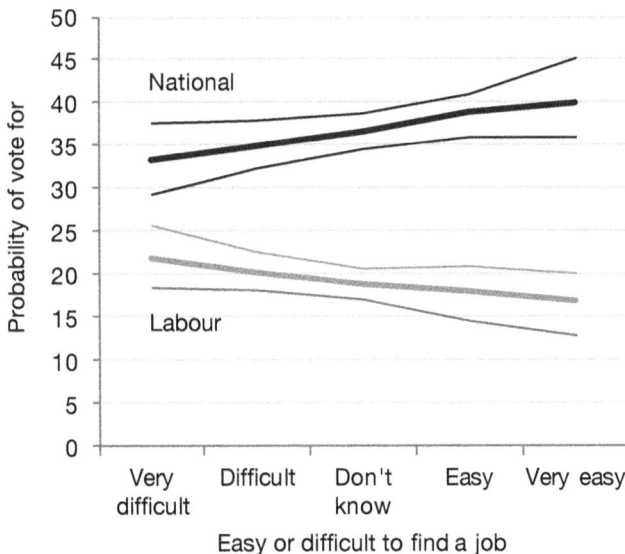

Figure 4.9: Confidence in getting a new job, National and Labour vote choice

Source: Appendix, Table 4.A3.

Figure 4.9 illustrates how expectations of finding a new job, if one was needed, affect the National or Labour vote. Expectations of finding a new job had no significant effect on people's probabilities of voting Green or New Zealand First, so the slopes for these two parties are not plotted. Confidence in getting a new job if necessary made people more likely to vote National and less likely to vote Labour, by about 6 per cent in each case. But people who were most concerned about finding a job were still more likely to vote National than Labour, even after having taken into account their perceptions of the state of the economy over the previous year.

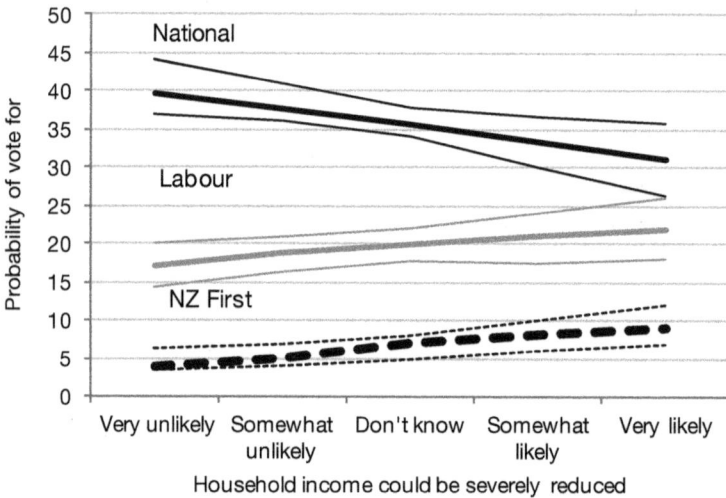

Figure 4.10: Perceptions of loss of income and vote choice
Source: Appendix, Table 4.A3.

Figure 4.10 plots the association between fear of income loss and voting choices. Fear of income loss had no effect on the probability of voting Green, but related significantly to the Labour, National or New Zealand First votes, and did so much as expected. However, the slope for Labour is close to flat, with only a 3 per cent difference. Fear of an income reduction decreased the probability of a National vote by about 9 per cent, and increased that for New Zealand First by about 4 per cent. With unemployment well below its post–global financial crisis (GFC) peak, and economic prospects perceived to be strong in New Zealand in 2014, one would not have expected highly potent effects. The big effect on the probability of voting National is a hint of potential vulnerability, if the economy were to turn downward once more.

Left–right position is one of the major variables underlying our analysis. Preferences for free markets and minimal government on the right and for regulated markets and income redistribution on the left should shape public opinion about inequality and the policies that government might adopt to reduce it. Table 4.A4 in the Appendix shows the results of regressions on the left–right scale: the first with just the baseline social structure variables and the second including the security and aspirational variables. Model I on social structure 'explains' about 16 per cent of the variance, Model II adding the security/aspirational variables improves the fit to nearly 22 per cent. Figure 4.11 displays the significant effects for the social structure, security and aspirational variables on left–right position, leaving those for income and assets. The effects of their interaction are displayed in Figure 4.12 below.

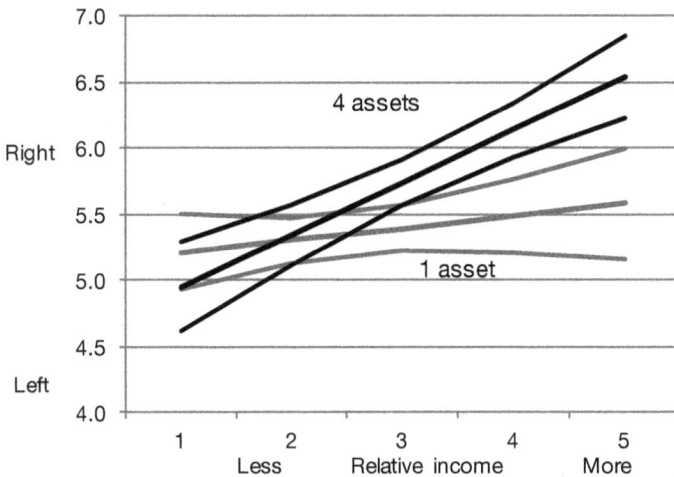

Figure 4.11: How baseline social structure, security and aspirations affect left–right positions

Source: Appendix, Table 4.A4, Model 2.

Figure 4.12 confirms that there is a strong link between asset ownership and left–right positions when conditioned by income. Relative income relates strongly and positively with a left–right position among those with multiple assets, propelling those with four assets and high incomes 1.5 points higher on the left–right scale than those with four assets and low incomes. By contrast, those with only one asset are largely unaffected by their incomes and are very close to the median and average voter positions. This provides support for the hypothesis that income does not affect the left–right positions of people who do not accumulate assets because people with fewer assets are more likely to be disposed toward collective risk-pooling. As we shall see in later chapters, support for such collective risk-pooling is found most clearly in New Zealand median voters' strong support for the universal provision of health, education and New Zealand Superannuation. Figure 4.12 stands in sharp contrast to Figure 4.7, which plotted the same relationship on the probability of voting Labour. Examining the foundations of left–right position, there seems some reason for confidence that income- and asset-based preferences for modest redistribution have the potential to be politically effective and carried into policy. But Figure 4.7 shows that in 2014 the Labour Party failed to mobilise those preferences into Labour votes.

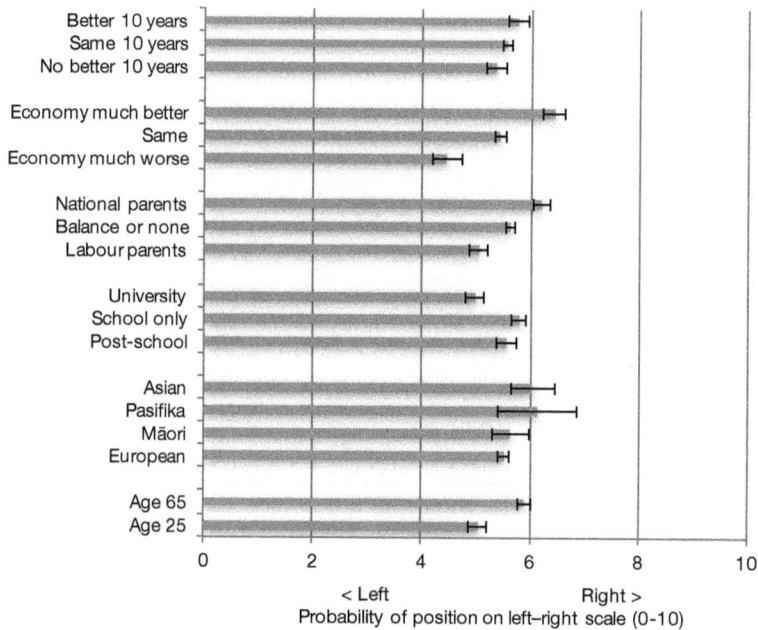

Figure 4.12: Left–right position, relative income and assets
Source: Appendix, Table 4.A4.

The difference between women and men on the left–right scale is too small to be significant, let alone substantive: women are to the left by only 1.5 per cent, and the male–female gap is well within confidence intervals. Older people tend to the right, younger people in the centre. All else equal, a person who is 65 is likely to be 0.8 further towards the right on the 10-point scale than a person who is 25. Persons of Asian ethnicity are likely to be 0.5 more to the right than a European, confirming claims that Asians tend toward the right. Māori and Pasifika differences are well within confidence intervals. People with only a school qualification tend to the right, people with university degrees to the left. People in union households tend to be more to the left, although this drops out of the second model where aspirations and security variables are added. Parental partisanship indicates the effects of socialisation; this is based on a five-point scale putting two National parents at the top, two Labour parents at the bottom, as on the horizontal axis of Figure 4.5. Occupation, sector of the economy, receipt of benefits, urban–rural and church attendance have no significant effects. In Model II, perceptions of a good economy over the last year and aspirational expectations of a better living standard in 10 years are the key variables; job insecurity or fear of income loss do not rate.

Inequality, the media and party funds

Around the world, as well as in New Zealand, party memberships have declined (Van Biezen, Mair and Poguntke 2012). Meanwhile, election campaign expenses have increased, and money matters more and more in electoral politics. Significant differences in the funds available for parties to organise and campaign may affect voters' choices, particularly over the long term. These differences are to be expected, given the propensity of some parties to gain the support of people with higher incomes and more assets than other parties. Parties with generous funding can effectively mobilise, research and target their appeals, identifying aspects of voter psychology they can seek to influence. Of course, a simple calculation of funds spent per vote by parties usually indicates no relationship between expenditures and party vote shares. This leads some to conclude that differences in funding between parties are irrelevant (Edwards 2006, 2008). Unpopular parties with plenty of money to spend do not necessarily make significant headway.

But campaign expenditure can have effects on the margins, as research on the United States Senate and House races confirms (Stratmann 2005). If all other factors shaping party vote share are equal, an intelligently used advantage in funding can be expected to make a difference. For example, advertising in the final week of the campaign in the most competitive and electorally important American states probably gave the Republican Party the edge in the 2000 Presidential election. In that final week, the Democrats could not match a Republican advertising barrage in those key states. Outside of the targeted states most crucial for the Electoral College, votes shifted to the Democrats. In the targeted states, the shift of votes was to the Republicans (Johnston, Hagen and Jamieson 2004: 99–100).

New Zealand law requires political news coverage on television to be balanced and impartial; political positions can be expressed in documentaries, interviews and debates, but all sides are expected to get their say over time (Broadcasting Standards Authority 2010). Television news formats are based on commercial principles that minimise their political content (Atkinson 2016). Outside of election campaigns, the incumbent government tends to dominate the coverage. Half of the 2014 NZES respondents followed the election often or sometimes on one or both of the two main television channels: One and TV3. New Zealand newspapers are generally nonpartisan and most are bound by a voluntary code under which they also agree to provide balanced political coverage (New Zealand Press Council 2017). Editorial positions on party choice are relatively rare and, if announced, are not sensationalised. There is no tabloid press but, equally, no 'quality press' either. Newspapers tend to have regional markets, although the biggest, the *New Zealand Herald* (Auckland) and the *Dominion Post* (Wellington), have greater penetration throughout the country, particularly through their comprehensive free-to-view websites. Of NZES respondents, 55 per cent followed election news in a newspaper during the campaign. Māori Television and Radio New Zealand (RNZ) are the only publicly funded sources of news in a public broadcasting mode that provides more in-depth balanced coverage. About a quarter of NZES respondents listened often or sometimes to RNZ's National Radio, while 10 per cent watched Māori Television. Talkback radio often has political content that tends to be more extreme and sensational: 28 per cent of 2014 NZES respondents listened 'often' or 'sometimes' during the campaign.

This media environment coupled with taxpayer funding and campaign spending limits partly level the playing field for New Zealand political parties, but the surface is far from flat. Research into the funding of political parties and political campaigns has been difficult to conduct in New Zealand since full party finance and membership statistics are, in contrast to most other advanced democracies, not publicly available. By contrast, incorporated societies far less important in New Zealand's public life are usually required to file an annual financial statement that must be approved by members at an annual general meeting and is available for public inspection. Since 1996, political parties seeking to stand candidates for the party vote have been required to register with the Electoral Commission, with a requirement that they have at least 500 members. Parties do have to report their donations on an annual basis, and the detail of their campaign expenditure in the three months prior to an election.

The Electoral Commission also has the task of allocating radio and television broadcasting expenditure between parties over the one-month election campaign, using a formula based on their vote at the previous election, party memberships, more recent polling information and some other factors. The total funds available for the 2014 election were NZ$3,283,250 (Electoral Commission 2015c). No advocacy of a vote by a political party can be broadcasted on radio or television except as funded through the Electoral Commission, and only during this period. Electorate candidates may buy broadcasting advertising out of their own funds within their own campaign expenditure limits, which apply over the 'regulated period' of three months before an election (NZ$25,700 in 2014), but it must be directed to their own electorate candidacy, although their candidature for a party can be indicated. Parties can buy advertising in newspapers and on digital platforms from their own funds within the overall campaign expenditure limits during the regulated period. Until 2016, it was understood that 'third party' organisations could advertise during campaigns, including on radio and television, but only in respect of policies, not explicitly for or against a party or group of parties. A legal decision has clarified that third parties can advertise for or against a party, with requirement to identify their promoter and an expenditure limit of NZ$315,000 over the three-month campaign period for those who spend over NZ$12,500. Overall expenditure limits apply only within the longer 'regulated' period, defined as three months before the election date. Parties can and do advertise prior to it, and sometimes have done so by means of billboards, but cannot do so on radio or television. In 2017, third-party advertisers will be able to advocate voting for or against political parties both inside and outside the campaign and regulated periods.

During the 2014 regulated campaign period, political parties could spend up to NZ$1.09 million plus another NZ$25,700 for each electorate contested. Regulated expenditure within the three-month campaign period is entirely and only related to direct communication with voters. The limits cover expenditure on television and radio production costs, other media advertising, including social media, and campaign materials such as pamphlets and billboards. Expenses incurred in in-house party polling, travel and consultants are not included, unless they are designed to directly encourage or persuade people to vote for one party or another. Expenses associated with party-paid staff or costs of volunteer assistance are also not included.

Figure 4.13 shows the total expenditure per party in the 2014 campaign, adding party, broadcasting and candidate expenditure as they were reported. The National Party spent almost twice Labour's budget. The second-highest spender, the Conservative Party, was principally funded by its leader, property manager Colin Craig. The Green Party spent a little more than Labour, but was able to so principally from a 10 per cent tithe on the salaries of its MPs (Davison 2014c).

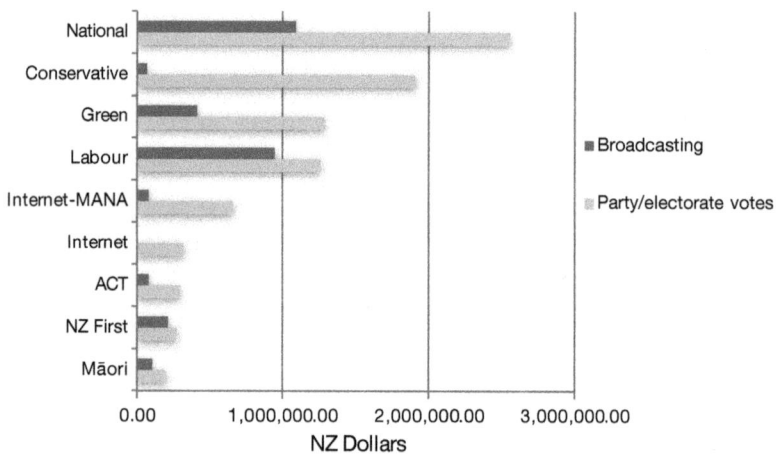

Figure 4.13: Campaign expenditure 2014 election by party (in NZ Dollars)
Source: Electoral Commission 2015b, 2015c.

Outside the regulated campaign period, parties are free to spend what they like, except on radio and television, and there is no publicly available information about how much they spend and on what they spend it. The parties maintain national, regional and electorate organisations, but there is little accessible information about their capacities and roles. Since 1993, the Electoral Commission has been charged with receiving returns of donations to political parties that are likely to comprise a significant part of their overall incomes, except for a residue of membership fees. Many traditional party fundraising activities are covered under the rubric of donations, including raffles, cake stalls and fundraising dinners.

In early years of reporting, transparency was limited by the use of trusts that would act as conduits for significant donations. By 2014, anonymous donations were limited to NZ$1,500, and 'transmitters' were required to disclose the original source of their donation if over the NZ$1,500 limit.

Figure 4.14 summarises the total named and anonymous donations from the period between the 2011 and 2014 elections. The second highest spender was the Conservative Party, almost entirely funded by one man, its leader in 2014, Colin Craig. Next, in terms of party income, was the Internet Party, again almost entirely funded by one man, Internet entrepreneur Kim Dotcom. As in Australia, a pattern seems to be emerging in New Zealand politics in which rich donors can set up or buy their own 'vanity' parties, with self-appointed leaders. The only exception for leadership was Kim Dotcom, who could not stand for election as he was not a New Zealand citizen. In November 2016, 'the Opportunities Party', to be funded and led by another rich donor, Gareth Morgan, appeared on the scene (Hehir 2016).

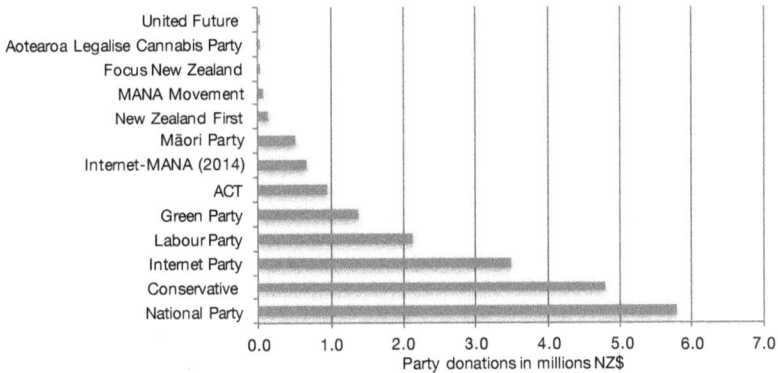

Figure 4.14: Donations to political parties, 2012–2014
Source: Electoral Commission 2016d.

Looking back to Figure 4.13, in campaign expenditure National outspent Labour by a ratio of over two to one; in terms of reported party income over the previous three years, the National–Labour ratio is closer to three to one. The gap in financial resources between the two major parties is bigger than the vote gap between them. While expenditure limits during the 'regulated period' place a ceiling on the disparity, they reduce but do not remove it. Some implications can be drawn from post-election commentary. The National Party could purchase a database of mobile phone numbers for use in the campaign. Labour could not afford to do so (Salmond 2015: 249). National could run extensive advertising on digital platforms at a cost of NZ$377,000, something Labour could not match (Barnett and Talbot 2015: 145). Labour's 2014 campaign has been described as being run on 'a shoe-string budget' (Trevett 2015).

The political parties keep their internal polling arrangements very much to themselves. It is known that the Labour Party used UMR Research, which seconded one of its staff, David Talbot, to work as campaign director in 2014. The National Party used David Farrar's Curia Market Research. Curia's 2014 pre-election polling questions have been reported by a person who was asked to participate and are standard for the territory (Brown 2014). Curia's work was supplemented by research and advice from Australian-based pollsters Crosby-Textor (Watkins 2014). John Key's relationship with Crosby-Textor goes back to 2006, when agency staff began making monthly visits to New Zealand to conduct focus groups designed to promote and define Key's public image, including strategic briefings from Mark Textor himself (Hager 2008). National's polling is considerably more intensive, regular and expensive than that of Labour. John Key has been recorded as saying that National is 'addicted to polling'—the party polls weekly (Hager 2014). John Key's responses to ongoing events were heavily informed by polling analysis and focus group reports.

Labour's funding deficit reflects a failure to maintain the strength of the party's organisation and its fundraising capacities during and after the period of the Helen Clark–led Labour Government (1999–2008). The party was in deficit in 2005 and the situation was made worse as Labour was obliged to pay a further NZ$800,000 back to government funds because Labour had unlawfully sought to use the funds to finance its 2005 election pledge card. By 2008, branch numbers and related income via fees were down, as was membership: from 12,000 in 2001 to 7,500 in 2008 (Franks and McAloon 2016: 241, 245). This is despite the record that shows that while in government Labour was mostly able to match the level of political donations flowing to the National Party (Edwards 2008). In opposition since, Labour's donations have fallen; expectations that businesses will give evenhandedly to both major parties have not been borne out. The claim that business donations have become of relatively low significance for party funding may have been evident up to 2008, with an average of only NZ$1 million a year. The recent data from 2012–2014 reported in Figures 4.13 and 4.14 shows a significant increase.

In 2014, National's electorate candidates collectively raised more than twice the amount raised by Labour candidates (Electoral Commission 2015d). A rare glimpse into usually confidential party finances can be gleaned from a Labour Party Financial Report 'obtained' by the *New Zealand Herald* in November 2015. The report showed that Labour ran a deficit in both 2013 and 2014, running down both its reserves and assets. The party reported day-to-day operating expenses on an annual basis of NZ$1 million in 2013 and $1.2 million in 2014, about half of which paid staff salaries. Internal levies on electorates and union affiliates in 2014 were NZ$636,000. Meanwhile, the National Party has an inbuilt advantage as a party that tends to reflect the interests of business and those with higher incomes and more assets, and as incomes and assets have increased most for those already at the top of those ladders, the party's advantage has increased since the 1990s. Declining numbers of unions and union members have also reduced what used to be one of the most stable and secure foundations of Labour Party funds (Edwards 2008: 7–8).

Of course, the parliamentary parties and the politicians they put into office receive a great deal of financial support from the taxpayer. Most of this benefits the incumbent government (Edwards 2006, 2008, 2016b). In New Zealand, both ministers and government departments have hired increasing numbers of public relations staff whose job is to present the policies of the government in the best possible light and, if necessary, do their best to bury information that would present a negative image (Edwards 2015a). The ability to get information under the Official Information Act (OIA) has been greatly reduced since about 2005 (Fisher 2014). As a result, regardless of all else, it may simply have become somewhat harder to dislodge an incumbent government than in the past. The opposition parties do have parliamentary staff that work to support their MPs and their party in general. They are outnumbered by those serving the government as party or ministerial officials who have much easier access to government information.

It has been argued that the increased number of staff serving MPs and the parliamentary parties is a form of state funding of parties and, in contrast, the revenues and expenditures of political parties and their sources pale into insignificance (Edwards 2008). While these funds are substantial, staff such as ministerial officials and secretaries spend only part of their time doing explicitly party politics. Electorate agents employed in MPs' offices around the country spend most of their time servicing constituents on everyday matters, although it would be naïve to imagine that agents can entirely avoid party political work. The use of parliamentary funds for party political or electorate purposes has become an increasingly sensitive subject since Labour tried to pay for its 2005 pledge card from taxpayer funds. For example, from 2011, MPs could no longer 'ask for money, votes, or party membership'. Current advice to MPs and officials draws the boundaries, although in practice there remains potential for overlap (New Zealand Parliamentary Service 2014). If governmental and parliamentary support for political parties is a form of 'state funding', it is the party in government that gets the lion's share.

The quality of the strategic advice given to political parties is almost certainly related to the money they can afford to spend. Labour's 2011 and 2014 campaigns failed to emphasise the respective party leaders and, in 2011, the crucial party vote. Whether Phil Goff or David Cunliffe might have benefited from Crosby-Textor-style 'grooming' is questionable: in Goff's case because he was already too well-known, and in Cunliffe's because his accession to the leadership was late. But the party almost certainly could not afford to pay much for the kind of research and advice that might improve a leader's presentation to the public. Labour's campaign slogan in 2014 was 'Vote Positive', widely derided for its vacuity and meaninglessness (Franks and McAloon 2016: 254), although still defended by some (Barnett and Talbot 2015: 140). Higher-quality advice based on more robust research would surely have exposed its weakness. The broadcasting allocation provided to parties pays for the time they are allocated; production costs must come from their own budgets. More funds can buy more professional advertising, and more entertaining variation in that advertising over the campaign will have a better chance of capturing public attention.

As noted earlier, a key feature of the political donation system in New Zealand is the absence of any limits per donor. Consequently, Colin Craig and Kim Dotcom were able to almost entirely fund the Conservatives and the Internet Party, respectively. In the latter case, it is unlikely to be coincidental that the Internet Party and its ally the MANA Movement managed to secure over 10 per cent of the media coverage during the campaign, despite gaining little or no polling traction and only 1.4 per cent of the party vote (Bahadar, Boyd and Roff 2016: 205–06). Money buys attention in the form of high-profile media events, such as the 'Moment of Truth' in which journalist Glen Greenwald was brought to New Zealand and Edward Snowden and Julian Assange were live-streamed into a packed Auckland Town Hall to reveal details about the how the Five Eyes intelligence network operates in New Zealand. This did Internet-MANA no good, and probably helped harden National party support in the last days of the campaign (Joyce 2015: 131–32). Meanwhile, Internet-MANA took attention away from the government's more potentially effective opponents. Comparing coverage of the two main party leaders by content analysis of the campaign media, Key had 47 per cent, almost exactly matching National's party vote; Cunliffe had 21 per cent, less than Labour's party vote (Bahadar, Boyd and Roff 2016: 205–06). Given that Cunliffe was the alternative prime minister, his coverage seems disproportionately low. Journalists and editorial staff were presumably already discounting the possibility that he could lead a government.

A key resource that can offset the financial advantages of large donations are party members—perhaps they can offset the advantages of 'big money' (Edwards 2008). There are claims that Labour party membership significantly increased as a result of the leadership campaign that elected Cunliffe. Party members have become able to vote in the Labour leadership elections since 2012, giving people an incentive to join. If it had more members to draw on, Labour would therefore be in a better position to beat National on the ground. Sophisticated 'micro-targeting' of voters might also have given Labour a slight edge in 2014, but National was not far behind (Salmond 2015). The National Party also claims a significant membership and on-the-ground activity. As no membership data is available for either party, we cannot compare. The most important test is active membership: those who are prepared to canvass or make telephone calls on behalf of a party. Chapter 11 reports the relevant data from the 2014 NZES, but it does not confirm a Labour advantage.

Conclusion

Despite increased concerns about economic inequality, after the 2014 election the National Party could form a government for a third term of office. The baseline models presented in this chapter demonstrate that relatively stable socio-structural patterns of voting persist, which are themselves the product of inequalities. Our focus here has been on the direct effects of patterns of inequality as they affected people's lives, opportunities and interests, to the extent that we can locate those in social group memberships, incomes and assets. The two main parties still have their traditional profiles: Labour more likely to attract lower income voters with limited assets, National more likely to attract those with higher incomes and more assets. Income and assets also provide the expected foundations for people's left–right positions, indicating potential support for the principle of collective risk-pooling, and thus policies favourable to income redistribution. But in 2014, the Labour Party failed to gain votes it needed from those on higher incomes who were more likely to be favourable to the principle of risk-pooling. Labour also failed to match National in the campaign funds that it secured and spent.

We also examined people's perceptions of their security in terms of jobs and living standards, as a potential source of disruption of previous patterns of vote choice. A sense of insecurity mattered, but only on the margins. In the context of a growing economy, those margins were not big ones. In the next chapter, we move on to discuss National's success in the context of the economy and other performance issues.

5

The winner! The National Party, performance and coalition politics

While inequality was an important theme of the 2014 election, it was sidelined by an even more salient issue: the economy. In Chapter 3, we argued that the effects of the economy on voting choices are complex. Perceptions of the state of the economy may be based on limited knowledge and can be biased by past loyalties and voting choices, as well as by cues shaped by those choices. People often resist new information that is not consistent with what they believe. The effects of the economy on voting choices are best addressed within a wider framework of 'performance' or 'valence' politics.

As explained in Chapter 3, the literature on electoral politics makes a distinction between 'valence' and 'positional' issues. *Positional issues* are issues about which individuals have different values or interests. While some voters are in favour of increasing taxes, others are not. In terms of interests, voters calculate their utilities and compete with others over scarce resources, with some winning and others losing. In the language of game theory, positional issues are 'zero-sum' games. If taxes are increased, supporters win and opponents lose. Increased inequality is one of the results of how such 'games' have played out politically over recent decades.

Valence issues can be understood as 'non-zero-sum' games: everybody can potentially benefit because the debate is about how to best enhance shared values or interests. The most obvious shared interest for most people is a growing economy. Effective and competent leadership is another.

Perceptions of the 'ability to deliver' on positional issues also shape valence perceptions (Green and Jennings 2012). Valence and positional issues often interact (Clark and Leiter 2014); for instance, people may agree with a party's policies, but doubt its ability to implement them effectively.

This chapter shows how the National Party won the 2014 election because of perceptions that the party was competent and well led. Its success relied mainly on valence issues. The economy mattered, but as part of a wider package of perceptions associated with competence and leadership, and above all because people who had voted National before saw no reasons to stop doing so.

National's path to victory was not without obstacles. The government's reputation for competence and good leadership was challenged by the book *Dirty Politics* (Hager 2014), and by the campaign run by a new political competitor, internet entrepreneur Kim Dotcom. National Party leader John Key's integrity was put in doubt. Publication of *Dirty Politics* may have cost National a single-party government, although other marginal factors that counted against National may have had the same effect. Meanwhile, Dotcom's intervention accentuated a problem of lack of coordination on the left, but may not have made it much worse.

The economy

In January 2014, Hong Kong and Shanghai Banking Corporation (HSBC) economist Paul Bloxham expressed a consensus among economic commentators, coining a much-repeated phrase: 'We think New Zealand will be the rock star economy of 2014. Growth is going to pick up pretty solidly this year' (Fairfax Media 2014). The year 2014 could hardly have begun better for an incumbent government. The rebuilding of the earthquake-hit city of Christchurch was reaching its peak, the Auckland housing market was booming and prices for dairy products, one of New Zealand's biggest export products, were high on international markets. At the beginning of 2014, the New Zealand economy was projected to grow at one of the fastest rates in the developed world.

Looking back over the last few years, the picture had been very different. In mid-2007, just before the election of the first Key Government, New Zealand's economic growth was beginning to falter as the result of a drought hitting farming production. Not long after, the effects of the global financial crisis (GFC) began to bite. New Zealand's mainly Australian-owned banks were not badly exposed, although a number of finance companies went bankrupt (Oram 2015). Global effects on trade and investment put the economy into recession throughout 2009. The Labour-led government under Helen Clark had already initiated a counter-cyclical fiscal response before it left office at the end of 2008. It continued to spend despite declining tax revenues, and began to incur government debt to do so. A similar approach was continued under John Key's incoming National-led government. New Zealand's recession was not as deep and long as that in most other countries. By 2011, an economic recovery was well under way, reaching an annual rate of 3.3 per cent by the end of 2014. Figure 5.1 tells the story.

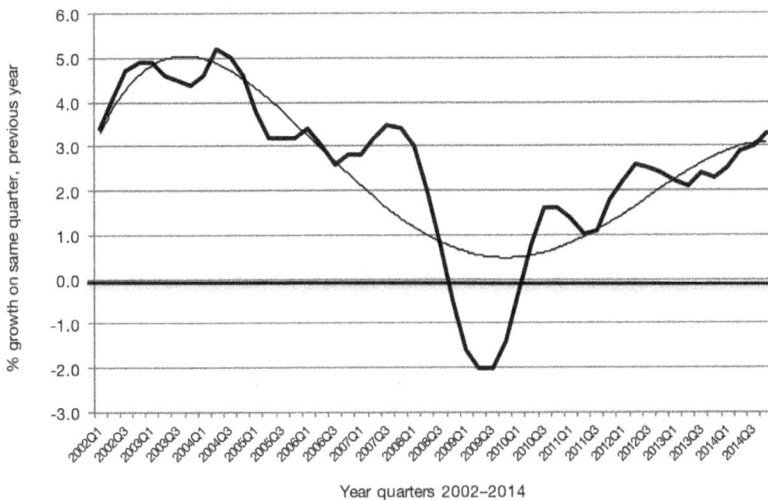

Figure 5.1: Quarterly economic growth (annual, on previous quarter), 2002–2014

Sources: Reserve Bank of New Zealand 2017; their data is drawn from Statistics New Zealand and Haver Analytics.

The statistics on growth are underpinned by evidence of public perceptions about the economy as measured monthly by Colmar Brunton research for TVNZ's *One News* program, displayed in Figure 5.2. Comparing to Figure 5.1, it is striking that while growth was stronger in the period prior to the GFC, optimism appears lower. This is because the question asked is a relative one, so when growth is strong 'the same' is as optimistic a response as 'better' (see Figure 5.2). Conversely, when growth is low, a 'better' response is paradoxically somewhat more likely.

As discussed in Chapter 3, the international literature on economic voting identifies the approval or disapproval of the economic performance of incumbent governments as one of the principal indicators of democratic accountability (for example, Anderson 2007; Duch and Stevenson 2008; Fiorina 1981). The theory tells us that a government perceived to have mismanaged the economy will be rejected by voters; one that has managed the economy well will be returned to office. Nearly one in five New Zealanders named the economy as the most important issue in the 2014 election, and nearly 80 per cent of those chose National as the party best able to deal with it. Relying on One News-Colmar Brunton polls, Figure 5.2 indicates that the trend of optimism has been upward since 2008, but particularly so from 2011 onward. A rising tide of economic optimism gave the National-led government a clear advantage in the 2014 election.

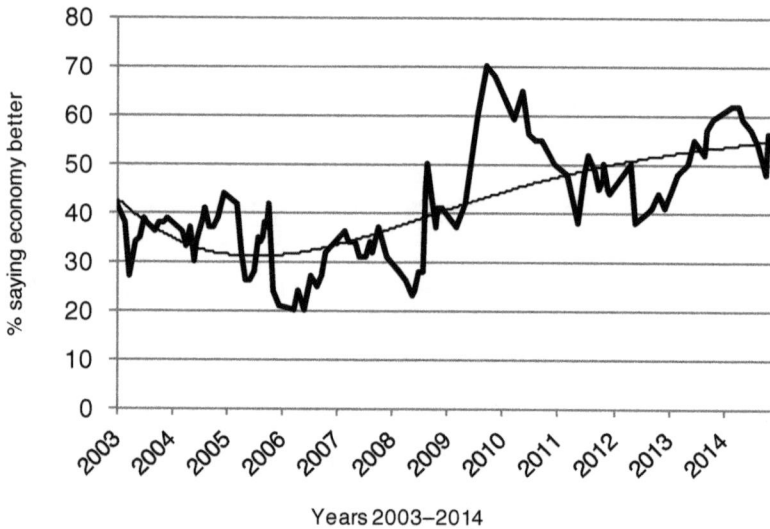

Figure 5.2: Economic confidence, 2003–2014

Note: The question was: 'Do you think during the next 12 months the economy will be in a better state than at present, or in a worse state?'

Source: Colmar Brunton 2014.

As we have explained above, there are difficulties in estimating the effects of the economic vote. Discussed in Chapter 3, there is an extensive body of research in political psychology that tells us that many people have preconceived opinions that colour how they interpret new information. Many voters have relatively low levels of political knowledge. Many people quite reasonably do not take the time to follow politics in any depth or detail, and tend to rely on bits and pieces of information they receive from sources that they trust. These sources will tend to confirm values rather than challenge them. The information voters receive often takes the form of cues that help them form their opinions on matters about which they would otherwise find it difficult to decide, and act as 'shortcuts'. Political parties are a particularly useful source of political cues.

The use of such shortcuts and voters' potential biases towards certain sources have important implications for measuring the economic vote. Regardless of the evidence by way of economic growth statistics, unemployment and so on, a party in government will always present its economic management in the best possible light. By contrast, parties in opposition will present the state of the economy negatively, and people with loyalties to those parties will take those cues (see Chapter 4, Figure 4.7). For this reason, despite objective evidence to the contrary (see Figure 5.1), 30 per cent of New Zealand Election Study (NZES) respondents indicated that they believed that the economy had got worse over the previous year, with another 25 per cent saying it had stayed the same.

According to the latest economic data released prior to the election and reported in newspapers, on the radio and on television, the economy had grown by nearly 3 per cent over the previous year, a very respectable figure by current international standards. Of the respondents, 45 per cent did agree that the economy had grown. One might expect that respondents' levels of political knowledge would be an important predictor of responses to this question. But political psychology suggests that party-generated cues will be the main source of responses to the question, rather than levels of political knowledge. Observing that so many voters for opposition parties had perceptions at odds with the economic data, we can infer that voters for the National Party were similarly cued in the other direction, and would have been so regardless.

Therefore, we estimate the extent to which people are primed or cued by prior party preferences in their responses about the state of the economy. Traditionally, whether or not people say they have a party identification has been used for this purpose, but there are doubts about the value of questions based on this concept. As explained in Chapter 3, the traditional model of party identification assumes it is based on long-standing loyalty to a party, either inherited from one's parents or otherwise acquired early in life. It is a loyalty from which people may temporarily diverge, but they will later 'come home'. The alternative theory conceives party identification as a 'running tally'. People will take cues from a party so long as they make sense; however, when they do not, they may go elsewhere and not necessarily return. Evidence from New Zealand research does indicate that party identification does 'travel together' with vote in a way more consistent with the running tally model (Aimer 1989).

Time series analysis shows that party identification tracks vote (Karp 2010; Vowles 2014b: 46–47). When people change their vote, they tend to change to the party they voted for when asked to which party they are generally close. When voters are asked about closeness to a party, the government party usually comes out ahead. When out of government, a party tends to lose that advantage. Because the NZES is a post-election survey, closeness to a party is measured after people have made their vote choice. There is too much possible error in assuming that this closeness is a result of a long or even a medium-term loyalty.

Recollection of parental partisanship may be a better indicator of long-term loyalties, although even this may be biased by recall. We use this as a control in many of our models. Using previous vote as an indicator of more recent cues is a more effective solution to this problem. Those who voted National in 2011 can be assumed to be most susceptible to its cues; those who voted for other parties are more likely to have taken cues from National's opponents. Testing this, the 'they would say that' theory wins out; previous vote is a powerful predictor of responses to the question on the previous year's economic performance. More importantly, it conditions the effect of the economy on the vote. Figure 5.3 is drawn from a logistic regression model where National voters are coded as 1, others as 0 in 2014, containing all the variables already discussed in earlier chapters and adding government performance, leadership and responses to 'Dirty Politics' (see Appendix, Table 5.A1).

Figure 5.3 confirms that the better their assessment of New Zealand's economic performance over the last year, those who voted National in 2011 were more likely to vote National again. But after the controls for overall government performance and leadership preferences are included, perceptions of the performance of the economy become too weak to be statistically significant or to fall outside confidence intervals. We cannot rule out an effect, but we cannot confirm one. A sceptic might point out that previous vote for National is based on recall that is sometimes prone to error. The model can be replicated using NZES panel respondents only, based on the vote they reported in the 2011 wave. It produces identical findings. Alternative models adding political knowledge do not produce significant findings, but indicate that there were no economic effects on low-knowledge voters. Any possible effects of economic perceptions were confined to those with higher knowledge. Research on the 2011 New Zealand election similarly showed that if the economic vote mattered it did so only in combination with other variables that reflected more general satisfaction with the government's performance (Vowles 2014c: 225).

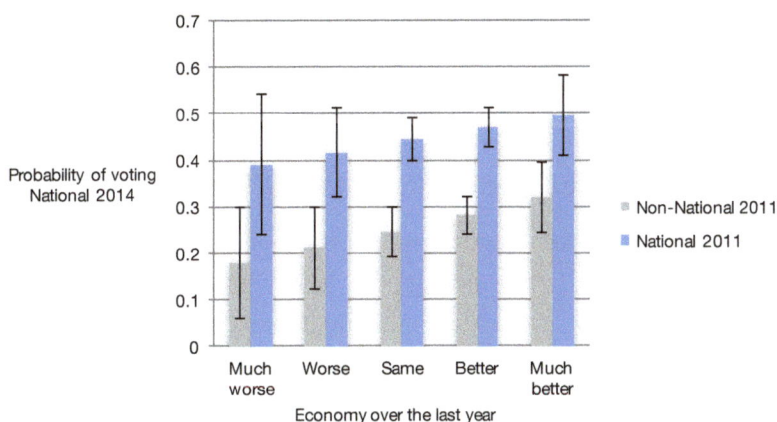

Figure 5.3: Effects of previous vote and perceptions of the economy on the probability of voting National

Note: Figure 5.3 plots probabilities from a logistic regression model on National vote versus the rest: the coefficients, standard errors, and significance statistics are in the Appendix, Table 5.A1.

Leadership and competence

As noted earlier, another key reason for National's election victory was strong approval of National's leader, prime minister John Key. Many voters trusted and liked him as a leader, and the NZES recorded John Key's score as preferred prime minister at 55 per cent (compared with only 13 per cent preferring Labour leader David Cunliffe in that role, closely followed by 10 per cent saying 'none of them').

John Key was brought up by a solo mother in a state house in Christchurch, but his family background was not working class. His mother was a Jewish refugee from a wealthy family, who fled Austria in the 1930s. Key was encouraged to take a business degree and thus in a sense work to restore the family fortune. He was very successful in doing so, embarking on a career as an international currency trader, during which he worked in Singapore, Ireland and New York. Key entered parliament in 2002. Despite having political ambitions from an early age, he had not been active in politics until he returned to New Zealand and joined the National Party in 1998. After his election, Key's parliamentary colleagues quickly recognised his talents and appeal. He was also a fresh face without political baggage from the past. In October 2003, National leader Bill English lost his job to former Reserve Bank Governor Don Brash, and Brash appointed Key as associate finance spokesperson. Key had not voted in favour of Brash in that leadership election because, as Key has explained, 'he was really, really, really right-wing, and I thought, "how do you win an election when you are at the fringe of your party's support?"' (Roughan 2014: 113). Brash regarded Key as his likely successor and, after National lost the 2005 election, Key challenged Brash and won the leadership in 2006.

Key's appeal had two important aspects. First, his personality and character resonated well with New Zealanders. He lacks 'charisma', a much over-used and misused word in politics, and a characteristic many successful political leaders manage to do without. People found him down-to-earth, easy to understand and relate to. He seemed the sort of person with whom one could have a pleasant conversation over a beer or at a barbeque. Key cultivated popularity by going on commercial radio regularly, with the objective of communicating with people who are not interested in politics. He tended to do relatively few interviews on radio or television news programs that cater to those with higher levels of interest, such as Radio New Zealand's program *Morning Report,* relying for exposure in those media outlets more than on coverage of press conferences or brief cameos. He was pragmatic, realistic and his supporters saw him as an achiever, both in his former financial career and as prime minister. As an election winner who maintained a consistently high level of popularity, he has been the most successful leader of the National Party since Keith Holyoake, who led National's four-term government between 1960 and 1972.

Key's second strength was a combination of his background and political moderation. Key did not vote for Brash in 2003 because Brash represented the hardline neo-liberalism of Roger Douglas and Ruth Richardson that many New Zealanders had rejected in the 1990s. As a young man, Key appreciated some aspects of former National Prime Minister Robert Muldoon's 'take no prisoners' leadership style. He is known to have supported the broad thrust of the market liberalisation of the 1980s and early 1990s. But after he began his political career, he expressed no intentions to take neo-liberal economic reform significantly further, if only because he believed that most New Zealanders had little taste for it.

John Key's childhood was not deprived, but neither was it prosperous. Not long after becoming leader of the National Party, Key expressed concern about the development of an 'underclass', and drew attention to communities where 'the rungs on the ladder of opportunity' had been broken. While Labour politicians and activists saw this as a cynical attempt to appeal to some of their voters, the 2014 post-election 'material hardship package' initiated primarily by Key himself now suggests there may have been some authenticity to Key's earlier statements. On taking office in 2008, National also committed to retaining some core policies of the former Labour Government; in particular, the Working for Families program, made up of tax credits for low- and middle-income families with children with a parent in employment, and not therefore applying to those on benefits. This was despite Key's statement, when in opposition, that Working for Families would create 'communism by stealth' (Taylor 2004). Working for Families has had an important role in halting the trend towards greater inequality in New Zealand. Key also pledged to maintain without changes New Zealand Superannuation, a universal pension available to all who qualify at age 65. Under Brash, National had taken quite a different tack. In sum, Key may be described as a moderate centre-right politician who supported many aspects of a welfare state.

Our data confirms that John Key had strong personal appeal as a leader, and the overall performance of National rated well in public opinion. The distribution of the responses to the questions featured in Figure 5.4 shows evidence of substantial approval both of John Key as prime minister and of the National Government in general. Eighty-one per cent took the positive position that John Key had been a fairly to very competent leader. Key's rating on 'trust' is a little lower, but still very high with 58 per cent of the people considering him either fairly or very trustworthy. This was a higher trust rating than that of the National Party itself (36 per cent). However, the party question is different, allowing a neutral 'neither' middle point between trustworthy and not trustworthy.[1] Many respondents who

---

1   The question in the NZES was: 'Thinking of the National Party, do you think that it is trustworthy or not trustworthy?', with answer categories: (1) Trustworthy, (2) Neither, (3) Not trustworthy, (9) Don't know.

are neutral or withheld judgement about the National Party were disposed to trust John Key 'fairly well'. Sixty per cent liked John Key, while only 24 per cent disliked him. On performance, 74 per cent of the respondents rated the government fairly to very good, although most of these did not take the very good option, plumping for the less generous 'fairly good'. While the three Key-related leadership items (liking John Key, trusting John Key and agreeing that Key is a competent leader) correlate strongly, the one with the biggest effect on vote choice turns out to be the simple 'like/dislike' scale.

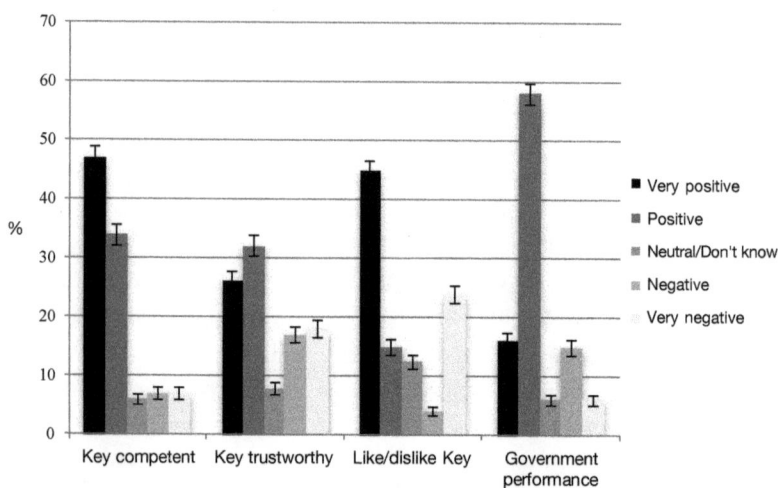

Figure 5.4: Perceptions of John Key and the National-led government

Notes: The questions were: 'How well does the following description apply to John Key: a competent leader?' (Very well (very positive), well (positive), don't know, not very well (negative), not at all well (very negative)); 'How well does the following description apply to John Key: a trustworthy leader?' (Very well, well, don't know, not very well, not at all well); 'How much did you like or dislike John Key?' (0–10 scale: very positive 8–10, positive 6–7, neutral/don't know 5, negative 3–4, very negative 0–2); 'Thinking about the performance of the government in general, how good or bad a job do you think it has done over the last three years?' (A very good job, a fairly good job, don't know, a fairly bad job, a very bad job).

Figure 5.5 shows that, after including all other variables in our model, evaluations of government performance only had a minor effect on those who voted National in 2011, if only because so few rated its performance poorly. Among non-National voters in 2011, though, government performance evaluations had a steep and significant effect. The contrast between Figure 5.5 and Figure 5.3 bears out the greater importance of overall evaluations of government performance, compared with those simply focusing on the economy.

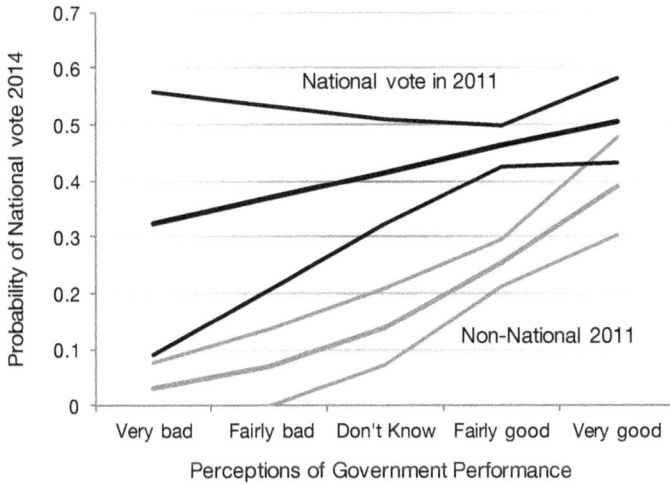

Figure 5.5: Effects of government performance evaluations, conditioned by previous vote, on the probability of voting National
Source: Appendix, Table 5.A1.

Key's reputation, as a politician who could be trusted and the leader of a competent government, came under question from two directions: first, the so-called 'dirty politics' affair; and second, political competition from an unlikely source, internet entrepreneur Kim Dotcom. Politicians are often vulnerable to sudden 'scandals', particularly during election campaigns, as a growing literature demonstrates (for example, Hirano and Synder 2012; Kumlin and Esaiasson 2012). Given how close National came to being able to form a single-party majority government in 2014, it is possible that the marginal effects of these challenges could have made a difference.

Dirty politics

Six weeks before the 2014 election, just before the campaign began, investigative journalist Nicky Hager published his book *Dirty Politics* (Hager 2014). The book was based on emails and Facebook postings from right-wing blogger Cameron Slater that Hager had been given by an anonymous hacker. Hager alleged that there were close contacts between the prime minister and other National Party politicians and a network of bloggers whose role was to seek out and aggressively attack the government's enemies. It was alleged that a strategy of manipulation and intimidation carried out on Key's behalf by others lay behind his apparently benign and affable exterior.

Three allegations were particularly challenging (for more detail, see McMillan 2015). First, Hager claimed that Key's office had colluded with the Security Intelligence Service (SIS) to accelerate the response to an Official Information Act (OIA) request from National Party–aligned blogger Cameron Slater that would reveal information damaging the reputation of then Labour leader Phil Goff prior to the 2011 election. Goff had denied the SIS had given him information about some Israeli spies in New Zealand. Goff had in fact been told but as a small part of a much wider briefing. A document confirming this was released to Slater in a way inconsistent with regular procedures, and in a way that maximised the damage to Goff. The SIS had sent the information to Slater within 24 hours, well before other journalists and mainstream media were given access. Someone in Key's office had almost certainly told Slater about the existence of the document in the first place (Hager 2014: 37–41).

The second allegation was that an official in the Prime Minister's Office had hacked into the Labour Party's website, and provided private information held in Labour Party data archives to be published through Slater's blog site. Both the SIS and the hacking incidents took place in John Key's office, for which he was nominally responsible. However, Key denied any knowledge or involvement.

The third allegation had the most impact, and concerned Judith Collins, the Minister of Justice. Hager claimed that she had divulged to Slater the name of a public servant whom Slater then identified incorrectly as having leaked to the Labour Party sensitive information about deputy prime minister Bill English's expenses as an MP. Death threats to that person subsequently appeared on Slater's blog site *Whale Oil*, and were removed only after police intervention. Collins had already been subject to earlier criticism about allegedly using a ministerial trip to China to promote her husband's business interests.

Key's response to the controversy was denial and dismissal of all Hager's claims, describing him as a 'left-wing conspiracy theorist'. But many journalists and commentators took Hager's claims seriously, and the prime minister's credibility was questioned. National had remained well ahead in opinion polls throughout the campaign, but there was evidence of damage by the end of August as more people came to believe that there was some truth in Hager's claims (One News 2014). Shortly after, Key put an end to Collins tenure as a minister, releasing information independent of Hager's allegations that purported to show that Collins had encouraged attacks against the chief executive of the Serious Fraud Office

(SFO), whose investigations were uncomfortable to some members of the business community. Well after the election, an investigation exonerated Collins from the charges related to the SFO but did not address those made by Hager. Collins rejoined the Cabinet as Minister of Corrections in December 2015.

Table 5.1 lays out the public response to *Dirty Politics* when the dust had settled, after the election. Post-election, most commentators took the view that the controversy did little or no harm to National's vote at the election, with Collins' resignation taking the sting out of the controversy. As a post-election snapshot, Table 5.1 provides no means of assessing the effects directly. It does show that over a third of voters did not know what to think about the matter. By the time that interest in the topic had mostly died after the election, there were very few who were prepared to declare that there was 'no truth' in the claims made by Nicky Hager in *Dirty Politics*, even among National voters. As expected, those who voted for opposition parties were more likely to believe that there was at least some truth in the allegations. Meanwhile, very few National voters ticked 'a lot of truth'. But slightly over half acknowledged 'a little' or 'some'. But this had not prevented them from voting for the party.

Table 5.1: Extent of truth in claims made in *Dirty Politics* by party vote

% by column	Non-vote	National	Labour	Green	NZ First	All
No truth	2	13	2	0	4	6
Don't know	55	31	26	29	31	36
A little truth	10	33	7	5	10	18
Some truth	23	20	33	26	31	24
A lot of truth	9	2	31	40	25	16
N	636	981	524	220	184	2,709

Note: The question was: 'How much truth do you think there is to the claims made by Nicky Hager in his recent book entitled *Dirty Politics*?'

Taking account of a robust collection of control variables (Appendix, Table 5.A1), Figure 5.6 does suggest that *Dirty Politics* may have had a more significant effect than commentators have acknowledged. *Dirty Politics* appears to have slightly attenuated the effect of liking John Key on the probability of voting National, mainly among the quite large group who acknowledged 'some truth' in the claims made in Hager's book. For the respondents who rated John Key moderately favourably at six or seven out of 10 on the like/dislike scale, the confidence intervals between the two probability estimates ('some truth' and 'no truth') just separate out, indicating a significant difference among these groups of voters. Those who believed that there was some truth and who scored John Key at six or seven were about 6–7 per cent less likely to vote National compared with those who claimed that there was 'no truth' in the book.

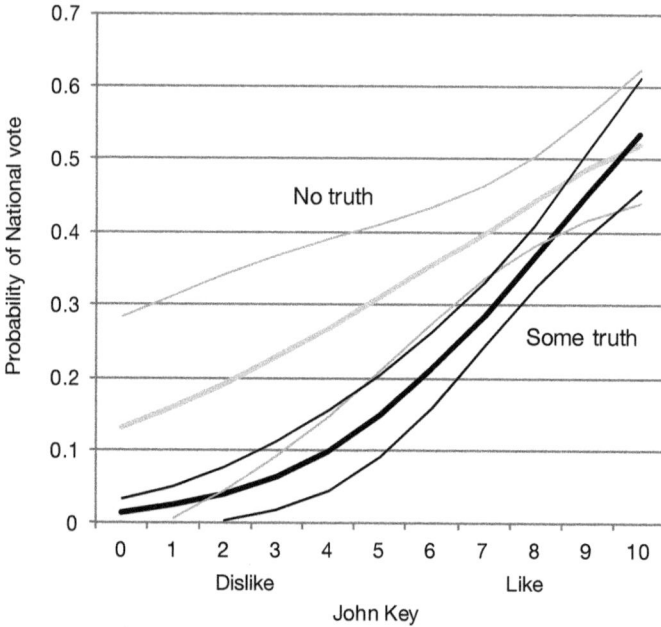

Figure 5.6: The effect of liking John Key, conditioned by assessment of truth in *Dirty Politics* on the probability of voting National
Source: Appendix, Table 5.A1.

One might also have expected *Dirty Politics* to have affected liking or disliking John Key. To test this, we again turn to the NZES panel respondents, comparing liking of John Key in 2011 with liking him in 2014. Among panelists, John Key's popularity was not statistically significantly different in 2014 and 2011 (6.16 in 2011 and 6.24 in 2014). *Dirty Politics* did not shift the general level of liking or disliking John Key. But it had effects: in the panel, controlling for 2011 like/dislike, and 2011 National vote, *Dirty Politics* did affect 2014 assessments of Key, making believers slightly less likely to like Key and disbelievers more likely to do so. But we can still conclude that a small but significant number of those who continued to like Key more than average, but not strongly, were less disposed to vote National if they thought there was some truth in *Dirty Politics*.

The Internet Party challenge and coalition building

Internet entrepreneur Kim Dotcom had moved to New Zealand in 2010, and was granted residency as an investor despite previous minor criminal convictions. Early in 2012, United States prosecutors charged him with infringement of intellectual property rights. He was alleged to have allowed his company to breach copyright by way of its popular file sharing service. The US Department of Justice initiated extradition proceedings and, in January 2012, the police raided Dotcom's house and seized much of his property and assets. The raid was later found to be based on invalid search warrants. The involvement of the New Zealand Government Communications Security Bureau (GCSB) in surveillance of Dotcom's activities was also found to breach the GCSB's legislative boundaries that then prevented it from spying on New Zealand citizens and permanent residents. The proven allegations of illegal spying eventually triggered a review of the GCSB, and was a matter of concern among civil libertarians, the legal profession and political activists who feared they might also be targeted.

John Key's management of the affair was widely criticised, and Key issued a formal apology. Dotcom went on to allege that Key had known of the possibility that the United States would seek to extradite him when Dotcom had been granted permanent residency. Key denied this, claiming no knowledge of Dotcom prior to the raid on his property. Dotcom later revealed an email message supposedly showing evidence of Key's prior knowledge, but the email was widely believed to be a forgery.

Dotcom formed the Internet Party to contest the 2014 election. Green party co-leader Russel Norman had visited Dotcom to urge him not to create a new party that could draw votes away from the Greens and other opposition parties. Dotcom went ahead and, even worse for the Greens, recruited left-wing activist and former left-wing Alliance MP and cabinet minister Laile Harré to lead the Internet Party. Harré had been working for the Green Party developing election policies, and her abrupt departure was unexpected and damaging. As a non-citizen, Dotcom himself could not stand for election. The Internet Party then formed a controversial alliance with the left-wing MANA Party led by Hone Harawira, who had held the Te Tai Tokerau electorate seat in parliament for the MANA Party since 2011. Harawira had previously held the seat for the Māori Party, from which he had been expelled. Because of the 'coat-tailing' provision in electoral law, if MANA had continued to hold the seat after the 2014 election, even a small party vote for the two-party alliance under the 5 per cent party vote threshold for representation could have delivered additional Internet-MANA representation in parliament.

There had initially been some public sympathy for Dotcom. His formation of a political party led many to question his motives, given his status as a non-citizen, allegedly involved in criminal activity and with his own interests to promote. The alliance with MANA was equally controversial, as it compromised the reputations of the Māori and left-wing activists who had agreed to it. To many, this was a cynical attempt to mobilise Dotcom's generous financial support to promote a left-wing movement that seemed to have forgotten its principles.

There were wider consequences. As one journalist put it, the appearance of the Internet Party could be seen to turn 'the left-wing bloc into a rabble of competing parties and interest groups' (Watkins 2014). It drew more attention to an 'extreme left' bogeyman for the National Party to exploit. The Labour Party found itself under pressure to confirm that it would exclude Internet-MANA from any government it might form, and eventually did so (Radio New Zealand 2014a). Had it been able to form a government after the election, Labour might have had to rely on MPs from Internet-MANA to secure a parliamentary majority, putting it in a difficult position that John Key did his best to exploit when talking about the dangers of a change of government (Trevett 2014).

Recent work in electoral studies in various countries with multi-party systems has found that a significant number of people vote for or against coalitions, rather than thinking purely in terms of voting for their favourite party (Bargsted and Kedar 2009; Duch, May and Armstrong 2010; Kedar 2005). In voting for or against a coalition, people may vote strategically for a party other than the one they most prefer in order to make a coalition more or less likely to be able to take office. Such a scenario has already been confirmed in the context of the 2002 New Zealand election (Bowler, Karp and Donovan 2010). Extending this logic, people could consider voting against a coalition that they feel could be unstable, even while having a preference for one of the parties that it is likely to contain.

Despite its own reliance on small parties to govern, National sought to use the possibility of a coalition consisting of Labour, the Greens, New Zealand First and Internet-MANA to instill unease during the campaign. While most New Zealanders prefer coalition to single-party majority governments (Vowles 2011), there is scepticism about coalitions among people on the centre-right. When asked whether a government formed by one party would be better at providing stability than a government formed by more than one party, NZES respondents were divided. National voters were almost twice as likely than others to prefer a single-party government (58 per cent compared to 32 per cent). The risks of a government having to rely on small parties to govern was one of the key concerns of those opposed to the Mixed Member Proportional (MMP) electoral system introduced in New Zealand in 1996. When asked whether there are too many, about the right number or too few political parties in the New Zealand Parliament, 45 per cent of the 2014 NZES respondents answered 'too many', and 38 per cent 'about right' or 'not enough'. National voters broke more strongly for 'too many', reflecting their relative lack of enthusiasm for MMP in general.

Looking at the preferred possible coalition partners, Table 5.2 identifies two groups of voters. The column labelled 'Preferred Government Party National' are those for whom National was their first choice as a government party; the column labelled 'Preferred Government Party Labour' includes those for whom the choice was Labour. The rows list the percentages of people in each group that expressed coalition partner preferences for other parties, or for no other party to join their most preferred major government party in power.

Table 5.2: Most preferred coalition party by preferred party in government (column percentage)

Preferred Coalition Party[2]	Preferred Government Party National[1]	Preferred Government Party Labour[1]
No other party	36	10
Green	17	58
NZF	15	32
ACT	12	1
United Future	15	2
Māori	19	16
Conservative	10	2
Internet-MANA	0	7
N	1,378	604

Notes: 1. The question was: 'on election day 2014, of all the parties, which one did you most want to be in government? (This was followed by a list of all the significant parties)'; 2. The question was: 'on election day 2014, in addition to your first choice of party, were there other parties you wanted to be in government?' (Also followed by a list of parties). Since respondents could specify more than one preferred coalition party, the columns do not add up to 100.

Of those wishing National to form a government, 36 per cent wanted National to govern completely alone. The majority of the people wanting National to lead the government expressed preferences for a variety of parties, with the Māori Party being the most preferred coalition partner. There was also support for the Green Party, New Zealand First and United Future, widely understood as opposition parties, as coalition partners. These three parties were also slightly more popular as coalition partners than National's closest partner, the ACT Party. Among those preferring a Labour-led government, preferences focused more clearly on the two most likely partners, New Zealand First and the Green Party, but the clear majority (58 per cent) in the Labour camp preferred the Greens. Only 10 per cent of those preferring Labour to lead the government wanted the party to govern on its own.

Figures 5.7 and 5.8 give slightly different estimates of overall popularities of the parties based on people's ratings of the parties. Figure 5.7 shows the percentage of respondents who most strongly disliked the various parties. The Internet Party was the most disliked party at 58 per cent, followed by MANA at 38 per cent. Then follow the Conservatives, and then the three smaller parties supporting National both before and after the 2014 election: ACT, United Future and the Māori Party. Figure 5.8 looks at the same information in a slightly different way: it presents the average scores on the 10-point dislike/like scale. The party order is more or less the same as in Figure 5.7, though National stands out with an average score of six. Labour and the Green Party rate somewhat higher that one might expect given their vote shares, at 4.8 and 4.6 respectively. This suggests that the result of the election was more an endorsement of National than a rejection of the two parties forming the most likely alternative.

The unpopularity of the Internet and MANA parties provides some provisional confirmation of the hypothesis that these parties' possible support for a non-National coalition might have pushed some people toward National in search of a stable government without needing to rely on those parties.

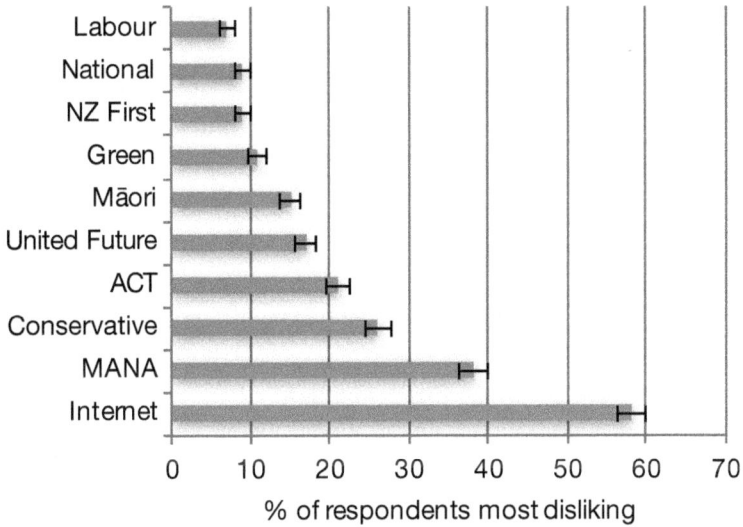

Figure 5.7: Most unpopular party (percentage disliking)

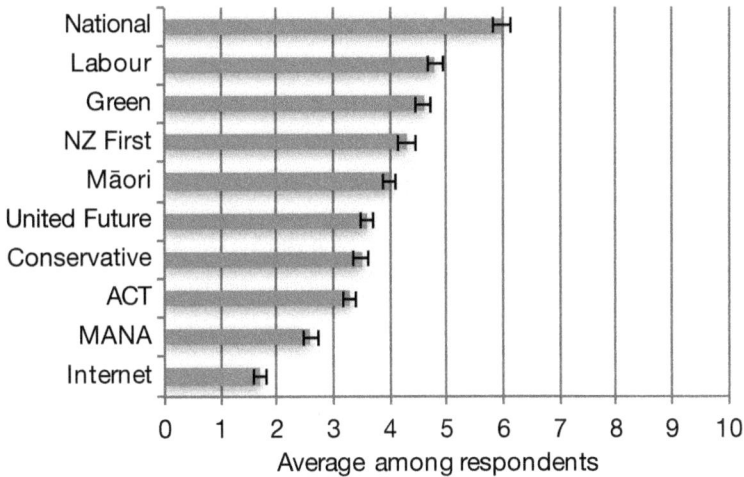

Figure 5.8: Mean score party popularities

Note: The question was: 'Please rate each party on a scale from 0 to 10, where 0 means you strongly dislike that party and 10 means you strongly like that party.' Figure 5.7 shows the percentage ticking 0, the most strongly disliked. Figure 5.8 shows the average rating respondents gave the various parties.

To explore this possibility, we use the model developed in this chapter to address the probability of voting National, and add liking or disliking the Internet Party. When doing so, we also need to test the possibility that there are other 'push' factors perhaps associated with the dislike of Labour's other two potential partners: the Green Party and New Zealand First. As a further control, we added respondent's self-placements on the left–right scale to reduce the chance that our findings would simply pick up right-wing bias toward the left. Appendix Table 5.A2 reports the full findings and Figure 5.9 displays the relationship between liking or disliking the Internet Party and the probability of voting National. Dislike of the Internet Party did have a minor significant effect on the National vote, but it is very small and well within confidence intervals, as Figure 5.9 shows.[2] The effects for disliking the Greens and New Zealand First (see Appendix, Table 5.A2) were not significant.

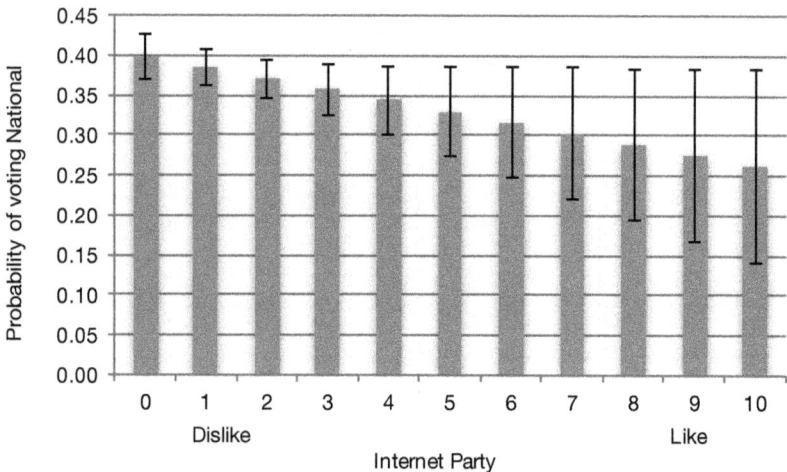

Figure 5.9: The effect of (dis)liking the Internet Party on the probability of voting National

Source: Appendix, Table 5.A2.

---

2   A similar approach was used to investigate whether dislike of National's coalition or support parties might have harmed the National vote. Liking of United Future and ACT were positively associated with the National vote, and Māori Party negatively, but none came close to statistical significance.

Conclusion

As the 2014 election approached, the National Party and its leader John Key rode a wave of popularity, underpinned by a growing economy and public perceptions of a political leadership closely in touch with public opinion. Among some journalists, professionals and political commentators there had been considerable criticism of the government, much of which had been given a new impetus by *Dirty Politics*. The criticism was not just about increased public concern about inequality, to which the government seemed unwilling to respond. Mismanagement of the security services and concerns about privacy and civil liberties had provided some impetus behind the Internet Party, but failed to gain traction. Abuse of the OIA (Fisher 2014), concerns about the awarding of government contracts, accusations of pandering to 'vested interests' (James 2014) and neglect of environmental protection and climate change issues (Chapman 2015) also added up to a strong critique of the government's performance. But these were not the issues that concerned the majority of New Zealanders.

By reducing the potency of John Key's personal popularity, *Dirty Politics* may have affected enough voters to rob National of a single-party majority. The margin was indeed so close that it would not have taken very many more party votes for National to have been able to form a single-party majority. On the other hand, during the campaign *Dirty Politics* took up precious time in news programs and in the wider media that might have been used for further debate about inequality. Attention to the activities of Kim Dotcom and the Internet Party was another distraction from policy debate.

National also had an advantage in the politics of coalition-building. While attempts to gain votes by raising concerns about Labour's potential coalition partners only gained marginal traction, National was always in the better position to form a coalition, and in a position to dominate any such coalition. As we shall discuss in the next chapter, Labour had made little or no effort to establish a relationship with its potential coalition parties, despite there being strong support for the Green Party as a partner among those who wanted a Labour-led government.

Post-election, confident in its success, in conditions of a growing economy, and in the sustainability of tax revenues being generated, the National-led government boldly advanced into Labour's territory by announcing in its 2015 Budget a 'material hardship package'. The increases to benefits and to Working for Families tax credits were relatively small, and would not take effect until the following year. Disagreement remains about whether this shift is more accurately interpreted as a token gesture, or as a real effort to respond to the concern about inequality that had intensified during the election campaign. In his victory speech, John Key had signalled there would be such a response. There had been no increase in the real value of benefits since the 1970s. As we shall see in the next chapter, public opposition to benefit increases has constrained Labour from such a clear commitment, making it difficult for the party to develop its own plans to reduce inequality, and thus allowing National to step into the breach.

6

Still in Labour

Inequality as a principle and in practice formed the second most salient cluster of issues in the 2014 election, and the most salient 'positional' issues. In this chapter, we ask why Labour failed to benefit from New Zealanders' concerns about inequality, an issue left-wing parties have traditionally 'owned'. We examine people's opinions about priorities for government expenditure to address inequality and their attitudes around redistributive social policy, and we investigate how both relate to voting choice. We also assess claims made by internal and external critics of Labour: that the party promised too much, and that these promises failed to cohere into a convincing narrative. Some have also argued that Labour has been captured by 'identity politics' and has consequently failed to engage effectively with its traditional supporters (for example, Pagani 2013, 2016). We address this claim by examining the social foundations of attitudes about the place of Māori in New Zealand politics and the Treaty of Waitangi, the politics of female representation, and how these attitudes affect the Labour vote.

Furthermore, we examine how and why Labour's leadership mattered. After the 2011 election, Phil Goff, leader since 2008, stepped down. His replacement, David Shearer, was elected by a caucus vote in December 2011, having served as an MP for only two years. Under pressure over his performance as leader, Shearer resigned in August 2013. In September 2013, David Cunliffe became Labour leader under new party rules that allowed union affiliates and party members to vote—a change mandated at Labour's 2012 party conference. Cunliffe had been a successful cabinet minister in the Clark Government. He won despite lacking a majority among his parliamentary colleagues. Cunliffe's accession to the leadership was sometimes described as marking a shift to the left (Harman 2016; Trotter 2014), but at that late stage such a shift, real or imagined, could make little difference to the party's policies for the 2014 election.

Labour's program for change

An opposition party is usually expected to run on a program of policy change, and is most likely to be successful when presenting its alternatives with clarity and coherence. Labour's Policy Platform was long, complex and lacked a concise summary. Buried within it were modest policies to address inequality, including a capital gains tax that excluded the home. It proposed an increase in the maximum marginal rate of personal income tax to 36c from the current 33c in the dollar, although above a relatively high income threshold of $150,000 (approximately the top 2 per cent of income earners). Labour promised to build 10,000 houses at accessible prices for first home buyers, and to expand state housing for low-income families. To combat child poverty, Working for Families income tax credits would be extended to beneficiary families. An Inequality Summit would be convened to identify further policy priorities.

Labour's electoral difficulties in 2014 were not simply a short-term problem. Labour's traditional core voting base in the manual working class has shrunk over the last half century. Higher levels of unemployment have emerged compared with the 1950s and 1960s when there was almost no one wanting it who could not find paid work in New Zealand. But none of this necessarily spells electoral doom for centre-left parties. Between 1999 and 2008, the Labour-led government under prime minister Helen Clark governed effectively and developed economic, trade and social policies that addressed some of these challenges. Clark's government helped to heal many of the wounds suffered by the party in the aftermath of its promotion of market liberalisation in the 1980s, and public perceptions of the party recognised that it had shifted back to a position more to the left. But during the period of Clark's government, the international economic situation was relatively benign. The New Zealand economy grew, unemployment declined and the government could run budget surpluses and pay down its debt. That changed in 2007 and 2008. With economic hard times, tax revenues go down and needs for social expenditure go up.

Welfare and social policies

New Zealand's welfare state was initiated in stages from the early twentieth century through the late 1930s. Provision and policies expanded well into the 1970s. It is probably no coincidence that the 1970s and early 1980s were the period in which social and economic inequality in New Zealand hit an all-time low (see Chapter 2). But pressure was beginning to build on the welfare state, internationally and in Australia and New Zealand (Castles, Gerritsen and Vowles 1996; Curtin, Castles and Vowles 2006). While it is fashionable to interpret changes to the welfare state from the 1980s onward as simply an ideological expression of neo-liberalism, the reality is more complex. Most of the principles and values associated with the welfare state in New Zealand were established in the 1950s and 1960s, before it had developed fully. In those days, there was little or no poverty, the number of people unemployed and on benefits was small, and government funding of pensions was modest. Costs and burdens have increased since the 1970s and 1980s, and at the same time pressure increased on the New Zealand economy to be more competitive, government policies moved toward the market and unemployment increased. When those on benefits were few, there was less public concern about beneficiaries. As the numbers expanded, a growing core of people receiving benefit support were not moving out of dependency, and in some cases the problem was being passed on to their children (Welfare Working Group 2011). Communities containing large numbers of beneficiaries and others prone to be on low incomes and in insecure employment began to consolidate (Ministry of Social Development 2008: 29), in tandem with other social problems such as crime, domestic violence and family breakdown (Ministry of Justice 2014: 67).

Those on benefits have become a focus of political debate. Fundamentally, most people in the Labour and National parties probably agree that simply catering to the needs of beneficiaries is not the answer to poverty and inequality, and that people should get their incomes from paid work to the greatest extent possible. The very name of the Labour Party indicates its intention to represent working people, to ensure that they receive the payment they are entitled to for their labour. Policies to assist those out of work were not central to the welfare model developed by the Labour Party in the 1930s, based on what Frank Castles (1985) has called 'a wage earners' welfare state'. At a time when there was a wide consensus of support for the principles of the welfare state, the *Social Security Act 1964* had a clear focus on employment as the best means of ensuring economic and social wellbeing.

There has been a change of mindset. In the twenty-first century, many people think the Labour Party cares more about people not in work than about those who are in work. Labour is caught in a conundrum: its egalitarian principles demand that it address the problems of the poor, and the worst cases of poverty tend to be among beneficiaries. Nonetheless, when Labour established Working for Families it excluded beneficiaries, and directly addressed the problems of low- to middle-income working families. In 2014, Labour promised to extend the program beyond those in work, a proposal that could have significantly reduced poverty.

Arguments about social policy between the Labour and National parties are rooted in differences of principle. Labour tends to retain residual socialist assumptions that people's circumstances are socially constructed. Many people are born into less than ideal situations from which it is hard to escape. Others may simply be unlucky, losing their incomes or health through no fault of their own. With less consideration to the social context, National tends to take a conservative position based on liberal principles: that people are individuals who should be responsible for themselves and their families. That responsibility may need to be enforced by incentives and sometimes coercion to get people into work—a focus of National's social policy reforms since 2008 (Davison 2012).

With the expansion of the number of people on benefits, public opinion about unemployment and welfare has shifted toward the conservative view (Humpage 2014), even among many people voting Labour. It is notable that Labour's 64-page policy platform, approved in 2013, uses the phrase 'welfare state' only twice and that its welfare policies are presented under the label 'social development' (Labour Party 2013). 'Welfare' has become a word many seek to avoid, because it is too closely connected to the claim from the conservative right that many people receiving 'welfare benefits' do not deserve them. Another good illustration of this dilemma and the divisions it can generate within the Labour Party came to the surface in August 2012. A resident of his electorate had asked Labour leader David Shearer whether Labour approved of a neighbour on a sickness benefit being fit enough to have been seen painting the roof of his house. Shearer had responded with a definite 'no', and told this story to a public meeting. Criticism from the right followed, that Shearer had failed to explain how Labour would solve the alleged problem. From the left it was asserted that Shearer was following a tried and true rhetorical strategy of 'beneficiary-bashing' that the left should not emulate (Dominion Post 2012).

The 2014 New Zealand Election Study (NZES) asked questions about preferences for more or less government expenditure in key policy domains. Figure 6.1 displays the percentages of those who said 'less' or 'much less' across them. Unemployment and welfare benefits head the list for those wanting less. Only 12 per cent wanted 'more' or 'much more' to be spent on unemployment benefits, and 16 per cent wanted 'more' or 'much more' to be spent on welfare benefits.

We expect responses to these questions to cluster around different expenditure types. For example, those supporting government expenditure on welfare should also support government expenditure on unemployment. A factor analysis reported in the Appendix confirms this (Table 6.A1), and we refer to this dimension as *targeted* benefits since they are targeted to those without a job and those in need of welfare support. These targeted benefits have the strongest effects on income redistribution, thus promoting equality. The next dimension confirmed by the factor analysis are those benefits that are *universal*: health, education and New Zealand Superannuation. Almost everyone benefits from government expenditure on these services; they are therefore less redistributive, and support for the government to spend money on these services remains high, with little change over time.

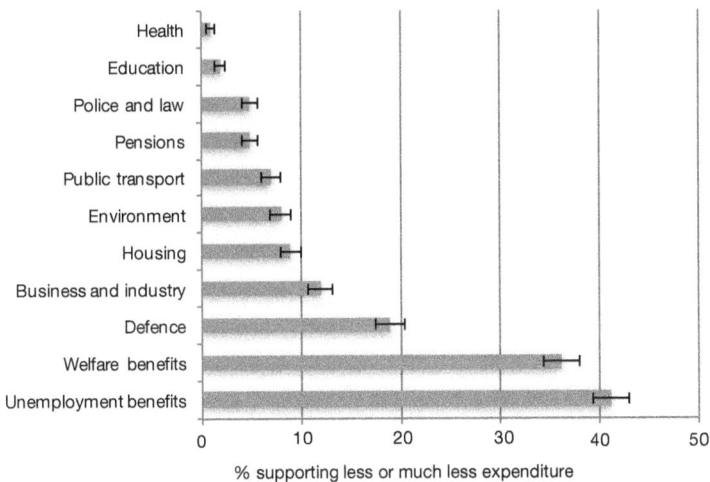

Figure 6.1: Less or much less government expenditure wanted on various items of public policy

Note: The question was: 'Should there be more or less public expenditure in the following areas. Remember if you say 'more' or 'much more' it could require a tax increase, and if you say 'less' or 'much less' it could require a reduction in those services.' The response options were: much more, more, same as now, less, much less, and don't know.

Source: New Zealand Election Study 2014.

We anticipate that these two underlying dimensions of expenditure preferences are related to party support. We focus on the two welfare dimensions of targeted and universal benefits. For ease of interpretation, we created additive scales combining the policy areas as shown in the factor analysis. Figure 6.2 shows, as expected, that National voters are significantly more likely to want less expenditure on welfare and unemployment benefits, with Labour, Green and New Zealand First voters taking more tolerant positions. Indicating support for expenditure on universal benefits, Figure 6.3 reveals that there is overall more consensus and support for universal benefits compared with the targeted benefits shown in Figure 6.2.

The Appendix tables for this chapter display the results of regressions of social, demographic and ideological variables on these two social expenditure preference variables (Table 6.A2). To summarise briefly, preferences for expenditure on universal services are spread widely among social groups, 'explaining' only just under 8 per cent of the variance in the preferences. Women, those on low incomes, those on the left, people in union households, those with Labour rather than National parents and those feeling insecure about their job situation or income are somewhat more likely than others to prefer higher rather than lower expenditures on universal benefits.

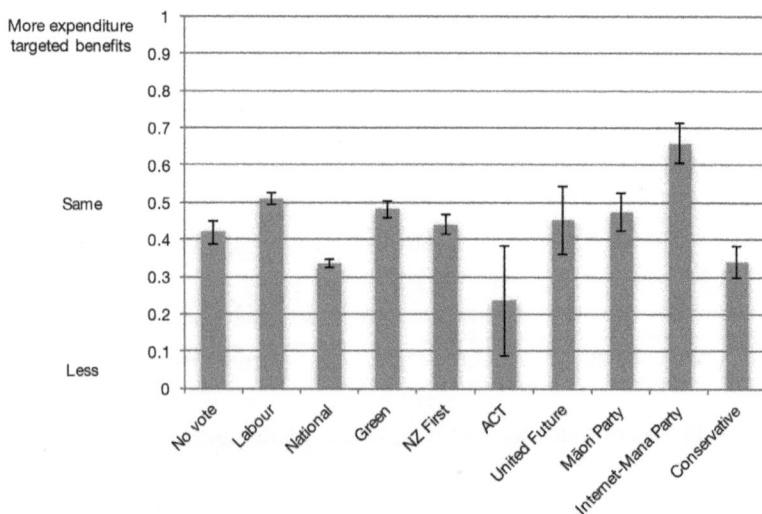

Figure 6.2: Average scores on expenditure dimensions by party vote 2014: Targeted benefits

Source: New Zealand Election Study 2014.

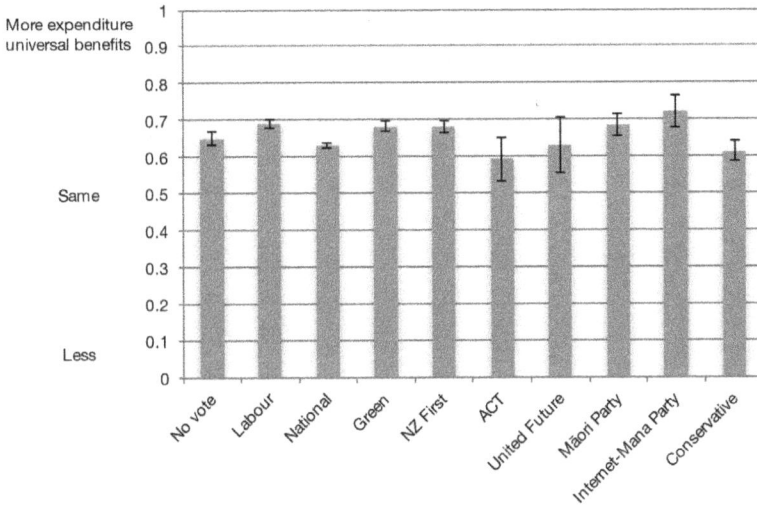

Figure 6.3: Average scores on expenditure dimensions by party vote 2014:
Universal benefits

Source: New Zealand Election Study 2014.

As one would expect, compared with preferences for universal benefits, preferences for expenditures on targeted benefits tend to be more structured around social group memberships and perceptions, 'explaining' nearly 24 per cent of variance. Those favouring higher targeted expenditures are the old, and Māori and Pasifika, but Asians are less likely to support this form of redistribution than the residual category of European and others. Compared to people with a non-university post-school qualification, people with only school qualifications and those with a university degree are more likely to favour targeted benefit expenditure. Those attending church frequently and those with few assets and/or on a benefit are also more likely to support more governmental expenditure on targeted benefits. Parents voting Labour, a left-wing position, and perceptions of job and income insecurity also all positively affect the likelihood of supporting targeted benefit expenditure. These are relatively stable patterns in New Zealand politics, predictably associated with partisan and left–right attitudes. We move on to specific policies that we expect to be more potentially important for short-term vote choices.

Raising the pension age

One of the elements of the universal benefits dimension is state pension provision, provided through New Zealand Superannuation. It pays the same pension to all who qualify by residence from the age of 65 and is funded by ongoing taxation. In terms of international comparison, New Zealand Superannuation is relatively generous, in most cases providing an acceptable standard of living for those solely dependent on it who own their own homes and have paid off their mortgage. For those in rental accommodation and with no other income, further income support is usually available. New Zealand Superannuation is not employment or contribution dependent. There is no discrimination against women or those who have had low incomes throughout their working lives.

As the New Zealand population ages and people live longer, funding New Zealand Superannuation is becoming more expensive. It is not means-tested, and those remaining in work after the age of 65 still receive it, even if they are on high incomes. Research on the affordability of the scheme has led to recommendations that the age of entitlement be increased. At the 2011 and 2014 elections, Labour promised to do so, with phased implementation, raising eligibility to 67 by the year 2030. The National Party opposed any change, with John Key making it clear that New Zealand Superannuation would remain untouched while he was prime minister.

In 2014, opinion on the issue had hardly shifted from 2011. A small plurality remained in favour of raising the age of eligibility (43 per cent in favour, 38 per cent against). Despite the reform being Labour policy, it had more support among National voters (49 per cent among National voters, 42 per cent among Labour). The results of further investigation of some of the socio-demographic correlations between socio-demographic variables and responses to this question can be found in Figure 6.4 and in Appendix, Table 6.A3. All baseline social structure variables were initially tested; we discuss only those for which there were significant findings.

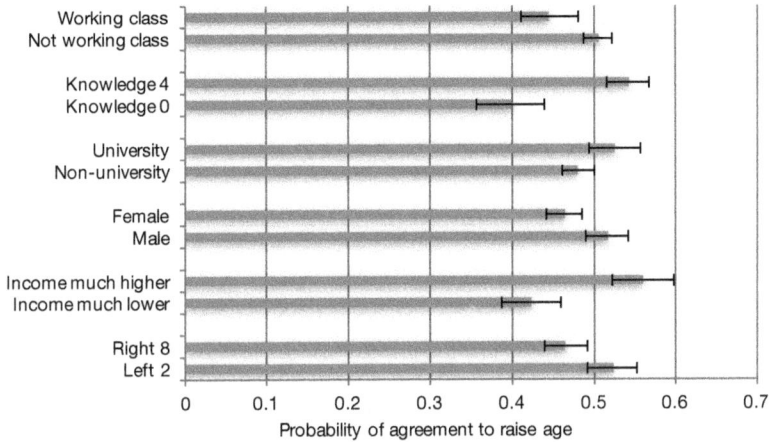

Figure 6.4: Raising the age of eligibility for New Zealand superannuation and socio-demographic variables

Source: Appendix, Table 6.A3.

Figure 6.4 shows how left–right position, gender, university education, political knowledge, subjective working class identification and relative income are related to opinion concerning eligibility for New Zealand Superannuation. Despite the partisan differences noted above, those on the left are slightly more likely to favour the change when other variables are taken into account. We compare a person in the middle of the left range (scored at 2) with a person in the middle of the right (8). We interpret this as a cueing effect.[1] People on higher incomes are more likely to be in favour of change than those on low incomes, by quite a large margin. Women are somewhat more likely to be opposed to change. Most of these differences are to be expected as the debate about the matter has focused on the disadvantages for women and those on lower incomes.

_____

1   This is a good example of a 'suppressor effect'. When simply correlating left–right positions and opinion on this question, there is no significant relationship. Because left-tending groups such as the young, Māori, women and those on low incomes have a tendency to be opposed to raising the age of eligibility, when we include these in the model, left–right position is found to have small effects in dragging some left-leaners toward supporting raising age-eligibility despite the interests associated with their social locations. This is not entirely unexpected; it is a reasonable left-wing position to want to target resources away from those who do not need them to those who do, particularly when there are pressures on social expenditure, and universal pension provision is among the most expensive of benefit programs.

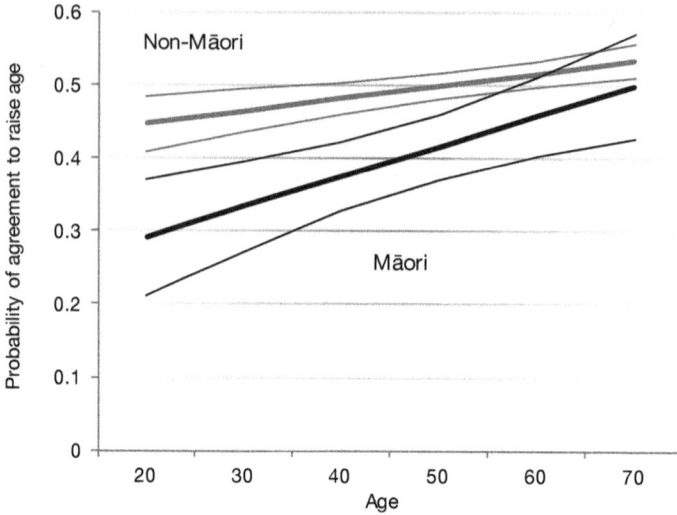

Figure 6.5: Age and Māori/non-Māori and raising the age of eligibility for New Zealand Superannuation
Source: Appendix, Table 6.A3.

Raising the age of eligibility for superannuation would have no effect on those aged 60 or above, and would have been phased in for the group currently in their late 40s. Everyone younger than 48 or thereabouts would qualify for superannuation at 67. We therefore expect an age-related effect on opinion on this question. Figure 6.5 confirms this, with unaffected older people being more likely to agree with an increase of the age of eligibility. This age effect is particularly strong among those identifying as Māori; stronger still if working class self-identification is left out of an alternative version of the model. Māori have tended to work in more physically demanding occupations, retire earlier and die younger than other New Zealanders. They are a group likely to lose as a result of raising the eligibility age. The age gradient for non-Māori is steep enough for statistical significance, but is not nearly so apparent.

While overall opinion is divided, social groups more likely to favour Labour are opposed to change in pension eligibility, notably those with lower relative incomes and Māori. National voters are more in support. The idea of raising the pension age is often welcomed as being fiscally responsible, and is in accord with the judgements of economists. Spending less on pensions for those still earning or with substantial incomes from other sources would promote greater equality if the funds saved were used on a more targeted basis. But if Labour could have won votes on this issue, it equally ran the risk of losing some among its traditional supporters. As we shall see later, it probably lost more than it gained. Labour leader since November 2014, Andrew Little, put himself personally on record as opposing any change to the age of eligibility. Labour has abandoned the policy for the 2017 election. After the retirement of John Key as prime minister and National Party leader in 2016, his successor Bill English announced that National would seek to change the age of eligibility if re-elected in 2017.

Capital gains tax

Another Labour Party policy in 2011 and 2014 that received support from Treasury and many economists was a capital gains tax, currently absent from New Zealand's repertoire of tax instruments. The Labour Party proposed the introduction of a flat rate of 15 per cent to apply to capital gains, exempting the family home (most other countries likewise exempt family homes). A capital gains tax would promote greater equality, although how much is a matter of debate. It is a policy in accord with traditional Labour principles.

Politically, the introduction of a capital gains tax presents risks. Labour's core voters should support it, but not necessarily the middle and upper-middle income median voters Labour wants to attract to increase its vote. The rising Auckland housing market over the two to three years prior to the 2014 election contributed to the feel-good tide that helped to float the National-led government back into office. Many New Zealanders have acquired rental property, most borrowing to do so, and significant capital gains have been made. A capital gains tax systematically applied to rental properties is unlikely to be popular among voters who are 'aspiring' to improve their standard of living by accumulating such assets.

'Aspiration' is not a new idea for Labour parties. As already noted, Labour's traditional role is as a party that represents the interests of workers, to ensure that they receive the incomes they deserve, and to create the opportunities for them to develop their capacities to the fullest potential. While New Zealand Labour's traditional role has been to advance aspirations through collective action and collective provision, its current language is individualistic, about 'doing well' and, as an option, 'starting your own business' (Labour Party 2015), adopting the same liberal and business-orientated language as that of the political right. This might appeal to some potential voters. But it is inconsistent with tradition and potentially in conflict with other Labour policies, giving credence to a criticism of policy incoherence.

In 2014, public opinion was almost equally divided on the merits or demerits of a capital gains tax: just over a third were in favour, another third against. When the question was asked in 2011, the distribution of responses was similar, with a slightly greater plurality against, but the 2011 question did not specify excluding the family home. Only 15 per cent of Labour voters and about the same proportion of Green voters opposed a capital gains tax, compared to 56 per cent of National voters, a predictable partisan split.

We investigated other variables expected to underpin attitudes to a capital gains tax. All variables in the baseline social structure model were tested against the question of support for a capital gains tax. The reported results in Appendix Table 6.A4 and displayed in Figure 6.6 are the ones that attained statistical significance. The strongest effect was people's left–right positions, capturing partisan as well as ideological differences. As expected, those who aspire to a better standard of living in the next 10 years are less likely to be in favour of a capital gains tax than those who do not. People in union households are about 15 per cent of respondents and were about 5 per cent more likely to be in favour of a capital gains tax than those with no union member in the household. Parental partisanship also had significant effects, again indicating that this dimension of opinion taps into traditional differences between the Labour and National Parties.

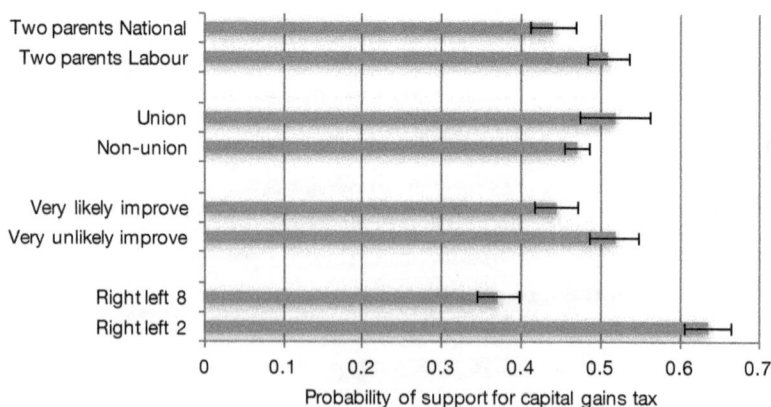

Figure 6.6: Social structure, ideology and opinions on a capital gains tax
Source: Appendix, Table 6.A4.

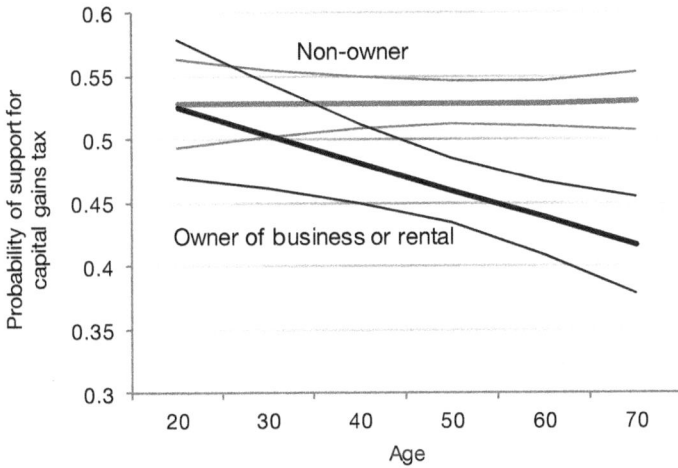

Figure 6.7: The effects of age on support for capital gains tax, conditional on ownership of a business or rental property
Source: Appendix, Table 6.A4.

The most striking finding is the result of interacting age with owning or not owning a business or a rental property (see Figure 6.7). In this model, this item replaces the assets index. For non-owners, age has no effect. Non-owners tend to be in favour of a capital gains tax. Among owners, the likelihood of supporting a capital gains tax decreases substantially with age. This is almost certainly the result of the accumulation of assets as people age. Owners of businesses or investors in rental property may be more accepting of a capital gains tax during the struggling or aspirational period in their lives, and only become stronger opponents when their assets accumulate later in life. Across all age groups, the 'owners' are about 30 per cent of the sample, of which 75 per cent are over the age of 35.

'Identity politics'

For some time, internal and external critics have been accusing the Labour Party of an excessive emphasis on 'identity politics' (Phillips 2014). The critics have asserted that Labour was placing too much emphasis on supporting the causes of minority, under-represented or less recognised groups (Edwards 2013a, 2016a). Of course, Labour's principles dispose it to take this stance. As a party of equality, collective action and fairness, Labour has sought and gained the support of ethnic minorities, who as a group tend to be socially disadvantaged. For example, as Pasifika peoples began to migrate to New Zealand in the 1960s and 1970s, Labour organised to mobilise their support, working with their community leaders and churches and forming a Pacific Island Council within the Labour Party (Franks and McAloon 2016: 193), with a significant electoral payoff (Iusitini and Crothers 2013). Labour has not formed such strong bonds with recent Asian immigrants, who tend to gravitate toward parties in government (Park 2006).

As discussed in more detail in Chapter 10, Labour has a long history of receiving substantial electoral support from Māori, but Māori loyalty to Labour has been severely tested in recent decades. Māori suffered more than most from the market liberalisation of the 1980s under Labour. Labour's Foreshore and Seabed Legislation in 2004 deprived *iwi* of the right to claim for maritime indigenous property rights. By 2014, Labour had reverted to its normal strong support for Māori rights and for the Treaty of Waitangi. Indeed, in July 2014, Labour leader David Cunliffe stated his personal view that Labour should apologise for passing the Foreshore and Seabed Act. By 2016, the party had not yet made any official statement to that effect (Radio New Zealand 2014b).[2] Treaty of Waitangi issues remain contested in New Zealand politics. New Zealand First actively campaigns against the Treaty being part of the law. Labour is vulnerable to some of its socially conservative voters finding New Zealand First's anti-Treaty rhetoric attractive. Indeed, as Chapter 1 shows, Labour's vote share has fallen back since 2008, while New Zealand First has gained ground.

Asked to agree or disagree with the statement 'reference to the Treaty of Waitangi should be removed from the law', 42 per cent agreed and 32 per cent were against. Figure 6.8 shows that when broken down by 2014 party vote, National and New Zealand First voters were equally likely to agree with the proposition, at 55 per cent. Of Labour voters, 29 per cent agreed, as did 22 per cent of Green voters.[3]

---

2 A proposal that the party apologise was removed from the party's conference agenda for its 2015 party conference (Stuff 2015).
3 On the other hand, retention (or expansion) of the number of Māori electorate seats has near majority support, at 48 per cent, compared with abolition at 39 per cent.

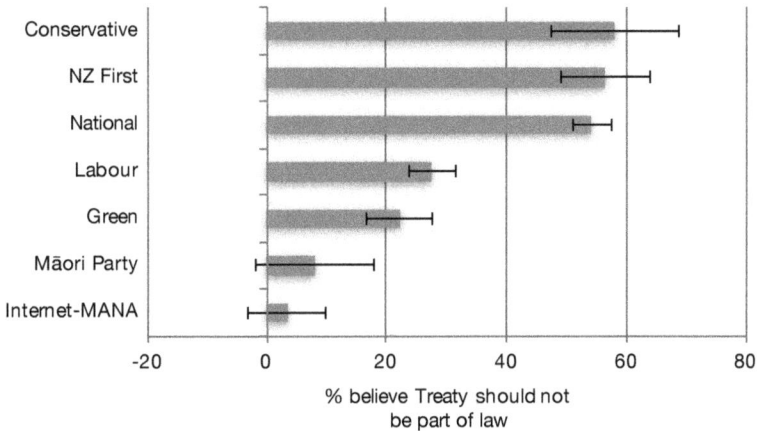

Figure 6.8: The Treaty should not be part of the law by party vote
Source: New Zealand Election Study 2014.

We might also expect Māori and non-Māori to differ on this issue and to see age effects. Acknowledgement of the Treaty of Waitangi and the promotion of Māori language and culture have increased in the education system in recent decades; younger non-Māori might be more likely to support the Treaty. On the basis of a simple regression interacting Māori/ non-Māori and age, and reversing the question response categories, Figure 6.9 shows that Māori across all age groups are strongly in favour of the Treaty remaining recognised in the law, but older Māori are 9 per cent less likely to express that position—a difference well within confidence intervals. There is a steeper age slope for non-Māori. From 18 to 30, non-Māori New Zealanders are evenly split, but by the age of 70 the probability of support for the Treaty is down by about 14 per cent and the difference is well outside confidence intervals. Adding socio-demographic variables and ideology to the analysis explains about 20 per cent of the variance in attitudes to the Treaty. Figure 6.10 shows the effects of some of the main socio-economic variables on attitudes towards the Treaty.

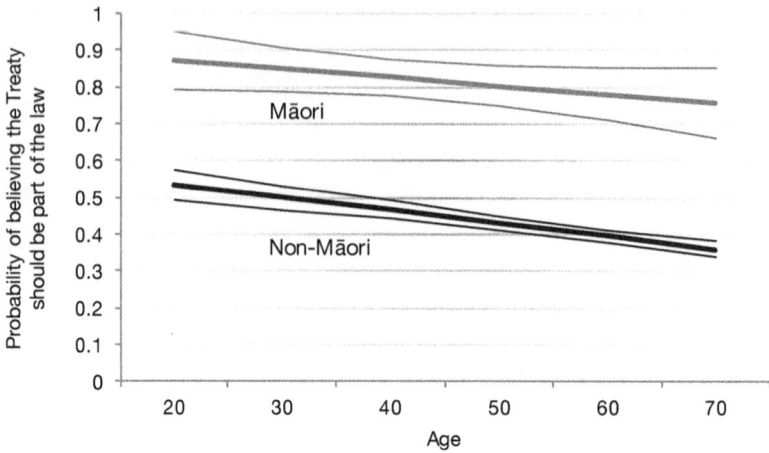

Figure 6.9: Support among Māori and non-Māori that the Treaty should be part of the law

Note: Post-estimation from an OLS regression on the question on Māori primary ethnicity versus all others, interacted with age.

Source: New Zealand Election Study 2014.

Figure 6.10 reveals that women are more in favour of keeping the Treaty as part of the law than men. Left and right positions also matter. Those who are income-rich are more in favour of the Treaty than the poor, but the asset-rich are less in favour than the asset-poor. Pasifika people are much more positive about the Treaty than Europeans, although not as much as Māori. Asian respondents cannot be distinguished from Europeans in their attitudes towards the Treaty. Both education and political knowledge increase support for the Treaty, giving some hope for those who feel that teaching New Zealand's colonial history in schools could have the effect of shifting attitudes eventually.

Feminism has also been a salient and long-standing theme of identity politics within the Labour Party. Labour MPs and politicians have been prominent in promotion of gay and lesbian rights. When the Labour Party debated the use of gender quotas in its candidate selection processes, right-wing journalists accused it of orchestrating a 'man ban' (Curtin 2013a; Edwards 2013b). Others within the party accused the party of paying too much attention to such issues, and ignoring other concerns that the wider public cared about more. Such criticisms construct perceptions of policy confusion and incoherence, and are explored in greater depth in Chapter 9. We assess the effect on Labour vote choice of both Māori and gender issues in the final section of this chapter.

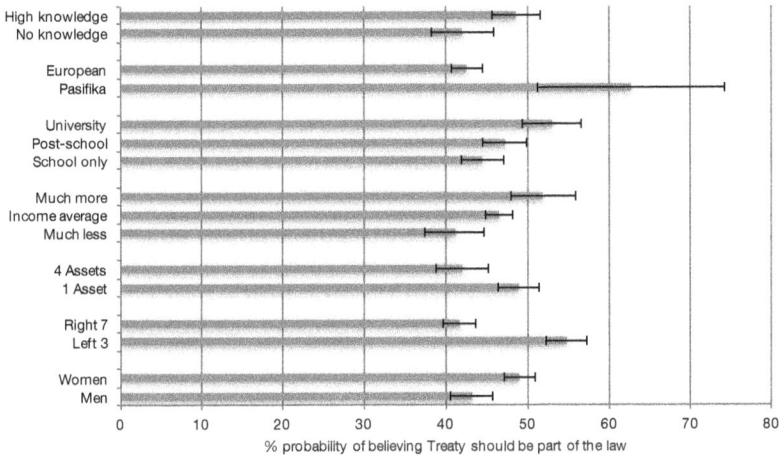

Figure 6.10: Probabilities of believing that the Treaty should be part of the law

Source: Appendix, Table 6.A5.

The leadership

Labour's biggest challenge in 2014 was leadership. Opposition leadership is a hard task, even more so when political news coverage is truncated and personality-focused, and when opposition politicians struggle for attention (Boyd and Badador 2015). In their search for stories, journalists look for drama. Hints of party disunity are blown up to their maximum. Polling news is badly interpreted, and small changes in leader evaluations or party support are made into headlines, despite being well within margins of error. Labour's leadership instability generated and was intensified by this kind of media coverage.

The shift to David Cunliffe as party leader in late 2013 was coupled with a new means of leader selection that widened the party's selectorate to members and Labour's union affiliates. Cunliffe's reliance on the union vote lowered perceptions of his legitimacy, particularly given his low support among Labour MPs. In the year of Cunliffe's leadership, it became clearer to the public why so many Labour MPs had opposed his election. Cunliffe often gave an impression of arrogance (Fox and Watkins 2014). Despite his obvious intellectual abilities, Cunliffe has been described as having a 'low emotional quotient'. Many of his colleagues came to see him as 'divisive, ambitious, self-absorbed and self-confident to a messianic level: all the time not picking up on how that was playing with those who had to work with him most closely' (Small 2016). He was prone to making poorly judged dramatic gestures, such as an apology for being a man at a conference about violence against women (see Chapter 9). Appreciated by the immediate audience, it was not well received generally, particularly when taken out of context by his opponents, as it was bound to be (Radio Live 2014). Meanwhile, National Party aligned bloggers and journalists pounced on Cunliffe's equivocations, framing him as untrustworthy (Armstrong 2014b). However, his biggest mistake was strategic. Cunliffe abandoned efforts to develop a cooperative relationship with the Green Party (Sunday Star-Times 2014). In the meantime, Labour continued to poll badly, and a polling upturn for New Zealand First further complicated the possible politics of an alternative coalition.

Table 6.1 confirms that voters did not see Cunliffe as a plausible leader, particularly when compared with Key. Only 3 per cent of the NZES respondents saw Cunliffe as competent, compared with 47 per cent for Key. Asked after the election which leader they would prefer as prime minister, only 13 per cent preferred Cunliffe as prime minister to Key's 55 per cent.

Table 6.1: Perceptions of David Cunliffe (percentages)

	David Cunliffe a Competent Leader (Percentage Difference with Key)	David Cunliffe a Trustworthy Leader (Percentage Difference with Key)
Very well/good	3 (–44)	6 (–20)
Fairly	21 (–13)	26 (–6)
Don't Know	12 (+6)	17 (+9)
Not very	34 (+27)	29 (+12)
Not at all well/good	30 (+23)	22 (+4)
N	2,788	2,763

Note: The two questions were: 'How well does the following description apply to David Cunliffe: a competent leader?'; 'How well does the following description apply to David Cunliffe: a trustworthy leader?'

Source: New Zealand Election Study 2014.

Inequality

When the issue of inequality emerged as a campaign issue, many observers expected a benefit to Labour, and were puzzled when Labour continued to fail to gain traction in opinion polls. Our data confirms that inequality was a matter of concern and that a majority of New Zealanders wished for a more egalitarian society. Table 6.2 indicates the distribution of responses to two statements measuring attitudes towards inequality. About two thirds of respondents agreed with each statement. Both questions were also asked in 2011. Between 2011 and 2014, there was a shift of about 6 percentage points towards agreement with both statements, confirming the growing concern about inequality. Transforming the responses into scales between 0 and 1, with 'don't know' scored with 'neutral', the differences over time are statistically significant.[4]

Table 6.2: Attitudes to inequality (column percentages)

	Differences in Income Too Large		Government Action to Reduce Income Differences	
	2011	2014	2011	2014
Strongly agree	27	33	24	27
Agree	34	34	34	37
Neither	15	13	13	12
Disagree	14	10	15	12
Strongly Disagree	4	5	9	5
Don't Know	6	5	4	6
N	2,411	2,735	2,401	2,745

Note: The questions were: 'Please indicate to what extent you agree or disagree with: Differences in income in New Zealand are too large'; 'Government should take measures to reduce differences in income levels'.
Source: New Zealand Election Study 2014.

Responses to the two questions correlate well at 0.67, and we therefore put them together as a scale designed to range between 0 (acceptance of inequality) and 1 (opposition to inequality). Figure 6.11 compares the means of this scale across the most significant parties in 2011 and 2014.

In 2014, the average party voter for all parties was on the agreement side, with scores of 0.5 and above. National Party voters are only just above, effectively halfway between indifference (represented by 0.5) and agreement (0.75). Green voters agreed most strongly with the principle, although the confidence intervals overlap with Labour just behind. New Zealand First voters and even Conservative voters are more likely than National voters to agree that inequality is high and that something

---

4   Making the same comparison among the panel respondents, the shift holds up and, indeed, it is somewhat stronger in the 2014 responses.

should be done about it. While differences in attitudes towards inequality between National and the other party votes were large in both 2011 and 2014, many National voters would have followed the shift in attitudes against inequality without abandoning National. Comparing Labour and Green voters in 2011 and 2014, we can see that the distribution of attitudes shifted too, while among New Zealand First and Conservative voters they did not.

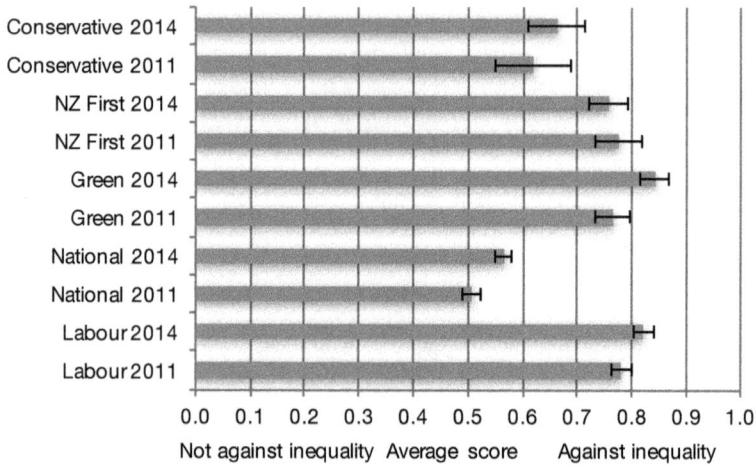

Figure 6.11: Attitudes towards inequality by party votes in 2011 and 2014 (averages)

Source: New Zealand Election Study 2014.

Figure 6.12 lays out the socio-demographic and attitudinal correlates of attitudes towards inequality in 2014 from a regression model on the inequality attitude scale. Older people are more opposed to inequality than younger people by a seven-point difference. As explained in previous chapters, we expect income and asset ownership to have strong effects, and they do. Church attendance is associated with opposition to inequality, consistent with a Christian social justice perspective. Self-positioning on the left–right scale has a major influence. As one would expect, those on the left are significantly more likely to oppose inequality than those on the right. Fears of reduced living standards and difficulty in finding jobs help drive opposition to inequality, as do higher levels of political knowledge. Surprisingly, there are no gender differences, nor any differences based on ethnicity; the latter is soaked up predominantly by the income and asset variables. Occupations, type of employment and even union membership do not appear to be significant either, although they probably have effects that run through the significant variables such as left–right position. Aspirational optimism for a better living standard in 10 years has no significant relationship with attitudes to inequality; aspirational people do tend to care marginally less about inequality, but not enough to matter.

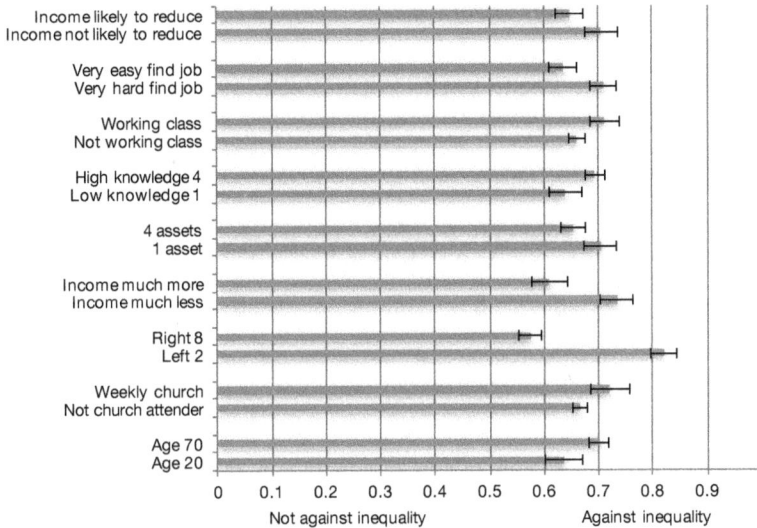

Figure 6.12: Correlates of attitudes opposing inequality (predicted probabilities)

Source: Appendix, Table 6.A6.

Vote choice

We have shown that Labour's policy distinctiveness on positional issues often presented a challenge for the party by way of conservative pushbacks on gender issues, on its reputation for more generous treatment of beneficiaries, and potentially the Treaty of Waitangi. On other issues, Labour's policies were distinctive from National's, especially with respect to New Zealand Superannuation, a capital gains tax and on other actions needed to address inequality. We investigate the effects on vote choice in a series of regression models reported in full in the Appendix.

We acknowledge that complex models of positional and valence vote choices are problematic since different theories assume different relationships between independent or explanatory variables. There are strong possibilities of reverse or reciprocal causality, 'chicken and egg' relationships or, in technical terms, of endogeneity. This means that causal order among independent variables or even between an independent and dependent variable can only be inferred by plausible assumptions, or from theory that may be contested. A plausible assumption is that age affects vote choice: we know that vote choice cannot affect age. On the other hand, union membership might affect vote choice, but having a tendency to vote Labour probably affects whether or not someone joins a union. Without even more complex models, equally contestable, we simply have to accept that we cannot avoid endogeneity, explore alternative model specifications as best we can, and make cautious inferences allowing for these uncertainties. The Appendix therefore contains four alternative models so that the implications of alternative assumptions are transparent.

The biggest problem is the question of reciprocal relationships between valence (competence) and positional (substantive issue) variables. Valence-driven preferences can cue a voter position. If someone liked David Cunliffe, and if they had uncertain views about a capital gains tax, they might be tempted to support Cunliffe's party's promotion of that policy. It may be more likely that causality operates in the other direction in more cases than not, but we must still be aware of the alternative.

Table 6.A7 in the Appendix represents the best attempt possible to address these concerns in the space available. The models have been stripped down to the variables that are statistically significant, but the findings are much the same with or without the full range of variables. We are interested in two main differences: first, what happens with and without valence variables in the models, and second, separating out those most likely to be cued by Labour loyalties, having voted Labour in 2011, and those less likely to have been cued, because they did not vote Labour in 2011. We are particularly interested in whether those two groups display different relationships between their positional preferences and their probability of voting Labour.

We focus on the positional variables discussed in this chapter. First, there are two unequivocal findings consistent across all four models included in Table 6.A7. Opinions about expenditure on universal social services and attitudes towards women's representation had no relationship with the Labour vote. Preferences for more expenditure on targeted benefits were significant only without including the valence/leadership variables, or without including previous vote. Support for targeted benefits is correlated with past Labour vote. It is not a preference that moved people toward or away from Labour in 2014. Support for targeted benefits also correlates strongly with disliking John Key; we suspect the causal directions here go both ways, but probably more from position to valence.

Opinion on change in pension eligibility is significant in three of the four models, but apparently not in the previous vote/valence model IV. Interacting pension change with previous vote exposes a relationship (Model VI). Plotting the post-estimation probabilities demonstrates it in Figure 6.13. If one voted Labour in 2011, one's opinion on pension reform made no difference to one's probability of voting Labour again; Labour loyalties prevailed over opposition to reform. For those who did not vote Labour in 2011, Labour's superannuation policy made them significantly less likely to shift to Labour—hardly the desired effect.

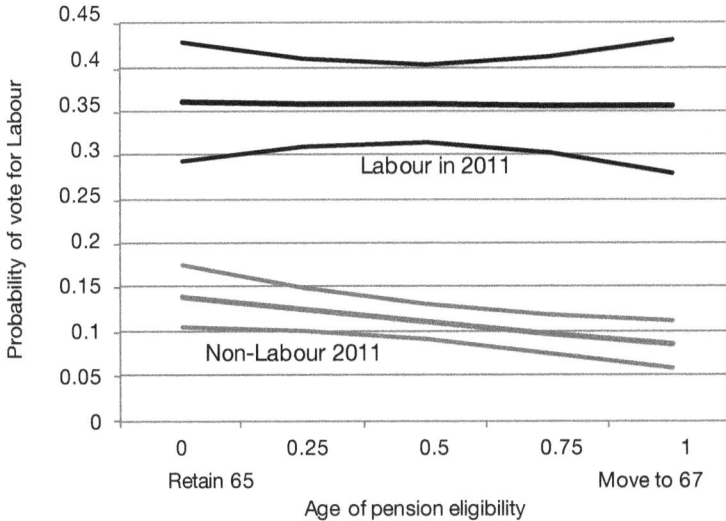

Figure 6.13: Probability of Labour vote by pension age reform
Source: Appendix, Table 6.A7, Model VI.

On attitudes towards the Treaty of Waitangi, Figure 6.14 shows that, all else being equal, Treaty opinion affected the probability of a 2014 Labour vote among those who had not voted Labour in 2011. The probability of an average non-Labour 2011 voter moving to Labour in 2014 was about 6 per cent. Support for the Treaty does seem to have been a pull factor for Labour among this group, limited only by the small number of Treaty supporters who did not already vote Labour in 2011. Whether they were unsympathetic or sympathetic to the Treaty, 2011 Labour voters were just as likely to stay with the party.

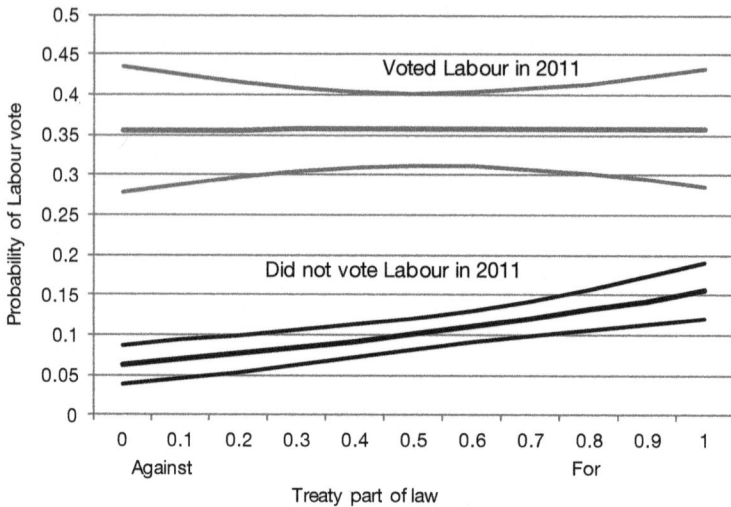

Figure 6.14: Probability of 2014 Labour vote by support or opposition to the Treaty conditioned by Labour vote or otherwise in 2011

Source: Appendix, Table 6.A7, Model VI.

Opinion on a capital gains tax also had consistent effects across all four models. For all the positional variables, in exploratory models we tested for non-linearity; in other words, whether the probability slope was a straight line or curved in some way, representing different slopes at different points of the curve. Capital gains tax was the only one that exhibited a non-linear relationship, in this case slightly concave. It is a subtle difference, but the slope among those in favour of a capital gains tax is about twice as steep as that among those opposed to it. Given that opinion on the proposed tax was evenly divided in the electorate, there may have been a slight advantage to the Labour vote. An interaction derived from Model VI shows the same slope for both 2011 Labour and non-Labour voters, both within confidence intervals, and widely separated, with the 2011 vote slope slightly steeper, suggesting that the policy was slightly better at holding on to previous Labour voters than gaining new ones. Plotting the non-interacted effect from Model IV confirms the relationship most clearly.

Opinion about inequality correlates strongly with the valence variables, particularly liking or disliking of John Key. Consequently, it drops out of models that include the two leadership variables. From Model V that does not contain the valence variables, but includes interactions with previous vote. We see in Figure 6.16 that inequality opinion apparently shifted non-Labour voters to Labour's probable benefit because there was more opposition to inequality than acceptance of it. However, controlling for the effects of the two leadership variables in Model VI, this slope becomes flatter and falls within the confidence intervals. Either liking John Key made people more accepting of inequality, or those accepting inequality were drawn to John Key on partisan or valence grounds; we cannot say which causal direction was stronger. In an alternative model, interacting inequality opinion with liking or disliking John Key does indicate that opposition to inequality somewhat reduced the negative effects of liking Key on the Labour vote.

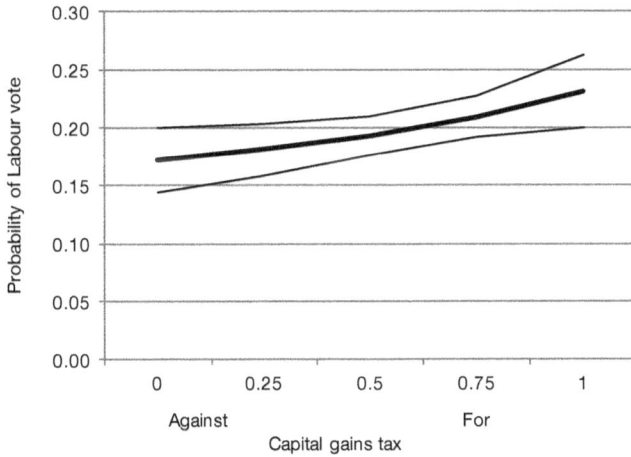

Figure 6.15: Probability of Labour vote by capital gains tax attitudes
Source: Appendix, Table 6.A7, Model IV.

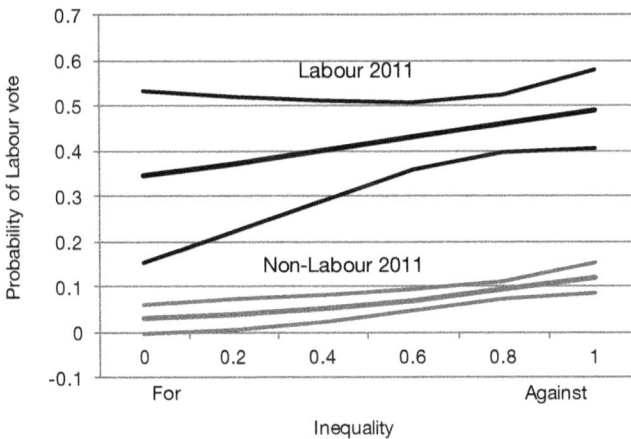

Figure 6.16: Probability of Labour vote by attitudes to inequality
Source: Appendix, Table 6.A7, Model V.

Conclusion

Opposition parties rarely if ever win elections on policies; they win because the incumbent government has run out of steam and voters have lost confidence in its ability to govern. As we have seen, the contrast between confidence and trust in the two major party leaders makes it clear that the government was in no danger of defeat on that score. But policies can make a difference on the margins. Our analysis of the effects of policy positions on vote choice finds little evidence that Labour policies gave the party much electoral traction in 2014—Labour was effectively spinning its wheels. For this, among other reasons, its vote fell back. In the late 1990s and early 2000s, Labour had an advantage over National in its reputation for adequate funding of universal services, particularly health and education. Our data indicates that in 2014, the National Party under John Key had neutralised that advantage. Support for benefits targeted to the unemployed and others unable to work is not strong enough to provide Labour with extra votes.

Labour's concern for 'identity issues' such as gender equality in its parliamentary representation seems to have no effect on vote choice. This may be because of low public interest in the matter, or because Labour downplayed the issue in the aftermath of conservative criticism. Labour's commitment to increase the age for receipt of New Zealand Superannuation appears in our analysis as a vote loser. Labour's positions on Treaty issues do not appear to have harmed the party in 2014 among its more consistent voters, and may have attracted some who had not voted Labour before, albeit marginally. National's close relationship with the Māori Party has taken pressure off this issue. There is no evidence the capital gains tax policy harmed Labour. The problem with this policy lies more in its inconsistency with Labour's pursuit of aspirational middle-income voters whose investments might be affected. Our analysis suggests that Labour both gained and lost votes on this policy, with a slight advantage toward vote gain. Finally, attitudes towards inequality did shape voting choice, but shifting attitudes did not necessarily deliver Labour much advantage. Those opposed to inequality did not move to Labour as much as the party might have hoped. Labour's leadership-based valence deficit was probably the reason.

7

Greening the inequality debate

The Green Party of Aotearoa/New Zealand is an environmental or ecological party that also favours a more equal society (Ford 2015). On the economic left–right dimension of the New Zealand party system, the Green Party occupies a position somewhat to the left of Labour. Some commentators argue that to become more politically successful, the Green Party should move to the centre by moderating its egalitarian and social justice principles. Others argue that the Green Party has already begun that process. On the social progressive–conservative dimension, the Green Party occupies a distinct space: as well as being an ecological party, the Green Party is a left-liberal or libertarian party and strongly defends social rights and individual freedoms.

Beginning this chapter with the historical background of the Green Party's development and ideology, we move on to an analysis of the party's innovative tax proposals that would have shifted current business taxes toward paying for pollution costs. In the context of claims that the tax policies shifted the party to the right, we examine how voters positioned the party, vote flows between the Greens and other parties, and vote splitting. We then examine the foundations of Green Party voters in the class structure. Next, we examine the proposition that values rather than social structure best explain the position of the Green Party, examining possible interactions between old politics and new politics ideological dimensions. This provides the foundation for an analysis of how the Green party's policies to address inequality, how the preferences of Green voters for action on that matter structured voting choice, and how attitudes about inequality interact with attitudes about environmental priorities within the Green vote. We conclude by discussing the party's coalition options and its lack of success in participating in governments hitherto.

Background and history

The beginnings of the Green Party of Aotearoa/New Zealand can be traced back to the establishment of the Values Party in 1972, the first Green Party in the world to contest a national election.[1] That year, Values won 2 per cent of the vote and three years later 5.2 per cent. The party's first manifesto addressed environmental quality, conservation and ecological sustainability, mounting a critique of the organisation, management and control of modern societies. The Values Party embraced the need to focus on people, communities and humanitarian values, rather than individualism, economic growth and profit (Dann 1999). Social equality through a moderately left-leaning collectivism was also an underlying principle.

In the late 1970s, the Values Party succumbed to conflict between those who took a moderately liberal or left approach and those who saw the party as eco-socialist. It contested the 1981 and 1984 elections but ran no candidates in 1987. Values activists instead concentrated on social movement politics and the campaign for proportional representation. In 1990, some former Values Party members and a new influx of activists formed the Green Party. It contested the 1990 election and gained nearly 7 per cent of the vote. In 1992, the Greens joined the left-wing Alliance, but withdrew in 1997 after the first election under the Mixed Member Proportional (MMP) electoral system. The party won just enough votes for parliamentary representation at the 1999 election. By 2008, the Greens had emerged as New Zealand's third largest parliamentary party, a position they continued to hold after the 2014 election, in which they won 10.7 per cent of the vote and 14 seats in the 121-seat parliament. This represented a slight dip in the Greens' vote share, down from 11 per cent in 2011. The party was disappointed with the result. Co-leader Russel Norman (2015: 147) had hoped to win 15 per cent. Polling had suggested the Greens might reach that goal.

---

1 Some Australian commentators contest this point, as the precursor to the Tasmanian Greens, the United Tasmania Group, was established in March 1972 and ran candidates in the state election held in April 1972.

Some New Zealand commentators sympathetic to the centre-right often seek to portray the Green Party as 'extreme'. The initial intake of Green Party MPs did include Sue Bradford and Keith Locke, both of whom had been active in socialist organisations in the past. But by 1999, both had left those groups to engage in broader, less sectarian political formations. Both Locke and Bradford became spokespeople for NewLabour after its formation in 1989, before joining the Greens (Bradford and Locke 1999). The Greens have come a long way since their reinvention in 1990, in terms of vote share, leadership and membership (Edwards and Lomax 2012). In 2014, this reinvention was best represented in announcements on building a 'Green economy' that spanned formal economic policy as well as sustainability, conservation and income equality.

From the outset, the Values Party had sought to develop an economic platform that represented a green alternative to both mainstream and social democratic economics. Environmental, ecological or green parties must inevitably engage with economics, because economic development often comes with environmental costs, both in terms of damage to natural ecosystems and to human health and wellbeing. In the days of the Values Party, much of the damage was also being done at the behest of government, with past Labour governments as much to blame as the business community. Under the influence of neo-liberalism, governments have drawn back from driving economic development directly. Contemporary Greens therefore direct their policies more toward the ways that government provides the incentives shaping business activity. This requires thinking more deeply about markets, taxation and the most effective means of affecting behaviour.

The breadth of Green thinking goes beyond the environment, and left and right in economic terms. It has another axis of human liberty. Homosexual law reform, the rights of indigenous peoples, a focus on youth representation and the rights of future generations have regularly featured in speeches and manifestos of the Green Party, just as they had earlier in those of the Values Party. Such values are common among Green parties globally (Ford 2015). Ecologism is central but supplemented with notions of respect and tolerance without violence, inclusivity, social justice and responsibility (Carroll et al. 2009; Talshir 2002). In Ronald Inglehart's (1990) terms, Green Parties are 'postmaterialist'. They stand for the liberation of human potential beyond the basic needs of economic and physical security that they also wish to ensure. Human beings should be free to create, to experiment and to live the lives they wish to live. This makes the Greens 'libertarian' as well as 'left'; indeed, in this sense, the Greens are much more extreme liberals than they are extreme left. This puts them strongly at odds with social conservatives whose ideas about human behaviour are conventional and traditional. The New Zealand Election Study (NZES) no longer estimates postmaterialist values but, in 1990, at the first election fought by the Green Party, it found that over half of its voters could be classified as postmaterialists or leaning in that direction, compared with 36 per cent overall among New Zealanders in general (Vowles and Aimer 1993: 143).

Tax and economic policies in 2014

Articulated in its 'Green charter' (Green Party 2014b), the Green Party's broad principles informed a raft of detailed policies in advance of the 2014 election. Rather than championing economic growth, co-leader Russel Norman (Green Party 2014d) announced their economic policy as one of economic transformation to support businesses to become 'smart, ethical and responsive'. He spoke of an economic plan that involved tackling unacceptable levels of inequality and environmental damage through reorienting taxation, regulating markets and bolstering environmental protection. The Greens' specific economic policy announcements during the campaign included establishing a government-owned and profit-making Green Investment Bank to act as an independent facilitator of private sector capital, a commitment to cheaper, sustainable energy sources, as well as encouraging organisations, public and private, to pay a living wage. Nonetheless, initially it was the carbon tax switch that attracted the media limelight.

Framed as an ecological tax reform by Norman, the idea was synchronous with Green Party principles. The reform would shift taxes off work and enterprise, and on to waste, pollution and scarce resources. The process was to begin with an Ecological Tax Commission that would review all existing taxes and discuss where eco-taxes would work best. This announcement did not undermine the Green Party's other aspects of its taxation platform: a progressive system that supplemented the goods and services tax (GST), a tax-free income threshold, adjustments to benefit abatement rates and the introduction of a capital gains tax, all aimed at reducing material inequalities. Most commentators, however, overlooked the latter, championing instead what they perceived to be the Greens' strategically smart decision to 'move just a little bit more towards the centre' (Edwards 2014c).

In contrast to the existing Emissions Trading Scheme (ETS), a measure the Greens had previously supported, the new carbon tax would result in costs for industry polluters: a tax of $25 per tonne of carbon, and a reduced rate of $12.50 per tonne for farmers. There would be a climate tax cut on the first $2,000 of income for households and businesses. When announced at the Greens conference, was greeted by 'rapturous reception' (Armstrong 2014c). Polling indicated that voters were not averse to the idea. UMR Research revealed that a 'personal tax cut funded by a charge on climate change polluters' would make 32 per cent of those surveyed 'a little more likely' to vote for the Green Party; 44 per cent said it would have no impact on their party choice, with 13 per cent indicating they would not vote for the Green Party anyway (Vance 2014).

Not everyone on the right expressed opposition to the Green Party's carbon tax proposals. National party supporters and political commentators Matthew Hooton and David Farrar, the Taxpayers Union and several economists argued that the shift away from the ETS towards a tax made good economic sense, and some businesses would ultimately benefit (Edwards 2014c). Both moderate and left-wing commentators concluded that with this initiative the Green Party had begun a raid on National's more centrist voters, who might think National's so-called Blue-Green group had not yet gone far enough to combat climate change. But given the proliferation of parties left of centre, and given the claim that those on lower incomes tend not to vote Green, the Greens' alleged repositioning on costing climate change could be hailed a strategic success story (Edwards 2014c). This reflects similar trends internationally. Green parties have regained momentum from the mid-1990s onwards, and have positioned themselves in ways that have opened up representation in both left- and right-leaning coalition governments in various parts of Europe (Dolezal 2010; Müller-Rommel and Poguntke 2002; van Haute 2016). In many European countries, centre-right parties have also come to recognise that more effective environmental policies are required, bringing them in closer proximity to Green parties.

Admittedly, the thrust of Green tax policies was not strongly redistributive, and there were non-party political grounds on which they could be justified that might appeal to wavering voters on the right (Campbell 2014).

Repetto et al. (1992) argued in the beginning of the 1990s for the use of 'Green Fees', which would begin to shift the tax burden away from worthwhile activities such as work, investment and clean, efficient production, onto activities governments would want to discourage, like pollution, inefficiency and waste. Since then there has been considerable comparative research into the economic viability of a carbon tax switch, which, if fiscally neutral, could result in wide ranging political support (Albrecht 2006; Speck 1999). In the end, the attention given to the economic and environmental possibilities associated with the carbon tax switch was fleeting at best. Unsurprisingly, business and farming interests believed it would be detrimental to their businesses (Vance 2014). A few mainstream outlets covered the prime minister's opposition to the idea, and the possibility that the Greens' initiative would produce tax cuts in 2017 in line with what the government was promising.

The *Dirty Politics* controversy (Hager 2014) and the 24-hour campaign news cycle also ensured it was difficult for the Greens' tax message to stay in the public eye. Russel Norman did his best to remind voters, arguing that the Greens were pro-market and that the major issues of sustainability could be 'solved by setting the right incentives and prices' (Rutherford 2014). Norman claimed that the Greens would be open to working with any government committed to implementing Green policies (Radio New Zealand 2014e). This was taken to be 'code' for working with National. There remained some journalistic scepticism about the Greens' capacity to go 'mainstream' (McLauchlan 2014b). The very low likelihood of the National Party moving to an environmentally based tax system seemed not to be considered. However much Green tax policies might potentially appeal to the intellectual centre-right, the odds of the New Zealand National Party adopting them were extremely low.

Party positioning, proximities and social structure

If the Greens intended their adoption of feasible, well-costed and innovative economic and tax policies to signal a shift to the right and attract National voters in 2014, the strategy failed. Figure 7.1 shows that in 2014 NZES respondents continued to view the Greens as a party marginally to the left of Labour. Meanwhile, National remained firmly to the right of centre, closer to the Conservatives and ACT than to New

Zealand First. Respondents placed three parties just to the right of centre (Māori, New Zealand First and United Future). Returning to the flow of the vote estimates discussed in Chapter 1, Table 1.2, we can note that about half of the 2014 Green Party vote was from those who had voted Green in 2011. While this data must be treated with caution, it suggests that the apparent stability of Green voting support is something of an illusion; as in a railway station, some got off and others got on the train, in this case in about equal numbers. The Green Party lost about 1 per cent to National and gained somewhat less from that source. It also may have lost a little more to Labour than it gained, but most of the inflow into the Green vote in 2014 was from Labour and previous non-voters.

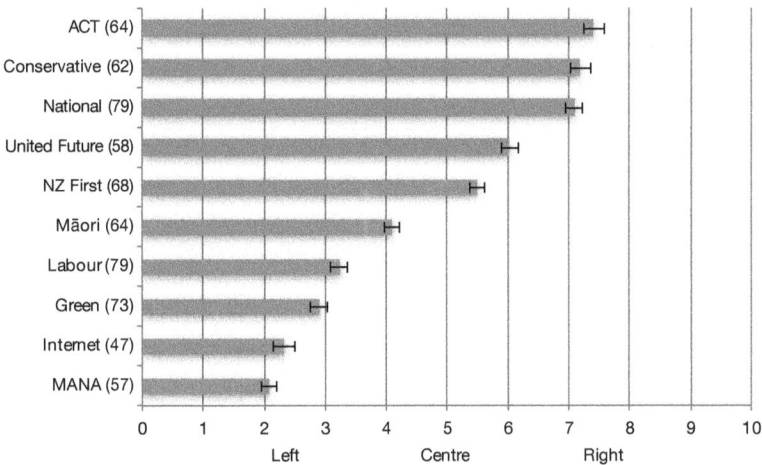

Figure 7.1: Left–right positioning of NZES respondents, 2014 election

Note: Labels include percentage of sample assigning a position to the various parties. Data excludes those not answering the question or who indicated don't know.

Figure 7.1 introduces the left–right positions of all the parties as ascribed by NZES respondents in 2014. The Labour and Green parties clearly remained much closer than the Greens and National. Split voting tells the same story, sourced from the official data produced by the Electoral Commission (see Appendix Table 7.A2). Green Party voters were 10.7 per cent of those who placed a ballot in the box. Those casting both party and electorate votes for the Greens were only 3.7 per cent, not much more than a third of the Green party vote. But no one expected any Green Party candidates to win an electorate, so it made sense for Green party voters to cast a vote for another candidate, assuming that they had a preference for one of those over another. That more preferred candidate was much more likely to represent Labour: 5 per cent of the voters cast a party vote for the Greens and an electorate vote for Labour. Only just under 1 per cent cast a party vote for the Greens and an electorate vote for National. In 2011, about 1.5 per cent did so (Vowles 2014b: 31). Fewer National Party voters gave an electorate vote to the Greens in 2014 than in 2011. Choices have tightened within the camps of National and Green voters, with fewer flows between the two votes across their boundaries. New Zealand voters did not see any convergence between the National and Green parties in 2014.

Some journalists have also suggested that the Greens' failure to attract voters on the right was less about the ability to demonstrate a capacity for economic management and environmental pragmatism, and more about how their position on issues of social justice connected or did not connect with their electoral support. For example, political commentator Duncan Garner (2014) argued that 'the Greens talk poverty and social justice, but the poor aren't listening—and they're certainly not voting for them'. He identified 'telling statistics' from party vote data across electorates: the Green Party polled much better in upper-income electorates than in those with high proportions of people on lower incomes. But Garner's observation is based on what is known as the ecological fallacy: it is dangerous to infer individual behaviour from differences between large groups of people such as those contained in electorates. At the individual level, as Chapter 4 has shown, the Greens were slightly more likely to gain votes from people on lower incomes than those on upper incomes.

Garner concluded that 'the Greens need to evolve and be open to formally supporting a National Government'. This evolution appeared to require a move away from a left position on social justice. This is not a particularly new claim. In 2009, Carroll et al. explored whether the New Zealand Green Party's left-of-centre social justice policies were stopping them from obtaining a much higher percentage of the vote and thus increasing potential to be a coalition partner (see also Batten 2005 and, for the Australian Greens, Manning 2002).

This argument is wide open to scepticism. Aside from the acceptability of Green tax proposals, there were equally significant policy differences between the Green Party and the National Party on core Green business: the environment. Cooperation between parties requires both to make a commitment. In 2008, the Green Party were not averse to working with the new National Government, and took part in a program to encourage home insulation and develop a New Zealand–based regulatory system for natural health products (Green Party 2009). After the 2011 election, cooperation continued on home insulation, the management of toxic industrial sites and the development of cycle ways. By 2014, most of these arrangements had lapsed and John Key sharply rejected a Green overture for continued and renewed cooperation after the 2014 election (Newshub 2014b).

Green voters in other countries tend to be employees in white-collar service sectors of the economy, and in the public sector, and are occupationally different from both the traditional 'old politics' economic cleavage (Dolezal 2010). In New Zealand, as shown in Chapter 4, Green voters are more likely to live in non-manual than manual households, but the probability estimates are not outside confidence intervals. Farmers are particularly less likely to vote Green. In New Zealand, the sector of the economy in which people work does not appear to matter for the Green vote. Other structural divisions of relevance for the Green vote are hypothesised to be gender, education and religion. As Chapter 4 has shown (Figure 4.4), education and absence of religiosity do matter in New Zealand. Dolezal (2010) suggests that Green supporters view ecologism as a form of religion, that there is an urban–rural divide (also confirmed in New Zealand) and that impact of age may be complex (youth versus the now ageing protest generation). Examining these characteristics alongside attitudinal factors in a multivariate analysis of 12 European countries, Dolezal's findings confirm that the stability of the Green vote in recent years is connected to shared social characteristics as well as values.

Green voters in New Zealand in 2014 were young, higher educated, tended to have a European ethnic identity, be a union member and live in an urban location. There is no evidence of an older 'protest generation' that bulges for Green voting. Contrary to Garner's claims, lower incomes and fewer assets are associated with Green voting. However, as Figure 7.2 shows, Green voters are not working class and do not see themselves as such. They also do not identify as middle class, given the width of the confidence intervals, mainly identifying with no class at all. The effect of identifying with no class on the probability of voting Green is statistically significant when compared with working-class identifiers. Yet the relationship between not identifying with a class and Green voting loses substantive and statistical significance once the socio-economic characteristics included in the basic social structure model are controlled for, indicating that social structural locations 'explain' these perceptions of class or non-class identification.

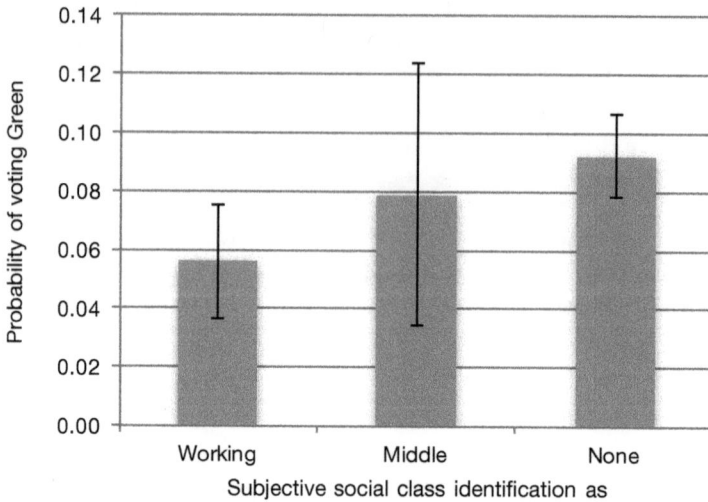

Figure 7.2: Probability of voting Green by subjective social class

Note: A simple regression of vote Green or not against the subjective social class categories.
Source: New Zealand Election Study 2014.

The Green Party and 'values'

Most of the debate about the positioning of the Green Party has focused on economic and social policies. But there is another side to the Green Party. As discussed in Chapter 3, materialism and post-materialism form one set of labels for a dimension that represents the 'new politics', as distinct from the 'old politics' reflected in the left–right dimension. One can define this dimension slightly differently as socially progressive against socially conservative, or simply as liberal versus conservative. As explained in Chapter 3, in the NZES we define it in terms of the difference between libertarian and authoritarian values.

The NZES measures authoritarianism with three questions, all soliciting agreement or disagreement with statements with which authoritarians will tend to agree. For this reason, it is biased somewhat in favour of authoritarianism, but measures its variation quite well. The statements are: 'Most people would try to take advantage of others if they got the chance'; 'A few strong leaders could make this country better than all the laws and talk'; and 'What young people need most of all is strict discipline by their parents'. We combine this into a 10-point scale with authoritarianism scoring high, libertarianism or social liberalism scoring low.

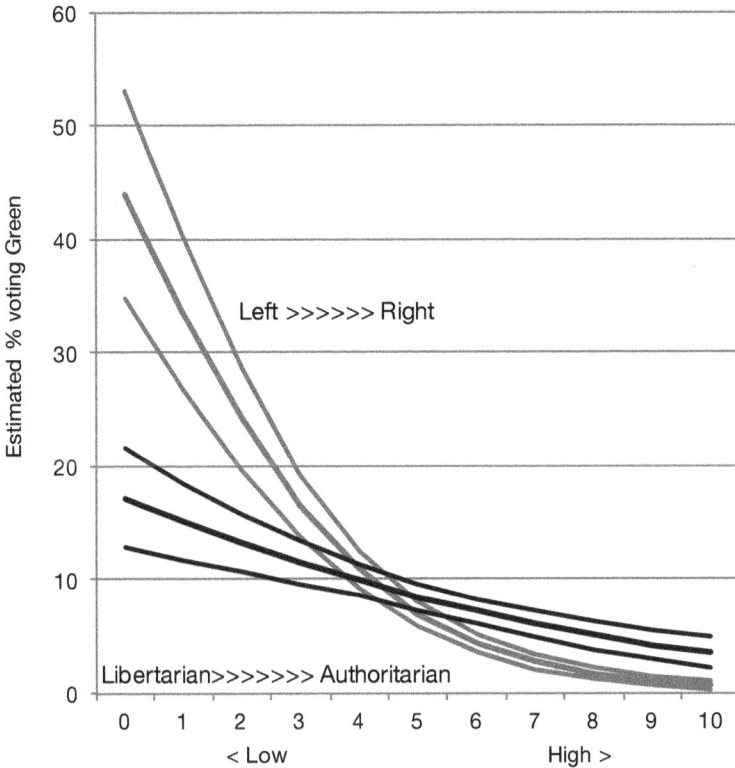

Figure 7.3: Left–right and liberal–authoritarian attitudes as predictors of voting Green, 2014 election

Note: Based on a logistic regression of left–right and libertarian–authoritarian positions on vote for the Green Party or not. The two scales are also interacted together, but Figure 7.3 shows the estimated probabilities generated by each scale leaving the interaction in the background. Each set of probabilities remain controlled for the effects of the other and the interaction between them.

Source: New Zealand Election Study 2014.

Libertarian–authoritarian attitudes correlate weakly (r=.15) with the left–right positions. Being economically right is associated with being authoritarian, and being economically left tends to be associated with libertarianism. This is consistent with NZES findings from previous elections (Vowles 2004b) and the nature of party systems in most developed democracies (Bornschier 2010). However, the correlation is modest. The most authoritarian person is likely to be only 1.5 higher on the 10-point left–right scale than the person who is most libertarian or liberal. Left–right and libertarian–authoritarian therefore form two underlying dimensions of the party system.

Figure 7.3 shows that both the left–right and libertarian–authoritarian position predict voting for the Green Party quite strongly. The strongest effect on the Green vote is the left–right position, with those who are most to the left voting for the Green Party at a probability of 30 per cent or higher. Those at 8 or higher on the left–right scale have a less than a 2 per cent probability of voting Green. The libertarian–authoritarian slope is not as steep as the left–right scale, but libertarians are nonetheless three times more likely to vote Green than authoritarians.

Figure 7.4 plots the interaction between left–right and libertarian–authoritarian. The combination of being right (8 and above) and authoritarian produces a flat line; as already noted, a person scoring 8 on the left–right scale has a less than 2 per cent chance of voting Green, and this is almost regardless of where they sit on the libertarian–authoritarian scale. People on the right who have libertarian values seem to extend those values into their position on the role of the state in the economy. For this reason, this flat line running parallel and very close to the X-axis is not plotted in the figure, and Figure 7.4 only presents the interaction between left–right and libertarian–authoritarian for people leaning towards the centre-left (score 4 on the left–right scale) or left (score 1 on the left–right scale).

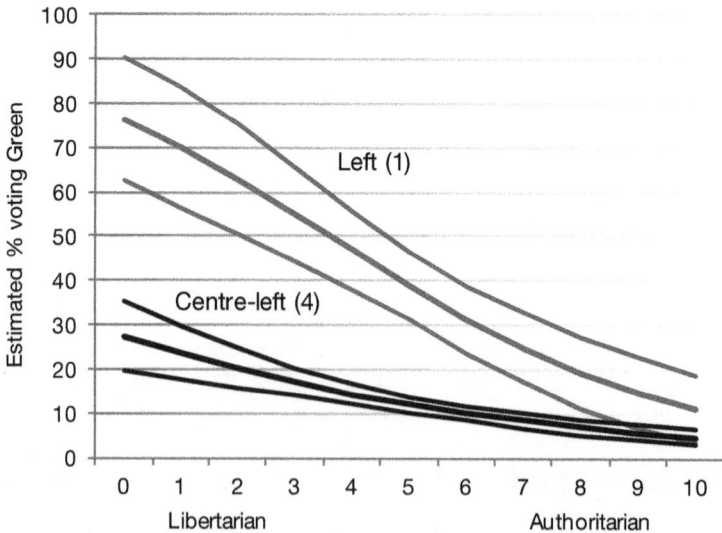

Figure 7.4: The interactive effects of libertarian–authoritarian positions and left positions on the probability of voting for the Green Party
Source: New Zealand Election Study 2014.

Figure 7.4 reveals that the combination of being economically left and socially libertarian has a potent effect on voting Green. The Greens are a majority party on the libertarian left: more than 75 per cent of the left-libertarian electorate supports the Green party. But this is, of course, a very small slice of society. Libertarian attitudes pull the centre-left towards the Greens too, but not as strongly. These findings are robust even after the baseline social structure variables are added as controls. Although both libertarian and economic left attitudes are important in predicting voting for the Green Party, being left is about three times more important than being libertarian (see Figure 7.3). While most Green voters do not feel that they belong to the working class, they are to the left in their political attitudes and tend to care about those who are less fortunate than they are.

The Green Party and the issue of inequality

This all casts considerable doubt on claims in the post-election media analysis that the Green Party needed to reassess its principles and add a 'more blueish tint to their supposedly red-green hue' (Edwards 2014d). We return to the two questions on income inequality included in the NZES: 'Differences in income in New Zealand are too large'; and 'Government should take measures to reduce differences in income levels'. Put together in Chapter 6, these two questions form a scale in which action to reduce inequality is the highest value with a theoretical maximum of one, and no action at all is a theoretical minimum of zero. As Figure 6.11 indicated, voters for the Green Party were significantly more likely to want action on inequality in 2014 than they were in 2011, and indeed they were slightly more concerned than Labour voters. Differences between the Greens, National, New Zealand First and Conservative voters were statistically significant, and hold even with controls for socio-demographic characteristics.

Around the world, Green voters tend to reject income inequality and believe that the government should seek to reduce it. Significant correlations can be found between willingness to pay increased taxes for social services and greater social equity, and a willingness to pay increased taxes to ensure environmental protection (Carroll et al. 2009). Contrary to Batten (2005), Carroll and co-authors concluded that the Greens would not necessarily fare better electorally by confining themselves to environmental issues and taking a less committed position on social justice and inequality, arguing that the Greens' left-of-centre social policies might prove even more attractive to those for whom environment was a priority. In our data, as reported in Chapter 6 (Figures 6.2 and 6.3), we also found strong support among Green Party voters to pay for universally provided services such as health, education and taxpayer-funded pensions, equivalent to the level of support among Labour voters. Green voters were also only slightly less supportive of expenditure on targeted benefits, such as unemployment and other welfare benefits than Labour, and significantly more supportive than National voters and voters of other parties to the right.

The Green Party did address the issue of inequality and poverty during the election campaign. The headline of a 'Billion-dollar plan' included a commitment to harnessing additional tax from high-income earners and trusts by creating a top tax rate of 40 per cent, and redistributing it through a children's credit, a parental tax credit and additional investment in child health and education (Green Party 2014a). Several weeks later, the Greens launched a document titled 'Fair reward for fair effort' (2014b). Their proposals included increasing the minimum wage to NZ$18 per hour, and introducing a living wage for core government and contracted workers. They also appealed to union members, through their commitment to making workplace bargaining more democratic and requiring companies to report on the income gap between the highest and lowest paid employees. While the Greens argued their policies were pro-market in advancing a Green economy, they remained firmly interventionist on creating a fairer economy. They promised to set benefits 'at a level such that beneficiary income is sufficient for all basic needs' (Green Party 2014a)

The environment

Despite its suggestions for new tax policies and the attention given to issues of social justice and inequality, the Green Party's focus remained firmly on the environment. Among its policy highlights for the 2014 election was strong action to restore freshwater quality; a response to high levels of water pollution as a result of urban development and, in particular, the rapid expansion of the dairy industry. The Greens demanded rivers in which people could swim safely; National regarded the ability to wade in them safely to be sufficient. Air pollution followed in Green priorities, with particular emphasis on the emissions from road transport. The Greens promised to stoutly defend the Resource Management Act from which the National-led government was seeking to remove some key principles underpinning environmental protection. The Green Party strongly opposed exploration for deep-water offshore oil, which was also strongly encouraged by National. All these policies stood in stark contrast to those of the government that, at best, promised slow and incremental action to address environmental problems.

The 2014 NZES asked respondents whether environmental protection should be prioritised over economic development (or vice versa). Reversed from its original questionnaire order, the scale ranges between 1 and 7 where '1 indicates do more to encourage economic development' and 7 refers to 'prioritising protecting the environment'. Figure 7.5 presents average scores for each party.

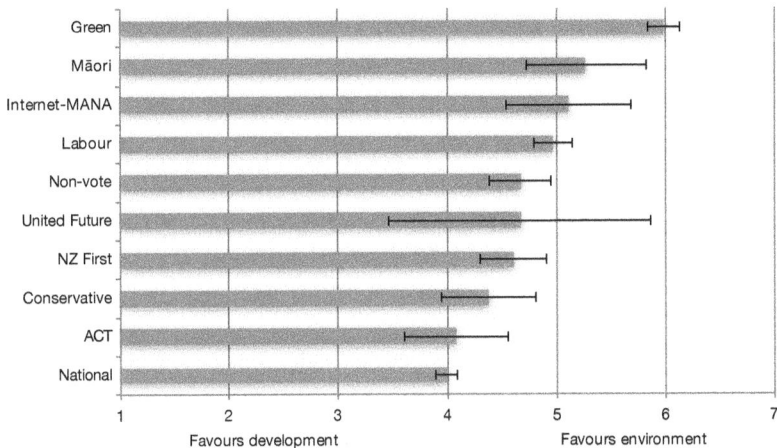

Figure 7.5: Environment versus economic development (comparison of means) per party choice
Source: New Zealand Election Study 2014.

Figure 7.5 indicates that the average National voter was the least likely to prefer environmental protection over economic development, compared with all other parties' voters. Environmental protection is not unimportant to many National voters, who score at 4 on average. Yet they show the largest difference of all party vote groups with Green voters. Unsurprisingly, the Green voters are most likely to be in favour of environmental protection, followed by supporters of the Māori Party and Labour. Even if the Greens dropped their economic 'leftism', their current voters are significantly different from National voters on environmental issues, and, while there is still a gap, Green voters are closer to Labour voters.

As argued above, Green Party principles articulate strongly both protection of the environment and promotion of social equality. If these opinions are correlated among voters, particularly among those who vote for the Greens, the claim that the Greens could drop their left-leaning policies and widen their support will not stand up to scrutiny. The 2014 NZES indicates that opposition to inequality and a desire to protect the environment do positively and significantly correlate (r=.20). Those who are strongly against inequality tend to be more supportive of protecting the environment than encouraging economic development. As Figure 7.6 shows, both attitudes also positively and significantly relate to Green voting and interact together.

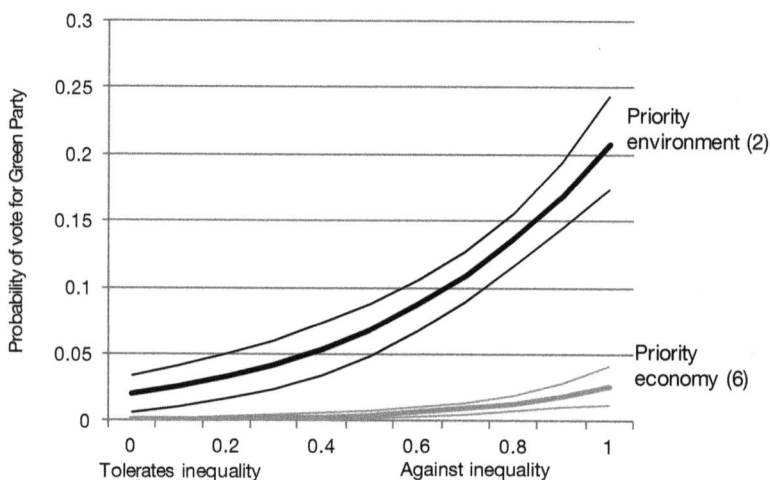

Figure 7.6: The interactive effects of environmental opinions and preferences about reducing inequality on the probability of voting for the Green Party

Source: New Zealand Election Study 2014.

Figure 7.6 reveals that the likelihood of voting Green increases significantly the more one is against economic inequality. The effect of not tolerating inequality is substantially stronger among those who prioritise protecting the environment than among those who are supportive of developing the economy. If the Greens move to the right, they might well lose rather than gain votes. Admittedly, parties to some extent shape the opinions of their supporters. A shift to the centre or right might carry some Green voters with it, but that remains speculative at best. Core Green support is based on a left environmental ideological base.

Seeking government: Office versus votes

While Green parties have entered governments around the world, Katz and Mair (1995) have argued that governing parties such as Labour and National in New Zealand operate in ways that will preserve their dominance as *formateur* parties. They seek to prevent new entrants encroaching on their access to office, media and political donors (on Australian, see also Brenton 2013; on New Zealand, see also Curtin and Miller 2011). The assumption is that Green demands will ultimately be accommodated and co-opted by the major parties without the need to include the party in government.

Alongside this, Green parties are often assumed to be less office-oriented than other types of parties, primarily because of their focus on grassroots participation and their early scepticism of the capacity of governments to make change. *Formateur* parties prefer to work with parties that are prepared to trade policy for office and have a centralised leadership structure (Warwick 1996). Participation in government is likely to present electoral challenges for Green parties, when their supporters criticise them for becoming captured by the system, and for sacrificing policy and participatory principles for incremental gains (Carter 2007; Dumont and Bäck 2006; Poguntke 2002).

Dumont and Bäck (2006) go on to hypothesise that Green parties are only likely to enter government under certain conditions: when a surplus majority government is formed, when they win a large proportion of non-major party seats in parliament, and have longevity in parliamentary experience. In terms of type of government, Dumont and Bäck suggest that inclusion of the Greens in government is most likely to occur when the policy distance between themselves and the *formateur* party's left–right position is small, and when the main party of the left wins government. These arguments build on early theories that maintain the importance of ideological proximity, whereby coalitions will be formed between parties that are ideologically 'connected' along a policy dimension, with minimal ideological diversity. Using a dataset comprised of 51 government formation opportunities where the Greens were represented in parliament in Europe, Dumont and Bäck conclude that longevity in parliament, experiencing vote loss and ideological proximity to a *formateur* party on the left are significant in explaining the cases where the Greens have succeeded in entering government. By September 2014, nine countries had experienced Green parties in government (Little 2016).

Entering government was one of New Zealand Green Party's objectives in 2014—and it was not unrealistic, given what is theoretically required. They had been in parliament continuously for 18 years, and had experienced both gains and losses in term of vote share since 1996. Party positioning, vote flow and split voting data examined above do also indicate a proximity to the Labour Party that is close enough to make coalition an option.

Prior to 2014, the working relationship between Labour and the Greens was seldom smooth. Although the Green Party supported Labour-led governments on confidence and supply in 1999 and 2002, they agreed only to abstain between 2005 and 2008, and there has been ongoing tension over a range of policy issues of significance to Green voters and party members. Of these, the most problematic has been the question of genetic modification of animals and plants, particularly for human consumption (Bale and Bergman 2006; Ford 2015). Differences between Labour and the Greens put the parties at odds in 2002, and while the Greens did support the Labour-led government formed that year, it almost certainly destroyed the best opportunity hitherto for the Green Party to have been fully included in a New Zealand government. This has meant that the Greens have never received the benefits of additional ministerial staff, or similarly enabling resources, despite the advent of minority governments, where they could have held the balance of power. Instead, they have watched other parties take up ministerial posts in government. In 2005, both New Zealand First and United Future demanded the exclusion of the Greens from ministerial positions as part of the price of their support for Labour. Nevertheless, the Green Party has continued to position itself on an increasing number of issues of public policy and as a potential governmental partner.

In advance of the 2014 election campaign, the Greens made it abundantly clear that they were interested in working alongside Labour during the campaign with a view to forming a Labour/Green government. The proposal sought agreement that Cabinet posts would be in proportion to the number of seats won by the respective parties, and to build a common strategy to facilitate a relationship with New Zealand First, should the latter's support be required. On 10 April 2014, Labour leader David Cunliffe rejected the proposal. He said that Labour wanted to be open to *all* prospective partners joining a *Labour-led* government, and cited Labour's 100-year history of independence. That history of independence had not prevented Labour from campaigning with the Alliance in 1999, presenting themselves as a government-in-waiting (Campbell 2014).

Some media commentators suggested it was a lost opportunity for Labour, a position Cunliffe admitted to be a mistake after National won and reclaimed government (Watkins, Rutherford and Kirk 2014).

As previously examined in Chapter 5, Table 5.2, the 2014 NZES asked three questions about coalition preferences: 'On election day 2014, between National and Labour, which party did you most want to be in government?'; 'Of all the parties, which one did you most want to be in government?'; and 'In addition to your first choice of party, were there other parties you wanted in government?' Table 7.1 shows all those who indicated 'Green' in the second and third questions tabulated in row percentages against the responses to the 'Labour or National' question. The table thus shows to what extent those who preferred a Labour-led government and those who preferred a National-led government also wanted the Greens in government. The right column of Table 7.1 presents the overall percentage of people wanting a National-led or Labour-led government in the form of percentages by column.

Table 7.1: Major party most wanted to be in government and preferences for Greens to be in government

Major party most wanted in government	Greens in government		Labour or National in government
	No	Yes	
	Row %		Column %
Labour	36	64	29
National	80	20	56
Neither	57	43	9
Don't know	91	9	6
Total	65	34	
N			2,807

Source: New Zealand Election Study 2014.

Table 7.1 indicates that nearly two-thirds of those who wanted Labour in government rather than National also wanted the Green Party in government with Labour. Among those supporting a National rather than Labour government, only 20 per cent also wanted the Greens in government. In all, 34 per cent of respondents wanted to see the Greens in government. Going through the list of the National-led government's support partners, estimated in the same way as for the Green Party, this contrasts well with the 7 per cent who wished to see ACT in government, the 9 per cent who wished to see United Future in government, the 18 per cent who wished to see the Māori Party in government and the 25 per cent who wanted New Zealand First. Of the minor parties, the Green Party was thus clearly the most preferred party to enter government.

Ultimately, the Greens' fate in terms of government formation is likely to be tied to the electoral success of Labour. In the medium term, at least, the Greens will not be in a position to be the *formateur* party in the process of coalition formation, but Green parties are not power-shy (Strøm 1990). In 2014, the fragmentation of the left undermined the potential success of the Greens, with Internet-MANA and Labour determined to appeal to both the left and the centre. Green policy positions on the environment, the economy and on inequality were well received by commentators and the Greens' core voters, but the party's hope to achieve 15 per cent of the vote may prove difficult to attain. Elsewhere, Green parties have rarely exceeded a 10 per cent seat share in national parliaments, and their ideological proximity with parties on the left restricts their coalition options. More than other types of party, Green parties tend to make major decisions through processes of internal party democracy, such as whether or not to enter a coalition government (Little 2016). Thus, when Green parties are presented with strategic choices between maximising votes, achieving policy gains or taking part in government, votes, and sometimes policy, tend to win out over government.

Conclusion

If the Green Party were to take the advice of political commentators and weaken its commitments to promoting social equality and social justice, its cause would be significantly weakened. In the context of a trend towards greater public concern about inequality and poverty in New Zealand, it seems odd advice for a vote-seeking political party to abandon its commitment to help address the problem.

Admittedly, the Green Party's promises to address inequality in 2014 were secondary to its tax proposals that would have shifted current business taxes toward paying for the costs of pollution. In emphasising the connection between climate change and economic policy reform, commentators from both the left and right assumed that the Greens were looking to reach beyond their traditional base of support, appealing to the liberal centre as well as the progressive left. If that was indeed the objective, the Greens made no progress in achieving it. While Green voters tend toward lower incomes and fewer assets than average, apart from opposition from farmers, the Green Party vote largely transcends the 'old politics' manual/non-manual cleavage. Greens tend not to see themselves in class terms, or otherwise, like most others, consider themselves 'middle class'.

This does not mean that Green voters form an incoherent group. They come together on a combination of left-liberal/libertarian and environmental values that are mutually reinforcing and consistent. For a Green voter, being left tends to mean being liberal on social values and wanting more action to protect the environment. Many of these values are held outside as well as inside the Green tent. Pulling back from any one of those value sets runs the risk of weakening rather than strengthening the Green vote. The Green Party commitment to a more equal society is almost as important in its objectives and principles as its commitment to protecting the natural environment.

8

Conservatives compared: New Zealand First, ACT and the Conservatives

Across the left–right dimension, New Zealand Election Study (NZES) respondents agree with most political analysts and commentators: from the left, the New Zealand party system runs from the MANA Party, the Greens and Labour, through the centre to the Māori Party, New Zealand First and United Future, and to the right through National, the Conservative Party and ACT. Party policies and the opinions of each group of voters are largely consistent with this ideological continuum in their positions on the role of the state, the role of the market and what to do about inequality.

Continuing our discussion from the previous chapter on the Green Party, and as discussed in earlier chapters, we also observe that there is a second dimension on which the parties can be aligned. This dimension runs from libertarianism to authoritarianism, and has become increasingly important when explaining voting behaviour in advanced post-industrial democracies over recent decades. As earlier chapters have argued, political arguments across the authoritarian–libertarian dimension may act as 'wedge' issues, moving attention away from left–right debates that highlight the various dimensions of inequality.

In this chapter, we focus on three broadly defined 'conservative' parties that were in contention for votes in the 2014 election, not just with other parties but among themselves: New Zealand First, ACT New Zealand

and the Conservative Party.[1] We expect preferences for these parties to be most strongly associated with the authoritarian–libertarian dimension, and with the potential to mobilise 'wedge' issues. On the other hand, their positions on the left–right dimension, and those of their voters, also need to be taken into account. New Zealand First, in particular, attracts more egalitarian voters than ACT or the Conservatives. If in a centre left–leaning government or supporting one, New Zealand First would be more likely than the two other conservative partes to agree to at least some policies to promote greater equality.

Gaining 8.7 per cent of the votes and 11 seats in parliament, New Zealand First has consistently been the most successful party in this group since its formation in 1993. The Conservative Party, established in 2011, and led and funded by property developer Colin Craig, received almost 4 per cent of the vote in 2014, up from 2.7 in 2011. Because the Conservative Party failed to gain the necessary 5 per cent of the party votes, it won no seats in parliament. While the ACT Party only received 0.7 per cent of the votes in the 2014 election, with the encouragement of the National Party it won the electorate seat of Epsom, thereby crossing the threshold for representation and ensuring its presence in parliament.

This chapter briefly outlines the histories of these parties, examines where voters position them and provides profiles of their voters. It pays particular attention to two key policy areas: abortion and immigration, two main issues on the libertarian–authoritarian dimension, while also continuing our inquiries into the salience of Treaty opinions and attitudes to inequality.

Histories and positions

International analysts tend to define New Zealand First as a 'radical' right populist party (Betz 2005). This is because New Zealand First tends to take socially and culturally conservative policy positions and advocates reduction of current levels of immigration into New Zealand. It is often argued that the party should be seen as more centrist than 'radical'

---

1   The United Future Party led by Peter Dunne is not included in this analysis for several reasons. It is not a conservative party and is usually defined as a centrist liberal party. More to the point, while Dunne won his electorate seat in 2014, the party gained only 0.2 per cent of the party vote. Only seven respondents to the 2014 NZES reported voting for the party. In 2013, United Future briefly lost its status as a registered party as its records could not confirm that it had the required 500 members (Trevett 2013).

or 'right', because it occupies a pivotal position that has enabled it to enter governing arrangements with both the centre-left and centre-right major parties at different times: with National between 1996 and 1998, and Labour from 2005 to 2008 (Joiner 2015). In the aftermath of New Zealand First's support of Labour, in 2008 and 2011 National Party leader John Key explicitly ruled out working with New Zealand First (Trevett 2011b). In January 2014, National moderated its position. John Key indicated that a post-election working relationship was very unlikely with New Zealand First, but would not rule out the possibility (Davison 2014b). As the 2017 election was approaching, the National leadership was again not ruling out an accommodation with New Zealand First.

The leader of New Zealand First, Winston Peters, has long been one of the most recognisable party leaders in New Zealand politics by reason of his long and often colourful political career. Winston Peters is of Māori and Scottish descent. Elected to parliament for the first time in 1978 as a National Party electorate MP, Peters' career reflects a mix of 'old' and 'new' politics. He has been a consistent opponent of neo-liberal economic policies but also a defender of social and cultural conservatism. He was appointed to the National Government Cabinet in 1990, but after consistently criticising government policies was sacked by prime minister Jim Bolger in 1992. He continued to criticise the government's neo-liberal direction from the backbenches. After the National Party excluded him from the candidate selection process for his electorate for the 1993 election, he resigned from the party and from parliament, causing a by-election at which he stood again and won as an Independent.

Winston Peters created New Zealand First to fight the 1993 election. New Zealand First has won seats at all subsequent elections except for that of 2008. Peters lost his Tauranga electorate seat in 2005 but was returned as a list MP in 2005, 2011 and 2014. In 2015, Peters won the safe National seat of Northland in a by-election, robbing the National–ACT combination of a majority in parliament, and thus requiring the government to require the support of either United Future or the Māori Party to pass legislation. Since then, New Zealand First poll ratings have continued to remain relatively strong (Keall 2016), enough to lead many commentators to anticipate that New Zealand First will be able to take a 'kingmaker' role after the 2017 election. Peters is one of the few politicians whose 'brand' is so strong that he is often referred to simply by his first name (Levine and Roberts 2015: 336). Indeed, six months out from the 2014 election, one headline read 'The first major poll of the election year can be summed up in one word—Winston' (Gower 2014b). In 2014, 32 per cent of NZES respondents found Winston Peters likeable, compared with Labour leader David Cunliffe at 22 per cent.

The contrast between New Zealand First and the ACT Party is conspicuous and considerable. ACT leans well to the right on the economic dimension, with a strong ideological emphasis on neo-liberal free market principles, but has varied its positions on social and cultural issues, normally leaning towards social conservatism (Edwards 2015: 266). More recent ACT leaders such as Don Brash and Jamie Whyte have taken more libertarian positions, sometimes to the discomfort of other party members. The ACT Party was formed in 1995, from an earlier brief incarnation in 1994 as the Association of Consumers and Taxpayers, from which the party's name is derived. Former Labour finance minister Roger Douglas and former National Party minister Derek Quigley led the formation of the party. ACT has been able to capture the economic, social and libertarian right, leaving National to focus on winning over moderate median voters to the right of centre. ACT leader Rodney Hide (2004–2011) won the formerly safe National electorate of Epsom in 2005, aided by strategic voting by National Party supporters that has become increasingly orchestrated at more recent elections, and at which successive ACT candidates have retained the seat. A National candidate stands, but does not actively campaign, except for the National party vote (Robson 2014). This process guarantees National at least one partner in government. Ironically, had National won the Epsom electorate in 2014 it would have gained an extra list seat from the party vote count and won majority government on its own (Farrar 2014a).

ACT has been a support partner for National-led governments since 2008, rewarded by a ministerial position outside Cabinet for Rodney Hide (2008–2011), an associate minister position for his successor John Banks (2011–2014) and a parliamentary under-secretary role for its current Epsom MP and leader of the party since 2014, David Seymour. ACT reached its highest vote in 2002 at just over 7 per cent. In 2014, its vote fell to 0.7 per cent, its lowest-ever share. Its leader Jamie Whyte was not elected to parliament. ACT's strongest showing coincided with National's disastrous party vote collapse to just under 21 per cent in 2002. Indeed, it is evident that the National and ACT party votes are closely aligned: as one waxes, the other wanes. At its first election in 1996, ACT carved out a niche of voters who had the characteristics of heartland National Party voters (Aimer 1998; Vowles 2002b). By 2014, most of them had returned to National (Aimer 2014).

The remaining significant conservative party in the New Zealand party system is the Conservative Party. The Conservative Party takes strong conservative stances on cultural and social issues, and emphasises a traditional model of the family (Edwards 2015: 267). Established, led and funded by property developer Colin Craig, the party looked like it might reach the threshold of 5 per cent in 2014. John Key acknowledged that the Conservative Party could have been a potential support partner, but without great enthusiasm (Davison 2014b). The Conservative and National parties toyed with the idea of an electorate seat deal that might have given Craig a seat, but National backed off. In the dying days of the election campaign things began to go awry for the Conservatives. Craig became increasingly erratic, offering strange answers to straightforward questions, missing media appearances and running a billboard campaign that some called 'creepy'. When his female press secretary with whom he had formed an apparently close relationship resigned two days before the election under mysterious circumstances, Craig's image began to unravel. Doubts began to emerge that he was really a 'wholesome, out-there sort of a bloke, that's all encompassing … the sort of person we should be looking up to' (Dougan 2014). Had Craig's reputation not been tarnished by these events, it is possible that the Conservative Party might have received more votes, perhaps even enough to have surmounted the 5 per cent threshold.

The three conservative parties in New Zealand—New Zealand First, ACT and the Conservative Party—can be found at different locations across the libertarian–authoritarian cleavage as well as on the economic left–right dimension. On the left–right dimension, respondents to the NZES place ACT and the Conservatives closely together: ACT at 7.4, the Conservatives at 7.2, with National not far away on 7.1. New Zealand First is more distinct, only a little to the right of centre at 5.5 (see Chapter 7, Figure 7.1).

Figure 8.1 displays the average positions of each group of party voters on a standardised version of the authoritarian–libertarian scale.[2] Compared with the economic left–right differences, we would expect smaller gaps between the parties and between their voters on these cultural or social values. This is because New Zealand political parties have a practice

---

2   Because of the direction of the 'agree–disagree' statements from which it is constructed, the unmodified scale is biased towards authoritarianism (with a mean of 5.9 when maximum authoritarian is 10, and libertarian is 0). By standardising and thereby putting the mean at 0, we can partly correct for this. The standardisation also amplifies the differences between the parties, meaning that on the unstandardised scale they would be much closer.

of allowing their MPs 'conscience votes' on the kind of issues that are included in this libertarian–authoritarian dimension: abortion law reform, legal recognition of sexual orientation, marriage equality, control of alcohol and gambling and the disciplining of children (for data and more information on the practice of conscience voting in New Zealand, see PCVD 2016; Lindsey 2006, 2008, 2011). One could assume that because parliamentary parties allow for differences of opinions on these matters, party vote choice is largely unaffected by the positions taken by MPs. But parties at the two ends of the libertarian–authoritarian dimension do tend to take clear stances on these issues. Voters for these parties may be expected to occupy the more distinct positions on these issues those for Labour and National.

Figure 8.1 confirms that voters for the Greens are the most libertarian. Internet-MANA voters also fall on the libertarian side, but their small number in the sample make the confidence intervals very wide. Labour and National voters are both close to the average. Non-voters, New Zealand First and Māori Party voters tend to cluster on the authoritarian side of the average. Unsurprisingly, New Zealand First voters form the most consistently socially conservative cluster.

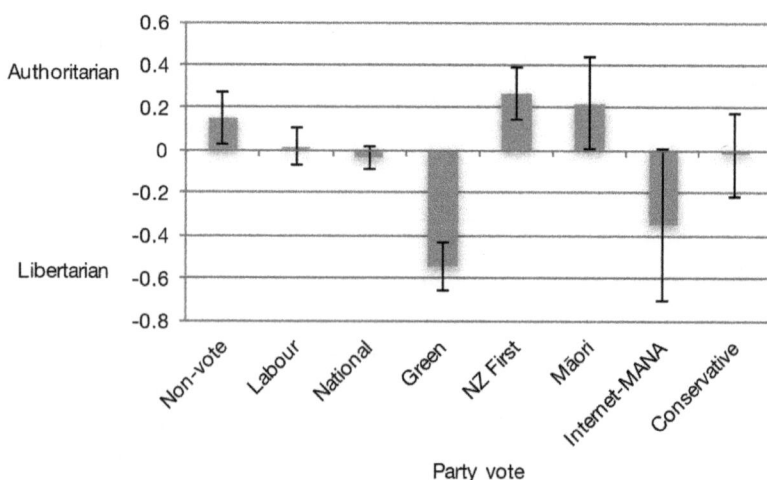

Figure 8.1: Authoritarian–libertarian attitudes by party voting groups (standardised scale)[3]
Source: New Zealand Election Study 2014.

3   Given the small number of ACT NZ respondents in the NZES, and thus the unreliability of these data, this party is not included in the figure.

While the Conservative Party took conservative positions on various cultural and social issues during the 2014 campaign and supported traditional family values, its voters tend to be close to the average on the libertarian–authoritarian scale. This location of the average Conservative voter compared with those for other parties on the right merits further investigation. The number of Conservative voters in our sample is small, and the confidence intervals are wide and go either side of the average on the scale. This means sampling errors or other kinds of bias might explain our finding. We can re-examine the influence of the small Conservative cell size on the results by drawing on other questions. Rather than simply relying on party choice we can investigate the likes and dislikes of political parties that all respondents were asked to record. Taking this analytical strategy also allows us to examine the potential support for other parties with only a small percentage of the vote, such as ACT and United Future.

Table 8.1 both confirms and modifies our earlier findings. When we take into account the libertarian–authoritarian positions of all New Zealanders and correlate them with party 'likes' and 'dislikes', Labour, Green, National and New Zealand First remain in more or less the same relative positions. The Māori Party moves to the libertarian side. This is probably because many non-Māori people of a liberal disposition like the Māori Party even though they do not give it their vote. Liking or disliking the Conservative Party has the second strongest relationship with libertarian–authoritarian attitudes. It is liked by authoritarian-leaning voters of other parties, and disliked by liberals who are very unlikely to vote Conservative. Those who do vote for the Conservative Party are somewhat less authoritarian than we might have expected.

Table 8.1: Correlations: Standardised libertarian–authoritarian scale by likes and dislikes of political parties

	r	significance
Green	–0.17	**
Māori	–0.14	**
Labour	–0.04	*
National	–0.04	
United Future	–0.01	
NZ First	0.11	**
ACT	0.11	**
Conservative	0.15	**

Notes: *p<0.05 **p<0.01.

Source: New Zealand Election Study 2014.

Figure 8.2 identifies the significant correlates of authoritarian and libertarian values in social structure (see the Appendix, Table 8.A1). The index of authoritarianism and libertarianism used here is the standardised scale applied earlier.

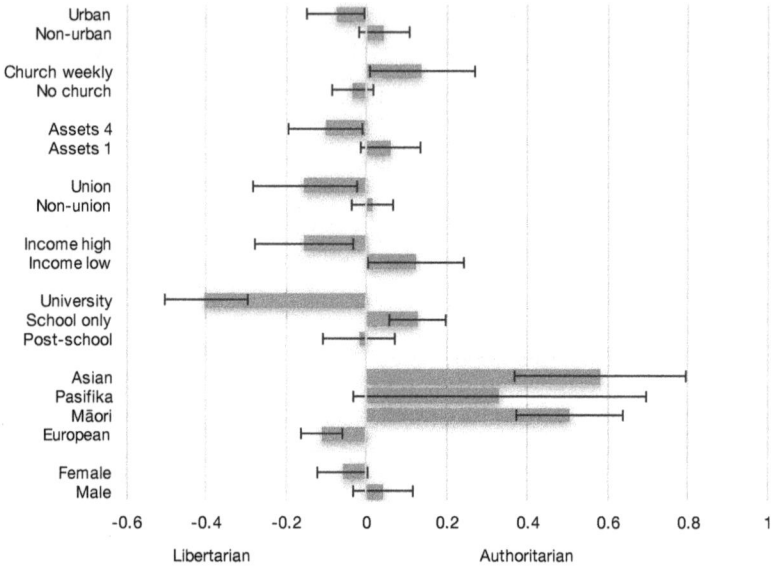

Figure 8.2: Correlates of authoritarianism–libertarianism by socio-demographic groups

Source: Appendix, Table 8.A1.

All else being equal, ethnic minority voters are somewhat more likely than the European majority to lean to authoritarianism. Māori voters are likely to be just over one point higher on the scale than European voters. While receiving benefits does not significantly relate to libertarian–authoritarian attitudes, income does matter. People on the lowest incomes are appreciably more likely to be authoritarian than those on the highest incomes. Similarly, the more assets one owns, the more libertarian one is. Church attendance is positively associated with authoritarianism. Men are marginally more likely to be authoritarian than women. Employment-related variables have no effect, but union households are less likely to exhibit authoritarian leanings. As expected, education has a significant and negative effect. The relationship with education is consistent with findings from international literature (for example, Bornschier 2010; Flanagan and Lee 2003; Inglehart 1984; Houtman 2003; Van der Waal, Achterberg and Houtman 2007). Those who embrace social liberalism tend to have ample cultural capital and high levels of education.

Higher education tends to instill democratic values, increases cognitive skills, undermines a belief in such things as a 'natural' social order and fosters greater openness and tolerance towards nonconformity and unconventional cultural patterns. Education is a cultural resource that deeply affects people's world views and has been found to be strongly related to the social liberalism–conservatism dimension (Van der Waal, Achterberg and Houtman 2007).

In Chapter 5 (Figure 5.9), we have already displayed the extent to which the various parties are liked or disliked by NZES respondents. Parties are scored on a scale where 0 represents strongly disliking a party and 10 strongly liking that party. Among the three conservative parties studied in this chapter, New Zealand First had the highest average favourability score with 4.3 (the fourth most liked party after National, Labour and the Green Party). The Conservatives were lower at 3.5, placed seventh most liked and ACT at 3.3 as eighth.

In terms of policy and campaign rhetoric, the three conservative parties profiled in this chapter tend to aim for the same group of socially conservative voters. We therefore expect to see some clustering among their voters, with those liking one of the conservative parties tending to also like the other conservative parties, though New Zealand First is likely to be a possible outlier given its more left-leaning position on economic issues compared with the other conservative parties.

A correlation matrix displayed in Table 8.2 indicates how party likes and dislikes among voters are distributed across the various parties. The correlation between liking/disliking the Conservative Party and liking/disliking ACT is particularly strong (r=0.53). The correlations between New Zealand First and ACT (r=0.11), and the New Zealand First and Conservative Party (r=0.16) are appreciably less strong. Liking New Zealand First relates positively with liking Labour (r=0.28), whereas it is related a little less strongly to disliking National (r=–0.17). Liking ACT and the Conservative Party relate positively with liking National (r=0.35 and r=0.23, respectively), but correlated negatively with Labour (r=–0.10 and –0.16, respectively). Respondents tend to consistently like or dislike ACT and the Conservative Party. Liking ACT or the Conservatives also tends to mean liking National and disliking Labour. This is all as expected given party histories and policies. New Zealand First is again distinct from ACT and the Conservatives in its closer proximity to the left; the correlation between likes/dislikes of New Zealand First and of the Green Party is 0.28, not that far behind that with Labour.

Table 8.2: Correlations between liking and disliking political parties in New Zealand, 2014 election

	NZ First	ACT	Conservative	Labour	National	Green	United Future	Māori	MANA
ACT	0.11								
Conservative	0.16	0.53							
Labour	0.28	-0.10	-0.16						
National	-0.17	0.35	0.23	-0.50					
Green	0.24	-0.05	-0.16	0.52	-0.42				
United Future	0.12	0.69	0.47	-0.06	0.30	0.01			
Māori	0.18	0.26	0.19	0.18	-0.03	0.28	0.40		
MANA	0.24	0.16	0.14	0.33	-0.32	0.43	0.19	0.47	
Internet	0.21	0.22	0.21	0.24	-0.28	0.32	0.22	0.29	0.67

Source: New Zealand Election Study 2014.

'New politics' attitudes: Immigration and abortion

The NZES gauges opinions on two examples of public opinion that fall into the new politics or libertarian–authoritarian dimension: immigration and abortion. Immigration is a highly salient issue in New Zealand. It does not have the same force as in countries that find it more difficult to control their borders such as European countries or, closer to New Zealand, Australia, with its longer coastline and closer proximity to sources of illegal entrants. The distance of New Zealand from other land masses strongly discourages uncontrolled passage by sea. Nonetheless, prior to the 2014 election, New Zealand was experiencing high levels of inward immigration. While New Zealand's uneven economic growth record tends to create fluctuations in the number of immigrants, the difference in numbers between arrivals and departures in the year to October 2014 was nearly 50,000: equivalent just over 1 per cent of the New Zealand population of 4.5 million, and the highest level since 2003 (Dixon 2014).

Since the 1990s, increasing numbers of immigrants to New Zealand have come from non-western countries, and New Zealand society has become more ethnically diverse. Māori are New Zealand's indigenous people, having migrated to New Zealand during the twelfth and thirteenth centuries. Europeans followed from the early nineteenth century, and settled in larger numbers, with Pasifika and Asian immigrants entering the country in significant numbers from the mid to late twentieth century onwards. In 2013, about 75 per cent of the population identified within the broad category of European, 12 per cent as Asian, 8 per cent as from a Pacific Island country, and 16 per cent as Māori. Observant readers will note that these numbers add up to more than 100 per cent: 11 per cent report more than one ethnic identification (Statistics New Zealand 2016c). According to the 2013 census, in Auckland, New Zealand's largest city of 1.4 million people, 56 per cent identified as European, 22 per cent Asian, 14 per cent Pasifika and 10 per cent Māori (Statistics New Zealand 2016d). Since New Zealand is one of the few countries that allows non-citizens to vote after they have been accepted as permanent residents and have lived in the country for a year, many of the newly arrived immigrants have the right to vote.

Figure 8.3 presents voters' attitudes towards the presence of immigrants, an issue not subject to conscience votes, by the groups of party voters. New Zealand First voters form the first column: 70 per cent of them would like to see less immigration. This finding is entirely expected. Since its formation in 1993, New Zealand First has been the party most critical of New Zealand's relatively liberal immigration policies. The party is committed to what it describes as a rigorous and strictly applied immigration policy that serves New Zealand's interests and prioritises jobs for New Zealanders.

Party vote

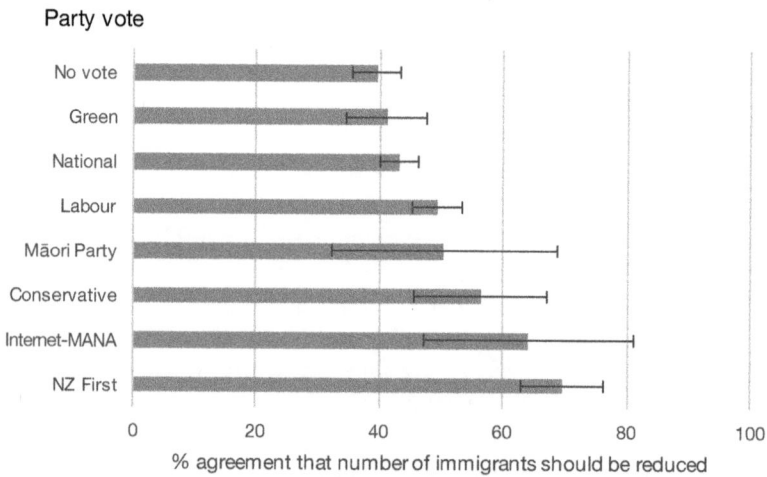

% agreement that number of immigrants should be reduced

Figure 8.3: Attitudes towards the number of immigrants by party vote (in percentage)

Note: The question was: 'Do you think the number of immigrants allowed into New Zealand nowadays should be increased a lot (1), be increased a little (2), be about the same as now (3), reduced a little (4), reduced a lot (5), or don't know? (9)' The percentage of agreement presented in the figure combines the answers 'reduced a lot' and 'reduced a little'.

Source: New Zealand Election Study 2014.

Criticism of current levels of immigration and attempts to draw attention to some negative consequences often attracts the accusation of 'racism'. But there are evidence-based arguments against high levels of immigration approaching those recently experienced in New Zealand. Large numbers of children for whom English is a second language or who may need to learn it from the beginning can put pressure on schools for which there is little or no recognition in terms of extra funding or support (for example, Duff 2014). While fears that immigration may depress wages are exaggerated, small effects are possible and may be larger on those local workers who compete for jobs with recent immigrants (Poot and Cochrane 2005). Importing skilled immigrants reduces the incentives for New Zealand employers to train New Zealand workers. Short-term effects may increase unemployment (Armstrong and McDonald 2016). A high volume of immigration drives up house prices, particularly where there is undersupply of housing in the areas where immigrants tend to settle (McDonald 2013; Fry 2014: 37). In Auckland, in particular, former National Party finance minister and current Prime Minister Bill English recognised in 2015 that house prices had reached levels that put home ownership out of reach for many people on low and middle incomes, with long-term implications for inequality (Edwards 2015b). Economic analysis finds that the effects of immigration enhance growth, but not necessarily per capita growth. In other words, a country may get richer, but wealth and income per person may not increase because there are more people to share that wealth and income (Rutherford 2015). Those with lower socio-economic status are often less likely to support high levels of immigration, and immigration policy has a strong potential to act as a 'wedge' in electoral politics and thus disrupt voting patterns, particularly if centre-left parties fail to listen to those who feel they are adversely affected.

Figure 8.4 shows the relationship between attitudes towards the presence of immigrants and opinions about economic inequality. Immigration attitudes are estimated on a scale of 1 to 5. The threshold for being more for or more against immigration is therefore a score of 2.5. If egalitarian attitudes are driven by values of fairness, we might expect egalitarians to support immigration. On the other hand, if egalitarians are concerned entirely about income differences, and are worried about some of the distributional effects of immigration explained above, we might expect the opposite. As the questions measuring attitudes to inequality focus on income differences, the latter hypothesis is more likely to be confirmed. And it is. Based on a simple regression of the inequality attitude scale against the immigration attitude scale, Figure 8.4 shows egalitarians are slightly but significantly more likely to oppose immigration.

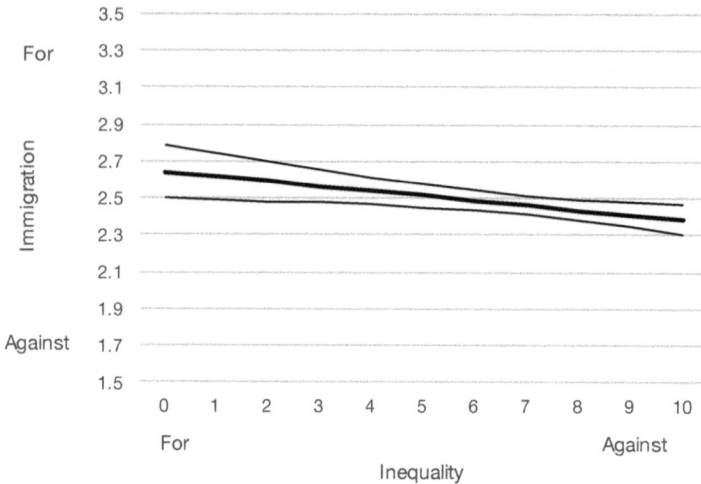

Figure 8.4: Inequality attitudes and immigration attitudes
Source: New Zealand Election Study 2014.

However, we might expect the relationship of inequality and immigration to 'wash out' when controlling for people who are in positions that could make them fear the consequences of high immigration. Figure 8.5 displays the significant correlates of attitudes about immigration in social structure and attitudes in the form of predicted probabilities, derived from a regression model in the Appendix, Table 8.A2.[4] We find that economic concerns do seem to drive much opposition to immigration. Those lacking aspirations for a better standard of living in 10 years tend to be opposed to immigration. Confidence in finding a job and a positive assessment of the economy over the last year tends to make people in favour of an increase in the number of immigrants, while those fearing job loss and who are not so confident about the economy tend to be opposed to greater immigration. Left–right and authoritarian–libertarian positions also matter: the left favouring immigration, the right being more likely to oppose it, as are authoritarians. Attitudes to inequality are not significant in this model; they are accounted for entirely by low or frustrated aspirations, low job security and low economic confidence.

4   An initial model without controls for aspirations, security and the economy (not shown) found young people more opposed to immigration than the old; when the aspirations and security variables are added, their stronger effects on the young shift age into non-significance. Employment variables and assets have no effects, even in the stripped-down model, casting some doubt on claims and the expectation that competition for jobs or investment opportunities might affect attitudes to immigration. However, income does have significant effects. Compared with Europeans, Māori tend to be significantly more opposed to immigration, while Asian New Zealanders are more in favour.

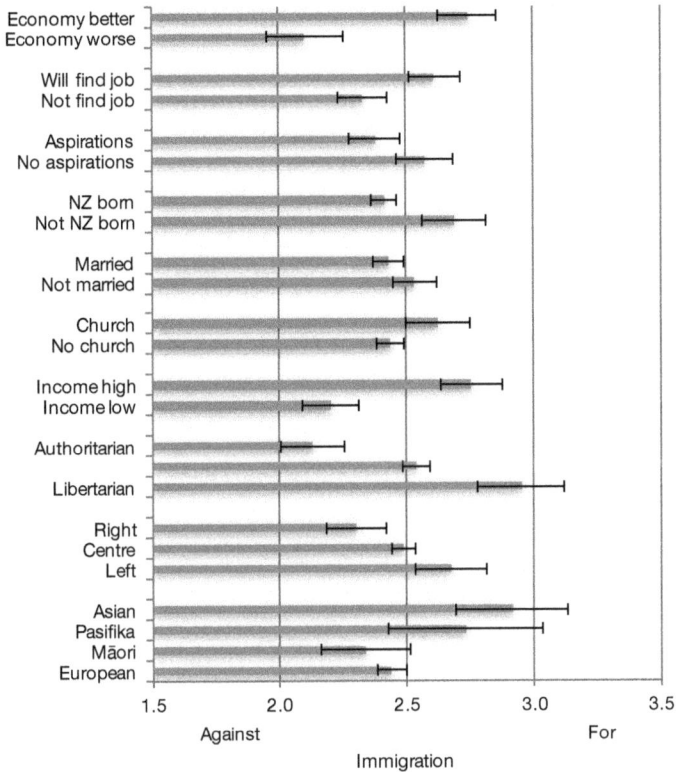

Figure 8.5: Correlates of immigration attitudes by social groups, aspirations and security

Note: The question was that shown for Figure 8.3. Don't know responses were re-coded to 3. Income, aspiration, job security and economy variable effects are estimated comparing the bottom and top of their five-point scales categories.

Source: Appendix, Table 8.A2.

In contrast to immigration, abortion is traditionally a conscience issue. While most political parties do not take positions, votes in parliament on such issues do tend to cluster on partisan dimensions. Indeed, although immigration is a matter of party policy and abortion is not, when using party vote as a predictor of positions on these issues, both have about the same effect, in both cases a pseudo R-squared of about 0.03. New Zealand's abortion law is conservative in principle, controlling the practice under the Crimes Act, but liberal in practice with two doctors required for approval on mental health grounds that are almost never refused. Early in 2017, there were indications that this compromise between conservative and liberal positions was increasingly unacceptable to liberals, foreshadowing future reform efforts in the case of a change of government. The abortion issue has been debated twice in the last 15 years. In an amendment to the *Care of Children Act 2004*, anti-abortionists sought to insert a provision that would require parental consent to abortion for those under the age of 16. In that parliament, Labour and Green MPs voted overwhelmingly against that principle. Despite positioning itself as a libertarian party, ACT's nine MPs split evenly, reflecting the party's appeal to social conservatism at that time. New Zealand First MPs voted 11 to 2 for the principles of parental consent, as did Māori Party MP Tariana Turia. National MPs were also divided, voting 19 to 8 in favour of the principle (PCVD 2016).

The issue of abortion was raised again in April 2011 by way of an amendment to a government resolution. Māori Party MP Tariana Turia sought to appoint a conservative on abortion issues to the Abortion Supervisory Committee, the administrative body responsible for supervising the process. Labour and Green MPs unanimously opposed the amendment; National MPs were close to evenly split and the four ACT MPs voted against. New Zealand First had no parliamentary representation at the time.

The question asked in the 2014 NZES sought agreement or disagreement across a five-point scale on a hardline anti-abortion position: 'Abortion is always wrong'. Figure 8.6 shows that Conservative Party voters were significantly more likely than those of all other parties other than the Māori Party to oppose abortion in all circumstances. New Zealand First and Labour voters do not look very different from each other, and have similar attitudes as those who do not vote. National Party voters tend to be slightly more liberal than this group, while Green voters are the most liberal of all.

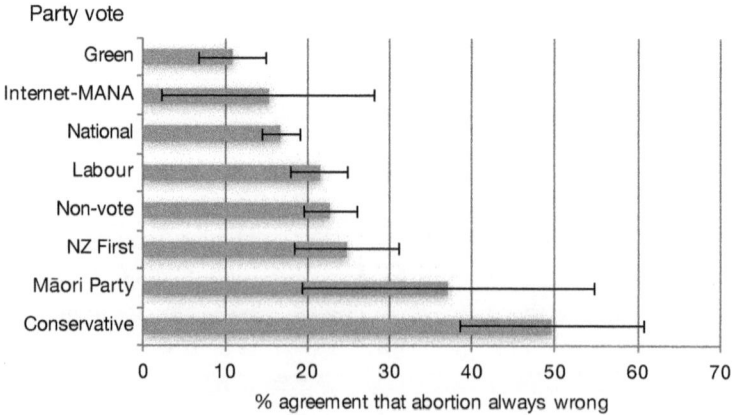

Figure 8.6: Abortion is always wrong by party vote, 2014
Source: New Zealand Election Study 2014.

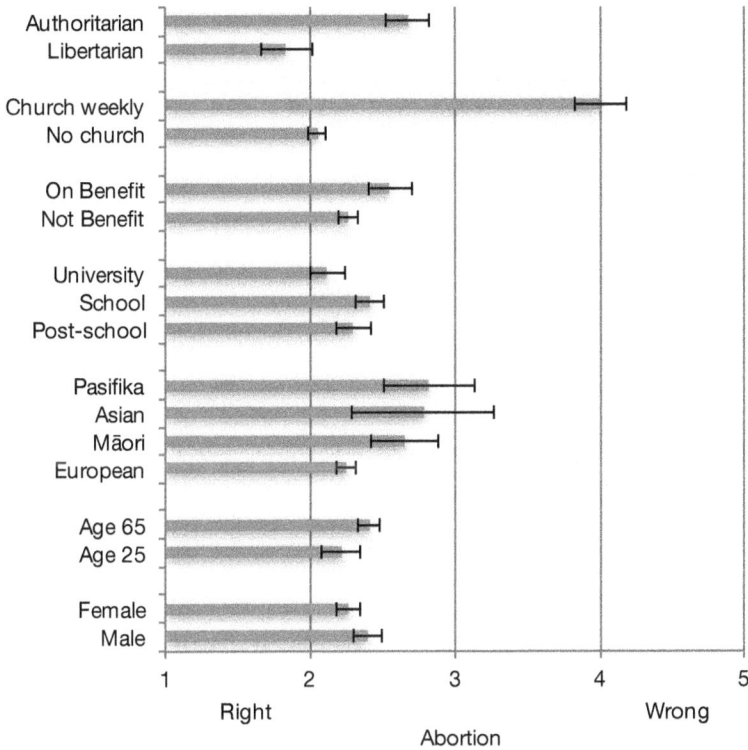

Figure 8.7: Attitudes towards abortion by social groups and the authoritarian–libertarian dimension

Source: Appendix, Table 8.A3.

Opposition to inequality could be associated with opposition to abortion if socially conservative Christians followed Christian values into social and economic policy preferences as does, for example, Catholic social teaching. But there is no significant relationship between these two sets of preferences. Figure 8.7 shows predicted probabilities from the regression model in the Appendix, Table 8.A3. As one would expect, the correlates of abortion attitudes in social structure highlight the importance of church attendance. Someone who attends church more than once a week is likely to be nearly two points higher on the 1–5 abortion attitude scale than someone who never attends at all. Women are less likely to be opposed to abortion, but the difference between women and men is only 0.15 on the five-point scale. Age also has a significant effect. A person who is 65 is more opposed than a person of 25, while those who are highly educated are less likely to be opposed. Those on benefits are somewhat more opposed to abortion than those not. Authoritarianism also leads people to oppose abortion, but there is no relationship between abortion attitudes and left–right position. Finally, there are significant differences in attitudes towards abortion between various ethnic groups. Europeans are less likely to oppose abortion compared with ethnic minorities, who, along with those on benefits, are more opposed to abortion.

Another issue of high salience for the conservative parties is that of the Treaty of Waitangi. As Figure 6.8 in Chapter 6 shows, New Zealand First and Conservative voters have much in common on this issue, and share their positions with that of National Party voters, tending to agree with the statement: 'The Treaty of Waitangi should not be part of the law'. New Zealand First has always had a conservative position on Treaty issues despite its leader, Winston Peters, being of Māori and Scottish descent. New Zealand First emphasises the principle of Article 3 in the Treaty, that of equal citizenship. Consequently, New Zealand First opposes any legal recognition of Māori rights as such, and would, if it had its way, remove all references to the principles of the Treaty from the law (New Zealand Parliament 2006). Like National and the Conservative Party, New Zealand First would abolish the Māori electorates, and no longer runs candidates in them. Analysis of the attitudes to the Treaty by social groups can also be found in Figures 6.9 and 6.10 in Chapter 6.

In Chapter 6, we examined how voters line up on the two scales that represent attitudes to social expenditure: universal versus targeted benefits (Figures 6.2 and 6.3). New Zealand First voters are closer to Labour in their relatively strong preferences for expenditure on universal benefits. Conservatives, if anything, are less keen on increasing expenditures than National voters, but the average voter for all parties on this dimension tends towards 'more', even amongst the small number of ACT voters. As far as targeted benefits are concerned, there is considerably more difference. The average Conservative lines up with National and ACT, while the average New Zealand First voter is closer to Labour or the Greens, although definitely still on the 'less' side of the scale. We can thus confirm that New Zealand First voters tend to be economically left of those who voted ACT or the Conservative Party. New Zealand First voters are more supportive of government spending on social issues such as welfare, unemployment, education and health compared with those supporting ACT and the Conservative Party. These latter two parties align quite closely with the National Party on those issues.

Summary models

To clarify further the social and ideological bases of New Zealand First and Conservative Party voting, we construct regression models on vote choice for these two parties (Figures 8.8 and 8.9). There are insufficient ACT voters in our sample, so we model on the like/dislike scale for ACT (Figures 8.10 and 8.11). Tables reporting coefficients and standard errors for all variables included are in the Appendix, Tables 8.A4–8.A6.

Beginning with New Zealand First, after controlling for the baseline social structure variables already discussed in Chapter 4, Figure 8.8 reveals that Treaty and immigration attitudes come through as strong predictors for the New Zealand First vote in the expected directions, with aspirations and fear of income loss retaining some potency but largely within confidence intervals. This does not refute earlier findings that left–right, libertarian–authoritarian, social policy and inequality are associated to varying degrees with the New Zealand First vote. Their effects are simply absorbed by other variables that have a closer proximity to vote choice. Opposition to inequality also fails to be significant in the full New Zealand First vote model. Correlated and regressed alone on vote or not for New Zealand First, opposition to inequality remains associated with the New Zealand First vote. Social spending attitudes and attitudes to abortion do not relate significantly to voting for New Zealand First.

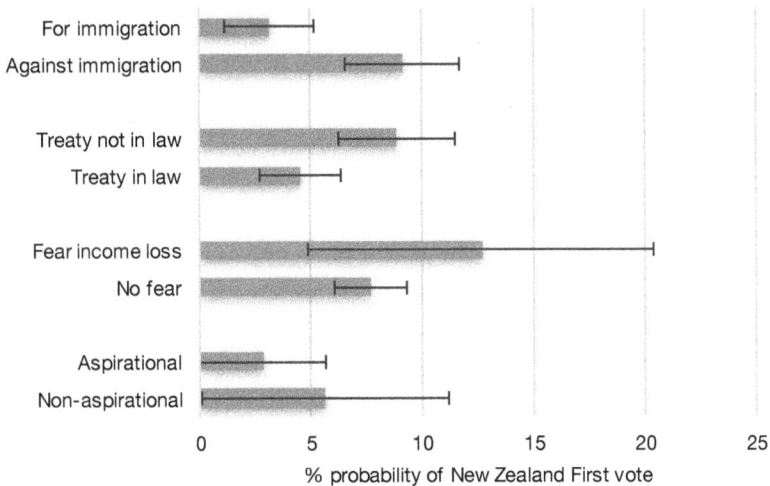

Figure 8.8: Vote choice for New Zealand First or not

Source: Appendix, Table 8.A4.

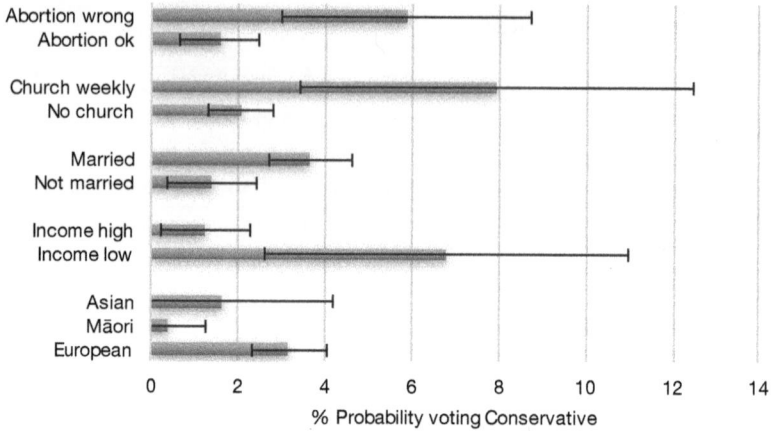

Figure 8.9: Vote choice for the Conservatives or not
Source: Appendix, Table 8.A5.

The ideological and socio-cultural values added here have the strongest effects in raising the explanatory power of the New Zealand First vote model up to 12 per cent. This confirms findings of research on populist 'radical right' voting that consistently shows a major impact of cultural attitudes on supporting such parties (for example, Lubbers, Gijsberts and Scheepers 2002; Mudde 2007; Norris 2005; Rydgren 2007; Van den Berg and Coffé 2012; Van der Brug, Fennema and Tillie 2000). At the same time, perceptions of economic insecurity and pessimism also help drive the vote for New Zealand First, but not as strongly.

As for the Conservatives (Figure 8.9), Māori and Pasifika people are significantly less likely to vote for the party than Europeans. Indeed, there were no Pasifika voting for the Conservatives in our sample, so no estimate is possible. People on low incomes are more likely to vote Conservative than those on higher incomes. Church attendance is a major predictor of the Conservative vote. A person attending church once or more than once a week is about 10 per cent more likely to vote Conservative than someone who never attends. The Conservative Party has a strong base among church attenders. According to New Zealand census data, the percentage of those affiliating as Christian decreased by 6 percentage points between 2006 and 2013, but evangelical Christians increased as a proportion of the total (Statistics New Zealand 2013). A person who is married was 3 per cent more likely to vote Conservative than someone who was not. Opposition to abortion also comes through very strongly. A baseline social structure model produces the same results as the expanded model for those variables. Gender, age, education, occupation, sector of the economy, union membership, whether or not New Zealand born, assets and benefits either wash out of the baseline model or had little or no relationship to begin with. In Model II, left–right is non-significant, although only marginally; Conservatives do line up on the right. Libertarian–authoritarian, social spending attitudes, immigration, the Treaty and opinions on inequality are all non-significant. We ran an exploratory model that included the security and aspirational variables, both simply on top of the Model I variables, and in Model III. None were statistically significant, and added only very marginally to the variable explained. Economic insecurity and low aspirations mattered for the New Zealand First vote but not apparently for the Conservative vote.

Analysing liking or disliking the ACT Party, we discuss two models here: a baseline containing social structure and group variables, and another adding aspirations/security and ideological and policy opinion variables (see Appendix, Table 8.A6). The most obvious inference from our analysis confirms ACT's relative unpopularity; all the probability estimates are on the 'dislike' side of the 10-point scale. From the baseline model (Figure 8.10), the most unexpected finding is that women are more likely to like ACT than men, although the effect is a small one. The effect actually rises to about 4 per cent in the full model. Younger voters, Pasifika and Asians tend to like ACT more than older voters, or Europeans or Māori. ACT appeals to those on higher incomes and with assets, but not to public sector workers, union members or those with university degrees.

Figure 8.11 reports the findings when the aspirational/security and socio-cultural and attitudinal variables are added. The social structure variables included in the baseline remain as controls. Those who like ACT tend to be aspirational, those who dislike ACT do not; if anything, they are pessimistic about their futures. The more right wing a person, the more likely they will like the ACT party. Those who like the ACT party tend to be against the Treaty, those who dislike it tend to be in favour. Those who like the ACT party are quite strongly against universal benefits. People who like ACT are also in favour of immigration.

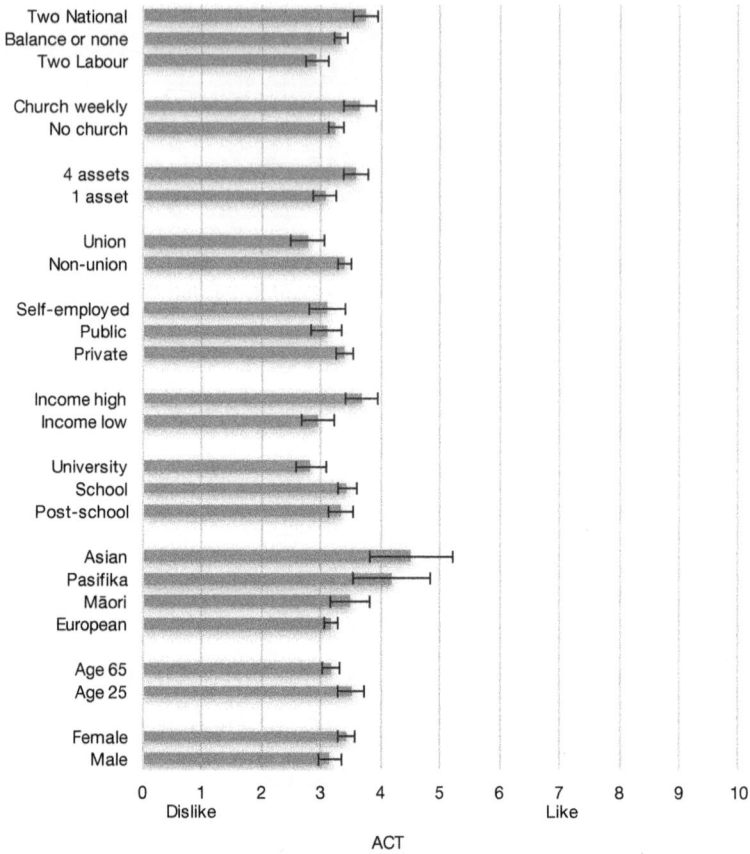

Figure 8.10: Liking or disliking the ACT Party: Baseline social, demographic and group variables: Model I.

Source: Appendix, Table 8.A6, Model I.

While we must be a little cautious when comparing a vote choice model for New Zealand First and a like/dislike model for ACT, all indications are that voters and supporters of the two parties are a long way apart, except on opposition to the Treaty of Waitangi being in the law. Immigration is the biggest difference. Favouring an increase of the number of immigrants relates positively to supporting ACT but negatively to voting New Zealand First. ACT comes across as clearly on the ideological economic right. The opposition of those who like ACT to universal social services (the services from which all benefit) stands out. The most likely explanation is that ACT supporters are drawing on a belief that all such services should be privatised and left to the market. This runs against majority public opinion that largely favours the current system of universal services.

The Key National Government has a record of maintaining those services with sufficient levels of public funding to effectively neutralise political debate on health and education. Ironically, it is the Labour party that raised the issue of superannuation reform, almost certainly to its political detriment (see Chapter 6). Only on the margins has the Key Government moved toward the ACT agenda on public services. The best example is ACT's most highly visible policy of Charter Schools (Sherman 2016). But even Charter Schools rely on public rather than private funding.

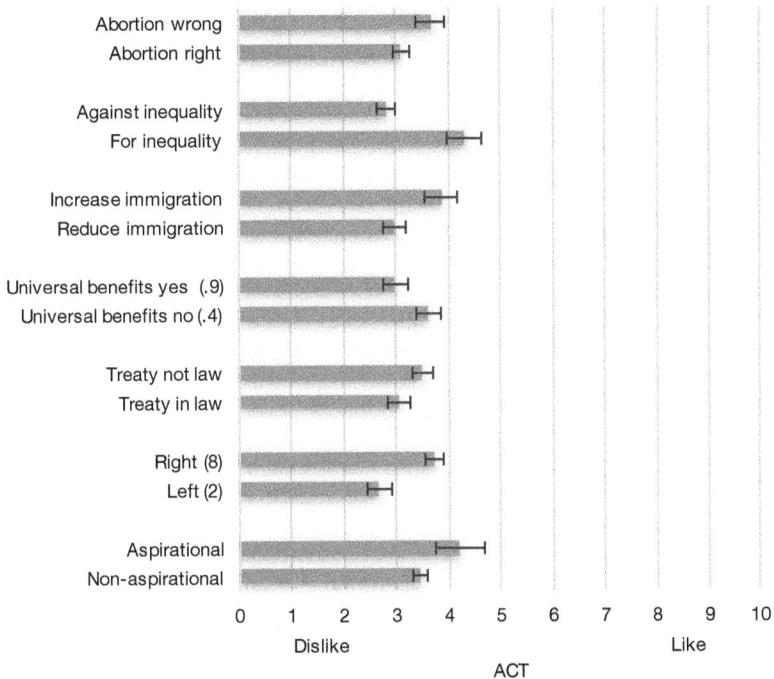

Figure 8.11: Liking or disliking the ACT Party: Model II
Source: Appendix, Table 8.A6, Model II.

Conclusion

Three New Zealand parties stand out in their presentation of alternate conservatisms. As we have seen, they exhibit policy and ideological differences and similarities, as do their voters. ACT has the profile of a classic right-wing liberal party, but most of those who support ACT feel equally at home in the National Party. Indeed, two of the party's former leaders, John Banks and Don Brash, previously served as National

Party MPs, and Brash also led the National Party between 2003 and 2006. The Conservative Party is similar in terms of many of its economic positions, but its support appears to be more strongly rooted in church attendance and right-wing Christian conservatism, although it also takes a populist position on a number of economic and moral issues. In terms of reducing inequality, neither ACT or the Conservatives can be expected to take positions to reverse the trend.

New Zealand First is the odd one out and also the most electorally successful. While the party is the one most critical of immigration and shares its nationalist approach towards the economy with 'radical right-wing populist' parties around the world, it is not a radical party—it is predominantly a socially conservative populist party of the centre. New Zealand First and its supporters value an older vision of New Zealand, one aspect of which includes a more egalitarian society than the one that is emerging in the twenty-first century. However, their notion of equality is not particularly liberal or tolerant. Nor does it embrace a culturally diverse society that continues to offer both economic and social challenges to the alternative conservative parties.

9

The gender dimension of inequality

During Labour's period in opposition since 2008, discussions of economic inequality and gender inequality have often been portrayed as at odds with each other. The former is framed as material, meaningful and representative of a class politics that, if addressed, would remedy inequality. By contrast, the latter is framed as a variation of 'identity politics', whereby material wellbeing is eschewed in favour of a politics of presence (Edwards 2009, 2011, 2013a). This is not a new standoff: the old left in New Zealand has a long history of resisting feminist politics, while Labourist feminism has an equally long history of championing women's economic equality. Women parliamentarians have been the conduit for some of the more significant reforms (Coney 1993; Curtin 2008; Curtin and Sawer 1996; Curtin and Teghtsoonian 2010; Davies 1984, 1997; Grey 2002; Nolan 2000; Wilson 2013).

Gender equality in political power and economic resources in post-industrial democracies has grown tremendously in the past 50 years. Over recent decades, women have sought, and in many countries gained, greater access to the labour market, equality before the law and social reforms that impact their everyday lives. Alongside this, more women are running for and being elected to national parliaments than ever before, and a record number of women hold executive positions within their nations' governments (Curtin and Sawer 2011; Lovenduski 2005; Paxton, Kunovich and Hughes 2007).

However, gender inequalities remain. In 2006, the World Economic Forum began an annual assessment of the global gender gap in women's empowerment and employed measures that sought to capture the economic, political and social dimensions of women's lives. In 2014, the Global Gender Gap Index ranked New Zealand as 30th on equality in economic participation and opportunity, a composite indicator drawing on five variables: labour force participation, wage equality for similar work, estimated earned income, the proportion of women managers and senior officials, and the proportion of professional occupations. While women had reached parity with men on the latter variable (thus boosting the overall score), New Zealand ranked 67th on women's estimated earned income. By contrast, when Labour's fifth term in government ended in 2008, New Zealand was ranked seventh on the economic dimension. While this ranking is also dependent on the performance of other countries, it shows that New Zealand has fallen behind while other countries have moved ahead.

The forum's index explicitly recognises that improving gender parity in the economic sphere is also connected to women's engagement in public life. Women's voice and descriptive presence in the political arena results in the advocacy and prioritisation of issues that have broad societal implications for the economy, the family, education and health. Moreover, women's engagement in public life is considered to foster 'greater credibility in institutions, and heightened democratic outcomes', with evidence to suggest that women's political leadership and wider economic participation are correlated (World Economic Forum 2015). This conclusion reflects scholarly research that shows that the descriptive representation of women relates significantly to the substantive representation of women's interests, including the gendered dimensions of economic inequality (Bolzendahl and Brooks 2007; Carroll 2001; Curtin 2008; Schwindt-Bayer 2006; Swers 2002; Waring, Greenwood and Pintat 2000).

If women's representation matters to women's material equality, it is unsurprising that international research indicates that women's political attitudes tend to differ from men's. For example, women have been found to be more supportive of social service spending (Manza and Brooks 1998). While women used to be more likely to vote for the right, as a result of their increasing rates of labour force participation and their apparently positive attitudes towards social spending, in recent decades women have turned to the left in most post-industrial societies (Inglehart and Norris 2000). Women might have higher concern for the needs and rights of minorities and be more aware of discrimination that women themselves often experience. Cross-national research indicates nuanced interactions between self-interest and women's attitudes to social injustice, much depending on context such as the former East–West division (Davidson, Steinmann and Wegener 1995). Further explanations suggest that the development over time of women's greater likelihood to lean to the left can be explained by women's greater insecurity associated with the decline of marriage (Edlund and Pande 2002), but this may vary according to the labour market opportunities available to them (Iversen and Rosenbluth 2006).

Despite women's increased influence and representation at the highest levels, research on a number of Western industrialised democracies also finds a persistent gender gap in political participation, with women less politically engaged than men (for example, Burns 2007; Coffé and Bolzendahl 2010; Schlozman, Burns and Verba 1999). This is crucial, since political participation is a central component of democracy, and people who participate in politics are more likely to have an influence (Verba, Schlozman and Brady 1995). This is particularly relevant and important since international evidence indicates, as suggested above, that women and men tend to differ in their party choices and policy ideas (for example, Giger 2009; Inglehart and Norris 2003; Manza and Brooks 1998). In addition, while some scholars note that gender differences in political participation are often small in comparison to other cleavages such as education or age (Burns 2007; Norris 2002; Parry, Moyser and Day 1992), gender is a cleavage that cuts across these other areas of stratification, making it salient for everyone (Martin 2004; Risman 1998).

These international findings confirm that a review of gender differences in vote choice, political attitudes and knowledge, and the significance of women's political representation, might help us understand the puzzle of the 2014 election. If women voters are more likely to vote for the party that will advance the material wellbeing of families and those less fortunate, why was Labour unable to benefit from this predisposition? In order to answer this question, we address theoretical and empirical claims that women and men tend to have different opinions on social issues relevant to inequality, and on the representation of other distinct groups.

Gender gaps in party choice and political attitudes

Leading up to the 2014 election in New Zealand, feminists had made considerable efforts to provoke parties to address gender inequality in their campaign promises. A Women's Election Agenda Aotearoa (2014) presented a 100-point plan calling on parties to commit to de facto equality for women by 2020 (MacLennan 2014). The agenda laid out a range of policy issues and solutions necessary to progress gender equality. The report began with the policy issue of domestic violence, then moving on to key issues relating to women's economic inequality, including access to benefits, superannuation, pay equity, paid parental leave, a universal basic income and affordable child care.

The agenda formed the basis of a six-part television series on Face TV, a public access television channel. It was uploaded to YouTube and was also sent to the 10 main registered political parties with a request to advise which aspects they supported. The parties' responses were then marked out of 100, with five parties being ranked (Greens, Labour, National, Māori and United Future). Both the Green Party and the Māori Party amended their policies as a result (Walters 2014). By contrast, ACT NZ, MANA, the Conservatives and New Zealand First offered no response, while the Internet Party stated they were a 'feminist party' and would respond with their own policy. The 'feminist party' claim got some attention and drew some criticism (Ellipsister 2014), but for the most part gender inequality issues only took place around the margins of the campaign (Goldsmith 2014; Salient 2014).

In the end, despite this feminist campaign, there were only minor gender differences in party choice. As noted earlier, research on gender and voting behaviour across Western post-industrial nations has found that women have turned towards the left since the 1980s (for example, Giger 2009; Inglehart and Norris 2003; Knutsen 2001; Manza and Brooks 1998). However, in the case of New Zealand, gender differences in party preferences at the 2011 New Zealand general election were not significant (Coffé 2013a). Indeed, the only significant gender difference was for New Zealand First, with women being less likely than men to vote New Zealand First. This represents a change from the past. In the early days of election surveys in New Zealand, it was found that women were more likely to vote for the right than the left (Vowles 1993: 124). Between

1993–2011, significant gender differences in preferences for the two major parties appeared: men were more likely to lean right and women more likely to lean left (Curtin 2014). This overall pattern is consistent with international research that identifies a change towards a so-called *modern gender gap* in the 1980s, with women now being more left-wing compared with men, having been more right-wing in the past (Inglehart and Norris 2003). In terms of self-position on the left–right scale, there was no significant difference between women and men in New Zealand in 2014 (see Chapter 4).

The reasons for a lack of major gender differences in party choice in the most recent New Zealand elections merit further research. The leadership of Helen Clark (from 1993 to 2008) no doubt attracted women toward Labour, and her last election as Labour leader in 2008 was the most recent with a significant National–Labour gender gap. Yet Labour has continued to retain effective female MPs. Many Labour policies have been intended to attract women voters, so much so that they came under attack within the party as part of its alleged overemphasis on 'identity politics'. Policies leaning towards the interests of women have become framed negatively rather than positively.

Efforts to increase the number of women in parliamentary politics elsewhere have often used explicit quotas, some required in electoral law, or otherwise in party candidate selection rules. In New Zealand, only the Green Party requires a gender-blended list. Although Labour had rejected a process used in the British Labour Party for all women shortlists in its electorate candidate selection process, its adoption of a gender target in late 2013 provided fuel to anti-Labour bloggers during the campaign (Goldsmith 2014). Labour presented policies to address the gender pay gap and family and sexual violence, but the latter was overshadowed by Labour leader David Cunliffe's apology in early July for 'being a man'. Speaking at a Women's Refuge Event he stated: 'Can I begin by saying I'm sorry—I don't often say it—I'm sorry for being a man, right now. Because family and sexual violence is perpetrated overwhelmingly by men against women and children'. Many journalists and commentators viewed the apology as a mistake (Hosking 2014b; C. Robinson 2014; Watkin 2014), arguing that most of middle New Zealand did not recognise the concept of 'rape culture' and were ambivalent about the issue of sexual violence, despite New Zealand's high rates of family and domestic violence.

A few argued it was an important, albeit electorally risky, statement highlighting the male-on-female violence that underpins rape culture in New Zealand, an issue highlighted by the 'Roastbusters'[1] case (McLauchlan 2014c; Miller 2014). The risk was that traditional male voters in particular would see the statement as another of Labour's detours into 'identity' politics (Miller 2014; see also Edwards 2014g). It ensured Cunliffe received significant media attention ahead of the party's Congress, but much of it presented him as some sort of 'male hating wimp' (Bradbury 2014b) or worse, a lazy, ill-disciplined leader (Watkin 2014).

National leader John Key in his turn seemed unable to demonstrate empathy and support for a high-profile victim of sexual assault.[2] His position sat at odds with National's long-standing position on family and sexual violence that was a key feature of its women's affairs policy in 2014 (Chappell and Curtin 2013; Hosking 2014b). In contrast to its 2011 campaign to 'crack down' on sole parent beneficiaries, National's Women's Affairs Policy in 2014 was more positive, including commitments to increasing paid parental leave, family tax credits, offering free doctors' visits and prescriptions for children as well as broader rhetorical commitments to advance women's economic independence and representation on boards through the Ministry of Women's Affairs (National Party 2014b).

Evidence of a female response to the parties' positions on women's issues can be found, but there are no major apparent effects. Figure 9.1 displays our findings based on a simple cross-tabulation of gender against the party vote. There are small gender gaps for Labour and National, but these are not statistically significant, confirmed by the overlapping confidence intervals. Women were significantly more likely to have voted Green compared with men. This latter finding confirms an international pattern. For example, Knutsen (2001) has shown that Swedish women were significantly more likely to support the Green Party in the 1990s compared with men. Rüdig (2012) revealed a similar trend of a feminisation of the Green voters in Germany. Controlling for the social structure baseline variables (Chapter 4), the probability of women voting Green in 2014

---

1   The 'Roastbusters' were a group of young men who encouraged young women to become intoxicated and then subjected them to sexual abuse, from which the men concerned escaped prosecution.

2   A young woman was subjected to sexual abuse by a person with diplomatic immunity who was allowed to leave the country after being accused. After expressions of public outrage, he was returned to New Zealand for a successful prosecution (Davison 2014a).

falls short of statistical significance. This does not deny the Green gender difference, simply indicating the underlying reasons for it in the social structural foundations of the Green vote.

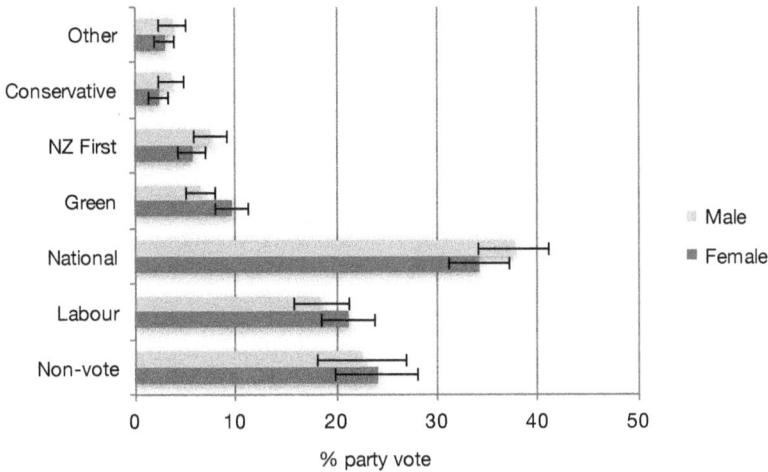

Figure 9.1: Percentage party votes for women and men
Source: New Zealand Election Study 2014.

There were reasons why women might find the Greens more consistently feminist than Labour. The Greens produced a comprehensive women's policy in June 2014. Linked to broader principles of equality, the document was the most comprehensive of the parties, in terms of its scope and specifics. Discussing the compounding effects of multiple variables in terms of 'intersectionality', it recognised that women were not a homogenous group as well as the need to undo structural discrimination, in terms of paid employment, family responsibilities and leadership (Green Party 2014c). Economic inequality was articulated in terms of the need for both equal pay and pay equity, alongside a living wage, while the broader pursuit of gender equality would involve mainstreaming gender analysis on all government bills and the development of a national action plan towards gender equality. Alongside this were policies addressing family and sexual violence, as well as bodily sovereignty.

Despite promising a range of initiatives to advance women's material wellbeing, the majority of the media attention was given to the Greens' position on abortion decriminalisation. Anti-abortion groups such as Family First, Men Against Abortion, Right to Life and the Salvation Army were quick to condemn the proposal. Nevertheless, this negative coverage did apparently little to dent the Greens' female support base. The party's female co-leader, Metiria Turei, is well liked by women, significantly more so than men. Women were, however, also more likely to prefer the male co-leader of the Greens at the 2014 elections, Russel Norman, compared with his male counterparts. Given women's greater support for the Green Party and the close link between supporting a party and liking that same leader's party, this should obviously not come as a surprise.

While Figure 9.1 shows no significant effects with respect to gender for New Zealand First, our multivariate analysis in Chapter 4 revealed a marginally significant male bias among voters for New Zealand First with the social and demographic controls. When we combine those who voted for New Zealand First with those who supported the Conservative Party and ACT, we also find that women are significantly less likely to vote for these parties (8 per cent female compared to 12 per cent for men). In this case, the estimate survives the addition of the controls for age, work and marital status. Finally, Figure 9.1 shows a non-significant difference for turnout: women may be slightly more likely to vote, but this is well within confidence intervals. Chapter 11 returns to turnout and gender; our null finding here is an artefact of the New Zealand Election Study (NZES) sample size. With larger samples, women can be identified as somewhat more likely to vote than men.

Gender differences in policy issue positions

The lack of a significant gender gap in vote choice for the major parties does not preclude women and men having different political attitudes and different policy positions. Figure 9.2 shows that there is a significant difference between women and men on whether or not the Treaty of Waitangi should be part of the law, with women being more likely to support the Treaty in the law. As reported in Chapter 10, there is also an age difference, with the young being more in favour of the Treaty. Figure 9.2 shows that this is predominantly the effect of younger women. Women aged 40 years and younger are significantly more pro-Treaty compared to their male counterparts. Controls for marital and work status do not influence this finding. Earlier New Zealand research on these questions drew on the 1990 NZES, and also found that women were more favourable to the Treaty of Waitangi than men and more opposed to sporting contacts with apartheid South Africa. In terms of issue salience more widely, women rated health and education to be more important political issues than men (Aimer 1993). All this was broadly consistent with findings in other comparable countries. Drawing on a cluster analysis based on political attitude questions (Vowles and Aimer 1993: 207–08; Aimer 1993: 122), this research found that women were more likely to be found in the small cluster to the furthest left, and men in another small cluster to the furthest right. Nearly 25 years later, this still accords with our findings in 2014.

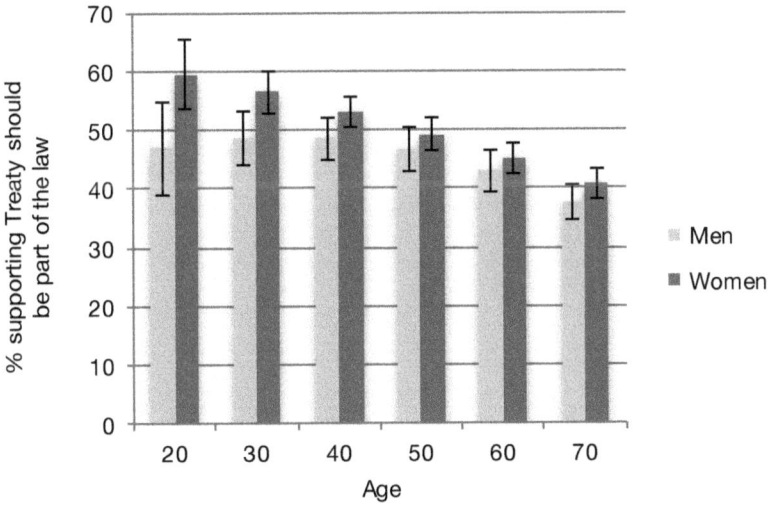

Figure 9.2: Percentage support that the Treaty of Waitangi should be part of the law by gender

Note: Results are based on an OLS regression model interacting gender with age and age-squared, with controls for Māori versus non-Māori primary ethnic identification.

Source: New Zealand Election Study 2014.

As discussed above, there was evidence in 1990 that women were somewhat to the left of men in their perceptions of issue salience, particularly in terms of the importance of health and education (Aimer 1993). If this pattern still holds, we might expect to find some evidence for women to be somewhat to the left on expenditure and distributional issues, as well as in their preferences for government action on inequality.

Figure 9.3 shows the probability of respondents disliking inequality. As in earlier chapters, it relies on a combination of the two NZES questions: 'The government should take measures to reduce differences in income levels'; and 'Differences in income in New Zealand are too large'.

Figure 9.3 shows that if there are any effects, they are most likely to be a result of age rather than gender, with older people being more likely to dislike inequality than the young.

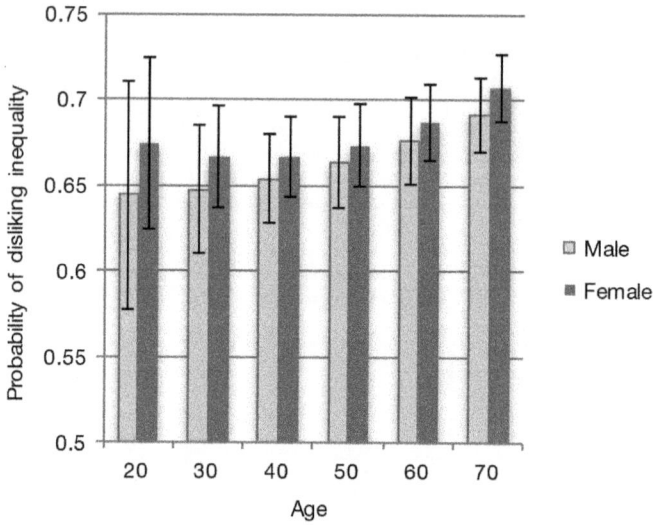

Figure 9.3: Preferences concerning inequality and gender
Note: Regression on female/male, age and age squared, with interactions.
Source: New Zealand Election Study 2014.

Turning to our measures of support for universal compared with targeted benefits, Figure 9.4 shows that there are gender differences in supporting expenditure on universal benefits such as health, education and taxpayer-funded pensions. These gender differences are particularly significant among those between around 40 and 60. Differences outside this age band are within confidence intervals, and thus not statistically significant. Adding the number of asset types and whether or not respondents feared their income would decline in the next year only marginally narrows the gap between men and women in the 40–60 age group. The gender differences in that age group cannot be explained by owning assets and fears of loss of income.

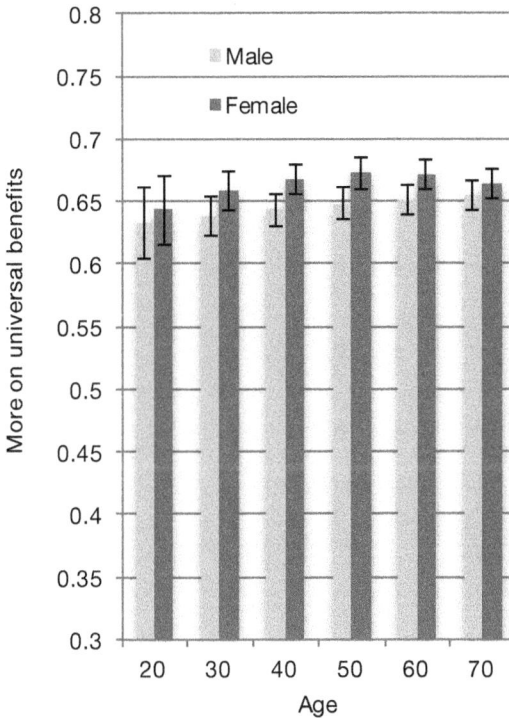

Figure 9.4: Preferences for expenditure on universal benefits by gender and age

Note for Figures 9.4 and 9.5: Regression on female/male, age and age squared, with interactions. Universal benefits: health, education and pensions (New Zealand Superannuation); targeted benefits: unemployment and social welfare.

Source: New Zealand Election Study 2014.

Figure 9.5 shows no significant gender differences within any of the age groups in response to questions about targeted benefits. Across the age and gender groups, women around the age of 20 are significantly more likely to favour targeted expenditure than anyone who is aged 40 and over, except perhaps those around 70. When controls for work and marital status are introduced, the gender gap opens more widely at age 70. Adding further controls for ownership of assets and fear of income loss reduces the tendency of young women to support targeted benefits, making it apparently insignificant. This means that young women are more likely than older women and men to be and feel economically vulnerable, and this vulnerability explains their greater preference for higher benefit expenditure. Being single or widowed and being out of the workforce increases support for targeted benefits regardless of age or gender, as self-interest would also suggest.

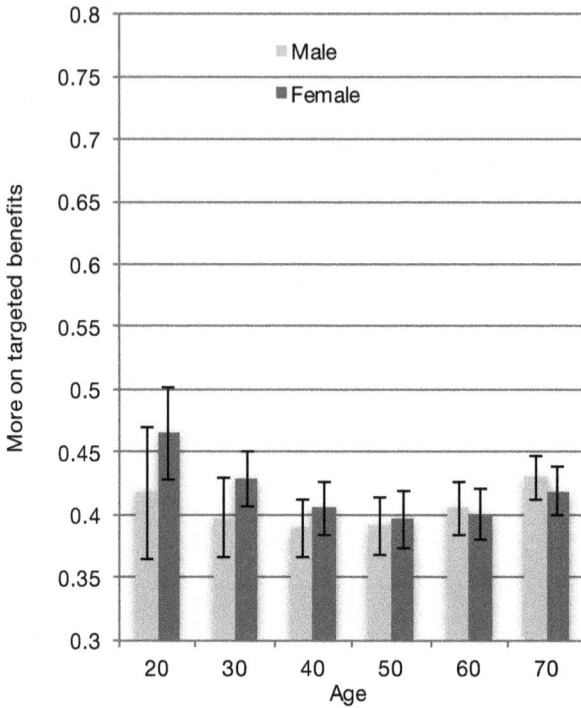

Figure 9.5: Preferences for expenditure on targeted benefits by gender and age

Source: New Zealand Election Study 2014.

Consistent with their greater support for the Green Party, women are significantly more supportive of doing more to protect the environment than men (Figure 9.6). On a seven-point scale (reversed from the questionnaire original)—with 7 meaning that 'we should concentrate more on protecting the environment, even it means lower economic development', and 1 meaning that 'we should concentrate more on encouraging economic development even if it is at the expense of the environment'—women score on average 4.7 whereas men have an average score of 4.4. While this is a relatively small difference, it is statistically significant. Applying controls indicates that stronger support for the environment among younger and more educated women helps to explain why women are more likely to support the Green Party than men. While we do see some gender differences in a range of political attitudes connected to social and economic inequality, as well as to the environment, these are small, and reflect the findings on the limited effect of gender on vote choice.

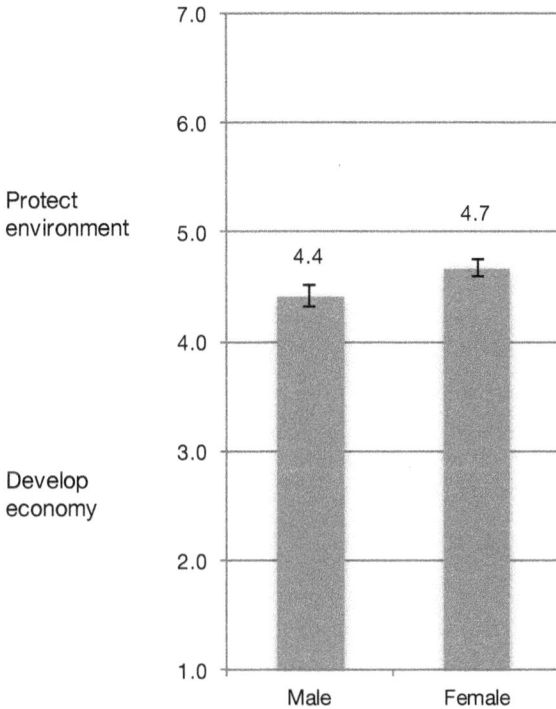

Figure 9.6: Means of protecting the environment versus economic development by gender

Source: New Zealand Election Study 2014.

Gender gaps in political interest and knowledge

A participatory and knowledgeable public is crucial for democratic responsiveness and is seen as an intrinsic democratic good, crucial for a well-functioning democracy (Verba 1996). As we will address more fully in Chapter 11, lower participation rates in politics is likely to intensify inequalities, particularly if low involvement is found among social groups already lacking power and resources. Hence, systematic and persistent patterns of unequal political interest, knowledge and participation along existing lines of stratification, such as gender, are threats to political equality, democratic performance and an egalitarian and fair society. Previous international research (for example, Coffé 2013b; Coffé and Bolzendahl 2010; Delli Carpini and Keeter 1996; Frazer and Macdonald 2003;

Verba, Burns and Schlozman 1997) has shown that women generally tend to be significantly less likely to engage with, be interested in and be knowledgeable about politics. Comparing interest in politics in New Zealand back to 1963 and up to 1990, Vowles (1993: 124) found that while a gap remained in 1990, it had narrowed considerably since 1963.

The gender gap in political interest was still significant in 2014. Figure 9.7 shows average scores on a 0 to 3 scale with 0 referring to being not at all interested in what is going on in politics, and 3 indicating a high interest in politics. As can be seen, women score on average 1.73, which is significantly lower than the 1.92 score among men. This difference remains after controls for age, work and marital status.

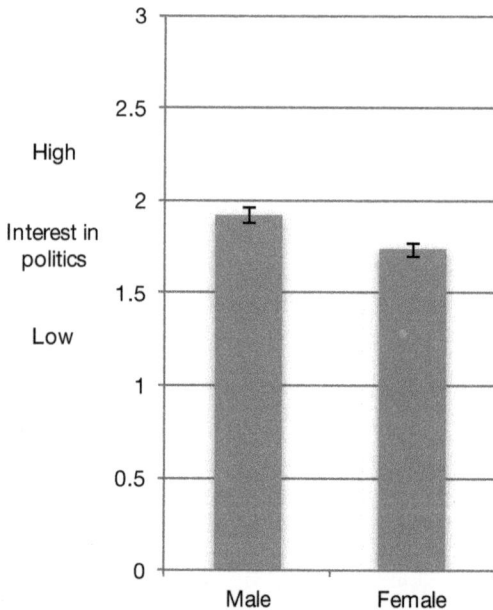

Figure 9.7: Interest in politics by gender
Source: New Zealand Election Study 2014.

The 2014 NZES also confirms that New Zealand men are significantly more knowledgeable about politics compared with women. The survey included four multiple choice questions, asking the name of the Minister of Finance before the 2014 General Election, the most recently released unemployment rate in New Zealand, the party that won the second largest number of seats in parliament at the 2014 General Election, and the name of the current Secretary-General of the United Nations.

When the four knowledge questions are combined into a 0–4 scale of political knowledge where each right answer is coded '1' and 'don't know' or a wrong answer scores '0', women score on average 2.3, whereas men score on average 2.7. Men thus outperform women when it comes to political knowledge as estimated this way. Women are also significantly more likely to opt for the 'don't know' option than men. This confirms other research showing that women are more risk-averse and disproportionally less likely to guess than men are (Lizotte and Sidman 2009; Mondak and Anderson 2004). With that in mind, once the 'don't know' option responses are eliminated, men no longer outscore women in knowing the Minister of Finance's name, and the gap on the knowledge scale narrows between women (2.9) and men (3.1). Controls for age, work and marital status do not affect these differences. However, some gender scholars argue that general indicators referring to 'politics' are gender-biased and treat politics as synonymous with the traditional arenas of electoral and legislative politics, resulting in an underestimation of women's political interest and knowledge in particular areas (Coffé 2013b; Dolan 2011; Stolle and Gidengil 2010). Acknowledging this critique, our emphasis here is on electoral and legislative politics. Broadening the range of inquiry beyond our present purposes, one might expect different findings.

Female political representation in New Zealand

The increasing gender gap in economic wellbeing since the election of National in 2008, explained at the beginning of this chapter and as measured by the Global Gender Gap Index, has not created a female backlash against the National Government. Labour has appeared unable to gain traction on the traditional economic issues of importance to women. This does not bode well for women's political representation or the promotion of gender parity in social and economic life. The current lack of progress is unexpected, given the long history of women's involvement in New Zealand politics. At the end of the nineteenth century, New Zealand led the world as the first country in which women obtained the right to vote in general elections. Since then, New Zealand has had two female prime ministers: Jenny Shipley (National, 1997–1999) and Helen Clark (Labour, 1999–2008), and three Governors-General. Thirty per cent of Helen Clark's first Cabinet were women, and women continue to make up 25 per cent of John Key's Cabinet. However, so far, women have formed no more than 34 per cent of any parliament elected under the Mixed Member Proportional (MMP) since 1996.[3]

Table 9.1: Women elected under MMP, 1996–2014

Election	Female List MPs as % List MPs	Female Electorate MPs as % Electorate MPs	Total Female MPs as % of All MPs
1996	45.5	15.4	28.3
1999	39.6	23.9	29.2
2002	29.4	27.5	28.3
2005	44.3	23.2	33.1
2008	42.3	27.1	33.6
2011	39.2	27.1	32.2
2014	32.0	31.0	31.4

Sources: www.elections.org.nz; Curtin 2014.

Table 9.1 also specifies the proportion of list and electorate MPs, an important distinction within MMP systems, in particular since electorate MPs are often considered to have more status and legitimacy than list MPs (McLeay and Vowles 2007). Since the start of MMP in 1996, women have been significantly more likely to be represented as list MPs than electorate MPs, although the differences were marginal in 2002 and after the most recent 2014 election.

The bias in the way that men and women are elected as list or electorate MPs has also been confirmed for Germany, which has a similar electoral system (Davidson-Schmich 2014). In electorate seats where only one candidate can be chosen, party selectors tend to opt for male candidates who are thought to be more likely to win a seat (Curtin 2014; Davidson-Schmich 2014). In Germany, the major political parties have adopted gender quotas for party lists, but they have not introduced a mechanism to increase the number of female candidates for electorate seats.

The gap between women's representation in list and electorate seats has narrowed since 2005. While women's share of list MPs tends to fluctuate, in recent years they have increased their representation as electorate MPs. Observing a similar trend in Germany, Davidson-Schmich (2014) suggests

---

3   Since the installation of parliament after the 2014 election, because of the retirement and replacement of list MPs a few changes have taken place in the composition of parliament. As of May 2016, the proportion of female MPs had increased to 33.9 per cent (N=41).

that the main reasons for this trend are the incumbency advantages that female electorate MPs experience and the openings presented when male incumbents retire. Increasingly, gender-aware parties can fill these vacancies with female candidates. While the overall percentage of female MPs was 31.4 per cent after the 2014 election, significant differences between the parties remain.

Table 9.2: Female MPs per party, 2014

Party	Number Female MPs	Percentage Female MPs
National Party	16	26.7
Labour Party	12	37.5
Green Party	7	50.0
Māori Party	1	50.0
NZ First	2	18.2
ACT	0	0.0
United Future	0	0.0

Source: www.elections.org.nz.

As can be seen from Table 9.2, women have the highest proportion of MPs within the Green Party and the Māori Party. The Green Party has a gender quota stipulating that women and men alternate up and down the order of their party list, and therefore exactly half of the MPs are women. The Māori Party had one female MP and one male MP after the 2014 election. While gender forms one of a set of its criteria in the party's candidate selection process, it does not have a formal quota. Prior to 2014, the Māori Party had only one woman MP, Tariana Turia, in a parliamentary caucus of four (in 2005), five (in 2008) and three (in 2011). Like the Green Party, the Māori Party appoints male and female co-leaders. The single MPs for both ACT NZ and United Future are male. The Internet Party failed to make any headway in the 2014 election, but it did have a female leader, former Alliance cabinet minister Laila Harré.

Of the two major parties, women are significantly better represented within the Labour Party (37.5 per cent) than within the National Party (26.7 per cent). Neither the National Party nor the Labour Party have adopted formal gender quotas, but after the introduction of MMP, the Labour Party instituted a so-called 'pause for an equity review' after each bloc of five candidates during the list selection procedure at regional conferences (McLeay 2006). The National Party also applies the principle of balance in its nomination process, but has never applied strict alternation on its lists or introduced quotas.

Within National, the proportion of female MPs was higher among the electorate MPs than the list MPs in 2014 (respectively 29 and 21 per cent). This pattern differs from the overall pattern shown in Table 9.1: that women are more likely to be a list MP than electorate MP. Within Labour, the representation of female MPs was slightly higher among list than electorate MPs (respectively 40 and 37 per cent).

The issue of gender quotas and women's political equality was hotly debated in 2013, when the Labour Party initially proposed and then rejected the adoption of an all-women shortlist option for candidate selection in electorate seats. Following the 2011 election defeat, the party established a Selection Working Group to provide recommendations about reforming its processes, with a view to increasing women's representation as electorate candidates. The group's report drew on the experiences of the UK Labour Party's strategy of all-women shortlists to achieve gender parity in the Labour Party caucus. A constitutional remit on the issue was planned for the annual conference in November but leaked to the right-wing blog site Whale Oil in early July (Robertson 2015). A media frenzy followed, with the proposed policy labelled a 'man ban' and commentators accusing Labour of discrimination, failing to select on the basis of merit and looking 'out of touch' with its rank and file (Curtin 2013a; Small 2013; Trotter 2013). Within a week of the leak, then leader David Shearer said the party was dumping the 'quota' but would retain its target of 45 per cent female MPs in 2014, a goal that was confirmed after the leadership moved to David Cunliffe in September 2013. For the 2017 election, Labour has a target of 50 per cent female MPs, one that it will find extremely difficult to achieve without a big increase in its vote. By November 2013, pollster Gary Morgan claimed the fall-out from the party's commitment to increasing women's representation had driven men away from Labour towards National (National Business Review 2013). While male vote intentions to vote Labour had fallen back compared with the last poll, no evidence was provided of a direct link.

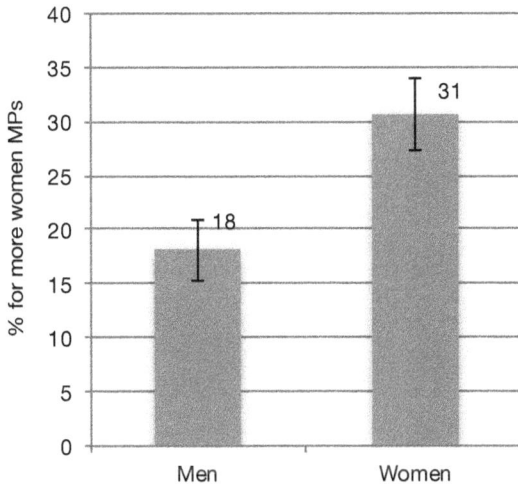

Figure 9.8: Percentage support for an increase in the number of female MPs by gender

Source: New Zealand Election Study 2014.

If there was a strong demand for greater female representation in politics, Labour's efforts to redress the balance among its MPs would be to its electoral advantage. But our data indicates that the demand that exists is relatively weak. The 2014 NZES data reveal that 24 per cent of people in New Zealand believe that there should be more women in parliament. Support for an increase in female MPs differs significantly between women and men. As can be seen from Figure 9.8, women are appreciably more likely than men to think that there should be more women in parliament. The gender gap is robust and remains significant even when various socio-economic and attitudinal characteristics such as political efficacy, and when controls are added for work and marital status.

Figure 9.9 displays an interaction effect between age and gender. We must be a little wary of it, because the confidence intervals are wide among the young, but they do not overlap significantly. The interactions indicate that both young men and young women are more likely to support increased women's representation than those who are old. The interactions also show that the gender gap is larger among the young. In particular, women and men differ more significantly in their attitudes towards the number of female MPs between those around the age of 30 than those at the age of 70. Support for greater women's representation is highest among women around the age of 20. Among this group of young women, about 50 per cent support an increase of women's representation.

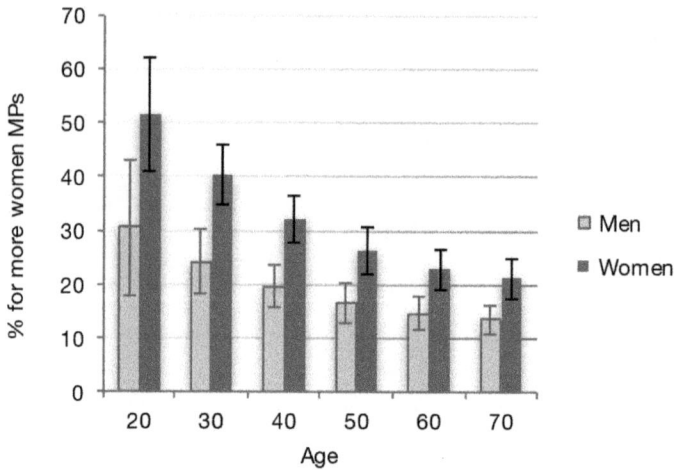

Figure 9.9: Percentage support for an increase in women's representation by age and gender

Source: New Zealand Election Study 2014.

Support for more female MPs also varies by party vote. Table 9.3 sorts the parties by level of support for 'more' compared with 'fewer or the same' number of female MPs. With the partial exception of a reversal between Labour and the Māori Party, the relationship is largely consistent with the parties' left–right ordering. Voters for left-leaning parties are more likely to support having more female MPs than voters for right-leaning parties.

Table 9.3: Support for more female MPs by party vote (in row percentages)

Voted	Fewer or the Same	More	N
Internet-MANA	52	48	31
Green	53	47	223
Māori	62	38	29
Labour	64	36	543
No Vote	79	21	637
NZ First	79	21	179
National	85	15	980
Conservative	88	12	82
ACT	96	4	15
Total	76	24	2,737

Source: New Zealand Election Study 2014.

One strand of theory suggests that women are socialised differently than men overall, and are thus more caring and empathetic than men (for example, Ridgeway 2011). If so, we might hypothesise that women will also be more likely to be supportive of an increase in representation for other groups who have been previously or currently marginalised or experiencing political inequality. Respondents were asked to what extent they believed that, besides women, the number of Asians, Pacific Islanders and Māori in parliament should be increased.

As can be seen from Figure 9.10, women only tend to show greater support for an increase of Māori MPs. They do not differ significantly from men in their support to increase the number of Asian or Pacific MPs—two ethnic groups whose presence, as a percentage of the population, has increased markedly in New Zealand society over the last couple of decades, but, particularly in the case of Asians, still lags behind in terms of representation in parliament. Women are significantly less likely to favour an increase in Asian MPs than for the other groups, while men are indifferent between the various ethnic groups.

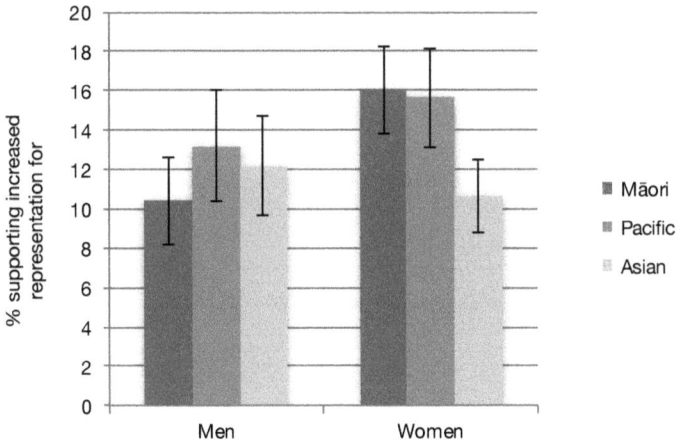

Figure 9.10: Percentage support for an increase in the number of various ethnic groups in parliament by gender
Source: New Zealand Election Study 2014.

Turning to the question of the extent to which people believe that more should be done to increase the number of female MPs and, if so, what should be done, Table 9.4 shows that a vast majority (61 per cent), believe that nothing should be done. They believe that there is no need to increase the number of female MPs, or that the number of female MPs will increase naturally. Here, too, substantial gender differences occur. Whereas more than 70 per cent of men believe that no effort should be done to increase the number of female MPs, 54 per cent of women believe that there is no need to increase the number of female MPs or that the increase of the number of female MPs will happen naturally. Figure 9.13 displays the data visually with confidence intervals. As with attitudes to women's representation more generally, the gender effect remains robust to a battery of controls.

Among those who believe that initiatives should be taken to increase the number of women in parliament, the 2014 NZES further shows that most believe that this should be achieved by encouraging more women to participate in politics (see Table 9.4 and Figure 9.11). The second most popular way to improve women's representation is by letting political parties make their own voluntary commitments to increase the number of female MPs. A small group, among both women and men, would prefer to legally require all political parties to select more women candidates by means of a 'quota'. Nonetheless, there is significant resistance towards the introduction of a quota; support is low among both women and men. In line with previous international research (Barnes and Córdova 2016; Gidengil 1998), it is significantly higher among women compared with men. As for overall support for the increase of female MPs discussed above, this gender gap may be due to both women's self-interest or more pro-social attitudes among women (Barnes and Córdova 2016).

Table 9.4: Percentage support for initiatives to increase women's representation in parliament by gender

	Men	Women	Total
No need to increase	19	12	15
Will happen naturally	51	42	46
Encourage women	21	29	25
Voluntary quota	7	12	9
Quota	2	6	4
N	1,350	1,485	2,835

Source: New Zealand Election Study 2014.

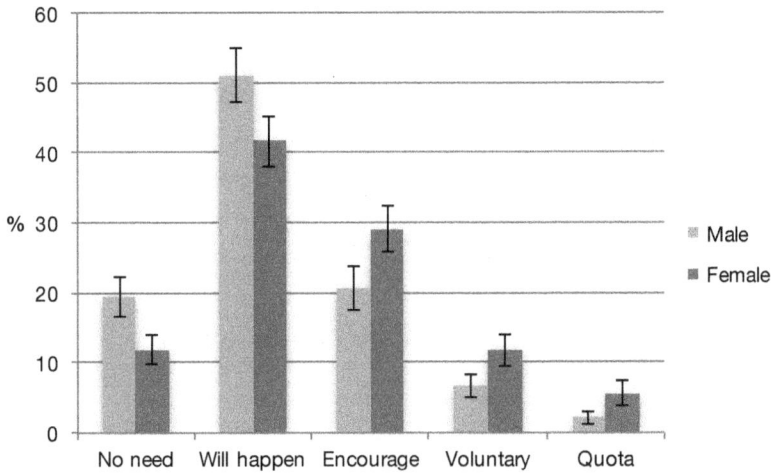

Figure 9.11: Percentage support for initiatives to increase women's representation in parliament by gender

Source: New Zealand Election Study 2014.

As significant differences exist between parties in the representation of female MPs (see Table 9.2), and in the initiatives they have taken to increase women's representation, we therefore expect to see differences between their voters in support for an increase of female MPs, and how this should be achieved. Table 9.5 reveals that compared with National voters, Labour and in particular Green voters are more likely to agree that efforts should be done to increase the number of female MPs. The support for legally requiring all political parties to select female candidates by means of a quota is small, even among Labour and Green voters. Even though the Green Party has gender quotas aiming at an equal representation of women and men, there is limited support among Green voters for a legal requirement that all political parties select female candidates by means of a quota. There is substantial support among Green voters for the idea that political parties should make their own voluntary commitments to increase the number of female MPs. Among all voters of all parties who believe that efforts should be taken to increase the number of female MPs, encouraging more women to participate in politics receives the greatest support.

Table 9.5: Women's representation options by percentages of party voters

% by Row	No Need	Will Happen	Encourage	Voluntary	Full quota	Don't Know	N
No Vote	11	37	22	9	5	16	635
Labour	13	31	33	11	6	6	537
National	19	45	23	7	2	4	964
Green	8	27	38	18	5	4	220
NZ First	22	43	19	8	5	4	176
Māori	14	28	31	12	5	11	28
Internet-MANA	17	24	33	20	6	1	30
Conservative	36	38	16	8	0	3	80
All	17	37	27	11	4	4	2,707

Source: New Zealand Election Study 2014.

Conclusion

We find small differences in the party choices of women and men in the 2014 election. On the margins, women are more likely to be on the left and men on the right, but this applies only to the relatively small groups who are furthest to the left or right. This is a pattern that was apparent as long as 25 years ago. Recent gender differences in party choices between the Labour and National parties have subsided from 2011 onwards. This contrasts with studies of other post-industrial societies where women are still found to be significantly more left-leaning than men. Women are significantly more likely to vote Green, a gap that can be accounted for by age, education and environmental attitudes. Men are more likely to vote for a bundle of conservative parties (ACT, New Zealand First and the Conservative Party) when put together, and similar controls do not reduce their tendency to do so.

We find that women are somewhat more to the left on the environment and on the Treaty of Waitangi; in the case of the Treaty, this is particularly so for younger women. Women tend to favour more expenditure than men do on universal benefits such as health, education and New Zealand Superannuation, particularly women between the ages of 40 and 60. The only gender difference apparent for targeted benefits for the unemployed and welfare beneficiaries is for younger women, who are significantly more in favour of higher expenditure than the middle-aged women and men. In line with international research, we find lower levels of political interest and knowledge among women. But this does not make them less likely to turn out to vote. Our findings also show that women are more likely to say that they do not know the answer on some political knowledge questions, and that allowing for this narrows but does not close the gap.

New Zealand was the first country that gave women the right to vote in general elections, and it has had two female prime ministers since 1997. In addition, in 1999 the two major party leaders were women and competed against each other in the election of that year. Since 2011, both major party leaders have been men. After the introduction of MMP delivered a boost in women's parliamentary representation, the overall representation of women in the New Zealand Parliament has stalled at around 30 per cent since 1996. There has been no significant increase over the last 20 years. One explanation is obvious: there have been no quotas to ensure woman MPs are selected, except within the Green party. There also does not seem to be strong support for quotas among New Zealanders, though the support is stronger among women than men, and younger women in particular. Along with greater support for the Treaty of Waitangi, women also tend to be more in favour of increased Māori representation than men, but have less support for increased representation of other ethnic groups, in regard to which they do not differ significantly from men.

Our findings echo some of the findings that have been found elsewhere, but we do not find any evidence to confirm that work and marital status account for gender differences, at least not at this point in time. We do, however, find considerable evidence that gender effects interact with age, indicating that women may respond to political socialisation and political events in different ways than men. There is some evidence of self-interest and some for greater vulnerability, particularly among younger women.

10

Against the tide? Māori in the Māori electorates

As in most ethnically diverse societies, for reasons of history and culture, inequalities of income and assets are not spread evenly among the various ethnic groups in New Zealand. The biggest and most robust differences that occur in New Zealand are between the European or Pākehā majority and the indigenous Māori population, which are also the two largest ethnic groups in New Zealand society. Māori social and economic disadvantages are evident in a wealth of data indicating their poor health outcomes, lower life expectancy and a disproportionate contribution to the prison population (McIntosh 2012). Figures 10.1 and 10.2 display the data from the 2014 New Zealand Election Study (NZES) sample, with distributions consistent with the general patterns of official data available (Statistics New Zealand 2014e).

The Māori population is significant because Māori are the largest ethnic minority, and more so because of their indigenous status, giving them rights both in international law and under the Treaty of Waitangi (see Chapter 2). In this context, the discourse widens into debates about group rights and affirmative action to address inequality that can cut across ideas based on individual rights and equality before the law. The political importance of Māori in New Zealand politics is further enhanced by the existence of seven Māori electorates, which make it possible for Māori to elect Members of Parliament who can directly speak to their interests. The Māori electorates are a special category of electorate that cover the whole of New Zealand and overlie the general seats. The 2005 election brought about a new development in Māori politics: the capture of a majority of the seats by a genuinely independent Māori Party with the potential to act as a pivotal player in government formation, particularly from the 2008 election onward.

The politics of the Māori electorates have implications for the pursuit of Māori aspirations that include but also go beyond simply raising Māori incomes and wealth to levels more equal to those of European New Zealanders. The political actors who compete in the Māori electorates tend to have two priorities: property rights and self-determination (bound up in Article 2 of the Treaty of Waitangi); and ensuring that Māori obtain a fair share of the benefits of New Zealand citizenship (Article 3). That is to say, their priorities are social and economic equality (Orange 2011; Stevens 2015).

In this chapter, we investigate these two dimensions by examining how both relate to the electorate and party vote in the Māori electorates, and explore how attitudes towards inequality and the Treaty relate to one another, both in the Māori and general electorates. We thereby show that while differences in voting patterns between Māori and Pākehā remain significant, diversity among Māori is also shaping their politics.

First, we provide a brief historical overview of Māori politics and a descriptive analysis of party competition within the Māori electorates.

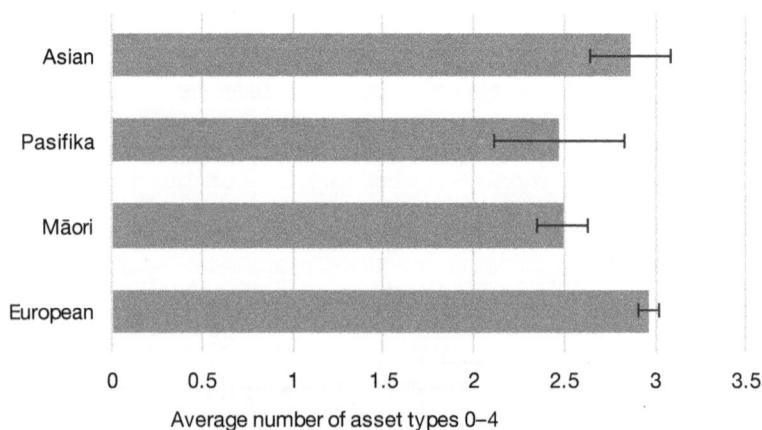

Figure 10.1: Average assets by ethnicity
Source: New Zealand Election Study 2014.

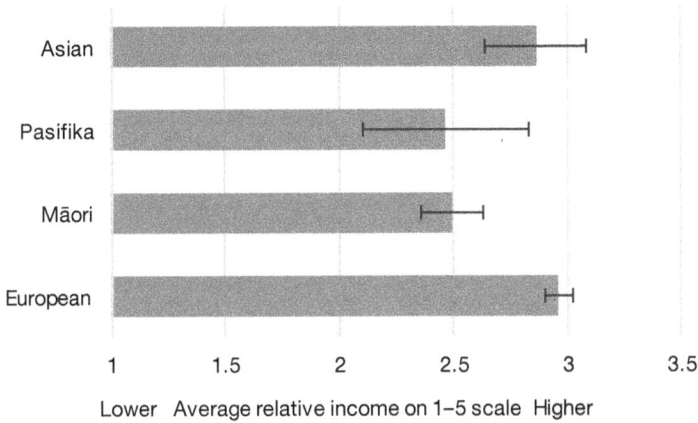

Figure 10.2: Average income by ethnicity

Source: New Zealand Election Study 2014.

The background of Māori electorates

When the *New Zealand Constitution Act 1852* (UK) established a House of Representatives, those eligible to vote included all men over the age of 21 who owned, leased or rented a property of a certain value, including Māori men. But because most Māori property was held in common, very few qualified. Four Māori constituency seats were then created in 1867 and universal suffrage for Māori men was introduced in 1869. At that time, eligibility to vote required some ownership of individual property and therefore still excluded most Māori from the vote. Separate Māori representation without that requirement was a way of sidestepping the problem. Only a few years after 1867, relaxation of the requirement of individual property ownership for eligibility to vote would have extended voting rights to Māori without the need for Māori seats (Wilson 2010), but the creation of those electorates had taken Māori politics in a different direction. Conservative European or Pākehā New Zealanders have consistently opposed the existence of the Māori seats, and liberal Pākehā have defended them. Their abolition remains National Party policy, although National has so far never implemented that promise.

With the development of party politics in the 1890s, Māori MPs became associated with the Liberal Party that governed from 1891 until 1912. After 1912, Māori MPs aligned first with the conservative Reform Party, but this shift to the right was later reversed with the rise of the Rātana

Movement. The Movement had emerged after World War One, its objectives being to restore the *mana* of the Treaty of Waitangi and to improve the social position of the Māori people. By the 1935 election, Rātana candidates had captured two of the four Māori seats, and in 1936 Rātana formally allied itself with the Labour Party. A third seat was won by Labour and Rātana in 1938, and the fourth in 1943 (Sullivan 2015). The National Party has had minor party status among Māori voters ever since. The Labour Party retained its dominance in Māori politics until the 1970s, reaching a peak of 80 per cent of the Māori electorate vote in 1972 (Chapman 1986).

Labour's command of the Māori vote soon became much wider than its foundations in the Rātana movement. As Māori moved into the cities in the 1940s and 1950s, many became employed in low-income manual occupations and became members of trade unions affiliated with the Labour Party. Māori politics and working-class politics converged. In office between 1972 and 1975, the Third Labour Government under Norman Kirk and Bill Rowling probably did more than any previous government to recognise the uniqueness and importance of Māori culture.

From 1893 until 1975, people whose ancestry was predominantly Māori had been required to register on the Māori roll. Those with less than half of their ancestry being Māori were required to be on the general roll. In 1975, Labour amended the law so that anyone who could claim any Māori descent could choose to enrol on either the Māori or the general roll. Labour also removed the limitation of the number of four Māori seats, making it possible for their number to vary according to Māori enrolment. That overdue change was needed to ensure that Māori votes would count equally to those cast in the general electorates. It was reversed by the National Government that took power in 1975, but reintroduced in 1996 as part of the Mixed Member Proportional (MMP) electoral system. The number of Māori electorates currently stands at seven.

Progress under Labour was not enough in the context of higher expectations generated from the Māori renaissance in the 1970s. Matiu Rata had served as Minister of Māori Affairs in the Kirk Government (1972–1975). He left the Labour Party in 1979 to form an independent Māori party, Mana Motuhake. At subsequent elections, Rata slowly chipped away at Labour's vote in the Northern Māori electorate. Ironically, he paved the way not for the victory of his own party but instead that of the New Zealand First party in 1993, in the form of its candidate Tau Henare (Sullivan and Vowles 1998).

The effects on Māori of the Fourth Labour Government (1984–1990) were very mixed. There was much greater recognition of the Treaty, with significant later effects. Treaty principles were embedded in legislation, with the effect that Treaty principles, if not the Treaty itself, have become recognised as part of New Zealand's 'unwritten' Constitution. But Labour's move to embrace the market in economic and social policy led to unemployment among the unskilled, disproportionately affecting Māori who tended to be concentrated in the manual working class (Statistics New Zealand 2016e). Mana Motuhake fought the 1990 election in a loose alliance with the NewLabour Party that had been formed by those who had left the Labour Party as a result of its shift to the right. In 1993, a more formal left Alliance came together including NewLabour, Mana Motukahe and the Green Party. The Alliance won two seats, one of which fell to Sandra Lee, Mana Motuhake's leader, but in a general rather than in a Māori electorate, Auckland Central.

The transition to the MMP electoral system was accompanied by the removal of the ceiling on the number of Māori seats. In proportion to population, and as a result of choices between Māori and general electorate enrolments, the number of Māori electorates increased to five in 1996, the first election under MMP, six in 1999 and seven from 2002 onwards. The seven seats at the 2014 election are displayed in Figure 10.3.

Electoral outcomes in Māori electorates since 1996

At the first MMP election in 1996, there was a seismic shift in Māori politics. All five electorates fell to the New Zealand First party. This was despite leader Winston Peters' and New Zealand First's relative conservatism on Treaty issues (see Chapter 8; also see Sullivan and Vowles 1998). In 1999, another political earthquake of equal dimensions returned all six seats to Labour, in tandem with the formation of a new coalition government of Labour and the Alliance, in which Mana Motuhake had three MPs (Sullivan and Margaratis 2000, 2002). In 2002, divisions in the Alliance led to the departure of Mana Motuhake and the loss of its parliamentary representation at the election that year.

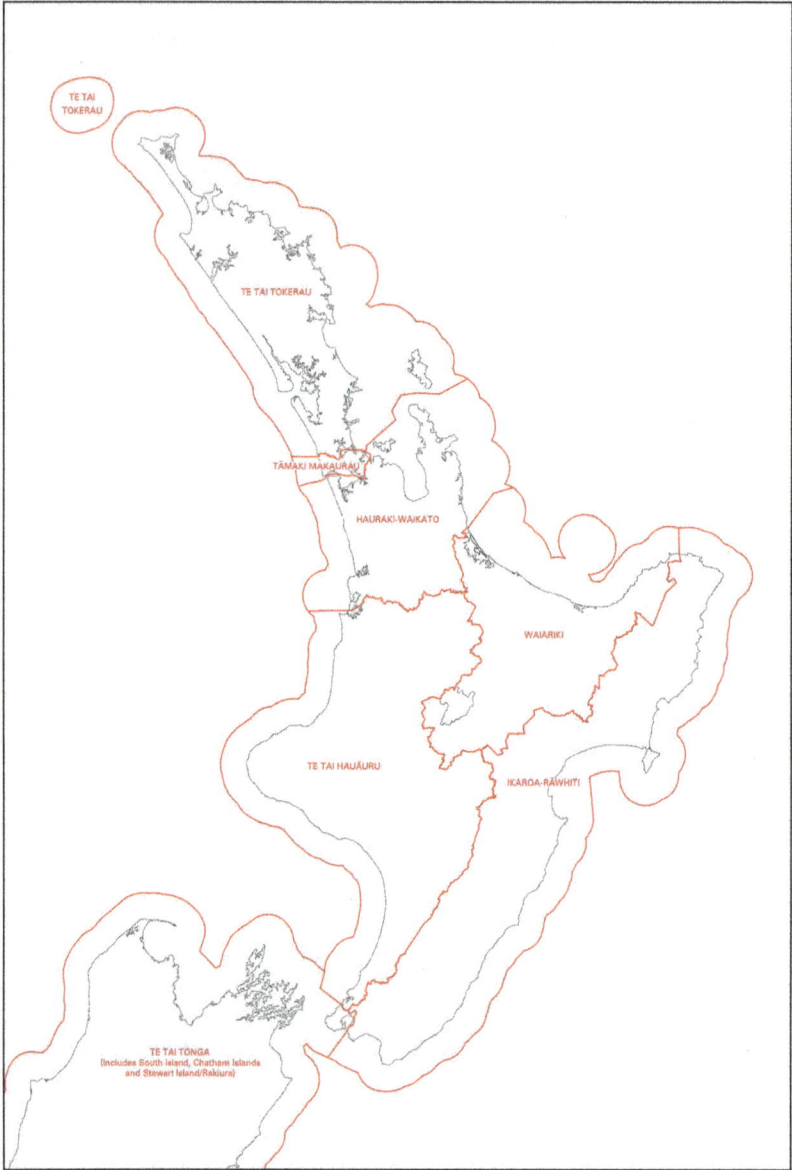

Figure 10.3: The Māori electorates in 2014
Source: Representation Commission 2014.

Dramatic at the time, Labour's loss of the Māori seats to New Zealand First in 1996 turned out to be temporary. The link between Māori politics and class politics was apparently reset in 1999, almost as if nothing had happened. What followed next stretched the relationship to breaking point. In 2003, the Court of Appeal ruled that Māori *iwi* (tribes) could make claims in the Māori Land Court for customary ownership of areas of the foreshore and seabed. Fearful of public opinion, and under pressure from the New Zealand First and National parties, the Labour-led government legislated to ensure Crown ownership of the foreshore and seabed except where it was already in private hands, while conceding some Māori customary rights where they could be established. This prevented Māori from contesting whether or not they could gain those customary property rights through the courts. Labour had used parliamentary supremacy to override principles of indigenous property rights recognised in international law, not to mention the Treaty of Waitangi. A trend of constitutional recognition of Māori rights over nearly 20 years had been stopped in its tracks, if not reversed. To many Māori, it felt as if the bad old days of government-sponsored theft of their property had returned. Labour lost the support and trust of many Māori, who felt they had been betrayed.

Labour's Māori MPs were put in a very difficult situation. Most stayed with the party and did their best to modify the law to allow the retention of some Māori rights. However, cabinet minister Tariana Turia left Labour and formed the Māori Party, which went on to capture four of the seven Māori seats at the 2005 election and won a fifth in 2008, when Labour lost office to the National Party. The Māori Party was not the first independent Māori party, but it has become more successful than any before, and was the first to form a significant relationship with a government on its own terms. For the time being at least, Māori politics had overcome class politics in the Māori electorates.

In 2008, the Māori Party became a support partner for the National-led government and this continued through to 2014, with Māori Party MPs Pita Sharples and later Te Ururoa Flavell taking the non-Cabinet position of Minister of Māori Affairs (Māori Development from 2014). The National Government repealed Labour's Foreshore and Seabed Act, replacing it with the Marine and Coastal Area Act. This transferred the foreshore and seabed Labour had declared to be in public ownership to a situation whereby no one has ownership, with guarantees of public access, confirmation of existing fishing and aquaculture rights, and reopening potential recognition of Māori customary title through the courts (Hickford 2015). In law, customary title is not understood as a property right that can be sold and does not exclude public access. The law also put into statute the previous common law understanding that such rights could only be established without substantial interruption in use since 1840.

With the government having dropped the claim of Crown ownership, Māori opinion was partly but far from fully accommodated. Critics argued that the new legislation was little different from that made under Labour. Māori Party MP Hone Harawira refused to support it and was forced out of the party. He formed the left-wing MANA Party, resigned his seat and won a by-election early in 2011, retaining the seat at the general election later that year. The MANA Party attracted some prominent Pākehā leftists as well as former members of Mana Motuhake. The splitting of the vote in 2011 between the two independent Māori parties provided an opening for Labour to recapture one seat from the Māori Party, bringing Labour's number of Māori seats back to three, from two in 2008. At the 2014 election, Harawira had allied MANA with Kim Dotcom's Internet Party, and lost his seat. It was reclaimed by Labour, giving Labour six of the seven Māori electorate seats. The Māori Party was left with only a single Māori electorate seat in 2014, that of Te Ururoa Flavell in Waiariki, plus one list seat held by Marama Fox.

Table 10.1: Electorate votes and electorate seats in the Māori electorates 1996–2011

	1996	1999	2002	2005	2008	2011	2014
Vote %							
Māori	-	-	-	48.7	57.9	31.5	26.7
Mana Māori/ MANA	4.6	1.7	7.8	-	-	21.2	20.4
National	4.5	3.9	6.9	-	-	-	-
Labour	28.8	48.9	63.8	43	37.5	40.7	43.1
Green	-	-	1.9	1.8	3.1	4.9	8
NZ First	48.8	14.4	-	-	-	-	-
Alliance	7.4	8.5	-	-	-	-	-
ACT	1.4	0.6	-	-	0.5	-	-
United	0	-	2.6	-	-	-	-
Independents	1.2	7.0	3.5	1.8	0.2	0.3	0.7
Other	3.3	14.8	12.4	4.8	0.8	1.4	1.1

	1996	1999	2002	2005	2008	2011	2014
Electorate Seats							
Labour	0	6	7	3	2	3	6
Māori	-	-	-	4	5	3	1
MANA	-	-	-	-	-	1	0
NZ First	5	-	-	-	-	-	-
Total	5	6	7	7	7	7	7
Valid Votes	101,377	103,782	104,639	129,289	132,797	122,408	142,867
Māori Overhang				2	2	1	
Effective N Parties	3.0	3.6	2.3	2.4	2.1	3.2	3.3

Note: Overhang effects arise when a party is entitled to fewer seats as a result of party votes than it has won constituencies.

Source: Electoral Commission 2016b.

Table 10.1 provides the official data for Māori electorate voting since the first election under MMP in 1996. The effective number of elective parties is an estimate of the number of parties weighted by their size (Laakso and Taagepera 1979): it starts at three, with Labour and New Zealand First as the main parties, but with a significant number of votes to Mana Māori, the Alliance and National. In 1999, Labour and several small parties benefited from New Zealand First's collapse; the effective size of the electorate-vote party system was rising again. Labour's recovery of dominance in the electorate vote in 2002 reduced the size of the effective party system to around two. Combined with the absence of National and New Zealand First candidates in the Māori electorates from 2005 onward, two-party competition between Labour and the Māori Party kept the effective number of parties around two until 2011. From then onwards, the appearance of the MANA Party has fragmented Māori electorate votes once more with the number of effective parties increasing to three.

Party by party, Table 10.1 documents the sharp drop in the Labour vote in 2005, Labour's loss of four seats to the Māori Party in 2005 and Labour's nadir both in terms of seats and votes in 2008. More to the point, it shows the weakness of Labour's recovery. By 2014, Labour's loss of electorate vote share in 2005 had not been recouped at all.

The split in the independent Māori vote is confirmed as the explanation for Labour's recapture of all but one Māori seat in 2014. The combined vote for MANA and the Māori Party still outpolled Labour in the electorate vote across all the Māori electorates in 2014. Within the electorates that

Labour won in 2014, the combined Māori/MANA vote outpolled Labour in three: Tamaki Makaurau, Te Tai Hauauru and Te Tai Tokerau. Promised coordination between the MANA and Māori parties in the 2017 election constitutes a serious threat to Labour's control of those Māori electorates.

Much of Māori politics remains inherently connected to communities defined by tribes (*iwi* and *hapu*) and *whanau* (family and kinship connections), meaning the personal vote may become as important as the party (Godfery 2015: 253–59). Indeed, in their analysis of voting in the Māori electorates in the 1996 general election, Sullivan and Vowles (1998) found large effects for liking or disliking the candidates on offer. These candidate preferences had big effects on voting for New Zealand First, and were therefore a key explanation of the party's success in capturing all the Māori seats. Comparable candidate effects in the general electorates were weaker. Analysis of the Māori electorate vote in 1999 told much the same story (Sullivan and Margaratis 2002).

Table 10.2 provides electorate-level detail on the changes that took place between 2011 and 2014. The differences between the electorates reflect incumbency, retirements, the death in 2013 of popular Labour MP for Ikaroa-Rāwhiti, Parekura Horomia, and a concerted campaign against MANA MP Hone Harawira in the Te Tai Tokerau electorate that was won by Labour's Kelvin Davis (Godfery 2015: 253–56). In 2014, Horomia's replacement as Labour candidate, Meka Whaitiri, was unable to claim much of Horomia's personal vote. The MANA Party made its only significant gains in that seat, although not enough to threaten Labour. Meanwhile, the retirement of the Māori Party's two senior MPs provided an opening for Labour; the most likely explanation of the successes of Labour's Peeni Henare and Adrian Rurawhe is the loss of Tariana Turia's and Pita Sharples' personal support. Whakapapa or family-based politics play a central role in Māori elections (Godfery 2015: 258–59). Penni Henare came with an advantage as his family has had a long and prominent history in Māori politics. He failed to shift as many votes to Labour as his colleague Adrian Rurawhe, but Rurawhe had the advantage of family connections to the founders of the Rātana Church. Rino Tirikatene, re-elected in Te Tai Tonga for Labour, has similar Rātana links. Meanwhile, long-standing Labour MP for Hauraki-Waikato, Nanaia Mahuta, is closely linked to the Māori King Movement and therefore the Tainui *iwi* leadership in the Waikato.

Table 10.2: Change between 2011 and 2014 in the seven Māori electorates

| | Change in 2014–2011 Vote Shares | | | Winner 2011 | Winner 2014 | 2011 Party holding seat > 2014 party holding seat |
	Labour	Māori	MANA			
Hauraki-Waikato	+3.18	+5.34	−7.11	Nanaia Mahuta	Nanaia Mahuta	Lab>Lab
Ikaroa-Rāwhiti	−14.44	−4.85	+9.82	Parekura Horomia*	Meka Whaitiri	Lab>Lab
Tāmaki Makaurau	+3.19	−9.55	−2.74	Pita Sharples**	Peeni Henare	Māo>Lab
Te Tai Hauāuru	+11.49	−14.9	+1.23	Tariana Turia**	Adrian Rurawhe	Māo>Lab
Te Tai Tokerau	+7.63	−4.73	−2.01	Hone Harawira	Kelvin Davis	Man>Lab
Te Tai Tonga	+2.3	−6.93	+1.96	Rino Tirikatene	Rino Tirikatene	Lab>Lab
Waiariki	+2.84	+2.51	−6.75	Te Ururoa Flavell	Te Ururoa Flavell	Māo>Māo
All	+2.4	−4.79	−0.75			

Notes:

* Died in office and succeeded by Meka Whaitiri at a by-election in 2013.

** Retired in 2014.

Source: Electoral Commission 2016b.

To test again if candidate effects tend to be higher in the Māori electorates, we focused on the link between liking the Labour candidate and the probability of voting for that candidate; Labour was the party running the most incumbent candidates, making this the best way to test the hypothesis (see Karp et al. 2002). If previous research was to be confirmed, first we would expect to find the net effect of most liking the Labour electorate candidate to both substantively and significantly affect the probability of a Labour electorate vote. Most of all, we also expect that effect to be greater in Māori than in general electorates.

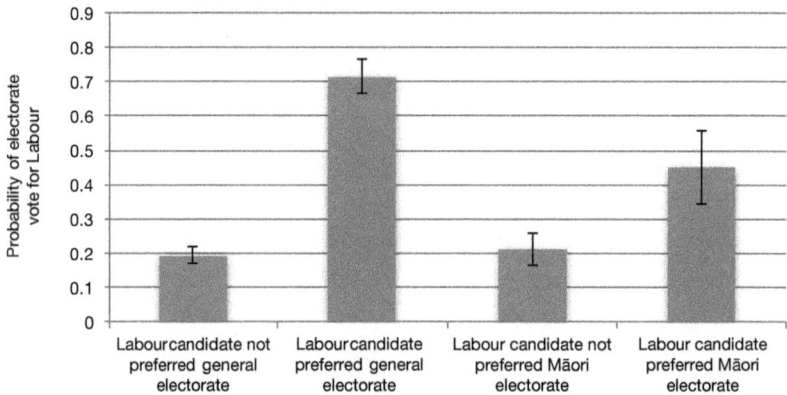

Figure 10.4: The effects of liking the Labour candidate the most across the general and Māori electorates
Source: Appendix, Table 10.A1.

Based on a multilevel random effects model with various control variables (see Appendix, Table 10.A1), the findings presented in Figure 10.4 show that the effects of preferences for or against Labour candidates are very strong, but unexpectedly are twice as big in general electorates as in Māori ones. This does not deny the possible effects of family-based politics or *whakapapa* (genealogy) in the Māori electorates, but indicates something else is going on in the general electorates that merits further research.

Table 10.3 provides the data for the party vote in the Māori electorates since 1996. With all registered parties recorded, the estimates of the effective number of elective parties summarise and display the greatly increased fragmentation of the party vote among Māori from 2011 onwards, confirming to a greater extent a pattern that was also found for the electorate vote (see Table 10.1). Labour's electorate vote had collapsed in 2005, but its party vote had held up. On the surface, this might seem puzzling. It makes sense in the context of the 2005 election. In 2005, the National Party was led by Don Brash, whose speech to the Orewa Rotary Club in January 2004 on the special status of Māori people had intensified Māori/Pākehā tensions and confirmed that National had even less sympathy than Labour for the protection of Māori property and political rights. This 'wedge' politics of 'us and them' galvanised voters. Labour only just managed to pull ahead of National in the party vote and form a government (Sawer and Hindess 2004). Many Māori found Brash's rhetoric and policy substance unpalatable, so had a strong incentive to give their party vote to Labour.

Table 10.3: The party vote, Māori electorates, 1996–2014

	1996	1999	2002	2005	2008	2011	2014
Māori	-	-	-	27.7	28.9	15.6	14.1
Mana Māori/ MANA	3.3	4.4	4.0	-	-	13	10.2
National	6.1	3.9	4.2	4.3	7.5	8.6	7.9
Labour	31.9	55.1	53.7	54.6	50.1	41	41.2
Green	-	5	10.7	3.3	3.9	10.3	11.2
NZ First	42.3	13.2	14.9	6	6.1	9.5	13
Alliance	8.5	6.7	-	-	-	-	-
ACT	1.1	0.8	1	0.2	0.5	0.2	0.2
United	0.1	0.7	2.5	0.5	0.1	0.6	0.1
Other	6.7	9.1	9.0	3.4	2.9	1.7	2.2
Valid Votes	101,630	104,660	108,270	134,452	138,054	129,209	149,259
Roll	141,929	159,400	194,114	208,003	229,666	233,100	239,941
Split Vote*	32.8	39.1	48.1	41.5	47.6	51.5	52.1
Non-standing %**	0.7	3.9	20.6	11.1	15.1	18.4	21.8
Real split	32.1	35.3	27.5	30.4	32.6	33.1	30.3
Effective number of parties	3.4	3.0	3.0	2.6	2.9	4.2	4.2

Notes:

* Percentage of those who cast both party and electorate votes.

** Percentage of (party votes for parties not standing candidates + electorate votes for non-list party candidates)/total party vote.

Source: Electoral Commission 2016b.

The electorate vote was a different story. Māori could afford to reject Labour in their electorates, and many did so. Many had 'a bob each way', splitting their votes between Māori and Labour, helping to push Labour ahead of National in the party vote and generating a two-seat overhang, a result of the Māori Party winning more electorate seats than the number warranted by its share of the party vote. Table 10.3 also provides the split voting data. Some Māori cast their party votes for National and New Zealand First despite those parties not running in their electorate seats. Taking these votes out, overall levels of split voting in the Māori electorates are quite close to those found in the general electorates. The overall effects of split voting in most general electorates go in all directions, so offset each other. In the case of the Māori electorates, more distinct patterns led to the overhang effects from 2005 and 2008 (two seats) through to 2011 (one seat). By 2014, the loss of all but one Māori electorate brought an end to the Māori overhang.

The drop in Labour's party vote in the Māori electorates did not occur until 2011. It appears that Labour's loss was the Green Party and New Zealand First's gain, although movements at the individual level were probably more complex. Māori conservatives were attracted to the revitalised New Zealand First Party that had re-entered parliament in 2011. Meanwhile, the Green Party had attracted some strong Māori MPs, including co-leader Metiria Turei. Indeed, the Green Party outpolled the MANA Party in the Māori electorate party vote in 2014. The Green Party strongly opposed the *Foreshore and Seabed Act 2004* and the replacement *Marine and Coastal Area Act 2010*, making it another possible destination for Māori disappointed with Labour and the Māori Party.

Electoral turnout in Māori electorates

A high level of non-voting has also long been a feature of the Māori electorates. Figure 10.5 displays the trends from 1987 onward, comparing turnout as a percentage of those enrolled with that on the general rolls. The gap is relatively constant over time, widening in 1990 and 1993, no doubt the result of a campaign by the Māori Council of Churches for Māori not to vote in 1990 in order to put pressure on the government to bring about Treaty-based justice for Māori.

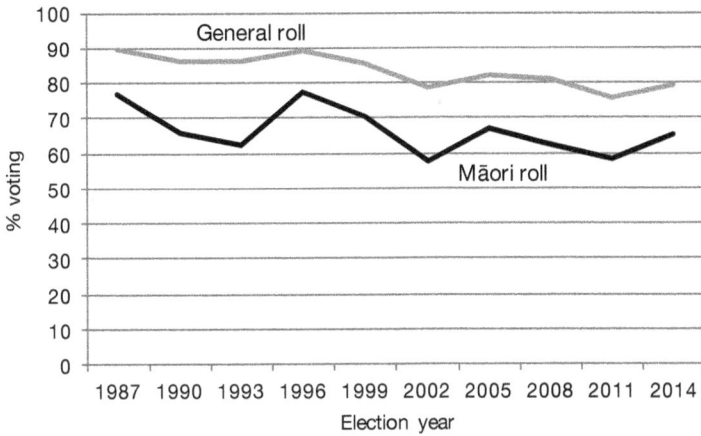

Figure 10.5: Electoral turnout as percentages of electoral enrolment, 1987–2014

Source: Electoral Commission 2002, 2016b.

There are several plausible explanations for the lower turnout in the Māori electorates than in the general electorates. Standard theories suggest that lack of competition in the Māori seats until 1996 would have provided low incentives for Māori to acquire a habit of voting (Franklin 2004). Turnout is also strongly affected by resources, defined broadly (Brady, Verba and Schlozman 1995). People in low-income households with low education are less likely to vote, whatever their ethnicity, and Māori have been more concentrated in those groups than others. Analysis in 1990 indicated that social structure and demographic variables accounted for about half the gap between Māori turnout and that of others, with the other half unexplained (Vowles and Aimer 1993: 54–56). With a narrower range of social structure controls, a persistent Māori effect can be found in longitudinal analysis ranging between 1963 and 2005 (Vowles 2010). On the other hand, more in-depth analysis of Māori turnout does find that age and demographics have bigger effects than culture (Fitzgerald, Stevenson and Tapiata 2007).

The advent of greater competition in the Māori electorates since the introduction of MMP might have been expected to increase turnout in 1996, when the five electorates were captured by New Zealand First. There may also have been an MMP effect associated with the expansion of the number of Māori seats. Post-MMP analysis indicates that variations in turnout in the Māori electorates are driven by closeness or distance in national-level competition between National and Labour, not at all by variations in competitiveness between the electorates themselves (Vowles 2015a). Admittedly, the steeper Māori turnout increase in 2005 compared with the general roll coincides with the Māori Party's first participation in a general election, but this was also in tandem with a very tight Labour–National race, with Māori issues highly salient in the campaign. Despite increased competitiveness in the Māori electorates, Māori turnout continues to be lower than turnout on the general roll, although the trend in turnout over time is similar in both. Variation in turnout between the Māori electorates and between elections is mainly the result of general electorate level campaigning and the intensity of national campaigns.

Data from the Electoral Commission's official records of voting and not voting show those on the Māori roll are less likely to vote than Māori on the general rolls, with Māori on the general rolls tending to sit midway between those on the Māori roll and non-Māori voters on the general roll. Being on the Māori roll is associated with lower turnout. Māori scholars hypothesise that the long-term effects of colonisation and the former marginal nature of the Māori seats continue to affect Māori political behaviour into the present. This is a plausible explanation that again emphasises turnout as a habit. It is also consistent with lower levels of political efficacy among Māori (Fitzgerald, Stevenson and Tapiata 2007). There may be an additional explanation since 1996, when numbers on the Māori roll first began to have an effect on the number of Māori electorates. Some may feel that choosing the Māori roll is an act of participation in itself as it helps to maximise the number of Māori electorates ensuring direct representation by a Māori MP.

A cross-cut cleavage?

While there is a distinct Māori/non-Māori cleavage in turnout and party preferences in New Zealand (see Chapter 4; also see Sullivan, von Randow and Matiu 2014), there is also considerable diversity among Māori in their political opinions and behaviour. Māori society itself is diverse, containing many actors with different interests. Migration out of rural tribal areas has led to the development of large urban clusters of Māori, some of whom who have lost connections to their *iwi*. Over the last 20 years, this trend has reversed with a high percentage of Māori now able to identify their origins (Kukutai and Rarere 2015). But not all Māori have been in a position to share the benefits associated with assets transferred to *iwi* as a result of the Treaty settlement process. Māori also vary in the depth of their immersion in Māori society and culture. Four out of five do not speak *te reo,* the Māori language, to a conversational level, and the proportion able to do so has declined over the last 15 years (Statistics New Zealand 2016f). The resources commanded by *iwi* also differ—some made early settlements and have become prosperous, others have been less successful.

There are also generational differences. These can be illustrated by differences in the proportions of age groups among people of Māori descent that chose between the Māori and general electoral rolls in 2014. Since 1996, that choice has taken on greater political significance, because the more who enrol on the Māori roll, the greater the number of Māori seats. A campaign to convince Māori to opt for the Māori roll was initially successful, increasing the number of seats from five to seven, but there has been no further increase since 2002.

Figure 10.6 shows the distribution of people of Māori descent between the Māori and general rolls at the 2014 election, broken down by four age groups defined by the three cut points: in 1976, when choice between the two rolls was permitted; in 1996, when the numbers opting to go on the Māori roll could result in a change in the number of seats; and in 2001, the closest point in the data to identify the 2004–05 events of the divisive Brash Orewa speech and the Foreshore and Seabed Act. The first age group whose members were able to choose between the two rolls was that entering voting eligibility between 1976 and 1996. They display an approximate 2:1 ratio favouring the Māori roll. This group also corresponds to the generation most caught up in the Māori political and cultural renaissance of the 1970s and 1980s. Despite the greater incentive to go on the Māori roll, the ratio drops from the age group becoming eligible in 1996 and afterward, although a significant majority still opt for the Māori roll. Post-2001, the year closest to the emergence of the Foreshore and Seabed issue given the age-band data available, the proportions opting for the rolls have moved even closer together. While the majority of the youngest age group of people of Māori descent opt for the Māori roll, many also choose the general roll.

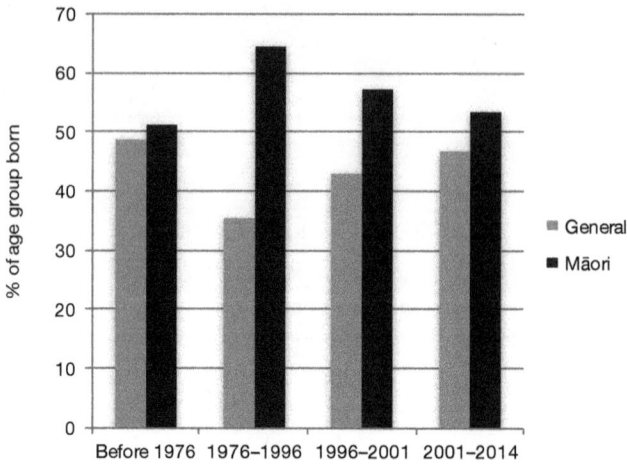

Figure 10.6: Percentages on the Māori roll by age groups defined by entry into voting eligibility, 2014

Source: Electoral Commission 2014b.

Besides generational differences in opting for the general or Māori roll, we would expect socio-economic diversity within the Māori community to be associated with differences in party preferences between various socio-demographic groups. Table 10.A2 in the Appendix displays the baseline social structure and demographic model for the electorate vote in the Māori electorates. Those who chose the Māori Party are older, suggesting that party's support draws more from the generation of the Māori revival, associated with speaking *te reo*, but not significantly with an *iwi* affiliation. Alongside this, Māori Party voters have lower education than Labour voters, and their parents are less likely to have been Labour voters. However, they have more assets than Labour voters. MANA electorate voters also tend to speak *te reo*, and are more likely to be found in manual households than Labour voters. Māori who chose to vote Green with their electorate vote are more likely to live in an urban area and have fewer assets compared to Māori who voted Labour. They are also less likely to have Labour-voting parents.

Based on this model, Figure 10.7 further explores the link between assets and the party preference for the electorate vote among the Māori electorates. Since the number of assets had no appreciable effect on the probability of voting MANA, those estimates are not reported. We see that having a high accumulation of types of assets decreases the likelihood of voting Labour or Green. The reverse is the case for the choice to vote for the Māori Party. Māori Party voters tend to be those who have become more successful in the era of Māori revival. The slope of the Labour probability line is not very steep with Māori more likely to support Labour, including those with assets. Moreover, there is no significant difference in the likelihood of voting Labour or the Māori Party among Māori voters with four types of assets.

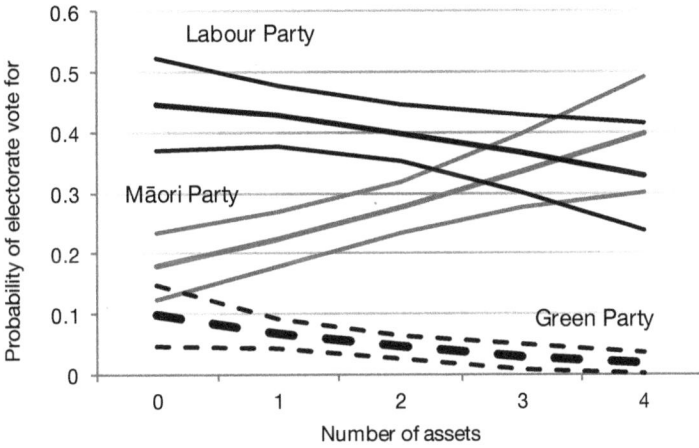

Figure 10.7: Asset ownership and the probabilities of an electorate vote for Labour, the Māori Party or the Green Party in the Māori electorates
Source: Post-estimation from Appendix, Table 10.A2.

As discussed in Chapter 4, people's party choices tend to be influenced by their parents' party choices. Party choice may be a habit passed down between generations (Jennings, Stoker and Bowers 2009). Earlier chapters have shown significant effects of recall of parental partisanship on vote choices and political attitudes. Figure 10.8 shows that such generational transmission of a Labour electorate vote is strong in the Māori electorates. Those who had two parents voting Labour when they were 14 had a 50 per cent probability of voting for Labour, compared to 30 per cent among those who parents did not vote Labour. The strong generational transmission reflects a hard core of Māori Labour loyalists, many of whom seem to have remained with the party after 2005, despite the Foreshore and Seabed legislation.

Shifting our attention to the party vote in the Māori electorates, we find that there are significant differences in the structure of Māori voting between the electorate vote and the party vote (Appendix, Table 10.A3). This is not surprising given the patterns of split voting in the Māori electorates based on official data (Electoral Commission 2016c). A third of those who voted Labour with their party vote, voted differently with their electorate vote. Specifically, 13 per cent of them gave their electorate vote to Internet-MANA and 11 per cent gave it to the Māori Party. Looking at the transfers in the other direction, a third of those who voted Labour with the electorate vote voted differently with their party vote: 13 per cent selected New Zealand First and 8 per cent chose the Greens. In the Māori electorates, a significant proportion of the voters thus split their vote, and the party vote model therefore differs from the electorate vote model.

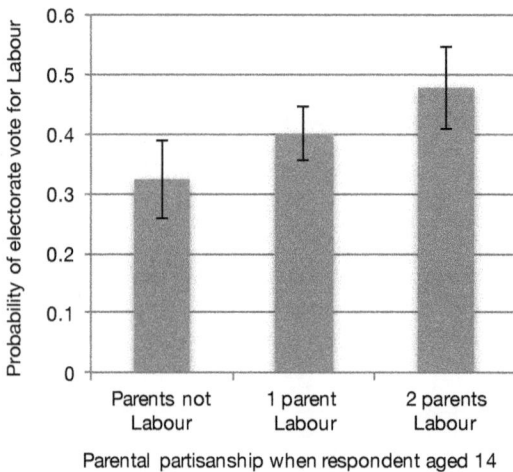

Figure 10.8: Parental partisanship and the Labour electorate vote in the Māori electorates

Source: Appendix, Table 10.A2.

Whereas age did not influence electorate vote choice, when looking at the party vote choice, age effects do occur. In particular, Internet-MANA appealed significantly more to older Māori, the Green Party more to the young, with middle-aged voters as likely to vote for the Green Party or for Internet-MANA (Figure 10.9). Other than the assets scale, the probability effects for which are plotted below in Figure 10.10, no other background variables had significant effects on the party vote, including *iwi* association. The null finding for parental partisanship is important here; past loyalties continue to anchor the Labour electorate vote among Māori, but not the party vote. In terms of assets, Labour appeals particularly to those with few assets. All other parties and non-voters tend to be found among those with more assets. In this sense, a class foundation for Labour's vote in the Māori electorates is evident in terms of both the electorate and party votes, but is strongest in the party vote.

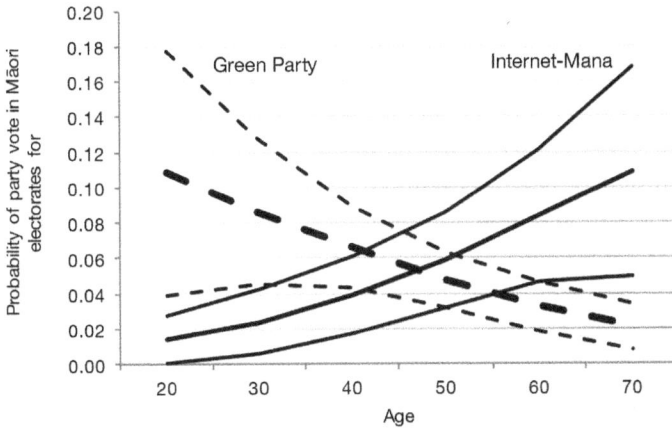

Figure 10.9: Age and the probabilities of a party vote for the Green and Internet-MANA parties in the Māori electorates

Source: Appendix, Table 10.A3.

We expand the analysis of the party vote in the Māori electorates to include political attitudes towards the legal status of the Treaty and to inequality, adding these to the baseline model (see Appendix, Table 10.A4). Whether the Treaty should be included in the law is based on a five-point scale reversal of the question: 'The Treaty of Waitangi should not be a part of the law'. It is worth noting here that the inclusion of the Treaty was the subject of a 'National Constitutional Conversation' held between 2011 and 2013. We find, however, that there is no significant variation on Treaty matters except for those Māori who vote National, who predictably tend to take a more conservative position than Māori who give their party vote to Labour.

As one might expect, higher toleration of inequality is associated with voting for National, but also with not voting. The higher the opposition to inequality, the greater the probability of Māori electorate voters to support Labour, the Green Party and even New Zealand First. Figure 10.11 plots the probabilities for not voting and for voting Labour. To better understand the alignment of Māori electoral politics on the two dimensions of Treaty rights and inequality, Figure 10.12 presents the mean or average positions of Māori electorate voters and non-voters on both dimensions. Figure 10.13 does the same for general electorate voters. When comparing both figures, it is evident that the opinions among general electorate voters are spread a little more widely than among the Māori electorate voters.

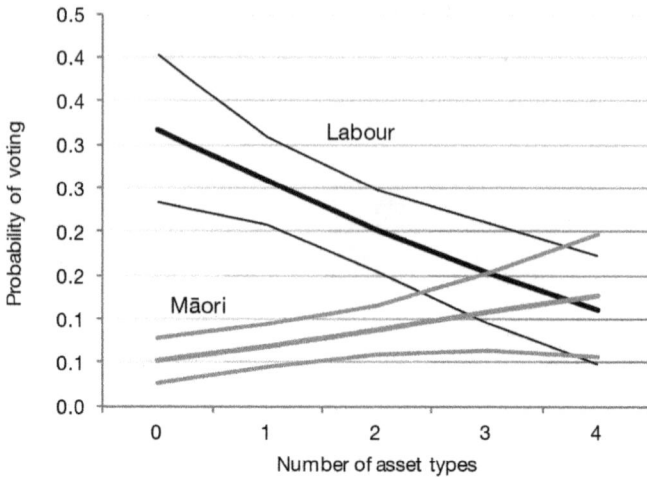

Figure 10.10: Assets and the probabilities of a party vote for Labour and the Māori Party in the Māori electorates

Source: Appendix, Table 10.A4.

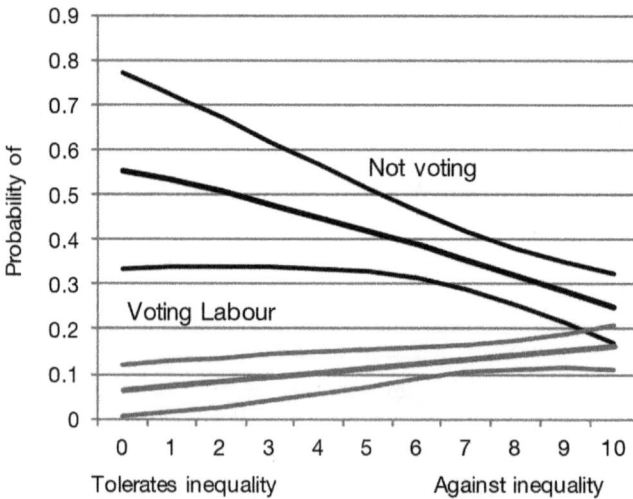

Figure 10.11: Inequality and the probabilities of a party vote for Labour or not voting in the Māori electorates

Note: Attitudes towards inequality are estimated by adding to what extent (five-point scales) respondents agree with two statements: 'Differences in incomes in New Zealand are too large'; and 'Government should take measures to reduce differences in income levels'.

Source: Appendix, Table 10.A4.

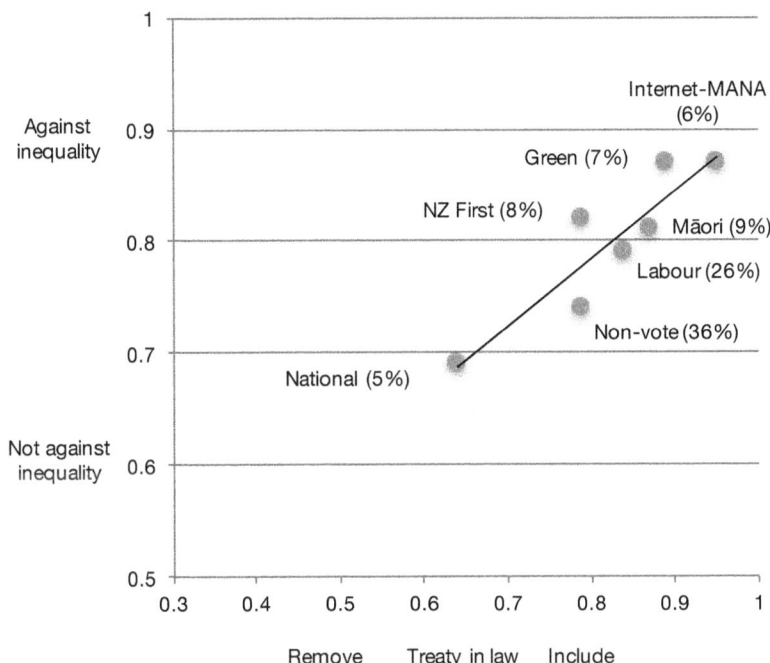

Figure 10.12: The alignment of voting groups on attitudes towards inequality and the Treaty in the Māori electorates

Notes: The Treaty/self-determination dimension is based on the question asking respondents to what extent (on a five-point scale) they agree that 'Reference to the Treaty of Waitangi should be removed from the law'. Original answers from 1 to 5 have been recoded to range between 0 and 1 and in such a way that a higher value refers to support for keeping the Treaty in the law. Percentages between brackets refer to percentage of voters.

Source: New Zealand Election Study 2014.

National voters stand out as less supportive of giving the Treaty legal status and are less opposed to inequality than other voters. The average New Zealand First Māori electorate voter is considerably more favourable to the Treaty than the New Zealand First party itself, given that the party has campaigned for the Treaty to be removed from the law. The key point to note is that the average positions across the two dimensions are correlated and clustered around a line that represents the slope of the relationship; that is, Māori electorate party voters can be seen as aligned on the two dimensions, and these are related.

As a comparison, Figure 10.13 presents the position of voting groups on the same attitudes towards inequality and the Treaty in the general electorates.

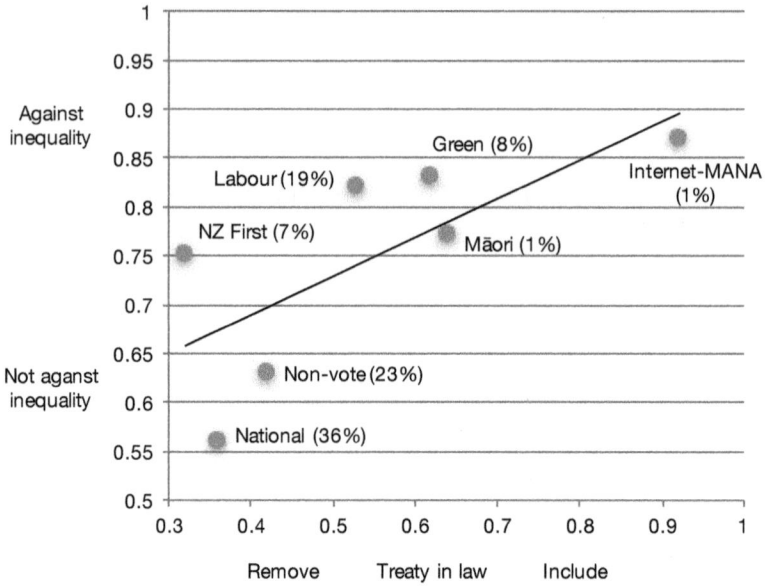

Figure 10.13: The alignment of voting groups on attitudes towards inequality and the Treaty in the general electorates
Source: New Zealand Election Study 2014.

Figure 10.13 shows that the two dimensions are less closely related in the general electorates than in the Māori electorates. The line that represents the slope of the relationship is not as steep and the average positions are further away from the line. When Māori electorate voters think about the Treaty and about inequality, they tend to see a closer relationship between the two issues than general electorate voters. In their party choices, they have clustered together in a way that confirms and strengthens a relationship, with support for inclusion of the Treaty in the law being related to rejecting inequality, that is a little less apparent among voters in the general electorates. This finding also confirms research on the 2011 election whereby those on the Māori electoral roll remain orientated to the left on policy issues such as opposition to privatisation of state assets (Sullivan, von Randow and Matiu 2014).

Conclusions

If the success of the Labour Party in recapturing almost all of the Māori electorates in 2014 was 'against the current', it was the ability of Labour to anchor itself in place that made the difference. The Labour Party did not regain significant headway in votes, particularly when one takes the extent of its 2005 loss as the benchmark. Labour's main rivals lost seats because they were competing for the independent Māori vote that the Māori Party had mobilised in 2005 but which has since fragmented. Labour's MPs and candidates had appeal, as did the only remaining Māori Party incumbent, Te Ururoa Flavell. With weaker candidates, Labour might have been less successful. Given the importance of incumbency, had Tariana Turia and Pita Sharples not retired from parliament, the Māori Party might have retained their seats, or at least come closer to doing so. The significance of parental party loyalties in underpinning the Labour electorate vote should not be forgotten; Labour was able to benefit from historic political capital. But this is an asset the value of which may depreciate over time.

The party system in the Māori electorates has become highly fragmented. Increasingly distinct from that of the general electorates, it is mobilised around the Treaty as a matter of difference over strength of opinion but not direction; there are very few Māori electorate voters who do not support the Treaty. As one might expect, Māori electorate voters connect their Treaty views a little more closely to their views about inequality than general electorate voters, and the way their votes are distributed emphasises this relationship.

Beneath the surface, the Māori Party appeals most to those Māori who have the most assets, and who belong to the first generation of the Māori revival, and who speak *te reo*. MANA electorate voters have a similar profile, but fewer assets and tend to be working class. Low-asset Māori tend to vote more for Labour and the Green Party, and the Green Party has an increasing appeal to young Māori voters, particularly in urban areas. We might therefore expect even more differences to emerge among Māori in the future around the two key Treaty dimensions that can be identified in their politics: self-determination and equality as citizens.

11

Inequalities in participation

Many political scientists argue that a participatory public is crucial for an effective democracy. They see threats to political equality and democratic performance in the form of systematic and persistent patterns of unequal participation by socio-economic status, age, gender and ethnic background (for example, Verba 1996). Debate continues about whether or not there are connections between low levels of turnout, changes in political participation in general and growing economic inequality. As noted in Chapter 1, several scholars have argued that there is a linkage between low turnout and increasing levels of inequality in advanced democracies (Boix 2003; Solt 2008), while others claim the link is tenuous at best (Stockemer and Scruggs 2012).

This chapter reviews some New Zealand evidence. New Zealand has experienced a combination of steady decline in turnout and increasing income inequality since the mid-1980s, making it a case well worth examination. We examine if there are biases in turnout, and whether they might be reduced by efforts to mobilise voters by traditional means or by new forms of media. We also address claims that some new forms of civic participation may become more significant than voting for new generations of New Zealanders in the twenty-first century.

Electoral turnout and inequality

Arend Lijphart has labelled low turnout the 'unresolved dilemma' of democracy, and has suggested that it makes the operation of electoral democracy unequal: some voices are heard and others are silent (Lijphart 1997: 1). However, others argue that this conclusion requires more analysis (for example, Lutz and Marsh 2007). Even though there may be apparent evidence of a connection in some cases, there may be other cases where there is none. It is sometimes suggested that non-voters may actually be satisfied with democracy, and thus lack the motivation to vote. This is refuted by European research that has found that non-voters tend to be less satisfied than voters (Grönlund and Setälä 2007), as was also the case in New Zealand in 2011 (Vowles 2015a: 290) and in 2014. However, the literature does not confirm a general finding that preferences of voters and non-voters are significantly different from each other, or that higher turnout would shift an electoral outcome consistently to the left (Grofman, Owen and Collet 1999; Bernhagen and Marsh 2007). The key issue does not seem to be partisan choice: if voters are consistently less likely to be young and poor, political parties whether of the right or left may be less likely to pay attention to their needs, and inequalities may persist or even increase.

Discussion of turnout loomed large in the months before and after the 2014 general election in New Zealand. A week after the election, a satirical story was posted on the Snoopman website with the headline, 'New Zealand PM John Key's suppressed "missing million" voters letter'. The 'letter' congratulated non-voters on helping to secure a third term for National (Snoopman 2014). The concept of the 'missing million' non-voters had entered political discourse in 2011 (Collins in Vowles 2014a: 53). While the official turnout rate in 2014 (76.7 per cent) was not as low as in 2011 (74.2 per cent), it was still lower than most earlier elections (Mitchell 2014).

Angst had been widespread since report of the low turnout rate in 2011. As Vowles (2014a: 53) noted, 'to find a New Zealand election with lower official turnout, one must go back to 1887, well before when women attained voting rights', making 'turnout in 2011 the lowest ever experienced in the country under conditions of full adult suffrage'. The 2011 election also represented a further drop in the Labour vote. In Australia and New Zealand, as elsewhere, it is often assumed that the majority of non-voters are likely to be on the left (Farrar 2014b; Jackman 1999; Salmond 2014) because they are also more likely to be young, lower educated, non-European and poor (Electoral Commission 2014c; Statistics New Zealand 2014c).

After the 2011 election, the New Zealand Electoral Commission identified low turnout as a problem to be addressed. For the Electoral Commission, increasing turnout is not about partisan or policy preferences but about maintaining 'a healthy democracy, which should be regarded as a matter of strategic national interest' (Electoral Commission 2014c). In May 2014, the Electoral Commission hosted a day-long conference titled 'Valuing our Vote'. The day received considerable media coverage and brought together local and international leaders in civic participation to consider how best to address voter decline in New Zealand (Electoral Commission 2014d). The Electoral Commission also did much more to encourage Advance Voting in 2014, and there was a significant increase: up from 15 per cent in 2011 to 29 per cent in 2014 (Electoral Commission 2015a: 4). It remains unclear whether or not those who took up this option were already likely to vote.

Various explanations for declining voter turnout in New Zealand have been canvassed elsewhere (Vowles 2002a, 2010, 2014a, 2015a). They focus on a mixture of individual and contextual factors. For example, age, income, education and ethnicity are often correlated with low turnout, with younger, lower income and lower educated people and those with a non-European background being less likely to vote. Contextual factors also matter: voter mobilisation by parties of those otherwise unlikely to vote; the extent to which party policies are polarised; and the competitiveness of a contest (Franklin 2004; Jaime-Castillo 2009).

The National Party's opinion pollster David Farrar analysed vote and turnout change in safe National seats between 2008 and 2011. He concluded that 'contrary to "received wisdom" it was National that suffered from the reduced turnout in 2011' (Farrar 2014b). A month later, at the National Party's conference, prime minister John Key told delegates that members should not take it for granted that it was only left-leaning voters who fail to turn out to vote. Drawing on Farrar, the prime minister stated that in 'the ten safe National seats where many people obviously thought it was a foregone conclusion, turnout fell by more than 6 percentage points compared to 2008, and if that happens again we could easily find ourselves on the opposition benches' (Radio New Zealand 2014c; The Nation 2016).

The concern with the implications of low turnout continued throughout the campaign. Various reports claimed that party strategists saw it as a major concern (Armstrong 2014d, 2014e; James 2014). Labour's strategists were worried that disillusionment with the party under Cunliffe's leadership would make Labour-leaning voters see simple abstention as the more comfortable option than switching to the Greens, Internet-MANA or New Zealand First.

High-profile attempts were made to get people under 30 out to vote, by not-for-profit organisations, computer application developers, the Electoral Commission and musical artist Lorde. Two weeks before the election, nearly 200,000 had not enrolled (Whelan and Hunt 2014). Young people are invariably less likely to vote than older people, but if the age gap grows (because voting is habitual and best acquired young, as they age young non-voters become older non-voters), we will see the generational replacements of keen voters with apparently more indifferent non-voters (Blais and Rubenson 2013; Franklin 2004; Vowles 2010; see also Rusk et al. 2004; Dalton 2007; Lyons and Alexander 2000; Wass 2007; Wattenberg 2007).

The small recovery in turnout in 2014 was a change in the right direction. Looking at the situation from a partisan angle, it did not seem to benefit Labour. One can inquire more deeply into this at two levels: electorate by electorate, as did Farrar for the 2011 election, or using the 2014 New Zealand Election Study (NZES) survey data. In the latter case, the numbers who shift are too small for anything more than speculation. Table 1.2 in Chapter 1 shows that net flows to and from non-voters for the two main parties between 2011 and 2014 may have been effectively zero, though flows to and from National into and out of non-voting were larger than Labour's. The Green Party and New Zealand First may have been the main beneficiaries of the turnout increase.

Like National Party pollster David Farrar in 2011, from official electorate voting data we can observe turnout changes in 2014 in strongly held Labour and National electorates. Because of boundary changes between 2011 and 2014, we rely on a subset of electorates where boundaries did not change. From those, Table 11.1 takes three more or less representative electorate seats held by each party, and compares change in enrolment and turnout. Doing this, we must again be wary of the ecological fallacy (see Chapter 7): the changes may not represent what individuals were doing. For example, voters for party A might be responsible for a change in turnout in an electorate held by party A; voters for party B might be equally responsible for the change. Table 1.11 tells us that official turnout was up in both National and Labour electorates. The table also shows us that enrolment was down, and down much more in Labour than in the National-held electorates.

Table 11.1: Change in turnout, enrolment base and change in enrolment, age-eligible base

Electorates	Turnout change	Enrolment change
National-held		
Pakuranga	3.6	0.9
North Shore	2.4	-4.1
Clutha-Southland	4.5	-2.0
Combined Change	*3.5*	*-1.7*
Labour-held		
Mangere	2.3	-5.3
Dunedin South	4.1	-3.2
Manurewa	3.1	-6.6
Combined Change	*3.1*	*-5.0*

Source: Electoral Commission 2014c, 2014f.

The enrolment rate is needed to estimate the *real* turnout rate that turnout on an enrolment basis fails to capture. In theory, enrolment to vote is compulsory in New Zealand. In practice, it is not enforced. Those eligible to vote are people 18 years and over, permanently resident in New Zealand for over a year, and not in prison after sentence since a legal change in 2010. Non-residents retain a right to enrol and register so long as they have returned to New Zealand once in the previous three years in the case of citizens, or in the year prior to the election for non-citizens. In 2014, 92.61 per cent of eligible voters in New Zealand were enrolled, compared to 93.74 per cent in 2011. This is about the same as the rate in Australia in 2013, although the enrolment rate in Australia has since increased to 96 per cent (Australian Electoral Commission 2013, 2016). In New Zealand, those less likely to be enrolled are people of Pasifika and Asian descent, and those aged 18–29 (Electoral Commission 2014c). As noted, official turnout went up in 2014, but about a third of this increase was illusory, as the enrolment rate was down by just over 1 per cent. The decline was concentrated among the young and, as it turns out, some not so young. Drawing on official data, Figure 11.1 shows a persistent gap between enrolment among those 18–29 and the rest since 1987 when data began to be collected. The picture is one of improvement up to the 2002 and 2005 elections, but in 2008 turnout among the youngest group begins to decline steeply. Among the not-so-young 30–39 group, there is a precipitous drop in 2014. The age gap in enrolment is widening.

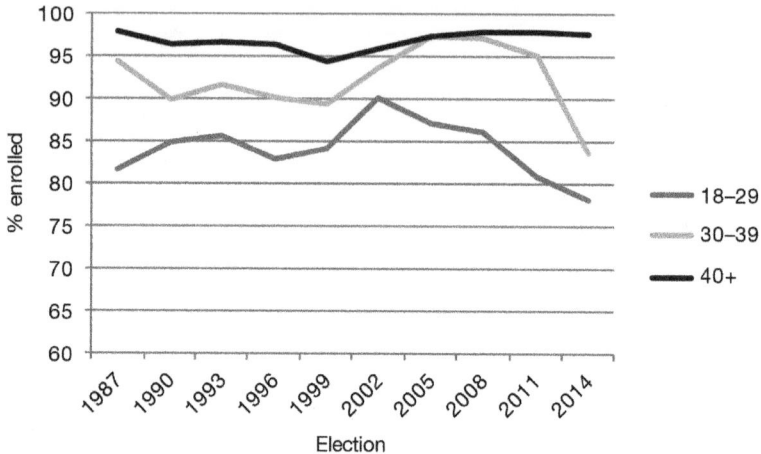

Figure 11.1: Enrolment on an age-eligible base, 1987–2014 by age groups
Source: Electoral Commission 2014g.

Younger voters (those under 30) have usually been less likely than those above 30 both to register and to turn out (Vowles 2015a). An age gradient in turnout is one of the most consistent findings in turnout research everywhere. As voters age, they participate in greater numbers. As turnout declines among the young, a 'footprint' remains that sets a lower baseline (Franklin 2004). Collectively, each generation starts from a lower baseline set by the habits its members acquired when young. As of 2014, in terms of enrolment, the ageing effect promoting voting as people get older appears to have become weaker among the 30–39 group, although until the next election we cannot be sure if this was a temporary phenomenon.

The age gap in turnout could be a constant. This would mean that turnout decline from one election to the next would be the responsibility of all age groups, with each group's turnout rate falling in tandem. Alternatively, turnout decline might be more strongly associated with the young, because their habits are less embedded and they are more sensitive to electoral contexts that might discourage voting (Franklin 2004). That is, as turnout goes down (or up), the age gap widens (or narrows), increasing or decreasing the bias towards older voters in the electorate. Figure 11.2

shows that this appears to be what has been happening in New Zealand since 1996. It is based on data taken from the official record, both from NZES respondents and non-respondents since 1996, and so suffers from no non-response bias. Focusing on people aged 25–65, Figure 11.2 reveals that in 1996, when the percentage of valid votes cast of the electoral roll was just over 78 per cent, a person aged 65 was about 16 per cent more likely to vote than someone aged 25. In 2011, when the valid vote/eligible turnout was down to 68 per cent, the 65–25 turnout gap was about 30 points. The figure shows a clear pattern of an increasing turnout gap between younger and older people as the percentage of valid votes decreases. If we were to take into account the enrolment gap displayed in Figure 11.1, the picture would be even worse (see Vowles 2015a).

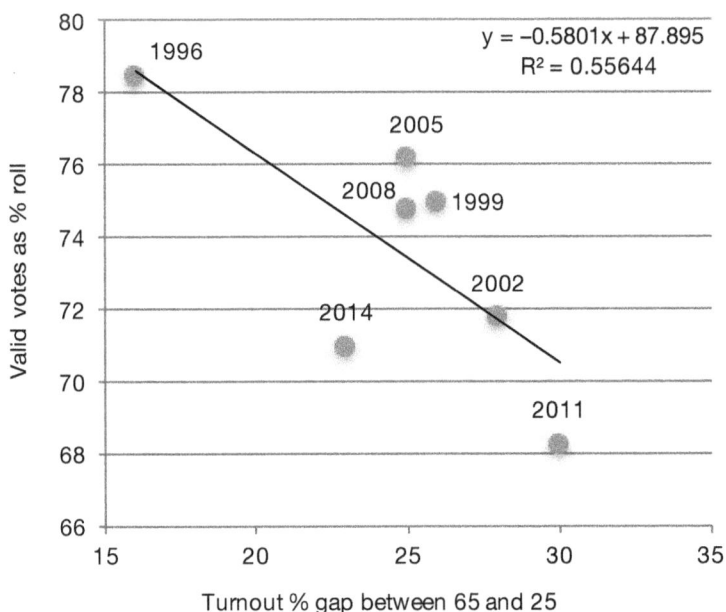

Figure 11.2: Age bias and turnout in New Zealand, 1996–2014

Note: The estimates are derived from logistic regressions of age and age-squared for each of the elections covered.

Source: For details of the data used here see Vowles 2015a: 295.

Widening our analysis further and returning our attention to the 2014 election, Figure 11.3 displays turnout behaviour by gender over the age gradient. Previous research on turnout based on NZES data has found no recent gender differences (Coffé 2013a; Vowles 1993). However, recent larger-sample General Social Survey data indicates that women are slightly more likely to vote than men (Statistics New Zealand 2014d). Here, using a new 'big data' sample of 30,000 people from the electoral rolls in 2014, again based on official voting data alone, we can bring in both age and gender. Figure 11.3 shows that young men are less likely to vote than young women, and this difference can be identified well into the 40–50 age bracket (see Appendix, Table 11.A1). We are unable to infer the extent to which these differences are based on the life-cycle events or are generational, but they do indicate that there is good reason to be concerned about low voter turnout amongst the young, and in particular among young men.

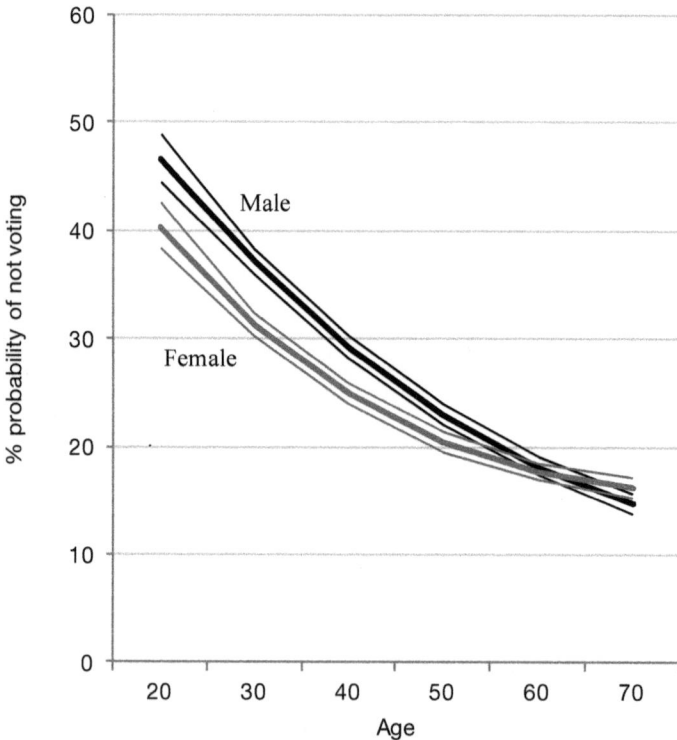

Figure 11.3: Non-voting by gender, 2014
Source: Appendix, Table 11.A1.

Our 'big data' contains few other individual-level variables, so we must return to the 2014 NZES for a more fully specified model (for the details, see Appendix, Table 11.A2). This model adds ethnicity, education, relative income and the assets scale, making it possible for us to address the question of inequality. One surprise emerges: relative income is not significant (nor is household income, which measures income more accurately but has more missing data). Indeed, exploration of NZES data since 1996 indicates that household income has little or no relationship with turnout. However, this finding is not consistent with other survey evidence, again based on a larger sample (N=8,500) and a higher response rate. Statistics New Zealand's General Social Survey has found that perceptions of income inadequacy correlated with reported not voting in 2011 and 2014, as did personal income, with people who felt they did not have enough money to meet everyday needs and with those with lower income being less likely to vote. (Statistics New Zealand 2014d).

Since 2011 and 2014, the NZES has asked questions about asset ownership, which comes through as a strong predictor: those with few assets are less likely to vote. Education and ethnicity also have significant effects. Those with a university degree are significantly more likely to vote than those holding any other post-school qualification. Compared with Europeans, those with a Māori and Asian background are significantly less likely to vote than Europeans.

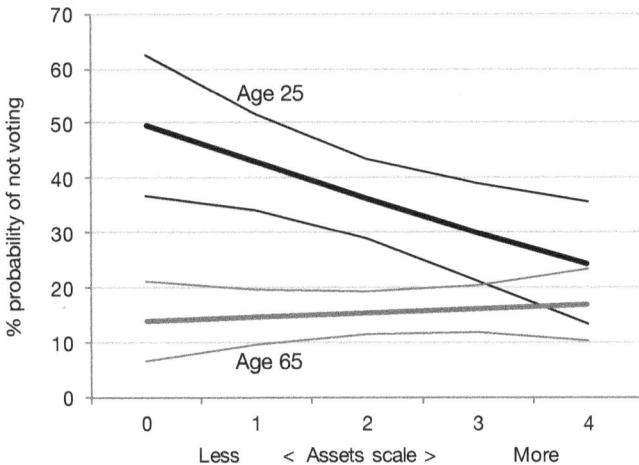

Figure 11.4: Probability of not voting according to number of asset types among 25 and 65 year olds
Source: Appendix, Table 11.A2.

We expected to find a relationship between ownership of assets and age; after all, people tend to acquire more assets as they grow older. Returning to the question of young voters, interacting age with the assets scale shows that ownership of assets predominantly affects the young (Figure 11.4).

Young people who begin adult life with significant assets are almost as likely to vote as people at 65. At 65, asset ownership makes little or no difference to turnout. The young who are asset poor face increasing difficulties in accumulating assets; many face repayment of loans for education, and purchasing a first home is becoming increasingly out of reach. The response of many is to fail to vote; roughly half of asset-less people around 25 years old. Again, this does not take into account the effects of non-enrolment, also concentrated among the young.

Figure 11.5 provides the estimates for ethnicity and education, consistent with well-known findings from previous New Zealand elections and elections in other countries (Vowles 2014a, 2015a). These findings mirror those of the Electoral Commission's post-election survey that found Pākehā voters and those over 50 most likely to vote. One explanation for the low voting turnout among ethnic minorities and young people may be a lack of understanding of the process. The commission's analysis of 1,310 respondents found that while the vast majority of respondents (93 per cent) had a good understanding of the voting process, of the 7 per cent that said they had a poor or very poor understanding of the process a significant proportion were those of Pasifika and Asian ethnicity and those aged 18–29 (Electoral Commission 2014c).

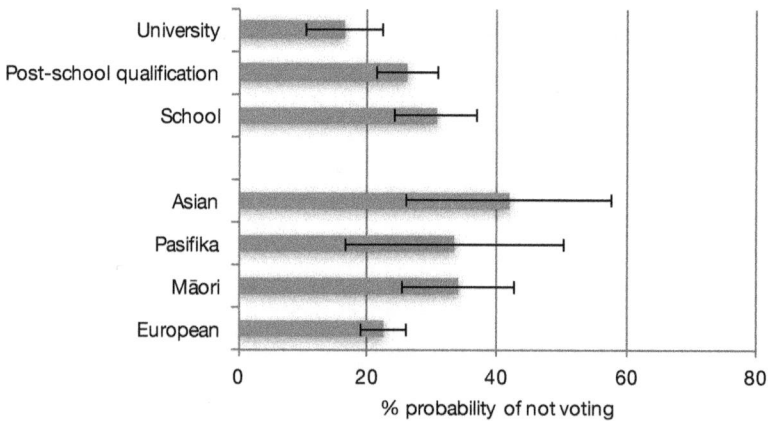

Figure 11.5: Not voting, ethnicity and education
Source: Appendix, Table 11.A2.

Our analysis of turnout among voters in the Māori electorates was presented in Chapter 10. Here we examine people who identify as Māori in both general and Māori electorates and compare them to other ethnic groups. While the confidence intervals slightly overlap, there is a clear difference between turnout among Europeans and among Māori and Asians in New Zealand. The Pasifika sub-sample is too small for any confidence in this estimate. As for education, the main difference is that those with a university degree are less likely to be found among non-voters.

We have seen above that a widening age gap does appear to be associated with lower levels of turnout. A widening income gap would confirm that turnout bias is also increasing between income groups. But as noted above, household income does not appear to have had consistent effects at any election since 1996. Our measure of household income is pre-tax and transfers, and does not take account of other differences between households, such as between those who own their homes mortgage free, those with a mortgage and those who rent. It may therefore not be a good indicator of people's circumstances.

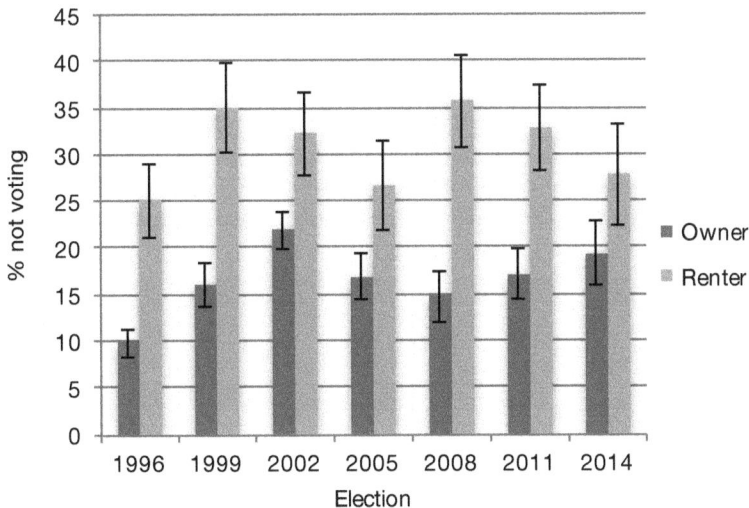

Figure 11.6: Home ownership, renting and roll-based turnout, 1996–2014
Source: New Zealand Election Study 1996–2014.

Since the NZES began to estimate differences in assets between households in 2011, differences with regard to this aspect of inequality have emerged, as described above. Unfortunately, the only information about assets we have before 2011 is home ownership. Figure 11.6 shows that since 1996, those renting their home have always been significantly less likely to vote than home owners. But there is no trend towards a greater gap between owners and renters associated with turnout decline. It is worth noting that home ownership has been declining in New Zealand over this period. Nonetheless, particularly since 2008 the turnout gap between renters and owners appears to have narrowed.

Another angle is to inquire what party non-voters might have chosen had they voted, although we are limited to the non-voters who responded to the NZES. Various studies in the international literature address this question. The 2014 NZES asked no question to directly collect such information. Instead, following Bernhagen and Marsh (2007) we use a process called multiple imputation to estimate the hypothetical probabilities of non-voters voting for the various parties, defining non-voters as having 'missing values'. We then generated a series of statistical models based on various models of vote choice, and examined the results. Most models found the Labour vote share almost identical to that recorded among voters. The same applied to the Green Party. However, National did consistently score a lower hypothetical vote share among the non-voters. The parties that did slightly better among non-voters than among voters were smaller parties, particularly the Māori Party and Internet-MANA, presumably reflecting the high number of non-voters among Māori. New Zealand First and the Conservative Party also did marginally better than among actual voters (Appendix, Table 11.A3). Had non-voters actually voted, the result of the election would have been little different, although government formation might have been somewhat more complicated. Details of the modelling behind these estimates can be found in the section of the Appendix for this chapter.

Addressing the problem of voter turnout

A commitment to finding solutions to low voter turnout depends on whether or not one sees it as a 'problem'. In 2013, there was a brief discussion of compulsory voting, in part a result of the Australian election (Curtin 2013b). The same 'moment' occurred again in July 2016 when Australian elections expert Antony Green visited New Zealand and advocated compulsory voting on television interview program *The Nation* (2016). Compulsory voting was picked up as a topic of interest at the 'Valuing our Vote' conference in 2014 (Farrell 2014). Chief Electoral Officer Robert Peden argued that the idea of compulsory voting had merit, but it was not a silver bullet (Radio New Zealand 2014d). Similar discussions have been had in the United Kingdom over the past decade (Birch 2009; Keaney and Rogers 2006).

Technically, Australia's electoral law requires all voters to attend a polling place rather than actually cast a vote. Most fulfil this obligation and turnout rates average about 94 per cent; they are even higher if informal votes are also counted. Some libertarian-leaning Australian commentators have questioned the paradox of having a compulsory voting attendance system in a democracy. Others question whether it is an effective cure for non-voting (Franklin 1999; for a counter perspective see Hill 2011). However, compulsory voting does have some advantages. If enforced, it significantly enhances turnout, and means that political parties of all persuasions have an incentive to appeal to as many voters as possible, whereas in a voluntary system parties might choose to target only those voters they expect will turn out (Birch 2009; Curtin 2013b; Hill 2002).

The New Zealand Electoral Commission takes the position that 'New Zealanders should vote because they want to vote, not because they have to' (Radio New Zealand 2014d). Similar sentiments were apparent in a debate on the issue in 2013 in New Zealand's weekly news magazine *The Listener*. The example of Australia tends to be criticised as less than desirable because of declining rates of enrolment and high rates of informal voting (Radio New Zealand 2014c). However, there is no way of knowing the reasons why people choose to spoil their ballot papers. Anecdotal evidence has suggested that some voters spoil their papers as a form of political protest (Green 2004, 2011; Orr 2015), while this kind of 'protest' can also take the form of non-voting in voluntary systems.

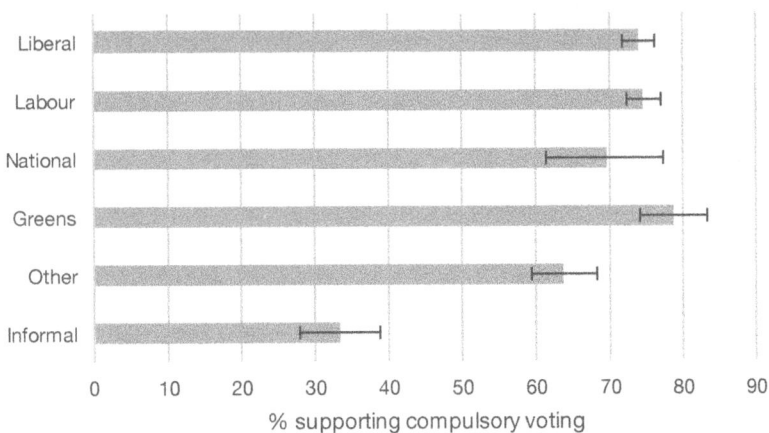

Figure 11.7: Percentage support for compulsory voting in Australia by Lower House vote, 2013

Source: Australian Election Study 2013.

The Australian Election Study has asked respondents about support for compulsory voting since 1967, and consistently since 1993. Over that time, those in favour has ranged from a low of 64 per cent in 1987 to a high of 77 per cent in 1969 and 2007. In 2013, 70 per cent of respondents supported compulsory voting (ANU 2014: 33). In 2013, support for compulsory voting sat at over 70 per cent for those who voted Liberal–National, Labour and Green. Those least likely to support compulsory voting supported independents, minor parties other than the Greens, or either voted informally or did not vote (Australian Election Study 2013).

Support for compulsory voting is lower in New Zealand than Australia. As Figure 11.8 shows, Labour voters are most supportive of compulsory voting, with more than 60 per cent of the Labour voters supporting compulsory voting. Support is lowest among the group of 'other' voters and National voters. Among National voters, only around 45 per cent support the idea of compulsory voting.

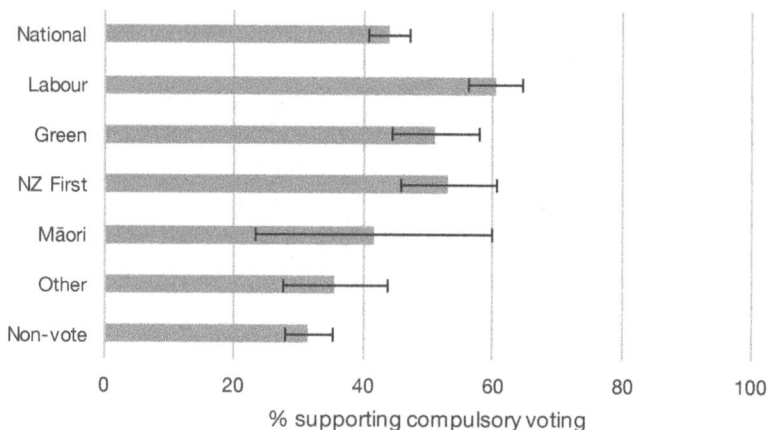

Figure 11.8: Percentage support for compulsory voting in New Zealand by party vote, 2014

Note: Excludes 'don't know' answers, the numbers of which were very small.

Source: New Zealand Election Study 2014.

The absence of compulsory voting puts more emphasis on parties' efforts to mobilise voters. The impact of party mobilisation efforts has become more central to the investigation of voter turnout in recent decades, with most showing that party mobilisation efforts can increase the willingness of voters to turn out and vote (for example, Karp, Banducci and Bowler 2008). In addition to greater efficiency and building a personal vote, efforts to 'get out the vote' are likely to pay the greatest dividends in elections that typically have low voter turnout. While the expectation is that mobilisation is more likely to be effective in systems like first past the post, proportional representation systems may also produce higher turnout because votes count wherever they are cast, and so both major and minor parties are incentivised to maximise a proportional representation vote.

Analysis of NZES data (Figure 11.9) indicates that the degree of contact experienced by respondents declined from 1993, reaching a low point in 2002, in tandem with turnout decline. Since then, the use of both personal visits and telephone contact has incrementally increased. These traditional modes of contact have been supplemented by email and social media options since 2011, but these have not replaced the work of party activists and candidates contacting voters in person.

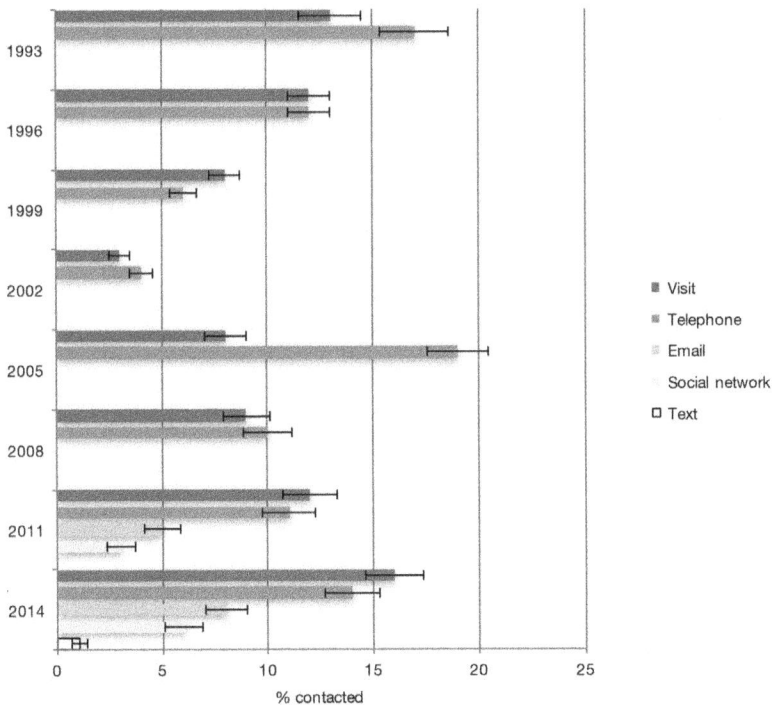

Figure 11.9: Campaign vote mobilisation by political parties, 1993–2014

Note: Contact by email and via social network was asked for the first time in 2011. Contact via text was only included in the most recent 2014 survey.

Source: New Zealand Election Study 1993–2014.

Party commitment to mobilisation is confirmed by Labour Party campaign director Dave Talbot. Labour was committed to a grassroots campaign to mobilise those who did not turn out in 2011; as he put it, 'To shift people who are reluctant voters you need to make personal connections. They're harder to reach via traditional media, so you have to get to them face to face' (Talbot, cited in Kirk 2014). By July 2014, the Labour campaign team claimed to have made five times more phone calls than it had at the same point in the previous campaign, surpassing the 200,000 mark (Kirk 2014). As we saw above, a turnout gap associated with renting or owning a home has not opened up along with turnout decline since 1996. If Labour was making more effective efforts to mobilise renters and beneficiaries, this may be one reason why. Meanwhile, on the National side, there had been much discussion of the decreased turnout in safe National seats in 2011. Prime minister John Key used the 2014 party conference to urge the party faithful to work to end complacency in safe National seats, and similar calls were made by Key and campaign director Steven Joyce throughout the campaign (Kirk 2014).

In Chapter 5, we presented evidence that the distribution of party funding and campaign expenditures between parties is far from creating a 'level playing field'. A key resource that can offset the financial advantages of large donations are party members; perhaps they can offset the advantages of 'big money' (Edwards 2008). There were claims that Labour party membership significantly increased as a result of the leadership campaign that elected David Cunliffe late in 2013. Party members have become able to vote in the Labour leadership elections since 2012, giving people an incentive to join. If it had more members to draw on, Labour would therefore be in a better position to beat National on the ground. Sophisticated 'micro-targeting' of voters might also have given Labour a slight edge in 2014, but National was not far behind (Salmond 2015). The National Party also claims a significant membership and on-the-ground activity. As no membership data is available for either party, we cannot compare. The most important test is active membership—those who are prepared to canvass or make telephone calls on behalf of a party. We can break down the personal and telephone contacts by party during the 2014 campaign as reported by NZES respondents. Figure 11.10 shows that Labour and National probably differed very little in their abilities to get their troops out on the ground or on the telephone. A larger and more active membership would have helped to offset the party-funding imbalance between the two main parties. However, in 2014 there was no apparent activist advantage for Labour compared with National. In terms of campaign resources, there is thus no doubt that 2014 was an unequal election. Figure 11.10 also displays Green and New Zealand First contacts. The percentage of NZES respondents who were contacted by either of the minor parties is, as expected, significantly lower than for the two main parties.

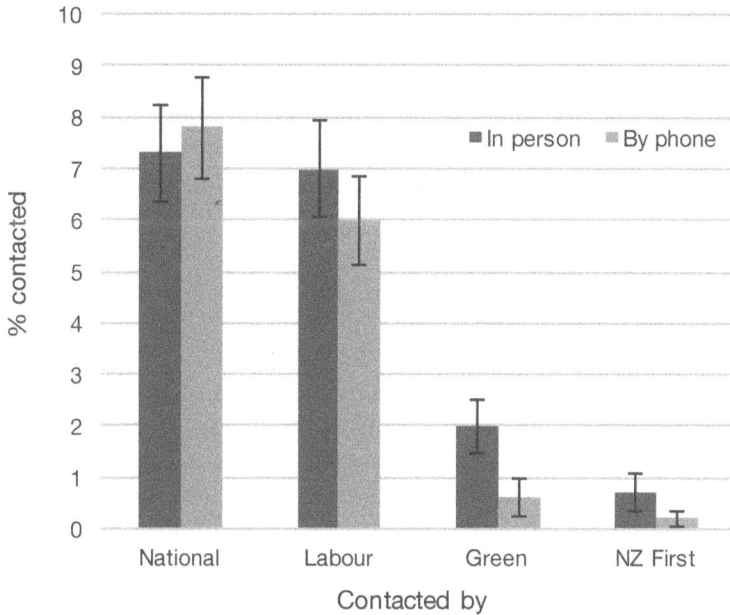

Figure 11.10: Personal visits and telephone contacts by party, 2014 election campaign

Source: New Zealand Election Study 2014.

As has been the case in Australia, third parties were also involved in campaigns to 'Get Out and Vote' in New Zealand in 2014. Coordinated by the New Zealand Council of Trade Unions, several unions combined to donate $220,000 for the campaign 'Get Out and Vote'. More than 5,000 volunteers and several paid staff were located at call centres across the country, working through a database of 100,000 union members (Armstrong 2014d). Campaign manager Conor Twyford said there was concern about the implications of a low voter turnout 'for democracy in general' but also for potential risks to people's industrial, social, economic and political rights.

Generation Zero and RockEnrol were particularly focused on getting young people engaged with the process of voting, without promoting any particular party. The former's central purpose was to lobby political parties to adopt policies to drastically cut carbon pollution. In July 2014, the group released their report titled 'The Big Ask', calling on political parties to set up an independent climate change commission and introduce carbon budgets (Generation Zero 2014). RockEnrol, derived from a similar organisational model in the United States, organised a series of events in the months leading up to the election including concerts and house parties featuring local talent and the support of Lorde. The concerts were free but only for those who had enrolled to vote, with the organisers emphasising the need to mobilise young people because the low turnout amongst that age cohort 'shows a real inequality and disconnect with how youth are being represented in Parliament' (McAllen 2014). Both organisations made significant use of new media to promote awareness and mobilise voters. However, social media was not a panacea. Laura O'Connell-Rapira, one of RockEnrol's founders, put it that part of the problem was the lack of political education in New Zealand schools: 'Unless you actively seek out what MMP [Mixed Member Proportional] means, how the government works and what your vote does you won't see the connection with who controls your driving age, or how much you can drink' (McAllen 2014). Analysis of the 2014 NZES indicates that texts, emails and social media contacts had no significant effects on turnout in 2014, either directly or as mediated by friends or other personal contacts forwarding relevant links to political content.

Automatic registration is a reform increasingly applied elsewhere but not yet given serious consideration in New Zealand. People could be automatically placed on the rolls where government data clearly indicates where they are living. Nearly 29,000 special votes were disallowed at the 2014 election, in most cases because those who cast them did not have their names on the electoral roll. If automatically registered, as many could have been, those people could have had their party vote counted. The feasibility of automatic registration in New Zealand is often questioned because of the need for people of Māori descent to opt for the general or Māori rolls. In order to cast an electorate vote, those enrolled automatically would still need to be contacted and respond in order to declare whether or not they should go on to the general or Māori rolls. But this is not a barrier that should prevent them from being registered to cast a party vote.

Modes of political participation

As is widely acknowledged in political science, political participation is not limited to the ballot box (Hayward 2006; Milbrath 1965; Verba, Schlozman and Brady 1995; Vromen et al. 2016). No political scientist would claim that voting is the only significant form of political participation. Alternative pathways may particularly apply to young people, many of whom define politics in ways that go well beyond party politics and that may exclude or minimise the value of voting, focusing more on discussion and voluntary civic engagement. Young people may seek out other means, particularly online, in the form of old strategies such as petitions and protests, and newer ones via Facebook, Twitter and Instagram amongst others (Anduiza, Cantijoch and Gallego 2009; Chapman and Coffé 2016; Norris 2001; Ross and Bürger 2014).

Despite turnout decline, voting remains the act of participation the largest number of people are likely to engage in. Those who are not voting may find other forms they consider equally valid that they believe can substitute for casting a ballot. Yet it is equally likely that those engaging in other forms of participation will also tend to vote, given that voting may require less energy and commitment than going on a protest march. The 2014 NZES included questions about various acts of participation. The results of a factor analysis displayed in Figure 11.11 show that activities tend to cluster in two dimensions: direct and indirect. All the forms of participation appear on both dimensions but, with the exception of protests, they are most strongly and clearly related to one or the other.

Direct acts include one-on-one contact with actors. Figure 11.12 shows that 'direct' participation acts are very rare; more than 75 per cent of the sample did not engage in any such activities over the past five years. Most people engaging in 'direct' acts also vote. Indirect acts are more frequent, although again more people vote than engage in any of these indirect activities. Voting is also an 'indirect' act, and tends to be associated with the other acts of indirect participation. Most people who engage in other forms of indirect participation also vote. About 17 per cent of people who engage in one or more alternative acts of indirect participation did not vote in 2014. But the more acts of such alternative indirect participation engaged in, the higher the likelihood of voting.

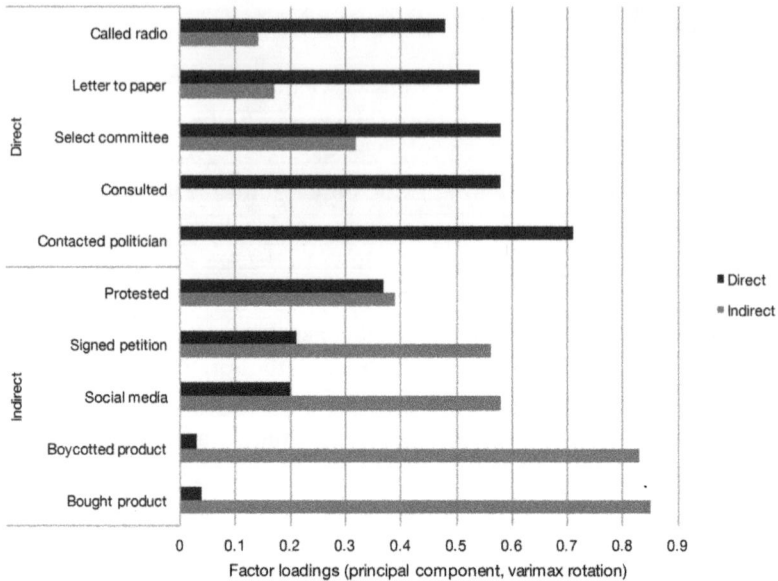

Figure 11.11: Modes of non-electoral political participation

Note: The question was: 'There are various forms of political action that people take to express their views about something the government should or should not do. Have you done any of the following, or would you consider doing them?' Response categories were: have done within the last five years, have done more than five years ago, have not done, might consider, have not done, would never. Forms of action: Signed a petition, made a select committee submission, taken part in a consultation with central or local government, written to a newspaper, gone on a protest march, demonstration, or *hikoi*, phoned a talkback radio show, not bought a product or service for political or ethical reasons, bought something to support its making or sale for political or ethical reasons, used Facebook, Twitter or other social media to promote an issue, been in contact with a politician or government official in person, writing or another way.

Source: New Zealand Election Study 2014.

The role of the internet in relation to young people's political knowledge and participation has attracted considerable scholarly and public attention (Bakker and De Vreese 2011). Pew Research on millennials in the United States reveals that the younger generation of potential voters are more likely to rely on Facebook for their political news rather than local television news, and are less likely to be familiar with more traditional sources of news (Mitchell et al. 2016). However, Facebook links often send users to traditional sources in print or video format. Barack Obama's campaign team's use of Facebook, Twitter and YouTube in the 2008 presidential election and the apparent increase in youth turnout went on to spark much discussion (Bakker and de Vreese 2011; Chen 2010, 2015; Curtin 2010).

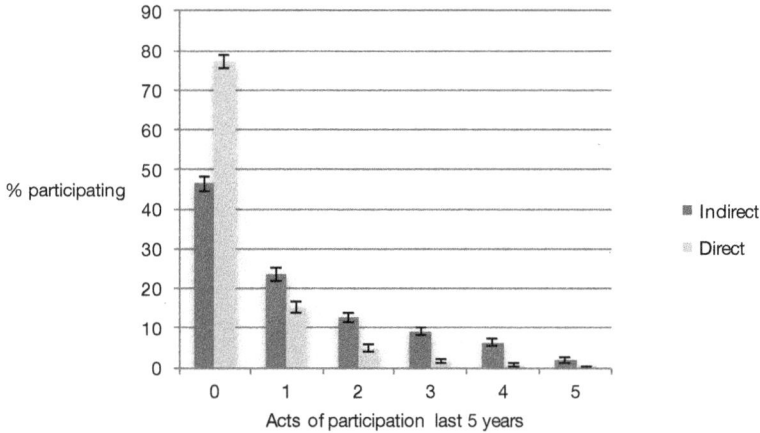

Figure 11.12: Acts of direct and indirect participation over the last five years
Source: New Zealand Election Study 2014.

We asked respondents about their internet use in the 2014 election campaign, although questions focused on blogs and YouTube rather than Facebook and Twitter. Only 6 per cent of respondents visited YouTube (14 per cent of those aged 18–30 did so) while 6 per cent accessed a political blog (with 12 per cent of 18–30-year-olds accessing information in this way). Young people thus tended to check blogs and YouTube more frequently for election information than the average.

When looking at internet usage more generally, Figure 11.13 shows that those respondents aged 18–30 are more likely than those over 65 to have internet access and appear significantly more likely to use it to gather information on the election. However, internet use is not limited to those labelled 'millennials'. It is apparent that those aged 31–45 also access the internet for political information, suggesting that parties would get good value from a multimedia strategy that reaches all voters. Although the numbers are relatively small, they reflect the Electoral Commission's findings, which showed those aged 18–29 were more likely to notice election advertising via social media, websites, signs and bus shelters (Electoral Commission 2014e). Those aged 30–49 were more likely to notice advertising on television, while those aged 50 years plus were likely to notice advertising via newspapers and pamphlets or fliers. Analysis of social media participation in the 2011 election in New Zealand indicated a tendency for top-down use by political parties (Murchison 2015; Ross and Bürger 2014). Young voters were more likely than those over 35 to use social media to engage in political activities and to source their political news (Diesing, cited in Murchison 2015: 527).

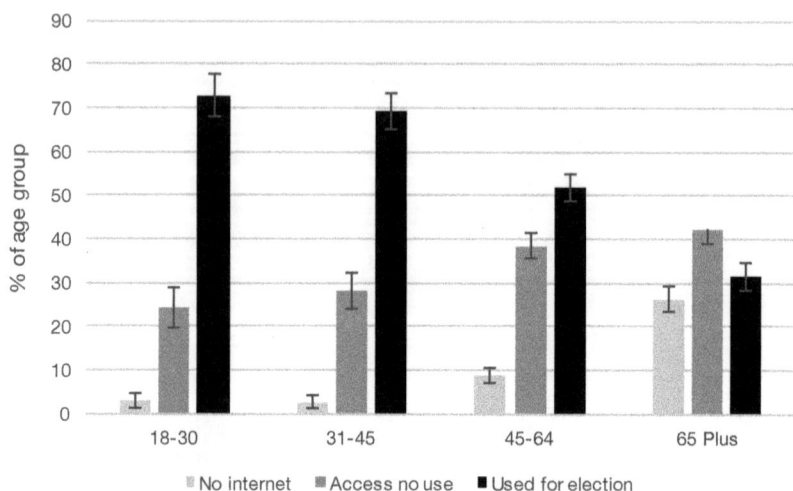

Figure 11.13: Percentage of respondents using the internet for election information, by age group
Source: New Zealand Election Study 2014.

In 2014, all the major and substantial small parties had Facebook pages. With 49,300 likes, the Greens were significantly more popular than the rest. The Internet Party was in second place with 19,100 likes. However, liking numbers do not always lead to success. The Pākehā Party was a Facebook phenomenon that received 42,000 likes within a month of going live in July 2013. Much of the discussion that ensued focused on whether the party was racist or not (Edwards 2014e; Manhire 2013), and whether 'liking' a page constituted a political activity. The party remains unregistered but still maintains a Facebook presence.

Media analysis from July 2014 indicates that in terms of engagement, Labour (16,000 fans) and the Greens were most popular among those aged 25–34 years of age, while the National Party appealed to a broader age group, those between 18 and 34 (14,000 fans). ACT NZ and the Internet Party both had a younger following. ACT's was significantly smaller at 2,000 fans, with the largest chunk of its engaged audience falling in the 18–24-year-old category, whereas the Māori Party appealed to those aged between 25 and 44. The MANA Party appeared to have the oldest Facebook audience among Kiwi political parties, appealing for the most part to 45–54 year olds (Venuto 2014).

The 2014 campaign was different to previous elections on the social media front. Social media was proclaimed to be the 'new campaign trail' (Gulliver 2014). Twitter was said to have made 'everyone a political pundit'. The *New Zealand Herald* published the top 100 tweeters to follow, including journalists, bloggers, politicians, comedians and a range of semi-anonymous others (Edwards 2014f). The 2014 election was also labelled the 'selfie' election (Murchison 2015). The Electoral Commission published guidelines on the appropriate use of the selfie during voting (Electoral Commission 2014e). Prime minister Key proved himself to be a popular selfie subject (Gulliver 2014). It was the Greens that were judged to be the most social media savvy party in the campaign (Manning 2014; Venuto 2014).

Given that social media appears to be pervasive in the lives of young people, many go on to make a case that voting should be made possible on the internet. We asked respondents about their preference for online voting versus the current polling booth option, and their confidence in the security of online voting. Figure 11.14 shows how the different age groups responded. Younger voters were more open to the use of online voting than the old. Around half of the respondents under 45 were sufficiently comfortable with the security and privacy of online voting. There is considerably less support for the online option amongst older respondents: only 20 per cent would opt for online voting if given the option. In 2013, the government established an independent working party to consider the feasibility of online voting in local elections, with a possible trial in 2016. Despite the working party recommending a trial, the government decided against this option, citing security issues for its decision (Radio New Zealand 2016). Online voting in New Zealand is therefore 'on hold'. This caution may be justified.

When asked if online voting would have changed one's likelihood of voting, 69 per cent of NZES respondents said it would have made no difference, 14 per cent that they would have been more likely to vote, offset by 10 per cent who said online voting would make them less likely to do so. The rest did not know. This suggests that online voting does not necessarily lead to significantly higher turnout, even among the young. Postal voting for New Zealand local elections was introduced to make voting easier and more convenient, but after a brief upswing, turnout continued downward. Some suggest that online voting may enhance rather than reduce turnout bias towards those with more resources. Were online voting to be adopted and opportunities to vote in person reduced, as has been the case with postal voting in local elections, such biases could be further exacerbated.

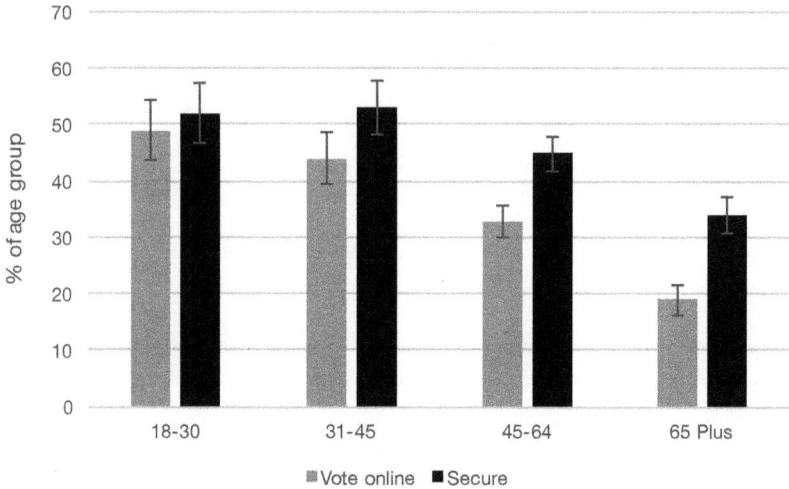

Figure 11.14: Interest in online voting by age groups (in percentages)

Note: The questions were: 'If you had a choice between voting on the internet or voting at a polling place, which of the two would you prefer?'; and 'If you were able to vote online, how confident would you be about the security and privacy of doing so?' For the second question, the chart indicates the percentage of those very confident or fairly confident in the security of online voting.

Source: New Zealand Election Study 2014.

Norway's experience of internet voting in local elections in 2011 found no turnout increase but also no biasing effects (Segaard, Baldersheim and Saglie 2013). Two sources report that Estonian experience has led to a small increase in turnout and no biasing effects (Madise and Vinkel 2014). Fears of biases have receded as uptake has increased (Vassil et al. 2016). But there is contrary evidence that online voters are 'more urban, richer, and better-educated than conventional voters and non-voters' (Lust 2015). Methodologically, when using observational data, the effects of internet voting are difficult to establish in a robust fashion due to the self-selection of those who choose to use it or not; experimental evidence comparing randomly assigned treatment and non-treatment effects would be preferable, but that raises questions of external validity. Of most importance, there is a broader consensus that the security of internet voting is poor and, that by the very nature of the technology, there is no easy fix (for example, Springall et al. 2014). At best, internet voting could enhance turnout slightly and perhaps make existing biases no worse, but its promise is modest at best.

What else can be done to reduce 'inequalities' in turnout? The Electoral Commission's survey findings reveal that the second biggest reason given for why people did not vote was a lack of interest: 27 per cent of non-voters said that they did not vote because of a lack of interest, up from 21 per cent in 2011 (Electoral Commission 2014c). The 2014 NZES makes it possible to classify non-voters into those who chose not to vote (26 per cent), those who didn't get around to it (28 per cent) and those who indicated in their survey response that they voted, but in fact did not do so according to the official record (39 per cent).

Both online and mainstream media pointed to young people's political apathy (Forschler 2014; M. Robinson 2014; Whelan and Hunt 2014). Certainly, the 2014 NZES finds significant relationships between age and political interest and political knowledge: the young have less of both than the old. But as political participation is learned behaviour, one would not expect anything else. Internationally, young people's lower rates of voting participation have often been attributed to declining interest in politics over time. Qualitative research conducted in Britain indicates that it is not that young people are disinterested in politics as such, but rather they feel 'disillusioned with, and alienated from formal politics' (O'Toole et al. 2005: 59; see also Dermody, Hanmer-Lloyd and Scullion 2010; Henn, Weinstein and Wring 2002). Other studies have also refuted the accusations that young people are politically apathetic (Loader 2007). Yet doubts remain about the kinds of alternative politics young people may identify as relevant, particularly where actions involved are more 'expressive' than 'instrumental'. Talk among groups of like-minded people does not necessarily translate into behaviour that may affect the actions of governments.

The 2014 NZES reveals that young people were unlikely to attend political meetings or rallies during the campaign, but respondents from other age groups were equally unlikely to do so. Similarly, as shown in Figure 11.15, young people said they discussed politics as much as older people. While the number of respondents under 30 was comparatively small, compared with the 46 plus and 65 plus categories, we see that a considerable percentage of young people talked about politics during the election campaign.

Why does this engagement in political discussions amongst those under 30 not translate into a vote on election day? As noted above, talk is not the same as action. Young voters are more likely to feel alienated or ambivalent about the value of voting than those who are older. Drawing on various NZES questions, we find that in New Zealand in 2014 young people were significantly less likely to believe that their votes would 'count', a little less likely to believe that voting makes a difference and that who is in power can make a difference, and a little more likely to believe that globalisation reduces government's 'room for manoeuvre'. Qualitative analysis could no doubt provide further evidence and insight (for example, Vromen et al. 2016). Lower turnout might also relate to more rational decisions about the lack of electoral competitiveness in 2014 or a sense that few of the parties had much to offer younger voters.

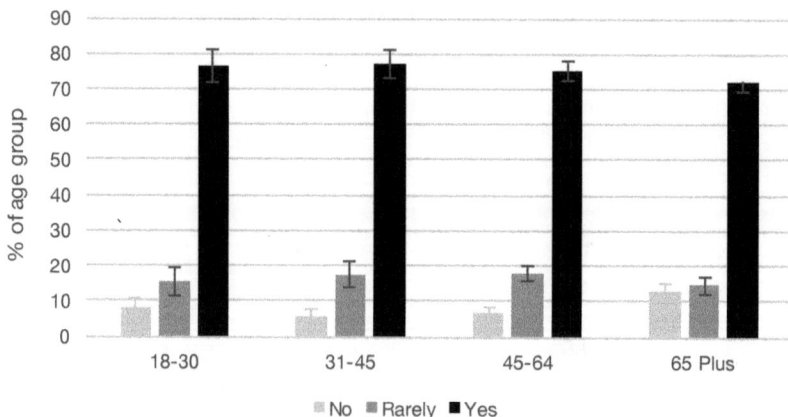

Figure 11.15: Discussing politics by age group (in percentages)

Note: The percentage referring to discussing politics ('Yes') combines those who said they discussed politics either occasionally or frequently.

Source: New Zealand Election Study 2014.

Conclusion

In 1971, National MP George Gair wrote in the *Nelson Evening Mail* that 'the chances of democracy failing … by a break in the atomic stalemate … is far less than the chances of us falling victim to the consequence of a suffocating apathy … Democracy belongs to the people, or it is not a democracy' (cited in Curtin 2013b). Forty years on, in 2011, National prime minister John Key remarked that 'if you don't vote you can't complain' and noted 'our [National] voters largely turned up'.

By 2014, Key and his party strategists were not so confident about their core voter turnout. Both major parties were keen to woo more voters to the ballot box. However, if Labour had imagined they could persuade anything close to a majority of the missing million to vote for them, they would have been sorely disappointed. As has been suggested both in the academic scholarship and in our chapter on the Māori electorates, the relationship between a concern about rising inequality and voter turnout is not straightforward. Those who own a house are more likely to vote than those who rent, but the turnout gap between these two groups has not grown in tandem with turnout decline. The proportion of renters to owners has been changing in favour of the former, making the differences more significant. Low asset ownership among the young is associated with low turnout in 2014, and the age gap is increasing as turnout declines. Because there is limited knowledge about those who are not enrolled to vote, we cannot confidently refute the hypothesis of progressive disempowerment of those on low incomes. But neither can we confirm it.

12

The unequal election

In this study of the 2014 general election in New Zealand, we have examined to what extent and how social and economic inequality shaped the campaign and the election outcome. As explained at the beginning of this book, the New Zealand general election of 2014 was an unequal election in several respects. First, in keeping with our theme, it was an election in which the issue of social and economic inequality and its various implications loomed large, and was only outranked by the economy. Second, the election was unequal in the sense that the National Party was by far the largest party in votes cast and seats won, and in its campaign outspent its main rivals by a considerable margin. Third, the election was unequal since, despite discussions about declining class voting in most post-industrial societies, economic inequalities continued to underpin the social foundations of voting choices between the parties. The traditional left–right dimension remained alive and well in New Zealand politics. But these economic inequalities and their associated patterns of vote choice intersected with and were intensified by social inequalities between women and men and between ethnic groups, most notably between indigenous Māori and the European or Pākehā majority. These group-based claims for rights interacted with and cut across debate about social and economic equalities, leading to criticisms of an excessive focus on 'identity politics', particularly within the opposition Labour Party.

Equality and inequality are complex concepts. Equality of respect is a starting point, implying equal rights and opportunities. Equal outcomes for all is an impossible goal, but too much inequality of outcomes makes it very difficult to promote equality of opportunity. Because recognition of equality has been delayed for some groups, collective claims for corrective action can confuse a discourse in which the primary definition of rights has tended to be individualist.

While the steep increase in social and economic inequality in New Zealand took place in the late 1980s and early 1990s, public concern about inequality was stronger and much more widespread in 2014 than at any recent election. The concern was generated by an international debate picked up by local commentators, and encouraged by an increased flow of information about poverty in New Zealand and its implications for health and life chances. But compared with other countries, New Zealand's experience of the consequences of inequality was less intense. Throughout the fall-out from the global financial crisis (GFC) after 2008, New Zealand did not become a poorer country and income inequality did not appreciably increase. For most New Zealanders, the debate on the global crisis and growing economic inequality was rhetorical. Even for those affected by low incomes, poor housing, related health consequences and family stresses and strains, experience of inequality was not easily and simply translated into political preferences and behaviour. Inequality was deemed an important issue, but only by a minority. Those among this minority believed that the election should have focused far more on the problem, or, at least, that the parties of the centre-left should have been able to gather more votes than they did. The main theme of this book has been to ask why not? In other words, why did inequality—an issue traditionally 'owned' by Labour—not result in a greater electoral success for that party?

According to one theory about how voting works, people are expected to vote for the party they perceive as best able to address the issue that those people consider most salient. This did not happen in New Zealand in the 2014 election for various reasons. The perceived competence of the sets of parties presenting themselves as alternative governments stands out most clearly. Using the best professional advice, the National Party had groomed John Key as a communicator and carefully developed his public image, although Key himself must take some credit for having an engaging personality to begin with.

Key and his party were also fortunate enough to take office after rather than before the GFC had hit New Zealand. With the advantage of low levels of public debt paid down by previous governments, the Key Government could maintain the modest stimulus package begun under

Labour that partly insulated New Zealand from the crisis. The economic shock was less intense than elsewhere, as New Zealand's biggest export markets were relatively less affected by the crisis than others. The major earthquake that hit the city of Christchurch in February 2011 gave the government another opportunity to take charge and appear to be successfully dealing with another crisis. As we showed in Chapter 5, there was an understandable cognitive bias among voters in their perceptions of National's competence that made it very difficult to shift its voters in other directions.

One of the most telling tables in this book is Table 1.3, in Chapter 1. It shows that about one third of the New Zealand Election Study (NZES) sample considered the economy the most important issue in the 2014 election. Of those, nearly 80 per cent favoured National as the party best able to manage the economy. Even more important, for those concerned about questions related to governance, 63 per cent favoured National and only a derisory 5 per cent favoured Labour. Worse (for Labour), while Labour was the most preferred party to address the problem of inequality in principle, and children and families, National was rated better in other areas of practical policy such as housing and jobs among those who thought those issues important. While Labour was favoured by 41 per cent as best to address inequality, this was short of a majority; 12 per cent said none, and 21 per cent the Green Party. Given Labour's traditions, one might have expected greater confidence in its commitment to combat inequality. But it was the Fourth Labour Government in the 1980s that presided over the steep increase in inequality that continued into the early 1990s under the Bolger-led National Government.

Many would argue that while in government between 1999 and 2008, the Labour Party returned to its social democratic roots and its commitments to fairness and equality (for example, Franks and McAloon 2016). There is reason to concur with this, if only in part. But after 2008, Labour failed to find its feet, went through a parade of leaders, and in 2014 failed to coordinate an alternative coalition of parties that could be presented as a government in waiting. Failing to conduct its own affairs effectively, and failing to signal a pathway to an alternative coalition, Labour fully deserved its poor rating on governance issues. A National Party campaign advertisement portrayed the opposition parties as chaotically trying to row a boat together, going nowhere with oars flailing in all directions. Even those intending to vote for opposition parties found it hard to deny the resonance of that metaphor.

Despite the salience of explanations such as leadership and perceptions of government competence, and the evidence for cognitive bias, the example of the National Government since 2008 still provides a cogent argument for the continued relevance of the economic or median voter model of electoral politics that we outlined in Chapter 3. Retaining the vote of the median voter has been, and continues to be, a major preoccupation of the National Party. Campaigning for office in 2008, John Key had removed almost all possible points of difference between National and Labour that could have provided reasons for voters considering a change to remain with Labour. Labour's reputation for better funding of universal provision of health and education than National, effective at previous elections, had been apparently neutralised by 2014. In office, the government was closely attentive to polling and focus groups, made policy changes accordingly, and introduced some policies that one would expect from a left-leaning party. For example, the 2014 Budget made some gestures towards child poverty, and the National Government introduced a 'material hardship' policy package after the 2014 election. If 2014, like 2011, was a 'valence' election about government competence, it was because positional issues remained in the background. This does not mean positional issues were unimportant; they retain a potential to be mobilised, particularly if the National Party were to move to the right. NZES respondents still put National as far to the right as Labour is to the left. If we had asked respondents where they put John Key, we might have found him placed closer to the centre. In 2017, for National under Prime Minister Bill English, the jury was still out.

NZES estimates of opinions about inequality indicate that values of fairness remain a part of New Zealand political culture. In Chapter 4, we confirmed that social groups shaped by the division of labour and a consequent unequal distribution of wealth and assets continue to provide structure to voting choices in New Zealand. Over and above these differences, ethnicity remains significant. These various divisions are constituted by an inter-related mixture of interests, values and identities. For example, higher education shapes more libertarian attitudes, bringing in the authoritarian–libertarian dimension, associated with Labour and Green voting in particular. Education also affects left–right positions.

Younger people are more attracted to the Green Party. While this may be in part a life-cycle effect, interests and a generational identity at least among a minority of this cohort are likely explanations. The Green Party's appeal is tilted more to those on lower incomes and with fewer assets, but subjective social class tells a slightly different story: those feeling they do not belong to a social class are particularly likely to support the Green Party. Education also appreciably and positively affects the likelihood of voting Green.

By interacting the effects of assets and income, we identified a problem that made a politics of redistribution more difficult to promote successfully in 2014. We expected and found that those with many assets would be less likely to vote Labour than those with few assets, regardless of their incomes. Assets provide people security on an individual and family basis. Those with fewer assets are more exposed to risk and might be expected to support the left even when their incomes rise. However, in 2014, as their incomes rose, people with low assets were not as likely to vote for Labour as we might have expected following that logic. Those with limited assets and high incomes were significantly less likely to support Labour than those with limited assets and low incomes. We did also find a pattern more consistent with expectations when testing our hypothesis against left–right position. In this case, income does not affect the position of those with only one asset, who, all else equal, tend to sit close to the median position. Those with several assets are strongly affected by income; those on high incomes and several assets likely to be well to the right. Stronger partisan mobilisation of left–right orientations could therefore strengthen political support for income redistribution, but only up to a point, as the average New Zealand voter has been moving to the right. The cause of equality requires changes in hearts and minds, and in voting choices. Unless the experience of a successful centre-left coalition pulls people back toward the left, mobilising the left alone will not be enough to strengthen it.

Economic insecurity should be at the heart of an economic model of voting. Perceptions of insecurity in jobs or in one's standard of living had predictable effects: the more vulnerable they perceived themselves, the more likely people tilted to the left. Even so, even the more vulnerable voted in greater numbers for National than for Labour. Insecurity slightly mobilised the New Zealand First vote, but there was no effect on the Green vote. Overall, given the relatively good state of the economy in 2014, modest effects for job insecurity were to be expected. Meanwhile, the social foundations of major party support give the National Party a strong financial footing because of its deep roots in the business community. By contrast, the main opposition parties had fewer resources to campaign and organise, less than parties like the Conservatives and the Internet Party, which were almost entirely funded, in each case, by a single rich donor.

In Chapter 5, we confirmed the effects of cognitive bias in economic voting and a relatively small net economic vote. Previous vote conditioned and reduced the significance of the economic vote in 2014, and positive perceptions of government performance in general outweighed the economy. The 2014 NZES also confirms high levels of confidence and trust in National Party prime minister John Key. This put Key in an excellent position to turn the voters' cognitive biases in his favour and refute the claims made in Hager's book *Dirty Politics* (2014). Using panel data, we found that there was no net change in how much people liked or disliked John Key between 2011 and 2014. Nonetheless, the NZES found only 6 per cent of respondents believing that the allegations contained no truth. The largest group of respondents ticked 'don't know'. While *Dirty Politics* had no *net* effect on the likelihood of liking or disliking Key, a small but significant number of those who continued to like John Key were less disposed to vote National if they thought there was some truth in *Dirty Politics*. Although the effect was not strong, it was perhaps enough to have robbed National of a single-party majority. But it was only a small bump in the road over which the bandwagon rolled, carrying National to another electoral victory.

We also sought a 'push' factor toward National, associated with disliking the Internet Party that campaigned primarily against the National Party. Some weak effects were found after controlling for other National 'push' factors associated with dislike of Labour's other two potential partners, the Green Party and New Zealand First. Those preferring a Labour to a National government were more disposed to coalitions than those favouring National. Only 10 per cent of those wanting a Labour government held out for a single-party Labour government, compared with 36 per cent of those wanting a National government wishing to see a government without a coalition partner.

In Chapter 6, we investigated how voters responded to the Labour Party's policies and performance. Labour failed abysmally on the latter and its policies failed to bite. Elections are rarely won or lost on policies. Policies can help on the margins and are significant if they can be anchored in identities that resonate with emotions and values. In 2014, Labour had no big policies. It had a 64-page policy document that very few people read. There was no concise pledge card summary of a set of simple and appealing policy proposals, of the sort that had worked well for the party in 1999 and 2002. Many economists approved of the superannuation and capital gains tax proposals, but there were few votes available among this small professional group. Labour's policy to raise the age of New Zealand Superannuation almost certainly lost votes.

An extension of Working For Families would have given extra money to beneficiaries with children. But Labour did not emphasise this policy proposal strongly in the campaign debate, or, at least, failed to communicate it effectively in the face of many distractions. Labour's potential vulnerability on the 'wedge issue' of the Treaty of Waitangi and its implications was neutralised by the National Government's partnership with the Māori Party. Labour kept its conservative voters despite their Treaty opinions, but was already at a low ebb. So-called 'identity' politics relating to Māori and women did not negatively affect the Labour vote. As Achen and Bartels (2016) argue, all politics is identity politics. The conservative male working-class vote that critics of 'identity politics' apparently believe Labour should primarily represent is as much based on its identity as any other social or demographic group.

Returning to our main theme, there was a shift between the 2011 and 2014 election on the issue of inequality. More people had become aware of the problem and were concerned about it. While shifting attitudes to inequality did shape voting choice, they did not deliver Labour an advantage. National voters disliking inequality tended to stay with National. There is no evidence the capital gains tax policy harmed Labour among those already well disposed to the party. The problem with a capital gains tax was more in its inconsistency with Labour's pursuit of aspirational middle-income voters whose investments might be affected. Labour's promise to build 10,000 homes was open to scepticism, given Labour's leadership and performance deficits and the obvious division within the party on these and other policy questions. Big shifts in performance evaluations tend to take place as governments age and lose momentum, and as opposition parties demonstrate a clear capacity to govern. It is obvious that no such shift was apparent at the New Zealand General Election of 2014.

The failure to coordinate with the Green Party was one of Labour's biggest failures. The Green Party campaigned against inequality, but its main thrust was a tax policy that would have shifted the burden of taxation on to producers who pollute, while seeking to maintain the overall tax take at its existing levels. Personal taxes would be reduced, but this would be offset by the increased costs of products produced by polluters. Like a capital gains tax policy, which the Greens also supported, the Greens' tax proposal gained approval from some academic economists but not from the business community. If this was a shift to the right as some assumed, it was not well targeted. When the Green Party got campaign attention, inequality tended not to be its focus.

The Green Party retained a significant pool of votes and would have supported a Labour-led government in efforts to reduce inequality. Were the Green Party to abandon its tilt to the left on inequality and focus on environmental politics alone, as some commentators have advised, Labour could well benefit, but not necessarily the overall left vote. Indeed, our data indicates that the Green Party would probably suffer electorally, because attitudes about environmental protection and social equality cluster together among Green voters. Those advancing the 'realist' school of theory in political behaviour might expect Green voters to follow their party if it cued such a policy shift and focused only on environmental issues (Achen and Bartels 2016; Lenz 2012). But Green Party identification is low, and people tend to move in and out of Green voting. We doubt that many would be cued to follow if the Green party moved to the right.

The biggest barrier in the way of a Green and National accommodation is environmental policy itself. How could the Green Party go into coalition with a party that aspired to strip all principles for environmental protection out of planning law, and was only prevented from doing so by its support partners? A small but still sizeable group of 20 per cent of National voters did see the Green Party as a desirable coalition partner. But if these are 'Blue Greens' voting for the National Party, and apparently available as potential Green voters, their Green credentials are open to scepticism.

The Green Party, like Labour, tends to draw on liberal/libertarian voters. On the other side of this dimension sit the conservative parties, who tend to draw on people with more authoritarian values. New Zealand First is the key player among the parties attracting authoritarian voters, with its voters tending to want less immigration, and hankering for a more conformist and egalitarian past that was much less libertarian and inclusive than New Zealand today. Immigration is another 'wedge' issue from which New Zealand First can benefit and from which Labour might suffer. It is no coincidence that since the 2014 election, Labour, and most recently even the National Government, have been moving somewhat toward New Zealand First in seeking to control or reduce immigration, and to address its apparent effects on the housing market (Walters 2015; Patterson 2016).

The international literature tends to show that women are more to the left than men (see Chapter 9). We therefore expected women to be more in favour of policies to promote equality. The evidence for a gender gap in voting has been inconsistent in New Zealand and only small effects could be found in opinions and behaviour at the 2014 election. On the left–right scale, in 2014 women aligned slightly more to the left than men but the difference was much too small to be statistically significant. While women are more in favour of the Treaty of Waitangi being part of the law than men and more in favour of environmental protection than men, contrary to expectations they are no more or less opposed to inequality. Between the age of 40 and 60, women are more likely to favour expenditure on universal services than men. Younger women are more in favour of targeted benefit expenditure than men or older women. Efforts to increase equality of 'voice' through the representation of women in parliament are stuck with the majority of New Zealanders accepting current levels of about 30 per cent, although women, and in particular younger women, are more likely to wish to see an increase.

Politics among Māori New Zealanders is a unique phenomenon and its parameters have shifted dramatically in the last 20 years. The Māori seats are important because the party that wins them may hold the balance of power in a close election. Most Māori remain more aligned to the left than the right in partisan terms, leading to expectations that increased Māori influence in politics should promote the cause of equality. The Māori Party's support and involvement in the National-led government since 2008 has created tensions that broke the party in two. Māori party politics is now more fragmented than New Zealand politics in general. Successive Treaty settlements have led to a burgeoning Māori economy, but not all can share equally in its benefits, and elements of class politics are emerging around asset ownership. While the Labour Party won six out of the seven Māori seats at the 2014 election, it has not recovered the votes it lost in the aftermath of the passage of the Foreshore and Seabed Act. While the Māori and MANA parties are unlikely to reunite, electorate accommodations announced for the 2017 election could see many Māori Labour MPs at risk of being defeated where MANA or Māori stand aside in favour of the other. But the Māori Party has not ruled out a shift from support of a National to a Labour-led government after the 2017 election if the votes make this possible.

At the beginning of this book, we suggested that inequality could have two effects. The first would be a sharpening of a political conflict between the asset/income 'poor' and the asset/income 'rich'. This would be reflected in greater polarisation between social groups in the party choices of those who identify as group members, with a shift to the left because the median voter has a lower income than the average voter. We have identified several reasons, summarised above, why New Zealand voters' behaviour at the 2014 New Zealand General Election did not confirm these expectations. The second effect would be a decline in turnout among the asset/income poor: a disempowerment thesis. The median voter tends to have more income or assets than the median citizen: the composition of those who vote is socially biased against the poor. By not voting, the asset/income poor do not have their need for policies to improve their living standards recognised by governments of any political stripe.

Chapter 11 confirms aspects of the disempowerment thesis, but only in part. Low assets are associated with not voting, but almost entirely among young voters. More generally, the strongest bias in voting is age, with young people being considerably less likely to vote than older people, and contributing more than their share to non-voting, particularly when overall voting turnout decreases. Estimating how non-voters might have voted, the data show that National would have gained slightly fewer votes, as it would tend not to do as well among non-voters as among voters. Labour and the Green Party would not do better or worse among non-voters than among those who voted. Smaller parties would have benefited most from increased turnout. The turnout gap between home renters and owners has narrowed since 2008. More intense mobilisation of the low-income vote by the Labour Party could be an explanation.

Left out of the model are those eligible to vote who are not enrolled that the NZES cannot sample. We know that the non-enrolled tend to be concentrated among ethnic minorities and the young. Data from the Electoral Commission indicate that a decline in enrolment between 2011 and 2014 was predominantly among those under 40, and perhaps more in Labour-held electorates than in those held by National, questioning the effectiveness of grassroots Labour organisation in getting its potential voters on the rolls. We also find that National mobilisation was probably as strong as that of Labour. Non-enrolment is likely to be associated with residential mobility, and therefore probably more among low income than upper income voters, making Labour's mobilisation effects more difficult than National's. Without incorporating the non-enrolled into our analysis, we cannot be confident that the disempowerment thesis should be rejected.

National won the 2014 election because this was the default option. There were insufficient reasons to change. The upsurge in income inequality had happened 20 or 30 years ago, along with the process that led to electoral system change. The renewed attention to inequality in 2014 was mainly based on talk. This is not to diminish the concerns raised in many quarters about child poverty, poor housing and increasing homelessness, and the accumulating evidence about the harm being caused. But those who were most concerned about inequality were already more likely to vote for the parties of the left.

Looking to the future, New Zealanders, like citizens of all post-industrial nations, live in a context of increasing uncertainty and doubt. The first two decades of the twenty-first century have not been good times for egalitarianism. The GFC hit at a time when centre-left governments were in office in many countries, including New Zealand, Australia and Britain. The destabilising effects of austerity politics in many European countries were later augmented by an unprecedented surge of refugees from Africa and the Middle East, spawning a wave of populism, mostly from the right. Even in the United States, despite a moderately successful economic stimulus in the wake of the 'great recession', populism in the form of Donald Trump's capture of the presidency has shifted the boundaries of political debate.

Against this background, politics in New Zealand is remarkably placid. Because of New Zealand's distance from sources of refugees, immigrants come legally for economic, social or family reasons. Despite high levels of immigration, there is little or no sign of a populist upsurge. Admittedly, New Zealand First shows some signs of increased activity and support. Its seat tally in 2014 was up by three, mainly at the expense of Labour. Winston Peters' capture of the Northland electorate from the National Party as the result of a by-election in March 2015 was unexpected, but as late as mid-2017 there was no sign of a consistent 'follow through' into polling for the party vote. Regional depopulation and lagging rural development may have potential to upset voting patterns in some parts of the country, but there has been little sign of this. The advance of right-wing populism in Europe and the United States has precipitated much political commentary in New Zealand that 'it might happen here'. While New Zealand lacks many of the drivers of resurgent populism, New Zealand First exemplifies the potential for its further advance, and could assume a pivotal position in government formation after the 2017 election.

Not long after the 2014 election, the inflating balloon of the housing market began to become an increasing focus of attention, bringing together concerns about young people and families, increasing inequalities in asset ownership and high immigration, a major contributing factor to the ballooning of housing prices under conditions of poor supply. Immigration continues to boost economic growth, but is generating increasing tension. John Key's resignation as prime minister in December 2016 generated even greater potential to change the political landscape. A commitment to co-ordination between the Labour and Green parties increases confidence in the possibility of an alternative government, albeit offset by the ambiguous position of New Zealand First. The replacement of Labour leader Andrew Little by his popular deputy Jacinda Ardern just seven weeks before the election could make a closer race more likely between the Labour–Green bloc and National and its allies. Thinking purely in terms of party competition, if 2014 was an unequal election, with the National Party firmly in charge, that of 2017 is likely to be a much more equal contest.

References

Achen, Christopher and Larry Bartels. 2016. *Democracy for realists: Why elections do not produce responsive government.* Princeton: Princeton University Press.

Adams, James. 2001. *Party competition and responsible party government.* Ann Arbor: University of Michigan Press.

Adams, James. 2012. Causes and electoral consequences of party policy shifts in multiparty elections: Theoretical results and empirical evidence. *Annual Review of Political Science* 15: 401–19. DOI: 10.1146/annurev-polisci-031710-101450

Adorno, Theodor W., Else Frenkel-Brunswick, Daniel J. Levinson and R. Nevitt Sanford. 1950. *The authoritarian personality.* Oxford: Harpers.

Aimer, Peter. 1989. Travelling together: Party identification and voting in the New Zealand general election of 1987. *Electoral Studies* 8(2): 131–42. DOI: 10.1016/0261-3794(89)90030-9

Aimer, Peter. 1993. Was there a gender gap in New Zealand in 1990? *Political Science* 45(1): 112–21. DOI: 10.1177/003231879304500108

Aimer, Peter. 1998. Old and new party choices. In Jack Vowles, Peter Aimer, Susan Banducci and Jeffrey Karp, eds, *Voters' victory? New Zealand's first election under proportional representation*, 48–64. Auckland: Auckland University Press.

Aimer, Peter. 2014. New Zealand's electoral tides in the 21st century. In Jack Vowles, ed., *The new electoral politics in New Zealand: The significance of the 2011 Election*, 9–25. Wellington: Institute for Governance and Policy Studies.

Albrecht, Johan. 2006. The use of consumption taxes to re-launch green tax reforms. *International Review of Law and Economics* 26(1): 88–103. DOI: 10.1016/j.irle.2006.05.007

Alesina, Alberto and Eliana La Ferrara. 2005. Preferences for redistribution in the land of opportunities. *Journal of Public Economics* 89: 897–931. DOI: 10.1016/j.jpubeco.2004.05.009

Alford, Robert R. 1962. A suggested index of the association of social class and voting. *The Public Opinion Quarterly* 26(3): 417–25. DOI: 10.1086/267115

Altemeyer, Bob. 1988. *Enemies of freedom: Understanding right-wing authoritarianism.* San Francisco: Jossey-Bass.

Anderson, Christopher. 2007. The end of economic voting? Contingency dilemmas and the limits of democratic accountability. *Annual Review of Political Science* 12: 271–96. DOI: 10.1146/annurev.polisci.10.050806.155344

Anderson, Gordon. 1991. The Employment Contracts Act 1991: An employers' charter? *New Zealand Journal of Industrial Relations* 16(2): 127–42.

Anduiza, Eva, Marta Cantijoch and Aina Gallego. 2009. Political participation and the Internet: A field essay. *Information, Communication and Society* 12(6): 860–78. DOI: 10.1080/13691180802282720

Ansell, Ben. 2014. The political economy of ownership: Housing markets and the welfare state. *American Political Science Review* 108(2): 383–402. DOI: 10.1017/S0003055414000045

Armstrong, Jed and Chris McDonald. 2016. Why the drivers of migration matter for the labour market. *Reserve Bank of New Zealand*, AN2016/2. Available at: www.rbnz.govt.nz/research-and-publications/analytical-notes/2016/an2016-02

Armstrong, John. 2014a. Labour's brutal week reveals Achilles heel. *New Zealand Herald,* 26 April.

Armstrong, John. 2014b. Opinion: National tries hard to paint Cunliffe as untrustworthy. *Otago Daily Times,* 1 February. Available at: www.odt.co.nz/news/politics/opinion-national-tries-hard-paint-cunliffe-untrustworthy

Armstrong, John. 2014c. Excitement the mark of a party whose time has come. *New Zealand Herald*, 2 June.

Armstrong, John. 2014d. Parties' final push: Getting punters out to vote. *New Zealand Herald*, 18 September.

Armstrong, John. 2014e. Politics will turn off youth until they find their voice. *New Zealand Herald*, 2 July.

Atkinson, Joe. 2016. The political role of television in New Zealand. In Geoff Kemp, Babak Bahador, Kate McMillan and Chris Rudd, eds, *Politics and the media*, 2nd ed. Auckland: Auckland University Press.

Australian Election Study. 2013. Available at: www.ada.edu.au/ada/01259

Australian Electoral Commission. 2013. 2013 Federal Election downloads and statistics. Available at: www.aec.gov.au/Elections/Federal_Elections/2013/downloads.htm#enrolment

Australian Electoral Commission. 2016. Enrolment statistics. Available at: www.aec.gov.au/Enrolling_to_vote/Enrolment_stats/

Aziz, Omar, Matthew Gibbons, Chris Ball and Emma Gorman. 2012. The effect on household income of government taxation and expenditure in 1988, 1998, 2007 and 2010. *Policy Quarterly* 8(1): 29–38.

Bahadar, Babak, Mark Boyd and Kate Roff. 2016. Media coverage of New Zealand elections 2008–14. In Geoff Kemp, Babak Bahador, Kate McMillan and Chris Rudd, eds, *Politics and the media*, 2nd ed. Auckland: Auckland University Press.

Bakker, Tom and Claes H. de Vreese. 2011. Good news for the future? Young people, Internet use, and political participation. *Communication Research* 20(10): 1–20. DOI: 10.1177/0093650210381738

Bale, Tim and Torbjörn Bergman. 2006. Captives no longer, but servants still? Contract parliamentarism and the new minority governance in Sweden and New Zealand. *Government and Opposition* 41(3): 422–49. DOI: 10.1111/j.1477-7053.2006.00186.x

Bargsted, Matias A. and Orit Kedar. 2009. Coalition-targeted Duvergerian voting: How expectations affect voter choice under proportional representation. *American Journal of Political Science* 53(2): 307–23. DOI: 10.1111/j.1540-5907.2009.00372.x

Barnes, Tiffany D. and Abby Córdova. 2016. Making space for women: Explaining citizen support for legislative gender quotas in Latin America. *Journal of Politics* 78(3): 670–86. DOI: 10.1086/685379

Barnett, Tim and David Talbot. 2015. The 2014 Labour campaign: A party perspective. In Jon Johansson and Stephen Levine, eds, *Moments of truth: The New Zealand general election of 2014*, 138–46. Wellington: Victoria University Press.

Bartels, Larry. 2008. *Unequal democracy: The political economy of the new gilded age.* 1st ed., Princeton: Princeton University Press.

Bartels, Larry. 2016. *Unequal democracy: The political economy of the new gilded age.* 2nd ed., Princeton: Princeton University Press.

Batten, Daniel. 2005. Greens must turn on and tune into the mainstream. *New Zealand Herald*, 6 October.

Bean, Clive. 1986. An inventory of New Zealand voting surveys 1949–1984. *Political Science* 38(2): 172–84. DOI: 10.1177/003231878603800206

Bean, Clive and Ian McAllister. 2012. Electoral behaviour in the 2010 Australian Federal Election. In Marian Simms and John Wanna, eds, *Julia 2010: The caretaker election*, 341–56. Canberra: ANU E Press.

Belich, James. 2001. *Paradise reforged: A history of the New Zealanders from the 1880s to the year 2000.* Auckland: Allen Lane Penguin.

Benabou, Roland and Efe A. Ok. 2001. Social mobility and the demand for redistribution: The POUM hypothesis. *The Quarterly Journal of Economics* 116(2): 447–87. DOI: 10.1162/00335530151144078

Bennett, Adam. 2014. Nationals ride post-Budget wave. *New Zealand Herald*, 26 May.

Berelson, Bernard R., Paul F. Lazarsfeld and William N. McPhee. 1954. *Voting: A study of opinion-formation in a presidential campaign.* Chicago: University of Chicago Press.

Bernhagen, Patrick and Michael Marsh. 2007. The partisan effects of low turnout: Analyzing vote abstention as a missing data problem. *Electoral Studies* 26(3): 548–60. DOI: 10.1016/j.electstud.2006.10.002

Bertram, Geoff, ed. 2014. *The Piketty phenomenon: New Zealand perspectives*. Auckland: Bridget Williams Books.

Betz, Georg. 2005. Against the system: Radical right-wing populism's challenge to liberal democracy. In Jens Rydgren, ed., *Movements of exclusion: Radical right-wing populism in the Western world*, 25–40. New York: Nova Science Publishers.

Birch, Sarah. 2009. *Full participation: A comparative study of compulsory voting*. Manchester: Manchester University Press.

Blais, André and Daniel Rubenson. 2013. The source of turnout decline: New values or new contexts? *Comparative Political Studies* 46(1): 95–117. DOI: 10.1177/0010414012453032

Boix, Carles. 2003. *Democracy and redistribution*. Cambridge: Cambridge University Press.

Bolzendahl, Catherine and Clem Brooks. 2007. Women's political representation and welfare state spending in twelve capitalist democracies. *Social Forces* 85(4): 1509–34. DOI: 10.1353/sof. 2007.0061

Bornschier, Simon. 2010. *Cleavage politics and the populist right: The new cultural conflict in Western Europe*. Philadelphia: Temple University Press.

Boston, Jonathan. 2013. What kind of equality matters? In Max Rashbrooke, ed., *Inequality: A New Zealand crisis*, 70–86. Auckland: Bridget Williams Books.

Boston, Jonathan and Simon Chapple. 2014. *Child poverty in New Zealand*. Auckland: Bridget Williams Books.

Bowler, Shaun, Jeffrey A. Karp and Todd Donovan. 2010. Strategic coalition voting: Evidence from New Zealand. *Electoral Studies* 29(3): 350–57. DOI: 10.1016/j.electstud.2010.03.001

Boyd, Mark and Babak Bahador. 2015. Media coverage of New Zealand's 2014 election campaign. *Political Science* 67(2): 143–60. DOI: 10.1177/0032318715609077

Bradbury, Martyn. 2014a. Why inequality needs to be on the political agenda. *The Daily Blog*, 13 May. Available at: thedailyblog.co.nz/2014/05/13/why-inequality-needs-to-be-on-the-political-agenda/

Bradbury, Martyn. 2014b. A tale of two men: Cunliffe's apology for rape culture vs Key's dismissal of it. *The Daily Blog*, 22 July. Available at: thedailyblog.co.nz/2014/07/22/a-tale-of-two-men-cunliffes-apology-for-rape-culture-vs-keys-dismissal-of-it/

Bradford, Sue and Keith Locke. 1999. Old reds defend their new green look. Letter to the editor. *National Business Review*, 26 November, 26.

Brady, Henry E., Sidney Verba and Kay Lehman Schlozman. 1995. Beyond SES: A resource model of political participation. *American Political Science Review* 89(2): 271–94. DOI: 10.2307/2082425

Brash, Donald. 2004. Nationhood. Speech to the Orewa Rotary Club. Available at: www.scoop.co.nz/stories/PA0401/S00220.htm

Brenton, Scott. 2013. Policy traps for third parties in two-party systems: The Australian case. *Commonwealth and Comparative Politics* 51(3): 283–305. DOI: 10.1080/14662043.2013.805538

Broadcasting Standards Authority. 2010. Controversial issues—viewpoints (balance) as a broadcasting standard in television. Wellington: Broadcasting Standards Authority. Available at: bsa.govt.nz/standards/practice-notes/balance-on-tv

Brown, Robin. 2012. Peter Mandelson calling Peter Mandelson a liar. Available at: robinbrown.co.uk/2012/01/calling-peter-mandelson-a-liar/

Brown, Russell. 2014. A call from curia. *Hard News*, 19 September. Available at: publicaddress.net/hardnews/a-call-from-curia/

Burns, Nancy. 2007. Gender in the aggregate, gender in the individual, gender and political action. *Politics & Gender* 3(01): 104–24. DOI: 10.1017/S1743923X07221014

Cameron, Sarah M. and Ian McAllister. 2014. *Trends in Australian political opinion: Results from the Australian Election Study, 1987–2013*. Canberra: Australian National University.

Campbell, Angus, Philip Converse, Warren Miller and Donald E. Stokes. 1960. *The American voter*. Chicago: University of Chicago Press.

Campbell, Gordon. 2014. The Green Party moves to the political centre … and vice versa. *Werewolf*, 11 June. Available at: werewolf.co.nz/2014/06/into-the-mainstream/

Carroll, Penelope, Sally Casswell, John Huakau, paul Perry and Philippa Howden Chapman. 2009. Environmental attitudes, beliefs about social justice and intention to vote Green: Lessons for the New Zealand Green Party. *Environmental Politics* 18(2): 257–78. DOI: 10.1080/09644010802682635

Carroll, Susan J., ed. 2001. *The impact of women in public office*. Bloomington: Indiana University Press.

Carter, Neil. 2007. *The politics of the environment: Ideas, activism, policy*. Cambridge: Cambridge University Press.

Castles, Francis. 1985. *The working class and welfare*. Sydney: Allen and Unwin.

Castles, Francis, Rolf Gerritsen and Jack Vowles, eds. 1996. *The great experiment: Labour parties and public policy transformation in Australia and New Zealand*. Sydney: Allen and Unwin.

Chapman, Harry and Hilde Coffé. 2016. Changing Facebook profile pictures as part of a campaign: Who does it and why? *Journal of Youth Studies* 19(4): 483–500. DOI: 10.1080/13676261.2015.1083962

Chapman, Ralph. 2015. *Time of useful consciousness: Acting urgently on climate change*. Wellington: BW Books.

Chapman, Robert M. 1981. From Labour to National. In William Hosking Oliver and Bridget R. Williams, eds, *The Oxford history of New Zealand*, 333–67. Wellington: Oxford University Press.

Chapman, Robert M. 1986. Voting in the Māori political sub-system 1935–1984. In Royal Commission on the Electoral System, *Report of the Royal Commission on the Electoral System: Towards a Better Democracy*. Wellington: Government Printer.

Chappell, Louise and Jennifer Curtin. 2013. Does federalism matter? Evaluating state architecture and family and domestic violence policy in Australia and New Zealand. *Publius. The Journal of Federalism* 43(1): 24–43. DOI: 10.1093/publius/pjs030

Chen, Peter. 2010. Adoption and use of digital media in election campaigns: Australia, Canada and New Zealand. *Public Communication Review* 1: 3–26.

Chen, Peter. 2015. New media in the electoral context: The new normal. In Carol Johnson, John Wanna and Hsu-Ann Lee, eds, *Abbott's Gambit: The 2013 Australian Federal Election*, 81–94. Canberra: ANU Press.

Chzhen, Yekaterina, Geoffrey Evans and Mark Pickup. 2014. When do economic perceptions matter for government approval? Examining the endogeneity of economic perceptions before and during the economic downturn. *Political Behavior* 36: 291–313. DOI: 10.1007/s11109-013-9236-2

Clark, Michael and Debra Leiter. 2014. Does the ideological dispersion of parties mediate the electoral impact of valence? A cross-national study of party support in nine Western European democracies. *Comparative Political Studies* 47(2): 171–202. DOI: 10.1177/0010414013488537

Clark, Terry Nichols and Seymour Martin Lipset, eds. 2001. *The breakdown of class politics: A debate on post-industrial stratification*. Baltimore: John Hopkins University Press.

Clarke, Harold D., David Sanders, Marianne C. Stewart and Paul Whiteley 2011. Downs, Stokes and the dynamics of electoral choice. *British Journal of Political Science* 41: 287–314. DOI: 10.1017/S0007123410000505

Coffé, Hilde. 2013a. Gender and party choice at the 2011 New Zealand general election. *Political Science* 65(1): 25–45. DOI: 10.1177/0032318713485346

Coffé, Hilde. 2013b. Women stay local, men go national and global? Gender differences in political interest. *Sex Roles* 69(5): 323–38. DOI: 10.1007/s11199-013-0308-x

Coffé, Hilde and Catherine Bolzendahl. 2010. Same game, different rules? Gender differences in political participation. *Sex Roles* 62(5–6): 318–33. DOI: 10.1007/s11199-009-9729-y

Collins. Simon. 2011. Investment hit closes gap between NZ rich and poor. *New Zealand Herald,* 3 August.

Collins, Simon. 2014. Poll finds rich–poor gap is the big election issue. *New Zealand Herald,* 29 August.

Colmar Brunton. 2014. ONE News Colmar Brunton Poll, 15–19 February.

Coney, Sandra. 1993. *Standing in the sunshine: A history of New Zealand women since they won the vote.* Auckland: Viking.

Converse, Philip E. 1964. The nature of belief systems in mass publics. *Critical Review* 18(1–3): 1–74. DOI: 10.1080/08913810608443650

Cowley, Philip, and Dennis Kavanagh. 2015. *The British general election of 2015.* London: Palgrave McMillan.

Curia. 2014. NZ Herald Digipoll July 2014. Available at: www.curia. co.nz/2014/07/nz-herald-digipoll-july-2014/

Curtin, Jennifer. 2008. Women, political leadership and substantive representation of women in New Zealand. *Parliamentary Affairs* 61(3): 490–504. DOI: 10.1093/pa/gsn014

Curtin, Jennifer. 2010. Youth participation. In Raymond Miller, ed., *New Zealand government and politics,* 5th ed., 559–70. Melbourne: Oxford University Press.

Curtin, Jennifer. 2013a. Parliament's gender balance. *The Listener,* 11 July. Available at: www.listener.co.nz/current-affairs/politics/coming-to-the-party-5/

Curtin, Jennifer. 2013b. Aussie rules: Compulsory voting. *The Listener,* 12 September. Available at: www.listener.co.nz/current-affairs/politics/aussie-rules-2/

Curtin, Jennifer. 2014. From presence to absence? Where were women in 2011? In Jack Vowles, ed., *The new electoral politics in New Zealand: The significance of the 2011 Election*, 125–39. Wellington: Institute for Governance and Policy Studies.

Curtin, Jennifer. 2015. Revisiting social liberalism and feminism in New Zealand. In Anna Yeatman, ed., *Feminism, social liberalism and social democracy in the neo-liberal era: Four essays*, 51–66. Whitlam Institute, Working Paper Series, June, University of Western Sydney.

Curtin, Jennifer and Heather Devere. 2006. Global rankings and domestic realities: Women, work and policy in Australia and New Zealand. *Australian Journal of Political Science* 41(2): 193–207. DOI: 10.1080/10361140600672436

Curtin, Jennifer, Francis G. Castles and Jack Vowles, eds. 2006. Globalising the Antipodes. Special issue. *Australian Journal of Political Science* 40(2): 131–288.

Curtin, Jennifer and Katherine Teghtsoonian. 2010. Analyzing institutional persistence: The case of the Ministry of Women's Affairs in Aotearoa/New Zealand. *Politics and Gender* 6(4): 545–72. DOI: 10.1017/S1743923X1000036X

Curtin, Jennifer and Marian Sawer. 1996. Gender equity and the shrinking state. In Francis Castles, Rolf Gerritsen and Jack Vowles, eds, *The great experiment: Labour parties and public policy transformation in Australia and New Zealand*, 149–69. Sydney: Allen and Unwin.

Curtin Jennifer and Marian Sawer. 2011. Oceania. In Gretchen Bauer and Manon Tremblay, eds, *Women in executive power: A global overview*, 45–64. Routledge.

Curtin, Jennifer and Raymond Miller. 2011. Negotiating coalitions: Comparative perspectives. *Political Science* 63(1): 3–9. DOI: 10.1177/0032318711403916

Dalton, Russell. 1996. Political cleavages, issues, and electoral change. In Lawrence Leduc, Richard G. Niemi and Pippa Norris, eds, *Comparing democracies: Elections and voting in global perspective*, 319–42. Thousand Oaks: Sage Publications.

Dalton, Russell. 2007. *The good citizen: How a younger generation is reshaping American politics.* London: Sage.

Dalton, Russell. 2008. *Citizen politics: Public opinion and political parties in advanced industrial democracies,* 5th ed. Washington DC: CQ Press.

Dalton, Russell. 2013. *The apartisan American: Dealignment and changing electoral politics.* Los Angeles: Sage/CQ Press.

Dalton, Russell. 2014. *Citizen politics: Public opinion and political parties in advanced industrial democracies,* 6th ed. Thousand Oaks: CQ Press.

Dalton, Russell and Martin Wattenberg, eds. 2000. *Parties without partisan: Political change in advanced industrial democracies.* New York: Oxford University Press.

Dann, Christine R. 1999. From earth's last islands: The global origins of Green politics. PhD dissertation, Lincoln University.

Dassonneville, Ruth and Marc Hooghe. 2011. Mapping Electoral Volatility in Europe: An analysis of trends in electoral volatility in European democracies since 1945. Paper presented at the 1st European Conference on Comparative Electoral Research Sofia (Bulgaria), 1–3 December. Available at: true-european-voter.eu/sites/default/files/Mapping%20electoral%20volatility_Dassonneville_Hooghe.pdf

Davidson-Schmich, Louise. 2014. Closing the gap: Gender and constituency candidate nomination in the 2013 Bundestag Election. *German Politics and Society* 32(2): 86–105. DOI: 10.3167/gps.2014.320206

Davidson, Pamela, Susanne Steinmann and Bernd Wegener. 1995. The caring but unjust women: A comparative study of gender differences in perceptions of social justice in four countries. In James R. Kluegel, David S. Mason and Bernd Wegener, eds, *Social justice and political change: Public opinion in capitalist and post-communist societies,* 285–322. New York: Aldine de Gruyter.

Davies, Sonja. 1984. *Bread and roses: Sonja Davies, her story.* Auckland: Australia and New Zealand Book Company.

Davies, Sonja. 1997. *Marching on.* Auckland: Random Hose.

Davis, Darren W. and Christian Davenport. 1999. Assessing the validity of the postmaterialism index. *American Political Science Review* 93(3): 649–64. DOI: 10.2307/2585580

Davison, Isaac. 2012. Welfare reform bill passed into law. *New Zealand Herald*, 19 July.

Davison, Isaac. 2014a. Diplomat case: Key under fire for not saying sorry. *New Zealand Herald*, 22 July.

Davison, Isaac. 2014b. Key refuses to rule out NZ First, Conservatives. *New Zealand Herald*, 21 January.

Davison, Isaac. 2014c. Wallets out … but can votes be bought? *New Zealand Herald*, 1 February.

Delli Carpini, Michael X. and Scott Keeter. 1996. *What Americans know about politics and why it matters.* New Haven: Yale University Press.

Dennison, James and Matthew Goodwin. 2015. Immigration, issue ownership and the rise of UKIP. In Andrew Geddes and Jonathan Tonge, eds, *Britain votes 2015*, 167–87. Oxford: Oxford University Press.

Dermody, Janine, Stuart Hanmer-Lloyd and Richard Scullion. 2010. Young people and voting behaviour: Alienated youth and/or an interested and critical citizenry. *European Journal of Marketing* 44(3–4): 421–35. DOI: 10.1108/03090561011020507

Dixon, Hugh. 2014. Net migration to New Zealand hits new record high. *BERL*, 25 November. Available at: www.berl.co.nz/economic-insights/jobs/migration/net-migration-to-new-zealand-hits-new-record-high/

Dolan, Kathleen. 2011. Do women and men know different things? Measuring gender differences in political knowledge. *Journal of Politics* 73: 97–107. DOI: 10.1017/S0022381610000897

Dolezal, Martin. 2010. Exploring the stabilization of a political force: The social and attitudinal basis of green parties in the age of globalization. *West European Politics* 33(3): 534–52. DOI: 10.1080/01402381003654569

Dominion Post. 2012. Editorial: Shearer missing the point. *Dominion Post*, 11 August. Available at: www.stuff.co.nz/dominion-post/comment/editorials/7457141/Editorial-Shearer-missing-the-point

Dougan, Patrice. 2014. Colin Craig's press secretary quits, reportedly calls him a 'manipulative man'. *New Zealand Herald*, 18 September.

Downs, Anthony. 1957. *An economic theory of democracy.* New York: Harper.

Duch, Raymond M., Jeff May and David A. Armstrong. 2010. Coalition-directed voting in multiparty democracies. *American Political Science Review* 104(4): 698–719. DOI: 10.1017/S0003055410000420

Duch, Raymond M. and Randolph T. Stevenson. 2008. *The economic vote: How political and economic institutions condition election results.* Cambridge: Cambridge University Press.

Duch, Raymond M. and Michaell A. Taylor. 1993. Postmaterialism and the Economic Condition. *American Journal of Political Science* 37(3): 747–79. DOI: 10.2307/2111573

Duff, Michelle. 2014. English is second language for majority of kids at this school. *Stuff*, 18 November. Available at: www.stuff.co.nz/national/education/in-our-schools/10767739/English-is-second-language-for-majority-of-kids-at-this-school

Dumont, Patrick and Hanna Bäck. 2006. Why so few, and why so late? Green parties and the question of governmental participation. *European Journal of Political Research* 45: 35–67. DOI: 10.1111/j.1475-6765.2006.00649.x

Easton, Brian. 2013. Economic inequality in New Zealand: A user's guide. *The New Zealand Journal of Sociology* 28(3): 9–66.

Economist. 2016. Post-truth politics: Art of the lie. *Economist*, 12 September. Available at: www.economist.com/news/leaders/21706525-politicians-have-always-lied-does-it-matter-if-they-leave-truth-behind-entirely-art

Edlund, Lena, and Rohini Pande. 2002. Why have women become left-wing? The political gender gap and the decline in marriage. *The Quarterly Journal of Economics* 117(3): 3917–61. DOI: 10.1162/003355302760193922

Edwards, Brent. 2015a. How cynical has NZ politics become? *Radio New Zealand News*, 25 August. Available at: www.radionz.co.nz/news/political/282617/how-cynical-has-nz-politics-become

Edwards, Brent. 2015b. House price rise increases inequality – English. *Radio New Zealand*, 22 July. Available at: www.radionz.co.nz/news/political/279353/house-price-rise-increases-inequality-english

Edwards, Bryce. 2006. Backdoor funding affects democracy. *New Zealand Herald*, 13 September.

Edwards, Bryce. 2008. Political finance and inequality in New Zealand. *New Zealand Sociology* 23(2): 4–17.

Edwards, Bryce. 2009. Identity politics versus class politics. *Liberation*, 15 December. Available at: liberation.typepad.com/liberation/2009/12/identity-politics-vs-class-politics-1-introduction.html

Edwards, Bryce. 2010. Does inequality matter? An upcoming Wellington forum. *Liberation*, 2 November. Available at: liberation.typepad.com/liberation/2010/11/does-inequality-matter-an-upcoming-wellington-policy-forum.html

Edwards, Bryce. 2011. NZ politics daily. *Liberation*, 18 October. Available at: liberation.typepad.com/liberation/2011/10/nz-politics-daily-18-october.html

Edwards, Bryce. 2013a. Labour's shift to identity politics. *National Business Review*, 5 July. Available at: www.nbr.co.nz/article/nz-politics-daily-labours-shift-identity-politics-ck-142501

Edwards, Bryce. 2013b. Labour's 'man ban' problem. *New Zealand Herald*, 5 July.

Edwards, Bryce. 2014a. What does the Labour Party want to be? *New Zealand Herald*, 28 April.

Edwards, Bryce. 2014b. Solving inequality and poverty with your vote. *New Zealand Herald*, 12 September.

Edwards, Bryce. 2014c. The strategically smart Greens. *New Zealand Herald*, 3 June.

Edwards, Bryce. 2014d. Will the gutted Greens go Blue? *New Zealand Herald*, 3 October.

Edwards, Bryce. 2014e. Coups, man bans, and pakeha parties. *New Zealand Herald*, 11 July.

Edwards, Bryce. 2014f. Top 100 tweeters to follow this election. *New Zealand Herald*.

Edwards, Bryce. 2014g. Labour's surprisingly smart and successful weekend. *New Zealand Herald*, 8 July.

Edwards, Bryce. 2015. The micro parties. In Janine Hayward, ed., *New Zealand Government and Politics*, 6th ed., 261–70. Melbourne: Oxford University Press.

Edwards, Bryce. 2016a. Advice for the Labour Party. Political roundup. *New Zealand Herald*, 19 April. Available at: www.nzherald.co.nz/nz/news/article.cfm?c_id=1&objectid=11625144

Edwards, Bryce. 2016b. Politicians, party professionals, and the media in New Zealand. In Geoff Kemp, Babak Bahador, Kate McMillan and Chris Rudd, eds, *Politics and the media*, 2nd ed., 219–37. Auckland: Auckland University Press.

Edwards, Bryce and Nicola Lomax. 2012. 'For a richer New Zealand': Environmentalism and the Green Party in the 2011 New Zealand general election. *Environmental Politics* 21(6): 994–1000. DOI: 10.1080/09644016.2012.724219

Electoral Commission. 2002. *The New Zealand electoral compendium 2002*. Wellington: New Zealand Electoral Commission.

Electoral Commission. 2008. Enrolment and voting statistics from the general election held on 8 November 2008. Available at: www.electionresults.govt.nz/electionresults_2008/e9/html/statistics.html

Electoral Commission. 2011. Enrolment and voting statistics from the general election held on 26 November 2011. Available at: www.electionresults.govt.nz/electionresults_2011/e9/html/statistics.html

Electoral Commission. 2014a. Enrolment and voting statistics from the general election held on 20 September 2014. Available at: www.electionresults.org.nz/electionresults_2014/e9/html/statistics.html

Electoral Commission. 2014b. ER180 scientific research extract. Data as at 2014–09–23. Wellington: New Zealand Electoral Commission.

Electoral Commission. 2014c. 2014 general election voter turnout statistics. Available at: www.elections.org.nz/events/2014-general-election/election-results-and-reporting/2014-general-election-voter-turnout

Electoral Commission. 2014d. Valuing our vote—2014 conference. Available at: www.elections.org.nz/voters/participation-2014-and-beyond/valuing-our-vote-2014-conference

Electoral Commission. 2014e. Use of social media. Available at: www.elections.org.nz/parties-candidates/all-participants/use-social-media

Electoral Commission. 2014f. Final enrolment statistics for 2014 by age group. Excel spreadsheet. Wellington: Electoral Commission.

Electoral Commission. 2015a. Report of the Electoral Commission on the 2014 general election. Available at: www.elections.org.nz/sites/default/files/bulk-upload/documents/report_of_the_ec_on_the_2014_general_election.pdf

Electoral Commission. 2015b. Broadcasting allocation 2014 general election. Wellington, New Zealand Electoral Commission. Available at: www.elections.org.nz/events/2014-general-election/2014-parties-candidates-and-third-parties/broadcasting-allocation-2014

Electoral Commission. 2015c. Party expenses returns 2014 election. Wellington, New Zealand Electoral Commission. Available at: www.elections.org.nz/events/2014-general-election/2014-parties-candidates-and-third-parties/party-expenses-returns-2014

Electoral Commission. 2015d. Candidate returns 2014 election. Wellington: New Zealand Electoral Commission. Available at: www.elections.org.nz/events/2014-general-election/2014-parties-candidates-and-third-parties/candidate-returns-2014

Electoral Commission. 2016a. Find my electorate. Available at: www.elections.org.nz/voters/find-my-electorate

Electoral Commission. 2016b. New Zealand election results. Available at: www.electionresults.org.nz/

Electoral Commission. 2016c. 2014 general election split voting statistics—Māori electorates. Wellington: New Zealand Electoral Commission. Available at: www.electionresults.org.nz/electionresults_2014/elect-splitvote-Maori.html

Electoral Commission. 2016d. Party donations by year. Wellington: New Zealand. Electoral Commission. Available at: www.elections.org.nz/parties-candidates/registered-political-parties/party-donations/party-donations-year

Electoral Commission. 2017. 2014 general election split voting statistics overall. Available at www.electionresults.org.nz/electionresults_2014/elect-splitvote-Overall.html

Ellipsister. 2014. Not a very feminist party. *Ellipsister*, 22 August. Available at: ellipsister.wordpress.com/2014/08/22/not-a-very-feminist-party/

Evans, Geoffrey. 2000. The continued significance of class voting. *Annual Review of Political Science* 3: 401–17.

Evans, Geoffrey and Robert Andersen. 2006. The political conditioning of economic perceptions. *The Journal of Politics* 68: 194–207. DOI: 10.1111/j.1468-2508.2006.00380.x

Evans, Geoffrey and Mark Pickup. 2010. Reversing the causal arrow: The political conditioning of economic perceptions in the 2000–2004 US presidential election cycle. *The Journal of Politics* 72: 1236–51. DOI: 10.1017/S0022381610000654

Eysenck, Hans. 1954. *The psychology of politics.* London: Routledge & Kegan Paul.

Fairfax Media. 2014. New Zealand 2014's 'rock star' economy. *Stuff*, 1 January. Available at: www.stuff.co.nz/business/industries/9583473/New-Zealand-2014s-rock-star-economy

Farrar, David. 2014a. What if? *Kiwiblog*, 7 October. Available at: www.kiwiblog.co.nz/2014/10/what_if.html

Farrar, David. 2014b. It seems it was more National voters who stayed home in 2011. *Kiwiblog*, 5 May. Available at: www.kiwiblog.co.nz/2014/05/it_seems_it_was_more_national_voters_who_stayed_home_in_2011.html

Farrell, David. 2014. Democracy fit for citizens? New Zealand in context. Valuing our vote conference, Parliament House, 29 May. Available at: www.elections.org.nz/voters/participation-2014-and-beyond/valuing-our-vote-2014-conference/valuing-our-vote-2014-0

Ferguson, Phillip. 2014. Thomas Piketty's ideas reach New Zealand. *Redline*, 29 April. Available at: rdln.wordpress.com/2014/04/29/thomas-pickettys-ideas-reach-new-zealand/

Fiorina, Morris. 1981. *Retrospective voting in American elections*. New Haven: Yale University Press.

Fisher, David. 2014. OIA a bizarre arms race. *New Zealand Herald*, 23 October. Available at: www.nzherald.co.nz/opinion/news/article.cfm?c_id=466&objectid=11347187

Fitzgerald, Eljon, Brendan Stevenson and Jacob Tapiata. 2007. Māori electoral participation: A report produced for the Electoral Commission. Palmerston North: Massey University. Available at: www.elections.org.nz/sites/default/files/plain-page/attachments/massey_report.pdf

Flanagan, Scott C. and Aie-Rie Lee. 2003. The new politics, culture wars, and the authoritarian–libertarian value change in advanced industrial democracies. *Comparative Political Studies* 36(3): 235–70. DOI: 10.1177/0010414002250664

Foley, Chris. 2014. Victorious New Zealand PM pledges more of the same, eyes 4th term. *Yahoo News*, 21 September. Available at: news.yahoo.com/polls-open-zealand-election-212405219.html

Ford, Geoffrey. 2015. The Green Party. In Janine Hayward, ed., *New Zealand government and politics*, 6th ed., 229–39. Melbourne: Oxford University Press.

Forschler, Henrike. 2014. Voting apathy. *Public Address*, 20 August. Available at: publicaddress.net/system/ourtube/voting-apathy/

Fowler, Anthony. 2013. Electoral and policy consequences of voter turnout: Evidence from compulsory voting in Australia. *Quarterly Journal of Political Science* 8: 159–82. DOI: 10.2139/ssrn.1816649

Fox, Michael and Tracy Watkins. 2014. How we really rate leaders. *Stuff*, 18 May. Available at: www.stuff.co.nz/national/politics/10056542/How-we-really-rate-leaders

Franklin, Mark. 1999. Electoral engineering and cross-national turnout differences: What role for compulsory voting? *British Journal of Political Science* 29(1): 205–16.

Franklin, Mark. 2004. *Voter turnout and the dynamics of electoral competition in established democracies since 1945.* Cambridge: Cambridge University Press.

Franks, Peter and Jim McAloon. 2016. *Labour: The New Zealand Labour Party 1916–2016.* Wellington: Victoria University Press.

Frazer, Elizabeth and Kenneth Macdonald. 2003. Sex difference in political knowledge in Britain. *Political Studies* 51: 67–83. DOI: 10.1111/1467-9248.00413

Fry, Julie. 2014. *Migration and macroeconomic performance in New Zealand: Theory and evidence.* New Zealand Treasury Working Paper 14/10. Wellington: New Zealand Treasury.

Garner, Duncan. 2014. Time for the Green Party to go both ways. *Radio Live*, 30 September. Available at: www.radiolive.co.nz/Duncan-Garner-Time-for-the-Green-Party-to-go-both-ways/tabid/674/articleID/55810/Default.aspx

Gascoigne, John. 2002. *The enlightenment and the origins of European Australia.* Cambridge: Cambridge University Press.

Gasper, John T. and Andrew Reeves. 2011. Make it rain? Retrospection and the attentive electorate in the context of natural disasters. *American Journal of Political Science* 55(2): 340–55. DOI: 10.1111/j.1540-5907.2010.00503.x

Generation Zero. 2014. The big ask. Available at: www.generationzero.org/thebigask

Gibbons, Matthew. 2011. New Zealand political parties' policies. *New Zealand Sociology* 26(1): 41–67.

Gidengil, Elisabeth. 1998. Gender and attitudes toward quotas for women candidates in Canada. *Women & Politics* 16(4): 21–44. DOI: 10.1300/J014v16n04_02

Giger, Nathalie. 2009. Towards a modern gender gap in Europe? A comparative analysis of voting behavior in 12 countries. *The Social Science Journal* 46: 474–92. DOI: 10.1016/j.soscij.2009.03.002

Godfery, Morgan. 2015. The search for stability. In Jon Johansson and Stephen Levine, eds, *Moments of truth: The New Zealand general election of 2014*, 252–63. Wellington: Victoria University of Wellington Press.

Goldsmith, Rachael. 2014. What is so threatening about standing up for women? *The Daily Blog*, 4 August. Available at: thedailyblog.co.nz/2014/08/04/what-is-so-threatening-about-standing-up-for-women/

Gower, Patrick. 2014a. Opinion: Labour's war room now Cunliffe's panic station. *Newshub*, 26 May. Available at: www.newshub.co.nz/opinion/patrick-gower/opinion-labours-warroom-now-cunliffes-panic-station-2014052610

Gower, Patrick. 2014b. Poll shows Winston Peters as kingmaker. *Newshub*, 2 February. Available at: www.newshub.co.nz/politics/poll-shows-winston-peters-as-kingmaker-2014020216

Green Party. 2009. Green and National parties announce shared policy initiatives. Available at: home.greens.org.nz/press-releases/green-national-parties-announce-shared-policy-initiatives

Green Party. 2014a. Green. Fair reward for fair effort. Available at: www.greens.org.nz/sites/default/files/policy-pdfs/Workers%20-%20full%20Green%20Party%20Policy.pdf

Green Party. 2014b. The Green charter. Available at: home.greens.org.nz/charter

Green Party. 2014c. Women's issues. Available at: home.greens.org.nz/women

Green Party, 2014d. Smart Green innovation. Wellington, Green Party. home.greens.org.nz/sites/default/files/econ-innovation-final.pdf

Green, Antony. 2004. Is voting really compulsory in Australia? *ABC*, 9 October. Available at: www.abc.net.au/elections/federal/2004/items/200406/s1140761.htm

Green, Antony. 2011. Strange things voters do to ballot papers. 1 November. Available at: blogs.abc.net.au/antonygreen/2011/11/strange-things-voters-do-to-ballot-papers.html

Green, Donald and Ian Shapiro. 1994. *Pathologies of rational choice theory: A critique of applications in political science.* New Haven: Yale University Press.

Green, Jane and Will Jennings. 2012. Valence as macro-competence: An analysis of mood in party competence evaluations in Great Britain. *British Journal of Political Science* 42(2): 311–43. DOI: 10.1017/S0007123411000330

Grey, Sandra. 2002. Does size matter? Critical mass and New Zealand's women MPs. *Parliamentary Affairs* 55: 19–29. DOI: 10.1093/parlij/55.1.19

Griffin, John D. and Brian Newman. 2013. Voting power, policy representation, and disparities in voting's rewards. *The Journal of Politics* 75(1): 52–64. DOI: 10.1017/S0022381612000862

Grofman, Bernard, Guillermo Owen and Christian Collet. 1999. Rethinking the partisan effects of higher turnout: So what's the question? *Public Choice* 99: 357–76. DOI: 10.1023/A:1018397327176

Grönlund, Kimmo and Henry Milner. 2006. The determinants of political Knowledge in comparative perspective. *Scandinavian Political Studies* 29(4): 386–406. DOI: 10.1111/j.1467-9477.2006.00157.x

Grönlund, Kimmo and Maija Setälä. 2007. Political trust, satisfaction, and voter turnout. *Comparative European Politics* 5: 400–22. DOI: 10.1057/palgrave.cep.6110113

Gulliver, Aimee. 2014. Social media the new campaign trail. *Stuff*, 11 September. Available at: www.stuff.co.nz/national/politics/10486540/Social-media-the-new-campaign-trail

Hackett-Fischer, David. 2012. *Fairness and freedom: A history of two open societies, New Zealand and the United States.* Oxford: Oxford University Press.

Hager, Nicky. 2008. Nat's secret advisers accused of dirty tricks in Aussie. *Sunday Star Times*, 29 June. Available at: www.stuff.co.nz/510500/Nats-secret-advisers-accused-of-dirty-tricks-in-Aussie

Hager, Nicky. 2014. *Dirty politics: How attack politics is poisoning New Zealand's political environment.* Nelson: Craig Potton Publishing.

Harman, Richard. 2016. Is Little looking to purge Labour's right-wing. *Politik*, 11 August. Available at: politik.co.nz/en/content/politics/903/Is-Little-looking-to-purge-Labour's-right-wing-Little-Leggett-Nash-Shearer-Peters-Labour.htm

Hayward, Bronwyn. 2006. Public participation. In Raymond Miller, ed., *New Zealand government and politics*, 4th ed., 514–24. Melbourne: Oxford University Press.

Hehir, Liam. 2016. Move from critic to 'arena' a daunting challenge for Gareth Morgan. *Stuff*, 6 November. Available at: www.stuff.co.nz/national/politics/opinion/86159395/move-from-critic-to-arena-a-daunting-challenge-for-gareth-morgan

Henn, Matt, Mark Weinstein and Dominic Wring. 2002. A generation apart? Youth and political participation in Britain. *British Journal of Politics and International Relations* 4(2): 167–92. DOI: 10.1111/1467-856X.t01-1-00001

Hickford, Mark. 2015. Law of the foreshore and seabed—Challenge and controversy. *Te Ara: The Encyclopedia of New Zealand*. Available at: www.TeAra.govt.nz/en/law-of-the-foreshore-and-seabed/page-4

Hill, Lisa. 2002. On the reasonableness of compelling citizens to vote: The Australian case. *Political Studies* 50: 80–101. DOI: 10.1111/1467-9248.00360

Hill, Lisa. 2011. Increasing turnout using compulsory voting. *Politics* 31(1): 27–36. DOI: 10.1111/j.1467-9256.2010.01399.x

Hillygus, D. Sunshine and Todd G. Shields. 2008. *The persuadable voter: Wedge issues in presidential campaigns.* Princeton: Princeton University Press.

Hince, Kevin and Martin Vranken. 1991. A controversial reform of New Zealand labour law: The Employment Contracts Act 1991. *International Labour Review* 130(4): 475–93.

Hirano, Shigeo and James M. Snyder Jr. 2012. What happens to incumbents in scandals? *Quarterly Journal of Political Science* 7: 447–56.

Hooton, Matthew. 2016. You've failed quite badly haven't you? *National Business Review*, 28 February. Available at: www.nbr.co.nz/opinion/you've-failed-quite-badly-haven't-you-mh

Hosking, Rob. 2014a. The meaning of Election 2014. *The National Business Review*, 26 September.

Hosking, Rob. 2014b. Soundbites, sanctimony and the Cunliffe apology. *National Business Review*, 7 July. Available at: bit.ly/1mzMRet

Houtman, Dick. 2003. Lipset and 'working-class' authoritarianism. *The American Sociologist* 34(1): 85–103. DOI: 10.1007/s12108-003-1008-8

Hubbard, Mark. 2014. Why there must be no compulsory Kiwisaver II: Inequality against men and Maori—personal choices and trade offs. #Individualism. 1 May. Available at: lifebehindtheirondrape.blogspot.co.nz/2014/04/why-there-must-be-no-compulsory.html

Hug, Simon. 2014. Further twenty years of pathologies? Is rational choice better than it used to be? *Swiss Political Science Review* 20(3): 486–97.

Hume, Tim. 2014. 'House of cards' in the South Pacific: New Zealand's dirty election campaign. *CNN*, 12 September. Available at: edition.cnn.com/2014/09/11/world/asia/new-zealand-elections-scandal/

Humpage, Louise. 2014. Do New Zealanders really support welfare reform? In Jack Vowles, ed., *The new electoral politics in New Zealand: The significance of the 2011 Election*, 75–98. Wellington: Institute for Governance and Policy Studies.

Humpage, Louise. 2015. *Policy change, public attitudes, and social citizenship: Does neo-liberalism matter?* Bristol: Policy Press.

Husted, Thomas A. and Lawrence W. Kenny. 1997. The effect of the expansion of the voting franchise on the size of government. *Journal of Political Economy* 105(1): 54–82. DOI: 10.1086/262065

Hyman, Prue. 2002. Fair/living/family/minimum/social wages: Historical and recent New Zealand debates. Labour, Employment and Work in New Zealand. Available at: ojs.victoria.ac.nz/LEW/article/view/1221

IMF (International Monetary Fund). 2014. *Fiscal policy and income inequality*. New York: IMF.

Inglehart, Ronald. 1977. *The silent revolution: Changing values and political styles among Western publics*. Princeton: Princeton University Press.

Inglehart, Ronald. 1984. The changing structure of political cleavages in Western society. In Russell J. Dalton, Scott C. Flanagan and Paul Allen Beck, eds, *Electoral change in advanced industrial democracies: Realignment or dealignment?*, 25–69. Princeton: Princeton University.

Inglehart, Ronald. 1990. *Culture shift in advanced industrial society*. Princeton: Princeton University Press.

Inglehart, Ronald and Pippa Norris. 2000. The developmental theory of the gender gap: Women's and men's voting behavior in global perspective. *International Political Science Review* 21(4): 441–63.

Inglehart, Ronald and Pippa Norris. 2003. *Rising tide: Gender equality and cultural change around the world*. Cambridge: Cambridge University Press.

Iusitini, Leon and Charles Crothers. 2013. Turnout and voting choices at general elections of Pacific Peoples in New Zealand. *Political Science* 65(2): 157–77. DOI: 10.1177/0032318713507206

Iversen, Torben. 2005. *Capitalism, democracy, and welfare*. Cambridge: Cambridge University Press.

Iversen, Torben and Frances Rosenbluth. 2006. The political economy of gender: Explaining cross-national variation in the gender division of labor and the gender voting gap. *American Journal of Political Science* 50(1): 1–19. DOI: 10.1111/j.1540-5907.2006.00166.x

Iversen, Torben and David Soskice. 2001. An asset theory of social preferences. *American Political Science Review* 95(4): 875–911.

Iversen, Torben and David Soskice. 2006. Electoral institutions and the politics of coalitions: Why some democracies redistribute more than others. *American Political Science Review* 100(2): 165–81.

Iyengar, Shanto and Jennifer McGrady. 2007. *Media politics: A citizen's guide*. Stanford: Stanford University Press.

Jackman, Simon. 1999. Non-compulsory voting in Australia? What surveys can (and can't) tell us. *Electoral Studies* 18: 29–48. DOI: 10.1016/S0261-3794(98)00040-7

Jacobs, David and Lindsey Myers. 2014. Union strength, neoliberalism, and inequality contingent political analyses of U.S. income differences since 1950. *American Sociological Review* 79(4): 752–74. DOI: 10.1177/0003122414536392

Jaime-Castillo, Antonio M. 2009. Economic inequality and electoral participation: A cross-country evaluation. Comparative study of the electoral systems (CSES) conference, Toronto, ON, Canada. Available at: ssrn.com/abstract=1515905 or dx.doi.org/10.2139/ssrn.1515905

James, Colin. 2014. Vested interests. Institute for Governance and Policy Studies Working Paper 14/02. Available at: igps.victoria.ac.nz/publications/files/49eb8333a6c.pdf

James, Colin. 2015. Election in a bubble. In Jon Johansson and Stephen Levine, eds, *Moments of truth: The New Zealand general election of 2014*, 70–87. Wellington: Victoria University Press.

Jennings, M. Kent, Laura Stoker and Jake Bowers. 2009. Politics across generations: Family transmission reexamined. *The Journal of Politics* 71(3): 782–99.

Johnston, Richard, Michael G. Hagen and Kathleen Hall Jamieson. 2004. *The 2000 Election and the foundations of party politics*. Cambridge: Cambridge University Press.

Joiner, Margaret. 2015. New Zealand First. In Janine Hayward, ed., *New Zealand government and politics*, 6th ed., 251–60. Melbourne: Oxford University Press.

Joyce, Stephen. 2015. The 2014 campaign: Working for New Zealand. In Jon Johansson and Stephen Levine, eds, *Moments of truth: The New Zealand general election of 2014*, 123–33. Wellington: Victoria University Press.

Jupp, James. 2012. Immigration issues in the 2010 Federal Election. In Marian Simms and John Wanna, eds, *Julia 2010: The caretaker election*, 267–78. Canberra: ANU E Press.

Jupp, James. 2015. Ethnic voters and asylum issues. In Carol Johnson and John Wanna, eds, *Abbott's gambit: The 2013 Australian federal election*, 323–40. Canberra: ANU Press.

Kahneman, Daniel. 2011. *Thinking, fast and slow.* New York: Farrar, Straus and Giroux.

Kahneman, Daniel and Amos Tversky. 1979. Prospect theory: An analysis of decision under risk. *Econometrica* 47(2): 263–91. DOI: 10.2307/1914185

Karp, Jeffrey A. 2010. How voters decide. In Raymond Miller, ed., *New Zealand Government and Politics,* 5th ed., 287–301. Melbourne: Oxford University Press.

Karp, Jeffrey A., Susan A. Banducci and Shaun Bowler. 2008. Getting out the vote: Party mobilization in a comparative perspective. *British Journal of Political Science* 38(1): 91–112. DOI: 10.1017/S0007123408000057

Karp, Jeffrey, Jack Vowles, Susan Banducci and Todd Donovan. 2002. Strategic voting, party activity, and candidate effects: Testing explanations for split voting in New Zealand's new mixed system. *Electoral Studies* 21: 1–22. DOI: 10.1016/S0261-3794(00)00031-7

Katz, Richard S. and Peter Mair. 1995. Changing models of party organization and party democracy: The emergence of the cartel party. *Party Politics* 1(1): 5–28. DOI: 10.1177/1354068895001001001

Kawharu, Hugh. 1989. *Waitangi: Maori and pakeha perspectives on the Treaty of Waitangi.* Auckland: Oxford University Press.

Kaye, Simon. 2015. On the complex relationship between political ignorance and democracy. London School of Economics and Political Science, 16 March. Available at: blogs.lse.ac.uk/politicsandpolicy/what-are-the-implications-of-political-ignorance-for-democracy/

Kayser, Mark Andreas and Michael Peress. 2012. Benchmarking across borders: Electoral accountability and the necessity of comparison. *American Political Science Review* 106(3): 661–84. DOI: 10.1017/S0003055412000275

Keall, Chris. 2016. Poll finds National support at lowest since 2014, NZ First highest since 1996. *National Business Review*, 27 April. Available at: www.nbr.co.nz/article/poll-finds-national-support-lowest-2014-nz-first-highest-1996-ck-188198

Keaney, Emily and Ben Rogers. 2006. *A citizen's duty: Voter inequality and the case for compulsory turnout.* London: Institute for Public Policy Research.

Kedar, Orit. 2005. When moderate voters prefer extreme parties: Policy balancing in parliamentary elections. *American Political Science Review* 99(2): 185–99.

Kelly, Paul. 2014. *Triumph and demise: The broken promise of a Labor generation.* Melbourne: Melbourne University Press.

Kirk, Stacey. 2014. Low voter turnout likely—poll. *Stuff*, 20 July. Available at: www.stuff.co.nz/national/politics/polls/10288601/Low-voter-turnout-likely-poll

Kitschelt, Herbert. 1994. *The transformation of European social democracy.* Cambridge: Cambridge University Press.

Knutsen, Oddbjørn. 2001. Social class, sector employment, and gender as party cleavages in the Scandinavian countries: A comparative longitudinal study, 1970–95. *Scandinavian Political Studies* 24(4): 311–50. DOI: 10.1111/1467-9477.00058

Koukoulas, Stephen. 2016. The economy of best perceptions. *Meanjin Quarterly*, Autumn issue. Available at: meanjin.com.au/essays/the-economy-of-best-perceptions/

Kriesi, Hanspeter, Edgar Grande, Romain Lachat, Martin Dolezal, Simon Bornschier and Timotheos Frey. 2008. *West European politics in the age of globalization.* Cambridge: Cambridge University Press.

Kuklinski, James, Paul J. Quirk, Jennifer Jerit, David Schwieder and Robert F. Rich. 2000. Misinformation and the currency of democratic citizenship. *Journal of Politics* 62(3): 790–816.

Kuklinski, James H. 2007. The limits of facts in citizen decision-making. Extensions, Carl Albert Congressional Research and Studies Center, University of Oklahoma, Fall, 1–6.

Kukutai, Tahu and Moana Rarere. 2015. Te ao jurihuri: Iwi identification in the census national institute of demographic and economic analysis brief, 5. Available at: www.waikato.ac.nz/__data/assets/pdf_file/0008/269216/NIDEA-Brief-No5-IwiIdentification.pdf

Kumlin, Staffan and Peter Esaiasson. 2012. Scandal fatigue? Scandal elections and satisfaction with democracy in Western Europe, 1977–2007. *British Journal of Political Science* 42(2): 263–82. DOI: 10.1017/S000712341100024X

Kymlicka, Will. 1990. *Contemporary political philosophy.* Oxford: Clarendon Press.

Laakso, Markku and Rein Taagepera. 1979. Effective number of parties: A measure with application to West Europe. *Comparative Political Studies* 12: 3–27. DOI: 10.1177/001041407901200101

Labour Party. 2013. *Policy platform.* Wellington: New Zealand Labour Party. Available at: www.labourparty.org.nz/sites/default/files/New%20Zealand%20%20Labour%20Party%20Policy%20Platform.pdf

Labour Party. 2015. We should all have the opportunity to live the Kiwi dream. Mail flyer. Wellington: New Zealand Labour Party.

Lange, David. 1986. Mackintosh memorial lecture: David Lange on politics the New Zealand way. *East Lothian Courier*, 13 June. Available at: www.jpmackintosh.ed.ac.uk/documents/DavidLangeCourierReport.pdf

Lansley, Stewart. 2006. *Rich Britain: The rise and rise of the new super wealthy.* London: Politico.

Lazarsfeld, Paul Felix, Bernard Berelson and Hazel Gaudet. 1944. *The people's choice: How the voter makes up his mind in a presidential campaign.* New York: Columbia University Press.

Lees-Marshment, Jennifer, Yannick Dufresne, Gregory Eady, Danny Osborne, Cliff van der Linden and Jack Vowles. 2015. Vote Compass in the 2014 New Zealand election: Hearing the voice of New Zealand Voters. *Political Science* 67(2): 94–124. DOI: 10.1177/0032318715609076

Lenz, Gabriel S. 2012. *Follow the leader? How voters respond to politicians' policies and performance.* Chicago: University of Chicago Press.

Leslie, Demelza. 2015. Fundraising 'wake-up call' for Labour. *Radio New Zealand*, 2 March. Available at: www.radionz.co.nz/news/political/267542/fundraising-'wake-up-call'-for-labour

Levine, Stephen, and Nigel Roberts, 2015. The general election of 2014. In Janine Hayward, ed., *New Zealand Government and Politics*, 6th ed., 334–44. Melbourne: Oxford University Press.

Lewis-Beck, Michael S. and Mary Stegmaier. 2013. The VP-function revisited: a survey of the literature on vote and popularity functions after over 40 years. *Public Choice* 157(3): 367–85. DOI: 10.1007/s11127-013-0086-6

Lijphart, Arend. 1997. Unequal participation: Democracy's unresolved dilemma. *American Political Science Review* 91(1): 1–14. DOI: 10.2307/2952255

Lindsey, David. 2006. Conscience voting. In Raymond Miller, ed., *New Zealand government and politics*, 4th ed., 186–98. Melbourne: Oxford University Press.

Lindsey, David. 2008. A brief history of conscience voting in New Zealand. *Australian Parliamentary Review* 23(1): 144–71.

Lindsey, David. 2011. *Conscience voting in New Zealand.* PhD thesis, University of Auckland.

Lipset, Seymour Martin and Stein Rokkan. 1967. *Party systems and voter alignments: Cross-national perspectives.* New York: The Free Press.

Lipson, Leslie. 1948. *The politics of equality: New Zealand's adventures in democracy.* Chicago.

Little, Conor. 2016. Green parties in government. In Emilie van Haute, ed., *Green parties in Europe*, 265–79. Abingdon Oxon UK: Routledge.

Littlewood, Michael. 2012. The history of death duties and gift duty in New Zealand. *New Zealand Journal of Taxation Law and Policy* 18: 66–103. DOI: 10.2139/ssrn.2439053

Lizotte, Mary-Kate and Andrew H. Sidman. 2009. Explaining the gender gap in political knowledge. *Politics & Gender* 5: 127–51. DOI: 10.1017/S1743923X09000130

Loader, Brian D. ed. 2007. *Young citizens in the digital age: Political engagement, young people and new media.* London: Routledge.

Lodge, Milton and Charles S. Taber. 2013. *The rationalising voter.* Cambridge: Cambridge University Press.

Lovenduski, Joni. 2005. *Feminizing politics.* Cambridge: Polity Press.

Lubbers, Marcel, Mérove Gijsberts and Peer Scheepers. 2002. Extreme right-wing voting in Western Europe. *European Journal of Political Research* 41: 345–78. DOI: 10.1111/1475-6765.00015

Lupia, Arthur. 1994. Shortcuts versus encyclopedias: Information and voting in California insurance reform elections. *American Political Science Review* 88: 63–76. DOI: 10.2307/2944882

Lupia, Arthur and Mathew D. McCubbins. 1998. *The democratic dilemma: Can citizens learn what they need to know.* Cambridge: Cambridge University Press.

Lupu, Noam and Jonas Pontusson. 2011. The structure of inequality and the politics of redistribution. *American Political Science Review* 105(2): 316–36. DOI: 10.1017/S0003055411000128

Lust, Aleksander. 2015. Online voting: Boon or bane for democracy? *Information Polity* 20(4): 313–23. DOI: 10.3233/IP-150373

Lutz, Georg and Michael Marsh. 2007. Introduction: Consequences of low turnout. *Electoral Studies* 26: 539–47. DOI: 10.1016/j.electstud.2006.10.001

Lyon, Rodney. 1982. *The principles of New Zealand liberal political thinking in the late nineteenth century.* PhD thesis, University of Auckland.

Lyons, William and Robert Alexander. 2000. A tale of two electorates: Generational replacement and the decline of voting in presidential elections. *Journal of Politics* 62(4): 1014–34. DOI: 10.1111/0022-3816.00044

Mackerras, Malcolm and Ian McAllister. 1999. Compulsory voting, party stability, and electoral advantage in Australia. *Electoral Studies* 18(2): 217–33. DOI: 10.1016/S0261-3794(98)00047-X

MacLennan, Catriona. 2014. Little progress on genuine equality for women. *New Zealand Herald,* 9 September. Available at: www.nzherald.co.nz/nz/news/article.cfm?c_id=1&objectid=11320994

Maddison, Sarah. 2006. Ideas from 'across the ditch'? Wedge politics in the 2005 New Zealand election. *Australian Journal of Political Science* 41: 427–35. dx.doi.org/10.1080/10361140600849018

Madise, Ülle and Priit Vinkel. 2014. Internet voting in Estonia: From constitutional debate to evaluation of experience over six elections. In Tanel Kerikmäe, ed., *Regulating eTechnologies in the European Union*, 53–72. Springer.

Mahler, Vincent A. 2008. Electoral turnout and income redistribution by the state: A cross-national analysis of the developed democracies. *European Journal of Political Research* 47(2): 161–83. DOI: 10.1111/j.1475-6765.2007.00726.x

Mainwaring, Scott and Edurne Zoco. 2007. Political sequences and the stabilization of interparty competition: Electoral volatility in old and new democracies. *Party Politics* 13(2): 155–78. DOI: 10.1177/1354068807073852

Mair, Peter. 2005. Democracy beyond parties. Center for the Study of Democracy, University of California, Irvine. Available at: cadmus.eui. eu/handle/1814/3291

Manhire, Toby. 2013. 'Pakeha Party' launched—a new voice for non-racism. *The Listener*, 9 July. Available at: www.listener.co.nz/culture/humour/the-internaut/pakeha-party-launched-a-new-voice-for-non-racism/

Manning, Ashleigh. 2014. Greens rated savviest in NZ's first truly social media election. *Newswire*, 19 September. Available at: www.newswire. co.nz/2014/09/greens-rated-socially-savvy-first-truly-social-media-election/

Manning, Haydon. 2002. The Australian Greens and the handicap of left legacies. *AQ: Australia Quarterly* (May–June), 17–20.

Manza, Jeff and Clem Brooks. 1998. The gender gap in U.S. presidential elections: When? Why? Implications? *American Journal of Sociology* 103(5): 1235–66. DOI: 10.1086/231352

Manza, Jeff, Michael Hout and Clem Brooks. 1995. Class voting in capitalist democracies since World War II: Dealignment, realignment, or trendless fluctuation? *Annual Review of Sociology* 21: 137–62.

Martin, Patricia Yancey. 2004. Gender as social institution. *Social Forces* 82(4): 1249–73. DOI: 10.1353/sof.2004.0081

Marx, Karl. 1875. *Critique of the Gotha Program*, reprinted in: *Marx-Engels-Werke* (MEW) vol. 19, Berlin 1978, and in: *Marx-Engels-Gesamtausgabe* (MEGA-B), Berlin 1975 ff., vol. I 25.

May, Robyn, Pat Walsh and Catherine Otto. 2003. Unions and union membership in New Zealand: Annual review for 2003. Available at: www.victoria.ac.nz/som/research/dhc-publtns/Unions_and_Union_Membership_2003.pdf

MBIE (Ministry of Business, Innovation and Employment). 2014. Minimum wage review 2014. Wellington: Ministry of Business, Innovation and Employment.

McAllen, Jess. 2014. Rocking the youth vote. *Sunday Star Times*, 25 May. Available at: www.stuff.co.nz/national/politics/10081413/Rocking-the-youth-vote

McAlister, Fiona, Debasis Bandyopadhyay, Robert Barro, Jeremy Couchman, Norman Gemmell and Gordon Liao. 2012. Average marginal tax rates for New Zealand 1907–2009. Wellington: New Zealand Treasury. Available at: www.treasury.govt.nz/publications/research-policy/wp/2012/12-04/twp12-04.pdf

McAllister, Ian and Clive Bean. 2006. Leaders, the economy or Iraq? Explaining voting in the 2004 Australian Election. *Australian Journal of Politics & History* 52: 604–20. DOI: 10.1111/j.1467-8497.2006.00435a.x

McAllister, Ian and Jack Vowles. 1994. The rise of new politics and market liberalism in Australia and New Zealand. *British Journal of Political Science* 24: 381–402. DOI: 10.1017/S0007123400006906

McDonald, Chris. 2013. *Migration and the housing market*. Wellington: Reserve Bank of New Zealand AN2013/10. Available at: media.nzherald.co.nz/webcontent/document/pdf/20147/an2013_10.pdf

McIntosh, Tracey. 2012. Māori sociology in New Zealand. *Global Dialogue* 2(3). Available at: isa-global-dialogue.net/maori-sociology-in-new-zealand/

McLauchlan, Danyl. 2014a. This actually happened. *The Dimpost*, 18 May. Available at: dimpost.wordpress.com/2014/05/18/this-actually-happened/

McLauchlan, Danyl. 2014b. Inevitable Labour pontification post. *The Dimpost*, 23 September. Available at: dimpost.wordpress. com/2014/09/23/inevitable-labour-pontification-post/

McLauchlan, Danyl. 2014c. On Cunliffe's apology for being a man. *The Dimpost*, 5 July. Available at: dimpost.wordpress.com/2014/07/05/ on-cunliffes-apology-for-being-a-man/

McLeay, Elizabeth M. 2006. Climbing on: Rules, values, and women's representation in the New Zealand parliament. In Marian Sawer, Manon Tremblay and Linda Trimble, eds, *Representing women in parliament: A comparative study*, 67–82. NY/London: Routledge.

McLeay, Elizabeth and Jack Vowles. 2007. Redefining constituency representation: The roles of New Zealand MPs under MMP. *Regional and Federal Studies* 17(1): 71–95. DOI: 10.1080/13597560701189628

McMillan, Kate. 2015. Black ops, glove puppets, and textual relations: The media's campaign 2014. In Jon Johansson and Stephen Levine, eds, *Moments of truth: The New Zealand general election of 2014*, 214–37. Wellington: Victoria University Press.

Meltzer, Allan H. and Scott F. Richard. 1981. A rational theory of the size of government. *Journal of Political Economy* 89: 914–27. DOI: 10.1086/261013

Merrill, Samuel III and Bernard Grofman. 1999. *A unified theory of voting: Directional and proximity spatial models*. Cambridge: Cambridge University Press.

Metge, Joan. 1967. *Rautahi: The Māoris of New Zealand*. London: Routledge and K. Paul.

Meyer, Thomas. 2013. *Constraints on party policy change*. Colchester: ECPR Press.

Milanovic, Branko. 2016. *Global inequality: A new approach for the era of globalization*. Cambridge: Harvard University Press.

Milbrath, Lester W. 1965. *Political participation: How and why do people get involved in politics?* Chicago: Rand McNally & Company.

Miller, Geoffrey. 2014. Three reasons why David Cunliffe's apology for being a man might have been a smart move. *Liberation.* Available at: liberation.typepad.com/liberation/2014/07/geoffrey-miler-three-reasons-why-david-cunliffes-apology-for-being-a-man-might-have-been-a-smart-move.html

Ministry for Women. 2016. Gender pay gap. Available at: women.govt.nz/our-work/utilising-womens-skills/income/gender-pay-gap

Ministry of Justice. 2014. 2014 Crime and Safety Survey: Main findings. Wellington: Ministry of Justice. Available at: www.justice.govt.nz/assets/Documents/Publications/NZCASS-201602-Main-Findings-Report-Updated.pdf

Ministry of Social Development. 2008. Briefing to the incoming government. Wellington: Ministry of Social Development. Available at: www.msd.govt.nz/documents/about-msd-and-our-work/publications-resources/corporate/bims/social-outcomes-bim-2008.pdf

Mitchell, Amy, Jeffrey Gottfried, Michael Barthel and Elisa Shearer. 2016. Young adults. Pew Research Center, 5 July. Available at: www.journalism.org/2016/07/07/young-adults/

Mitchell, Charlie. 2014. Voter turnout near record low. *Stuff,* 21 September. Available at: www.stuff.co.nz/national/politics/10526861/Voter-turnout-near-record-low

Moene, Karl Ove and Michael Wallerstein. 2001. Inequality, social insurance, and redistribution. *American Political Science Review* 95(4): 859–74. DOI: 10.1017/CBO9780511619793.014

Mondak, Jeffery J. and Mary R. Anderson. 2004. The knowledge gap: A reexamination of gender-based differences in political knowledge. *Journal of Politics* 66(2): 492–512. DOI: 10.1111/j.1468-2508.2004.00161.x

Mudde, Cas. 2007. *Populist radical right parties in Europe.* Cambridge: Cambridge University Press.

Mueller, Dennis C. and Thomas Stratmann. 2003. The economic effects of democratic participation. *Journal of Public Economics* 87(9–10): 2129–55. DOI: 10.1016/S0047-2727(02)00046-4

Mughan, Anthony. 2007. Economic insecurity and welfare preferences: A micro-level analysis. *Comparative Politics* 29(3): 293–310.

Müller-Rommel, Ferdinand and Thomas Poguntke, eds. 2002. *Green parties in national governments.* London: Frank Cass.

Murchison, Ashley. 2015. Social media and participation. In Janine Hayward, ed., *New Zealand government and politics*, 6th ed., 523–33. Melbourne: Oxford University Press.

Nagel, Jack. 1998. Social choice in a pluralitarian democracy: The politics of market liberalization in New Zealand. *British Journal of Political Science* 28(2): 223–67. DOI: 10.1177/003231878804000202

Nagel, Jack. 2012. Evaluating democracy in New Zealand under MMP. *Policy Quarterly* 8(2): 3–11.

National Business Review. 2013. Labour/Greens fall behind as 'man ban' drives men to National—poll. *National Business Review*, 14 November. Available at: www.nbr.co.nz/article/labourgreens-fall-behind-man-ban-drives-men-national-poll-ck-148704

National Party. 2014a. Policy 2014: Children and families. Available at: d3n8a8pro7vhmx.cloudfront.net/nationalparty/legacy_url/196/children-and-families-policy.pdf?1484559627

National Party. 2014b. Policy 2014: Women's affairs. Available at: national.org.nz/files/documents/womens-affairs-policy.pdf

New Zealand Companies Office. 2006. Union membership report 2006. Auckland: New Zealand Companies Office. Available at: www.societies.govt.nz/cms/registered-unions/annual-return-membership-reports/older-reports/Union-Membership-2006.pdf/view

New Zealand Companies Office. 2009. Union membership report 2009. Auckland: New Zealand Companies Office. Available at: www.societies.govt.nz/cms/registered-unions/annual-return-membership-reports/older-reports/union-membership-2009.pdf/view

New Zealand Companies Office. 2014. Union membership report 2014. Auckland: New Zealand Companies Office. Available at: www.societies.govt.nz/cms/registered-unions/annual-return-membership-reports/2014

New Zealand Election Study. 1987. Auckland, University of Auckland.

New Zealand Election Study. 1990. Hamilton: University of Waikato. Available at: www.nzes.org/exec/show/1990

New Zealand Election Study. 1993. Hamilton: University of Waikato. Available at: www.nzes.org/exec/show/1993

New Zealand Election Study. 1996. Hamilton: University of Waikato. Available at: www.nzes.org/exec/show/1996

New Zealand Election Study. 1999. Hamilton: University of Waikato. Available at: www.nzes.org/exec/show/1999

New Zealand Election Study. 2002. Auckland: University of Auckland. Available at: www.nzes.org/exec/show/2002

New Zealand Election Study. 2005. Auckland: University of Auckland. Available at: www.nzes.org/exec/show/2005

New Zealand Election Study. 2008. Auckland: University of Auckland. Available at: www.nzes.org/exec/show/2008

New Zealand Election Study. 2011. Auckland: University of Auckland. Available at: www.nzes.org/exec/show/2011

New Zealand Election Study. 2014. Wellington: Victoria University of Wellington. Available at: www.nzes.org/exec/show/2014

New Zealand Government. 2015. Regulatory Impact Statement: Budget 2015 package to address child material hardship in New Zealand. Wellington: Department of Prime Minister and Cabinet, Ministry of Social Development, and Treasury. Available at: www.msd.govt.nz/documents/about-msd-and-our-work/publications-resources/regulatory-impact-statements/ris-budget15-cmh-may15.pdf

New Zealand Herald. 2014. CEOs overwhelmingly back John Key. 11 September.

New Zealand Parliament. 2006. Principles of the Treaty of Waitangi Deletion Bill—First reading. Available at: www.parliament.nz/en/pb/hansard-debates/rhr/document/48HansD_20060726_00001143/principles-of-the-treaty-of-waitangi-deletion-bill-first

New Zealand Parliamentary Service. 2014. Publicity guidelines. Wellington: New Zelaand Parliament. Available at: www.parliament.nz/media/1408/publicity-guidelines-pdf-715-kb.pdf

New Zealand Press Council. 2017. Statement of principles. Available at: www.presscouncil.org.nz/principles

Newshub. 2014a. Decision 14 leaders debate – part 4. Available at: www.newshub.co.nz/politics/decision-14-leaders-debate---part-4-2014091021

Newshub. 2014b. John Key rejects the Green Party. *Newshub*, 12 September. Available at: www.newshub.co.nz/politics/john-key-rejects-the-green-party-2014091218#axzz4GudIbmnh

Newton, Lisa. 2008. *Illegal, alien, or immigrant: The politics of immigration reform*. New York: New York University Press.

Nolan, Matt. 2014. National's not alternative budget—Budget 2014. *The Visible Hand in Economics*, 16 May. Available at: www.tvhe.co.nz/2014/05/15/nationals-not-alternative-budget-budget-2014/

Nolan, Melanie. 2000. *Breadwinning: New Zealand women and the state*. Christchurch: Canterbury University Press.

Norman, Russell. 2015. Stable in the storm: The Green campaign. In Jon Johansson and Stephen Levine, eds, *Moments of truth: The New Zealand general election of 2014*, 147–52. Wellington: Victoria University Press.

Norris, Pippa. 2001. *Digital divide: Civic engagement, information poverty and the internet worldwide*. Cambridge: Cambridge University Press.

Norris, Pippa. 2002. *Democratic phoenix: Reinventing political activism*. Cambridge: Cambridge University Press.

Norris, Pippa. 2005. *Radical right. Voters and parties in the electoral market*. Cambridge: Cambridge University Press.

Nyhan, Brendan and Jason Reifler. 2010. When corrections fail: The persistence of political misperceptions. *Political Behavior* 32(2): 303–30. DOI: 10.1007/s11109-010-9112-2

O'Hara, Mary. 2015. *Austerity bites: A journey to the sharp end of cuts in the UK.* Bristol: Policy Press.

O'Toole, Therese, Michael Lister, Dave Marsh, Su Jones and Alex McDonagh. 2005. Tuning out or left out? Participation and non-participation among young people. *Contemporary Politics* 9(1): 45–61. DOI: 10.1080/1356977032000072477

OECD (Organisation for Economic Co-operation and Development). 2016. OECD income distribution database (IDD): Gini, poverty, income, methods and concepts. Available at: www.oecd.org/social/income-distribution-database.htm

One News. 2014. Belief in dirty politics claims growing—poll. 1 September. Available at: tvnz.co.nz/vote-2014-news/belief-in-dirty-politics-claims-growing-poll-6068795

Oram, Rod. 2015. New Zealand and the global financial crisis. In Janine Hayward, ed., *New Zealand government and politics*, 6th ed., 60–70. Melbourne: Oxford University Press.

Orange, Claudia. 2011. *The Treaty of Waitangi*, 2nd ed. Wellington: Bridget Williams Books.

Orr, Graeme. 2015. *Ritual and rhythm in electoral systems. A comparative legal account.* Abingdon Oxon: Routledge.

Ostry, Jonathan David, Andrew Berg and Charalambos G. Tsangarides. 2014. *Redistribution, inequality, and growth.* New York: International Monetary Fund.

Pacek, Alexander C. and Benjamin Radcliff. 1995. Economic voting and the welfare state: A cross-national analysis. *The Journal of Politics* 57(1): 44–61. DOI: 10.2307/2960270

Pagani, Josie. 2013. About that 'man ban'. *Pundit*, 4 July. Available at: www.pundit.co.nz/content/about-that-man-ban

Pagani, Josie. 2016. How the left should respond to Donald Trump's elected-presidency. *New Zealand Herald*, 17 November. Available at: www.nzherald.co.nz/opinion/news/article.cfm?c_id=466&objectid= 11749444

Page, Benjamin I. and Robert Y. Shapiro. 1992. *The rational public: Fifty years of trends in Americans' policy preferences*. Chicago: University of Chicago Press.

Page, Dorothy. 1996. *The National Council of Women: A centennial history*. Wellington: Bridget Williams Books.

Pakulski, Jan. 2005. Foundations of a post-class analysis. In Erik Olin Wright, ed., *Approaches to class analysis*, 152–79. Cambridge: Cambridge University Press.

Park, Shee-Jeong. 2006. *Political participation of 'Asian' New Zealanders: A case study of ethnic Chinese and Korean New Zealanders*. PhD thesis, University of Auckland.

PCVD (Parliamentary Conscience Votes Database). 2016. Available at: votes.wotfun.com/

Parry, Geraint, George Moyser and Neil Day. 1992. *Political participation and democracy in Britain*. Cambridge: Cambridge University Press.

Patterson, Jane. 2016. Govt out to reduce number of new migrants. *Radio New Zealand*, 11 October. Available at: www.radionz.co.nz/ news/political/315389/govt-out-to-reduce-number-of-new-migrants

Paxton, Pamela, Sheri Kunovich and Melanie M. Hughes. 2007. Gender in politics. *Annual Review of Sociology* 33: 263–84. DOI: 10.1146/ annurev.soc.33.040406.131651

Perry, Bryan. 2014. *Household incomes in New Zealand: Trends in indicators of inequality and hardship 1982 to 2013*. Wellington: Ministry of Social Development.

Perry, Bryan. 2015. *Household incomes in New Zealand: Trends in indicators of inequality and hardship 1982 to 2014*. Wellington: Ministry of Social Development.

Phillips, Jock. 2014. Ideas in New Zealand—identity politics. *Te Ara: The Encyclopedia of New Zealand*, 22 October. Available at: www.TeAra. govt.nz/en/ideas-in-new-zealand/page-8

Pickup, Mark and Geoffrey Evans. 2013. Addressing the endogeneity of economic evaluations in models of political choice. *Public Opinion Quarterly* 77(3): 735–54. DOI: 10.1093/poq/nft028

Piketty, Thomas. 2013. *Capital in the twenty-first century.* Cambridge: Belknap/Harvard University Press.

Poguntke, Thomas. 1987. New politics and party systems: The emergence of a new type of party? *West European Politics* 10(1): 76–88. DOI: 10.1080/01402388708424615

Poguntke, Thomas. 2002. Green parties in national governments: From protest to acquiescence. *Environmental Politics* 11(1): 133–45. DOI: 10.1080/714000585

Poot, Jacques and Bill Cochrane. 2005. *Measuring the economic impact of immigration: A scoping paper.* Population Studies Centre, University of Waikato Working Paper 48.

Popkin, Samuel L. 1991. *The reasoning voter: Communication and persuasion in presidential campaigns.* Chicago: University of Chicago Press.

Radcliff, Benjamin. 1992. The welfare state, turnout, and the economy: A comparative analysis. *The American Political Science Review* 86(2): 444–54.

Radio Live. 2014. David Cunliffe insists his apology for being a man was made in the context of domestic violence and is not a commentary on all New Zealand men. 4 July.

Radio New Zealand. 2014a. Cunliffe says no to Internet Mana. 25 May. Available at: www.radionz.co.nz/news/political/251425/cunliffe-says-no-to-internet-mana

Radio New Zealand. 2014b. Foreshore and seabed apology possible. 1 July. Available at: www.radionz.co.nz/news/te-manu-korihi/248680/foreshore-and-seabed-apology-possible

Radio New Zealand. 2014c. PM tells National voters to get out and vote. 28 June. Available at: www.radionz.co.nz/news/political/248446/pm-tells-national-voters-to-get-out-and-vote

Radio New Zealand. 2014d. Mandatory voting idea questioned. 25 May. Available at: www.radionz.co.nz/news/political/245351/mandatory-voting-idea-questioned

Radio New Zealand. 2014e. Labour 'not hurt' by Greens positioning. 12 September. Available at: www.radionz.co.nz/news/political/254400/labour-'not-hurt'-by-greens-positioning

Radio New Zealand. 2016. No online voting in 2016 local body elections. 19 April. Available at: www.radionz.co.nz/news/national/301851/online-voting-trial-won't-go-ahead

Rankin, Keith. 2014. New Zealand's income tax in the rollercoaster Muldoon years: 1967–84. Paper for Asia Pacific Economic and Business History Conference, Hamilton, New Zealand. Available at: unitec.researchbank.ac.nz/handle/10652/2880

Rashbrooke, Max. 2013. *Inequality: A New Zealand crisis.* Wellington: Bridget Williams Books.

Rawls, John. 1971. *A theory of justice.* Cambridge: Harvard University Press.

Rehm, Philipp. 2016. *Risk inequality and welfare states.* New York: Cambridge University Press.

Repetto, Robert, Roger C. Downer, Robin Jenkins and Jaqueline Geoghegan. 1992. Green fees: How a tax shift can work for the environment and the economy. World Resources Institute, November. Available at: www.actrees.org/files/Policy_Alerts/wri_greenfees.pdf

Representation Commission. 2014. Report of the Representation Commission 2014. Wellington, Representation Commission. Available at: www.elections.org.nz/sites/default/files/bulk-upload/documents/report_of_the_representation_commission_2014.pdf

Reserve Bank of New Zealand. 2017. Key graphs. www.rbnz.govt.nz/statistics/key-graphs.

Ridgeway, Cecilia L. 2011. *Framed by gender: How gender inequality persists in the modern world.* New York: Oxford University Press.

Risman, Barbara. 1998. *Gender vertigo.* New Haven: Yale University Press.

Robertson, Emily. 2015. No boys allowed: The Labour Party's 'man ban' and political party gender quotas in Aotearoa New Zealand. Unpublished dissertation, University of Auckland.

Robinson, Claire. 2014. If it wasn't laughable it would be a great first line in a romance novel. Available at: spinprofessor.tumblr.com/post/90799198069/if-it-wasnt-

Robinson, Matt. 2014. Voter apathy needs to end. *Stuff Nation*, 23 January. Available at: www.stuff.co.nz/stuff-nation/assignments/share-your-news-and-views/9641572/Youth-voter-apathy-needs-to-end

Robson, Sarah. 2014. National's Epsom candidate wants votes for ACT. *Newshub*, 29 August. Available at: www.newshub.co.nz/politics/nationals-epsom-candidate-wants-votes-for-act-2014082906

Rosenstone, Steven. 1982. Economic adversity and voter turnout. *American Journal of Political Science* 26: 25–46. DOI: 10.2307/2110837

Ross, Karen and Tobias Bürger. 2014. Face to Face(book): Social media, political campaigning and the unbearable lightness of being there. *Political Science* 66(1): 46–62. DOI: 10.1177/0032318714534106

Roughan, John. 2014. *John Key: Portrait of a Prime Minister.* Auckland: Penguin.

Rüdig, Wolfgang. 2012. The perennial success of the German Greens. *Environmental Politics* 21(1): 108–30. DOI: 10.1080/09644016.2011.643371

Rusk, Jerrold G., Harold D. Clarke, David Sanders, Marianne C. Stewart and Paul Whiteley. 2004. *Political choice in Britain.* Oxford: Oxford University Press.

Rutherford, Hamish. 2014. Greens pro-market: Russel Norman. *Stuff*, 27 August. Available at: www.stuff.co.nz/national/politics/10428953/Greens-pro-market-Russel-Norman

Rutherford, Hamish. 2015. Record migration boosts growth short term, but will it make NZ richer? *Stuff*, 24 November. Available at: www.stuff.co.nz/business/74358744/Record-migration-boosts-growth-short-term-but-will-it-make-NZ-richer

Rydgren, Jens. 2007. The sociology of the radical right. *Annual Review of Sociology* 33: 241–62. DOI: 10.1146/annurev.soc.33.040406.131752

Sachdeva, Sam. 2016. Labour leader Andrew Little dismisses Helen Clark's advice about 'commanding the centre ground'. *Stuff*, 25 September. Available at: www.stuff.co.nz/national/politics/84636485/Labour-leader-Andrew-Little-dismisses-Helen-Clarks-advice-about-commanding-the-centre-ground

Salient. 2014. Interviews with MPs on women's issues. 3 August. Available at: tinyurl.com/zd2jeb6

Salmond, Rob, 2014. Who do the 'missing million' look like? *The Standard*, 2 July. Available at thestandard.org.nz/polity-who-do-the-missing-million-like/

Salmond, Rob. 2015. Voter targeting: Developments in 2014. In Jon Johansson and Stephen Levine, eds, *Moments of truth: The New Zealand general election of 2014*, 239–51. Wellington: Victoria University Press.

Sawer, Marian. 2003. *The ethical state? Social liberalism in Australia*. Melbourne: Melbourne University Press.

Sawer, Marian and Barry Hindess, eds. 2004. *Us and them: Anti-elitism in Australia*. Perth: API Network.

Schlozman, Kay Lehman, Nancy Burns and Sidney Verba. 1999. 'What happened at work today?': A multistage model of gender, employment, and political participation. *The Journal of Politics* 61(1): 29–53.

Schlozman, Kay Lehman, Sidney Verba and Henry E. Brady. 2012. *The unheavenly chorus: Unequal political voice and the broken promise of American democracy*. Princeton: Princeton University Press.

Schwindt-Bayer, Leslie A. 2006. Still supermadres? Gender and the policy priorities of Latin American legislators. *American Journal of Political Science* 50(3): 570–85. DOI: 10.1111/j.1540-5907.2006.00202.x

Segaard, Signe Bock, Harald Baldersheim and Jo Saglie. 2013. The Norwegian trial with internet voting: Results and challenges. *Revista general de derecho público comparado*, 13. Available at: dialnet. unirioja.es/servlet/articulo?codigo=4658860

Sherman, Maiki. 2016. Allow state schools to become charter schools—ACT Party. *Newshub*, 31 August. Available at: www. newshub.co.nz/politics/act---allow-state-schools-to-become-charter-schools-2016083107

Simms, Marian and John Warhurst, eds. 2005. *Mortgage nation: The 2004 federal election.* Perth: Curtin University of Technology, API Network.

Sinclair, Keith. 1959. *A history of New Zealand.* Harmondsworth: Penguin.

Sinclair, Keith. 1967. *The Liberal Government, 1891–1912: First steps towards a welfare state.* Auckland: Heinmann Educational Books.

Small, Vernon. 2013. 'Man ban' dumped but gender target stays. *Stuff*, 7 July. Available at: www.stuff.co.nz/national/politics/8898625/Man-ban-dumped-but-gender-target-stays

Small, Vernon. 2016. Cunliffe was told to contemplate retirement—and finally takes the hint. *Stuff*, 1 November. Available at: www.stuff.co.nz/national/politics/opinion/85961450/cunliffe-was-told-to-contemplate-retirement--and-finally-takes-the-hint

Smellie, Pattrick. 2014. The book that hit like a bomb. *The Listener*, 26 May. Available at: www.listener.co.nz/current-affairs/the-book-that-hit-like-a-bomb/

Smets, Kaat and Carolien van Ham. 2013. The embarrassment of riches? A meta-analysis of individual-level research on voter turnout. *Electoral Studies* 32(2): 344–59. DOI: 10.1016/j.electstud.2012.12.006

Smith, Rodney, Ariadne Vromen and Ian Cook. 2006. *Keywords in Australian politics.* Port Melbourne: Cambridge University Press.

Snoopman. 2014. John Key's suppressed 'missing million' voters letter. *Scoop Independent News*, 5 October. Available at: www.scoop.co.nz/stories/HL1410/S00029/john-keys-suppressed-missing-million-voters-letter.htm

Solt, Frederick. 2008. Economic inequality and democratic political engagement. *American Journal of Political Science* 52: 48–60. DOI: 10.1111/j.1540-5907.2007.00298.x

Speck, Stefan. 1999. Energy and carbon taxes and their distributional implications. *Energy Policy* 27(11): 659–67. DOI: 10.1016/S0301-4215(99)00059-2

Springall, Drew, Travis Finkenauer, Zakir Durumeric, Jason Kitcat, Harri Hursti, Margaret MacAlpine and J. Alex Halderman. 2014. Security analysis of the Estonian internet voting system. Proceedings of the 2014 ACM SIGSAC conference on computer and communications security, 703–15.

Statistics New Zealand. 2013. 2013 Census QuickStats about culture and identity. Wellington: Statistics New Zealand. Available at: www.stats.govt.nz/Census/2013-census/profile-and-summary-reports/quickstats-culture-identity/religion.aspx

Statistics New Zealand. 2014a. 2013 Census QuickStats about education and training. Wellington: Statistics New Zealand. Available at: www.stats.govt.nz/Census/2013-census/profile-and-summary-reports/qstats-education-training/highest-qualification.aspx

Statistics New Zealand. 2014b. 2013 Census QuickStats about income. Wellington: Statistics New Zealand. Available at: www.stats.govt.nz/Census/2013-census/profile-and-summary-reports/quickstats-income/personal-income-ethnic.aspx

Statistics New Zealand. 2014c. Voter turnout. Available at: www.stats.govt.nz/browse_for_stats/snapshots-of-nz/nz-social-indicators/Home/Trust%20and%20participation%20in%20government/voter-turnout.aspx

Statistics New Zealand. 2014d. Nonvoters in the 2008 and 2011 general elections: Findings from the New Zealand General Social Survey. Wellington: Statistics New Zealand. Available at: m.stats.govt.nz/browse_for_stats/people_and_communities/Well-being/civic-human-rights/non-voters-2008-2011-gen-elections.aspx#data

Statistics New Zealand. 2014e. 2013 Census QuickStats about income. Available at: m.stats.govt.nz/Census/2013-census/profile-and-summary-reports/quickstats-income.aspx

Statistics New Zealand. 2016a. Household net worth statistics: Year ended June 2015. Wellington: Statistics New Zealand.

Statistics New Zealand. 2016b. New Zealand social indicators—unemployment. Wellington: Statistics New Zealand. Available at: www.stats.govt.nz/browse_for_stats/snapshots-of-nz/nz-social-indicators/Home/Labour%20market/unemployment.aspx

Statistics New Zealand. 2016c. Estimated resident population (ERP), national population by ethnic group, age, and sex, 30 June 1996, 2001, 2006, and 2013. Available at: nzdotstat.stats.govt.nz/wbos/Index.aspx?DataSetCode=TABLECODE7511

Statistics New Zealand. 2016d. 2013 Census tables about a place: Auckland region. Available at: www.stats.govt.nz/Census/2013-census/data-tables/tables-about-a-place.aspx?request_value=24394%20%20%20%20%20%20%20%20%20%20%20%20%20%20%20%20%20%20%20%20&reportid=14&tabname=Culturaldiversity

Statistics New Zealand. 2016e. Impacts of unemployment. Wellington: Statistics New Zealand.

Statistics New Zealand. 2016f. Speakers of teo reo Māori. Available at: www.stats.govt.nz/browse_for_stats/snapshots-of-nz/nz-progress-indicators/home/social/speakers-of-te-reo-maori.aspx

Stenner, Karen. 2005. *The authoritarian dynamic*. Cambridge: Cambridge University Press.

Stevens, Michael. J. 2015. Māori political history 1860–1960. In Janine Hayward, ed., *New Zealand government and politics*, 6th ed., 4–14. Melbourne: Oxford University Press.

Stockemer, Daniel and Lyle Scruggs. 2012. Income inequality, development and electoral turnout—New evidence on a burgeoning debate. *Electoral Studies* 31: 764–73. DOI: 10.1016/j.electstud.2012.06.006

Stokes, Donald E. 1963. Spatial models of party competition. *American Political Science Review* 57(2): 368–77. DOI: 10.2307/1952828

Stolle, Dietlind and Elisabeth Gidengil. 2010. What do women really know? A gendered analysis of varieties of political knowledge. *Perspectives on Politics* 8: 93–109. DOI: 10.1017/S1537592709992684

Stratmann, Thomas. 2005. Some talk: Money in politics. A (partial) review of the literature. *Public Choice* 124: 135–56. DOI: 10.1007/s11127-005-4750-3

Strøm, Kaare. 1990. *Minority government and majority rule.* Cambridge: Cambridge University Press.

Stuff. 2015. No controversial policy expected at Labour conference. 4 November. Available at: www.stuff.co.nz/national/politics/73686626/No-controversial-policy-expected-at-Labour-conference

Sullivan, Ann. 2015. Tōrangapū—Māori and political parties—National, New Zealand First, Māori and Mana parties. *Te Ara: The Encyclopedia of New Zealand.* Available at: teara.govt.nz/en/torangapu-maori-and-political-parties?source=rel_link

Sullivan, Ann and Dimitri Margaritis. 2000. Māori voting patterns in 1999. In Stephen Levine and Nigel Roberts, eds, *Left turn: The New Zealand general election of 1999*, 175–83. Wellington: Victoria University of Wellington Press.

Sullivan, Ann and Dimitri Margaritis. 2002. Coming home: Māori voting in 1999. In Jack Vowles, Peter Aimer, Jeffrey Karp, Susan Banducci, Raymond Miller and Ann Sullivan, eds, *Proportional representation on trial: The 1999 election in New Zealand and the fate of MMP*, 66–82. Auckland: Auckland University Press.

Sullivan, Ann and Jack Vowles. 1998. Realignment? Māori and the 1996 Election. In Jack Vowles, Peter Aimer, Susan Banducci and Jeffrey Karp, eds, *Voters' victory? New Zealand's first election under proportional representation*, 171–91. Auckland: Auckland University Press.

Sullivan, Ann, Martin von Randow and Aimee Matiu. 2014. Māori voters, public policy, and privatisation. In Jack Vowles, ed., *The new electoral politics in New Zealand: The significance of the 2011 election*, 141–60. Wellington: Institute for Governance and Policy Studies.

Sunday Star-Times. 2014. Labour's decision to fly solo could prove costly. 13 April.

Swers, Michele L. 2002. *The difference women make: The policy impact of women in congress.* Chicago: University of Chicago Press.

SWIID (Standardized World Income Inequality Database). 2016. Available at: myweb.uiowa.edu/fsolt/swiid/swiid.html

Talshir, Gayil. 2002. *The political ideology of green parties. From the politics of nature to redefining the nature of politics.* Houndmills: Palgrave Macmillan.

Task Force on Inequality and American Democracy. 2004. *American democracy in an age of rising inequality.* Washington DC: American Political Science Association.

Taylor, Kevin. 2004. National accuses Government of communism by stealth. *New Zealand Herald*, 11 June. Available at: www.nzherald. co.nz/nz/news/article.cfm?c_id=1&objectid=3571934

Television New Zealand. 2014. Vote Compass: Government should do more on inequality. *TVNZ*, 8 September. Available at: www.tvnz. co.nz/one-news/archive/vote-compass-government-should-do-more-on-inequality-6075440.html

The Nation. 2016. In search of the missing voters. *TV3*, 28 June.

Trevett, Claire 2011a. Key admits underclass still growing. *New Zealand Herald*, 8 October.

Trevett, Claire. 2011b. PM rules out any NZ First deal. *New Zealand Herald*, 2 February.

Trevett, Claire. 2013. United Future Party registration cancelled. *New Zealand Herald*, 31 May.

Trevett, Claire. 2014. Cunliffe denies double standards over deals. *New Zealand Herald*, 29 July.

Trevett, Claire. 2015. Election campaign funds: Labour outspent by Greens. *New Zealand Herald*, 24 February.

Trotter, Chris. 2013. The high peaks of principle: Thoughts on Labour's 'man ban'. *The Daily Blog*, 5 July. Available at: thedailyblog. co.nz/2013/07/05/the-high-peaks-of-principle-thoughts-on-labours-man-ban/

Trotter, Chris. 2014. Uncomplicated loyalties: Why Cunliffe and the Labour left cannot win. *The Daily Blog*, 24 September. Available at: thedailyblog.co.nz/2014/09/24/uncomplicated-loyalties-why-cunliffe-and-the-labour-left-cannot-win/

UMR. 2014. Inequality in New Zealand. Available at: umr.co.nz/sites/umr/files/final_inequality_mar-14_1.pdf

Van Biezen, Ingrid, Peter Mair and Thomas Poguntke. 2012. Going, going ... gone? The decline of party membership in contemporary Europe. *European Journal of Political Research* 51: 24–56. DOI: 10.1111/j.1475-6765.2011.01995.x

Van den Berg, Job C. and Hilde Coffé. 2012. Educational and class cleavages in voting behavior in Belgium: The effect of income, EGP class and education on party choice in Flanders and Wallonia. *Acta Politica* 47(2): 151–80.

Van der Brug, Wouter, Meindert Fennema and Jean Tillie. 2000. Anti-immigrant parties in Europe: Ideological or protest votes? *European Journal of Political Research* 37(1): 77–102. DOI: 10.1023/A:1007013503658

Van der Waal, Jeroen, Peter Achterberg and Dick Houtman. 2007. Class is not dead. It has been buried alive: Class voting and cultural voting in Western societies (1956–1990). *Politics & Society* 35(3): 403–26. DOI: 10.1177/0032329207304314

van Haute, Emilie, ed. 2016. *Green parties in Europe*. Abingdon Oxon: Routledge.

Vance, Andrea. 2011. Inequality report ignores tax cuts for rich—Goff. *Stuff*, 3 August. Available at: www.stuff.co.nz/national/politics/5379331/Inequality-report-ignores-tax-cuts-for-rich-Goff

Vance, Andrea. 2014. Greens launch climate change policy. *Stuff*, 1 June. Available at: www.stuff.co.nz/national/politics/10108920/Greens-launch-climate-change-policy

Vassil, Kristjan, Mihkel Solvak, Pritt Vinkel, Alexander H. Trechsel and R. Michael Alvarez. 2016. The diffusion of internet voting: Usage patterns of internet voting in Estonia between 2005 and 2015. *Government Information Quarterly* 33(3): 453–59. DOI: 10.1016/j.giq.2016.06.007

Venuto, Damien. 2014. How Kiwi political parties measure up on Facebook. *Stop Press*, 15 July. Available at: stoppress.co.nz/news/facebook-stats-politicians

Verba, Sidney. 1996. The citizen as respondent: Sample surveys and American democracy. Presidential Address, American Political Science Association, 1995. *The American Political Science Review* 90: 1–7. DOI: 10.2307/2082793

Verba, Sidney, Nancy Burns and Kay Lehman Schlozman. 1997. Knowing and caring about politics: Gender and political engagement. *Journal of Politics* 59: 1051–57. DOI: 10.2307/2998592

Verba, Sidney, Kay Lehman Schlozman and Henry E. Brady. 1995. *Voice and equality: Civic voluntarism in American politics.* Cambridge: Harvard University Press.

Victoria University of Wellington Election Study. 1963. Wellington: Victoria University of Wellington.

Victoria University of Wellington Election Study. 1975. Wellington: Victoria University of Wellington.

Vlastos, Gregory. 1962. Justice and equality. In Richard Brandt, ed., *Social justice*. Englewood Cliffs: Prentice-Hall.

Vote Compass New Zealand. 2014. Toronto: Vox Pop Labs.

Vowles, Jack. 1982. Liberal democracy: Pakeha political ideology. *New Zealand Journal of History* 21(2): 215–27.

Vowles, Jack. 1987. The Fourth Labour Government: Ends, means, and for whom? In Jonathan Boston and Martin Holland, eds, *The Fourth Labour Government: Radical politics in New Zealand*, 15–35. Auckland, Oxford University Press.

Vowles, Jack. 1990. Nuclear-free New Zealand and Rogernomics: The survival of a Labour Government. *Politics* (now *Australian Journal of Political Science*) 25(1): 81–91. DOI: 10.1080/00323269008402107

Vowles, Jack. 1993. Gender and electoral behaviour in New Zealand: Findings from the present and the past. *Political Science* 45(1): 122–35. DOI: 10.1177/003231879304500109

Vowles, Jack. 2002a. The puzzle of turnout. In Jack Vowles, Peter Aimer, Jeffrey Karp, Susan Banducci, Raymond Miller and Ann Sullivan, eds, *Proportional representation on trial*, 99–113. Auckland: Auckland University Press.

Vowles, Jack. 2002b. What happened at the 1999 Election. In Jack Vowles, Peter Aimer, Jeffrey Karp, Susan Banducci, Raymond Miller and Ann Sullivan, eds, *Proportional representation on trial*, 83–98. Auckland: Auckland University Press.

Vowles, Jack. 2004a. Estimating change during the campaign. In Jack Vowles, Peter Aimer, Susan Banducci, Jeffrey Karp and Raymond Miller, eds, *Voters' veto: The 2002 Election in New Zealand and the consolidation of minority government*, 33–47. Auckland: Auckland University Press.

Vowles, Jack. 2004b. Patterns of public opinion. In Jack Vowles, Peter Aimer, Susan Banducci, Jeffrey Karp and Raymond Miller, eds, *Voters' veto: The 2002 Election in New Zealand and the consolidation of minority government*, 117–33. Auckland: Auckland University Press.

Vowles, Jack. 2010. Electoral system change, generations, competitiveness and turnout in New Zealand, 1963–2005. *British Journal of Political Science*, 40: 875–95. DOI: 10.1017/S0007123409990342

Vowles, Jack. 2011. Why voters prefer coalitions: Rationality or norms. *Political Science* 63: 126–45. DOI: 10.1177/0032318711403917

Vowles, Jack. 2014a. Down, down, down: Turnout from 1946 to 2011. In Jack Vowles, ed., *The new electoral politics in New Zealand: The significance of the 2011 Election*, 53–74. Wellington: Institute for Governance and Policy Studies.

Vowles, Jack. 2014b. Putting the 2011 Election in its place. In Jack Vowles, ed., *The new electoral politics in New Zealand: The significance of the 2011 Election*, 27–52. Wellington: Institute for Governance and Policy Studies.

Vowles, Jack. 2014c. The 2011 election through a wide-angle lens. In Jack Vowles, ed., *The new electoral politics in New Zealand: The significance of the 2011 Election*, 217–36. Wellington: Institute for Governance and Policy Studies.

Vowles, Jack. 2015a. Voter turnout. In Janine Hayward, ed., *New Zealand government and politics*, 6th ed., 287–99. Melbourne: Oxford University Press.

Vowles, Jack. 2015b. New Zealand Longitudinal Turnout Study (NZLTS), First Wave. Dataset. Wellington, Vicoria University of Wellington.

Vowles, Jack. forthcoming. The Big Picture: Turnout at the Macro-Level, in ed. Justin Fisher, Marta Cantijoch, Edward Fieldhouse, Mark Franklin, Rachel Gibson, and Christopher Wlezien, *The Routledge Handbook of Elections, Voting Behavior and Public Opinion*. Oxford, Routledge.

Vowles, Jack, and Peter Aimer. 1993. *Voters' vengeance: The 1990 Election in New Zealand and the fate of the Fourth Labour Government.* Auckland: Auckland University Press.

Vowles, Jack, Peter Aimer, Helena Catt, Jim Lamare and Raymond Miller. 1995. *Towards consensus? The 1993 general election and referendum in New Zealand and the transition to proportional representation.* Auckland: Auckland University Press.

Vromen, Ariadne, Brian D. Loader, Michael A. Xenos and Francesco Bailo. 2016. Everyday making through Facebook engagement: Young citizens' political interactions in Australia, UK and USA. *Political Studies* 64(3): 513–33. DOI: 10.1177/0032321715614012

Walters, Laura. 2014. Parties adopt women-specific policies. *Stuff,* 25 May. Available at: www.stuff.co.nz/national/politics/10077682/Parties-adopt-women-specific-policies

Walters, Laura. 2015. Labour's 'half-baked' property data turns Chinese buyers into 'scapegoats'. *Stuff*, 11 July. Available at: www.stuff.co.nz/business/money/70155168/labours-halfbaked-property-data-turns-chinese-buyers-into-scapegoats

Ward, Ian. 2002. The Tampa, wedge politics, and a lesson for political journalism. *Australian Journalism Review* 24(1): 21–39.

Waring, Marilyn, Gaye Greenwood and Christine Pintat. 2000. *Politics: Women's insight.* Geneva: Inter-Parliamentary Union.

Warwick, Paul V. 1996. Coalition government membership in West European parliamentary democracies. *British Journal of Political Science* 26: 471–99. DOI: 10.1017/S0007123400007572

Wass, Hanna. 2007. Generations and socialization into electoral participation in Finland. *Scandinavian Political Studies* 30(1): 1–19. DOI: 10.1111/j.1467-9477.2007.00170.x

Watkin, Tim. 2014. Sorry, but ill-discipline still hounds Labour … Sorry. *Pundit*, 5 July. Available at: www.pundit.co.nz/content/sorry-but-ill-discipline-still-hounds-labour-sorry

Watkins, Tracy. 2014. Election battle lines drawn. *Stuff*, 2 March. Available at: www.stuff.co.nz/national/politics/9779949/Election-battle-lines-drawn

Watkins Tracy, Hamish Rutherford and Stacey Kirk. 2014. David Cunliffe admits mistake over Greens. *Stuff*, 23 September. Available at: www.stuff.co.nz/national/politics/10526624/David-Cunliffe-admits-mistake-over-Greens

Wattenberg, Martin. 2007. *Is voting for young people?* New York: Pearson Longman.

Welfare Working Group. 2011. Long-term benefit dependency: The issues. Wellington: Institute for Policy Studies. Available at: igps.victoria.ac.nz/WelfareWorkingGroup/Downloads/Final%20Report/WWG-Final-Recommendations-Report-22-February-2011.pdf

Westen, Peter. 1990. *Speaking equality*. Princeton: Princeton University Press.

Whelan, Megan and Elle Hunt. 2014. Sparking the youth vote. Wireless, Insight. *Radio New Zealand*. Available at: www.radionz.co.nz/national/programmes/insight/audio/20148525/insight-for-7-september-2014-sparking-the-youth-vote

Whitley Jr, Bernard E. 1999. Right-wing authoritarianism, social dominance orientation, and prejudice. *Journal of Personality and Social Psychology* 77(1): 126–34. DOI: 10.1037/0022-3514.77.1.126

Wilkinson, Richard and Kate Pickett. 2009. *The spirit level: Why greater equality makes societies stronger*. London: Bloomsbury Publishing.

Wilson, John. 2010. The origins of the Māori seats. In Maria Bargh, ed., *Māori and parliament: Diverse strategies and compromises*, 37–74. Wellington: Huia Publishers.

Wilson, Margaret. 2013. Impact of women's political leadership on democracy and development in New Zealand. In Farah Deeba Chowdhury, Margaret Wilson, Colleen Lowe Morna and Mukayi Makaya Magarangom, *Impact of women's political leadership on democracy and development*. London: Commonwealth Secretariat.

Women's Election Agenda Aotearoa. 2014. 100 steps on the road to equality for the women of Aotearoa. Available at: tinyurl.com/zs7pcst

World Economic Forum. 2015. The global gender gap report 2015. Geneva, World Economic Forum. Available at: reports.weforum.org/global-gender-gap-report-2015/

Wright, Erik Olin. 2009. Understanding class: Towards an integrated analytical approach. *New Left Review* 60: 101–16.

Young, Audrey. 2011. Head to head with National. *New Zealand Herald*, 29 October.

Zaller, John. 1992. *The nature and origins of mass opinion*. Cambridge: Cambridge University Press.

Appendix: Methods and tables

Statistical significance, confidence intervals and sources

In all Tables, ** indicates statistical significance at 0.01 or better (99 out of 100 possible samples) and * indicates significance at 0.05 (19 out of a possible 20 samples).

In most figures, confidence intervals at the 95 per cent level have been added. In post-estimation, sometimes statistically significant findings do have confidence intervals that overlap. We report this where necessary, leaving it up to readers to decide for themselves how reliable and robust they consider our findings to be.

All data is drawn from New Zealand Election Study (NZES) 2014, unless noted otherwise.

Weighting

Our dataset contains oversamples of young people and the Māori electorates and is affected by non-response bias that is based on political interest, political knowledge, education and turnout behaviour. We have weighted to correct for oversampling by gender, age and Māori electorates on a cell by cell basis, and on top of that by education, reported vote and validated turnout, on the basis of iterative weighting on the marginal frequencies. For users of the dataset, the weight variable is *dwtfin*.

Chapter 4

Table 4.A1: Multinomial logistic regression party choice at the 2014 election (reference category=National; N=2581)

	Not voting Coeff	r.s.e.	Labour Coeff	r.s.e.†	Green Coeff	r.s.e.	NZ First Coeff	r.s.e.	Conservative Coeff	r.s.e.	Other Coeff	r.s.e.
Female (male)	0.006	0.200	0.212	0.147	0.277	0.196	-0.401 *	0.203	-0.565	0.336	-0.278	0.366
Age (18 >)	-0.015 *	0.006	0.000	0.005	-0.038 **	0.006	0.004	0.007	-0.009	0.011	-0.003	0.011
(European and other)												
Māori	1.768 **	0.311	1.483 **	0.268	0.871 **	0.321	1.607 **	0.365	-1.202	1.073	3.663 **	0.344
Pasifika	1.686 *	0.653	1.584 *	0.643	-0.366	0.869	1.317	0.836	-15.169 **	0.625	2.360 *	1.093
Asian	0.729	0.382	-0.090	0.309	-1.858 **	0.523	-16.323 **	0.243	-0.817	0.728	1.410	0.781
(Mid-education)												
Low education	-0.225	0.227	-0.057	0.177	-0.309	0.246	-0.120	0.238	0.403	0.384	-0.217	0.359
High education	-0.552	0.296	0.566 **	0.202	0.869 **	0.219	0.002	0.297	0.295	0.391	0.248	0.491
Relative income (1-5)	-0.141	0.101	-0.508 **	0.085	-0.379 **	0.102	-0.551 **	0.122	-0.500 **	0.167	-0.617 **	0.236
(Private)												
Public sector	0.241	0.270	0.339	0.189	0.134	0.216	0.165	0.252	0.492	0.389	0.123	0.345
Self-employed	0.175	0.281	-0.184	0.226	0.487	0.273	-0.484	0.275	0.083	0.345	0.025	0.480
(Non-manual)												
Manual	0.231	0.240	0.631 **	0.177	0.000	0.257	0.145	0.250	-0.289	0.385	-0.582	0.408
Farming household	0.151	0.468	-0.644	0.544	-1.338 *	0.585	-0.924	0.590	-0.600	0.537	-0.108	0.753
No occupation Reported	0.442	0.484	-0.594	0.433	0.000	0.693	0.643	0.580	-1.838	1.108	-1.481	0.887
Union household	0.300	0.291	0.922 **	0.205	0.721 **	0.231	0.562	0.295	0.247	0.458	0.028	0.383

	Not voting		Labour		Green		NZ First		Conservative		Other	
	Coeff	r.s.e.†	Coeff	r.s.e.†	Coeff	r.s.e.	Coeff	r.s.e.	Coeff	r.s.e.	Coeff	r.s.e.
Church attendance (0–1)	-0.036	0.332	0.184	0.217	-0.810 *	0.386	0.373	0.297	2.010 **	0.333	-0.404	0.403
Assets scale (0–4)	-0.334 **	0.093	-0.389 **	0.073	-0.247 **	0.084	-0.097	0.104	0.139	0.183	-0.125	0.154
On benefit (not)	0.267	0.248	0.265	0.190	0.303	0.235	-0.271	0.310	-0.398	0.486	0.333	0.387
Major urban (not)	0.010	0.204	0.106	0.151	0.391 *	0.184	-0.331	0.212	-0.229	0.304	-0.080	0.321
Constant	1.285 *	0.568	0.929 *	0.456	1.431 **	0.539	0.196	0.613	-1.238	0.790	-0.492	1.361
R-squared	0.113											

Note: The baseline model employs multinomial logistic regression, with party vote for the National Party as the baseline category. This is one of the best forms of multivariate analysis for an unordered set of categories. By including not voting and all other parties in the model, all choices are accounted for and set against each other. The other category includes the Māori Party, Internet-MANA, the ACT Party, United Future and all other parties. Because these are a mixture of quite different parties, the category is in the model to be added into the overall pattern but are of little relevance in themselves. Not voting is also included, but will be discussed in chapter 11. The figures in this chapter and those following are usually post-estimation probabilities derived from the model, using the post-estimation command margins in Stata, the statistical analysis software primarily used for this book.

Significance: * p< 0.05; ** p< 0.01.

† r.s.e. = robust standard error.

Table 4.A2: Multinomial logistic regression party choice at the 2014 election, with parental party identification and income/assets interaction (reference category=National; N=2581)

	Not voting		Labour		Green		NZ First		Conservative		Other	
	Coeff	r.s.e.	Coeff	r.s.e.	Coeff	r.s.e.	Coeff	r.s.e.	Coeff	r.s.e.	Coeff	r.s.e.
Female (male)	0.005	0.201	0.228	0.155	0.266	0.195	-0.392	0.206	-0.564	0.345	-0.303	0.368
Age (18 >)	-0.015 *	0.006	-0.003	0.005	-0.042 **	0.007	-0.001	0.007	-0.007	0.010	-0.004	0.010
(European and other)												
Māori	1.574 **	0.316	1.170 **	0.282	0.565	0.336	1.224 **	0.368	-1.144	1.072	3.406 **	0.340

	Not voting		Labour		Green		NZ First		Conservative		Other	
	Coeff	r.s.e.	Coeff	r.s.e.	Coeff	r.s.e.	Coeff	r.s.e.	Coeff	r.s.e.	Coeff	r.s.e.
Pasifika	0.648 *	0.401	0.053	0.329	-1.640 **	0.520	-14.514 **	0.267	-0.777	0.731	1.245	0.769
Asian	1.339	0.663	1.354 *	0.623	-0.672	0.882	0.873	0.832	-13.395 **	0.652	1.409	1.163
(Mid-education)												
Low education	-0.287	0.226	-0.204	0.188	-0.428	0.247	-0.239	0.242	0.370	0.381	-0.249	0.365
High education	-0.527	0.295	0.597 **	0.213	0.861 **	0.226	0.071	0.306	0.281	0.387	0.337	0.484
Relative income (1–5)	-0.378	0.219	-0.702 **	0.190	-0.279	0.196	-0.217	0.283	-0.178	0.550	-0.828 *	0.323
(Private)												
Public sector	0.204	0.272	0.180	0.200	0.009	0.223	0.002	0.259	0.475	0.390	0.044	0.351
Self-employed	0.086	0.288	-0.251	0.233	0.428	0.264	-0.540	0.283	0.089	0.356	-0.082	0.493
(Non-manual)												
Manual	0.242	0.239	0.575 **	0.187	-0.079	0.253	0.071	0.252	-0.279	0.386	-0.588	0.411
Farming household	0.439	0.469	-0.145	0.517	-1.054	0.606	-0.409	0.589	-0.552	0.555	0.306	0.728
No occupation Reported	0.496	0.453	-0.502	0.435	0.185	0.675	0.809	0.576	-1.798	1.112	-1.366	0.872
Union household	0.317	0.302	0.980 **	0.220	0.751 **	0.233	0.595 *	0.296	0.223	0.458	0.025	0.392
Church attendance (0–1)	0.057	0.324	0.311	0.234	-0.681	0.385	0.481	0.311	1.972 **	0.328	-0.280	0.399
Assets scale (0–4)	-0.588 *	0.243	-0.605 **	0.213	-0.091	0.221	0.268	0.260	0.454	0.393	-0.298	0.486
On benefit (not)	0.253	0.251	0.317	0.202	0.394	0.235	-0.145	0.311	-0.342	0.492	0.355	0.369
Major urban (not)	-0.024	0.202	0.016	0.157	0.315	0.185	-0.394	0.215	-0.227	0.307	-0.129	0.295
Parents Labour (0–2)	0.045	0.125	0.567 **	0.097	0.657 **	0.120	0.660 **	0.133	-0.067	0.213	0.125	0.168
Parents National (0–2)	-0.532 **	0.148	-0.744 **	0.139	-0.223	0.123	-0.398 *	0.168	-0.123	0.173	-0.779 **	0.219

	Not voting Coeff	Not voting r.s.e.	Labour Coeff	Labour r.s.e.	Green Coeff	Green r.s.e.	NZ First Coeff	NZ First r.s.e.	Conservative Coeff	Conservative r.s.e.	Other Coeff	Other r.s.e.
Assets*income (interaction)	0.106	0.079	0.104	0.070	-0.043	0.070	-0.126	0.093	-0.114	0.166	0.094	0.155
Constant	2.081 **	0.784	1.468 *	0.667	1.116	0.742	-0.634	0.920	-2.112	1.384	0.229	1.244
R-squared	0.144											

Note: As for Table 4.A1.

Table 4.A3: Baseline model, plus security and insecurity, controlling for economic performance perceptions and aspirations

	Not voting Coeff	Not voting r.s.e.	Labour Coeff	Labour r.s.e.	Green Coeff	Green r.s.e.	NZ First Coeff	NZ First r.s.e.	Conservative Coeff	Conservative r.s.e.	Other Coeff	Other r.s.e.
Can find job	-0.129	0.085	-0.167 *	0.072	-0.048	0.091	-0.101	0.093	0.132	0.131	-0.141	0.141
Economy better	-0.800 **	0.116	-1.155 **	0.103	-0.929 **	0.107	-0.968 **	0.128	-0.497 **	0.174	-1.070 **	0.189
Better in 10 years	-0.016	0.090	-0.095	0.077	-0.394 **	0.090	-0.270 **	0.100	0.031	0.128	0.061	0.145
Fear income loss	0.112	0.082	0.184 **	0.070	-0.043	0.082	0.308 **	0.081	0.245	0.134	0.169	0.126
Constant	1.782 *	0.820	1.118	0.760	1.185	0.818	-0.981	0.947	-2.486	1.492	-0.391	1.240
N	2581											
R-squared	0.191											

Note: As for Table 4.A1. In addition, all variables in Table 4.A2 were also included in this model as controls, but are not shown here.

Table 4.A4: Left–right position, social structure and aspirations and insecurity

	Model 1			Model 2		
	Coeff		r.s.e.	Coeff		r.s.e.
Female (male)	−0.038		0.097	0.027		0.096
Age (25–65)	0.789	**	0.114	0.867	**	0.126
(European and other)						
Māori	−0.089		0.188	0.024		0.184
Pasifika	0.316		0.354	0.430		0.372
Asian	0.519	*	0.236	0.498	*	0.214
(Mid-education)						
Low education	0.264	*	0.117	0.235	*	0.115
High education	−0.600	**	0.125	−0.568	**	0.124
Relative income (1–5)	−0.009		0.112	−0.171		0.116
(Private)						
Public sector	−0.100		0.130	−0.105		0.128
Self-employed	0.071		0.141	0.049		0.139
(Non-manual)						
Manual	−0.174		0.114	−0.123		0.111
Farming household	0.463		0.330	0.423		0.298
No occupation Reported	−0.438	*	0.201	−0.311		0.205
Union household	−0.286	^	0.146	−0.164		0.142
Church attendance (0–1)	0.127		0.139	0.149		0.137
Assets scale (0–4)	−0.188		0.112	−0.277	*	0.114
On benefit (not)	−0.152		0.127	−0.171		0.124
Major urban (not)	−0.027		0.094	−0.046		0.090
Parents National/Labour (0–2)	0.336	**	0.037	0.290	**	0.036
Assets*income (interaction)	0.101	**	0.037	0.116	**	0.037
Can find job				−0.003		0.041
Economy last year				0.489	**	0.057
Aspirations				0.107	**	0.041
Fear income loss				−0.005		0.038
Constant	4.469	**	0.409	4.724	**	0.419
R-squared	0.159			0.216		
N	2,654			2,654		

Significance: * p< 0.05; ** p< 0.01.

Chapter 5

Table 5.A1: Valence model on the National vote

	Coeff		r.s.e.
Easy to find job	0.104		0.081
Improve in 10 years	−0.080		0.082
Income reduce next year	−0.118		0.074
Economy better or worse over last year	0.201		0.191
Like/dislike John Key	0.198		0.135
Dirty politics	−0.823	*	0.355
Dirty politics*Key like/dislike (interaction)	0.083		0.045
National 2011	2.009	**	0.409
Government performance	0.935	**	0.270
Performance*National 2011 (interaction)	−0.626		0.360
Economy*National 2011 (interaction)	0.037		0.266
Constant	−3.048	*	1.357
R-squared	0.460		
N	2,455		

Note: Controls for baseline social structure model applied but not shown.
Significance: * $p < 0.05$; ** $p < 0.01$.

Table 5.A2: Effects of liking or disliking Labour coalition/support parties on the National vote

	Coeff		r.s.e.
Left–right position	0.052		0.057
Like/dislike Green	−0.069		0.043
Like/dislike NZ First	−0.069		0.043
Like/dislike MANA	0.056		0.058
Like/dislike Internet	−0.115	*	0.059
Constant	−2.314		1.413
R-squared	0.469		
N	2,455		

Chapter 6

Factor analysis enables us to test correlations between these question responses. As Table 6.1 indicates, four factors or dimensions are apparent.

Table 6.A1: Dimensionality of government expenditure preferences

	Targeted benefits	Universal benefits	Environment	Security
Unemployment benefits	**0.898**	0.045	0.066	−0.055
Welfare benefits	**0.895**	0.067	0.130	0.024
Health	0.084	**0.878**	0.052	0.061
Education	0.024	**0.806**	0.249	−0.005
Superannuation	0.234	**0.474**	−0.050	0.427
Public transport	0.047	0.143	**0.766**	0.028
Environment	0.213	0.120	**0.716**	−0.062
Housing	0.379	0.273	**0.576**	0.075
Defence	0.117	−0.020	−0.144	**0.753**
Police and law	−0.155	0.284	0.075	**0.668**
Business and industry	−0.207	−0.121	0.369	**0.582**
% variance	26	16	11	10

Note: Principal component analysis, varimax rotation. Loadings in bold are those contributing the most to each factor.

The first dimension refers to the targeted benefits: unemployment and welfare; the second to universal services: health, education and New Zealand Superannuation. The third dimension relates to infrastructure (public transport and housing) and the environment. The last factor can be interpreted as tapping into preferences for security, most clearly through expenditure on defence, police and law enforcement, but also supporting business and therefore direct government investment in underpinning economic growth. The four dimensions amount together to a little under two-thirds of the total variation in responses among all the expenditure questions.

Table 6.A2: Correlates of opinions on universal and targeted benefits

	Universal			Targeted		
	Coeff		r.s.e.	Coeff		r.s.e.
Female	0.015	*	0.007	−0.012		0.011
Age	0.000		0.000	0.001	**	0.000
(European and others)						
Māori	−0.009		0.013	0.054	**	0.018

	Universal			Targeted		
	Coeff		r.s.e.	Coeff		r.s.e.
Asian	−0.015		0.013	−0.082	**	0.031
Pasifika	−0.037		0.024	0.065	*	0.031
(Post-school)						
School qualification	0.007		0.009	0.038	**	0.012
University	−0.011		0.009	0.056	**	0.014
Relative income	−0.009	*	0.004	−0.001		0.006
Wage/salary private						
Public sector	−0.004		0.008	−0.001		0.013
Self-employed	0.003		0.010	0.007		0.017
(Non-manual)						
Manual	−0.002		0.009	0.000		0.013
Farmer	0.001		0.019	0.016		0.030
No occupation	−0.039		0.026	0.099	**	0.029
Union house	0.042	**	0.009	0.001		0.014
Assets scale	−0.004		0.003	−0.021	**	0.005
Religious services	−0.012		0.011	0.047	**	0.014
On benefit	−0.010		0.009	0.070	**	0.013
Parental partisanship	−0.009	**	0.003	−0.008	*	0.004
Subjective working Class	0.003		0.009	−0.029	*	0.013
Could find job	−0.008	**	0.003	−0.018	**	0.005
Economy last year	0.002		0.005	−0.015	*	0.007
Better in 10 years	0.001		0.003	−0.004		0.005
Fears income loss	0.006	*	0.003	0.011	*	0.004
Left–right scale	−0.005	**	0.002	−0.023	**	0.003
Constant	0.708	**	0.022	0.491	**	0.031
R-squared	0.075			0.237		
N	2,672			2,672		

Notes: Age estimated in years. Left–right runs from 0–10, Relative income from 1–5, 3 being average income. University education vs not university educated. Working class: subjective working class 1, rest 0.

Significance: * $p < 0.05$; ** $p < 0.01$.

Table 6.A3: Agreement with raising the age of New Zealand superannuation

	Coeff	Sign.	r.s.e.
Age	0.002	**	0.000
Māori	−0.203	**	0.069
Age*Māori (interaction)	0.002		0.001
Female	−0.056	**	0.017
Right–left	−0.010	**	0.004
Relative income	0.034	**	0.009

	Coeff	Sign.	r.s.e.
University degree	0.045	*	0.020
Political knowledge	0.035	**	0.007
Working class	−0.059	**	0.020
Constant	0.320	*	0.048
R-squared	0.093		
N	2,807		

Notes: Ordinary Least Squares Regression on five-point scale indicating strong agreement (1) through to strong disagreement (0): 'Between 2020 and 2033, the age of eligibility for New Zealand Superannuation should be gradually increased to 67'. Age, education, income, left–right as Table 6.A1. The political knowledge scale is based on four questions, scored 1=right and 0=no or don't know. 'Which of these people was minister of finance before the 2011 election?' (Judith Collins, Bill English, Tony Ryall, or Nick Smith); 'What was the unemployment rate in New Zealand when it was recently released last month?' (four options, one correct); 'Which party won the second largest number of seats at the 2014 General election?'; 'Who is the current secretary-general of the United Nations?' (four recent secretaries, one of them the current). An alternative ordinal logit model produces almost identical results, as does an alterna'tive model including all the baseline social structure variables as controls (without interactions).

Significance: * p< 0.05; ** p< 0.01.

Table 6.A4: Social correlates of support for capital gains tax: Ordinary least squares regression

	Coeff		r.s.e.
Age	0.000		0.001
Left 0 (2)–right 10 (8)	−0.044	**	0.004
Own business or rental	0.037		0.048
Aspirational	−0.018	**	0.007
Union household	0.048	*	0.024
Parental party	−0.018	**	0.006
Age*business (interaction)	−0.002	*	0.001
Constant	0.759	**	0.032
R-squared	0.13		
N	2,807		

Notes: The question asked respondents on a 5-point scale to what extent they agreed or disagreed with the statement 'New Zealand needs a capital gains tax excluding the family home', rescaled to run between 0 and 1, with a higher score referring to supporting the introduction of a capital gains tax. 'Aspirational' relies on the question: 'Over the next 10 years or so, how likely or unlikely is it you will improve your standard of living?' Answering categories ranged between very likely (1) and very unlikely (5), but have been recoded in such a way that a higher value refers to believing that it is very likely that the standard of living will improve. An alternative ordinal logit model produces almost identical results, as does an alternative model including all the baseline social structure variables as controls (without interactions). The slope estimate for left–right is between 2 and 8 of the 0–10 point scale to reduce the apparent effect of extreme values.

Significance: * p< 0.05; ** p< 0.01.

Table 6.A5: The Treaty of Waitangi as part of the law

	Coeff	Sign.	r.s.e.
Ethnic background (*Reference*: European)			
Māori	0.346	**	0.076
Pasifika	0.171	**	0.059
Asian	−0.034		0.034
Age	−0.002	**	0.001
Māori*age (interaction)	0.001		0.002
Female	0.058	**	0.016
Left (0)–right (10)	−0.033	**	0.004
Assets	−0.023	**	0.008
Relative income	0.027	**	0.009
Level of education (*Reference*: middle education)			
Low education	−0.044	*	0.019
University degree	0.084	**	0.021
Public sector	0.037		0.020
Political knowledge	0.016	*	0.008
Constant	0.602	**	0.045
R-squared	0.22		
N	2,807		

Note: An alternative ordinal logit model produces almost identical results, as does an alternative model including all the baseline social structure variables as controls (without interactions).

Significance: * p< 0.01; ** p< 0.05.

Table 6.A6: Demographic and attitudinal correlates of opposition to inequality

	Coeff	Sign	r.s.e.
Age	0.001	**	0.000
University degree	0.029	*	0.015
Left (0)–right (10)	−0.041	**	0.003
Relative income	−0.031	**	0.007
Assets	−0.013	*	0.006
Political knowledge	0.014	**	0.005
Church attendance	0.055	**	0.021
Working class	0.052	**	0.016
Easy to find job	−0.019	**	0.005
Better in 10 years	−0.014	*	0.006
Constant	0.897	**	0.036
R-squared	0.209		
N	2,672		

Significance: * p< 0.05; ** p< 0.01.

Table 6.A7a: The Labour vote or not, 2014 by positional and valence variables

	Model 1			Model 2			Model 3			Model 4		
	Coeff		r.s.e.	Coeff		r.s.e.	Coeff		r.s.e.	Coeff		r.s.e.
Age	0.009	*	0.004	0.016	**	0.004	-0.002		0.005	0.005		0.005
Māori	-0.415		0.238	-0.673	**	0.251	-0.763	**	0.293	-0.897	**	0.308
Manual or service	0.588	**	0.153	0.503	**	0.167	0.564	**	0.180	0.481	*	0.191
Union	0.483	**	0.175	0.460	*	0.195	0.378		0.207	0.407		0.212
Parental party	-0.313	**	0.059	-0.256	**	0.069	-0.213	**	0.070	-0.189	*	0.075
Dislike/like Key				-0.220	**	0.026				-0.167	**	0.030
Dislike/like Cunliffe				0.329	**	0.036				0.283	**	0.040
Left-right	-0.298	**	0.044	-0.179	**	0.046	-0.177	**	0.045	-0.102	*	0.052
Authoritarian	0.096	*	0.039	0.103	*	0.041	0.073		0.043	0.083		0.044
Against inequality	1.400	**	0.364	0.606		0.399	1.216	**	0.440	0.648		0.463
Capital gains tax (exp)	0.520	**	0.135	0.347	*	0.152	0.500	**	0.149	0.378	*	0.157
Women MPs	0.250		0.181	0.195		0.195	0.251		0.205	0.245		0.221
Treaty	0.577	*	0.253	0.524	*	0.263	0.692	**	0.262	0.608	*	0.269
Pension age	-0.519	*	0.223	-0.485	*	0.238	-0.480	*	0.237	-0.362		0.246
Universal services	0.256		0.567	0.138		0.603	0.192		0.671	0.094		0.692
Targeted benefits	1.056	**	0.382	0.084		0.399	0.776		0.442	-0.055		0.454
2011 Labour vote							2.355	**	0.172	2.034	**	0.181
Constant	-3.996	**	0.646	-3.856	**	0.703	-4.549	**	0.734	-4.542	**	0.828
R-squared	0.213			0.325			0.360			0.422		
N	2,572			2,572			2,572			2,572		

Notes: Women's representation: A scale between –1 and 1 based on two questions: 'Should there be more efforts to increase the number of women MPs. If so, what means would you prefer?'; and 'Looking at the types of people who are MPs, do you think there should be more, fewer, or about the same number as there are now: women'. Capital gains tax opinion is estimated by an exponential form of the variable.

Significance: * p< 0.05; ** p< 0.01.

Table 6.A7b: The Labour vote or not, 2014 by positional and valence variables

	Model 5			Model 6		
	Coeff		r.s.e.	Coeff		r.s.e.
Age	−0.003		0.005	0.003		0.005
Māori	−0.678	*	0.267	−0.826	**	0.287
Manual or service	0.526	**	0.184	0.454	*	0.196
Union	0.358		0.201	0.400		0.210
Parental party	−0.194	**	0.072	−0.180	*	0.078
Dislike/like Key				−0.160	**	0.031
Dislike/like Cunliffe				0.286	**	0.040
Left–right	−0.162	**	0.045	−0.094		0.051
Authoritarian	0.069		0.042	0.079		0.044
Against inequality	1.620	*	0.715	0.766		0.699
Capital gains tax (exp)	0.445	*	0.218	0.311		0.221
Women MPs	0.207		0.209	0.206		0.224
Treaty	1.462	**	0.350	1.272	**	0.347
Pension age	−0.686	*	0.331	−0.725	*	0.342
Universal services	0.274		0.669	0.185		0.702
Targeted benefits	0.839		0.447	0.007		0.460
2011 Labour vote	3.594	**	0.819	2.540	**	0.870
Interactions:						
2011 Labour vote interacted with						
Against inequality	−0.923		0.932	−0.393		0.953
Capital gains tax (exp)	0.049		0.302	0.105		0.312
Treaty	−1.444	**	0.459	−1.258	**	0.481
Pension age	0.480		0.466	0.722		0.496
Constant	−5.173	**	0.916	−4.810	**	0.967
R-squared	0.368			0.427		
N	2,572			2,572		

Chapter 7

Table 7.A1: Likelihood of voting Green or not, logistic regression

	Coeff		Std. Err.	Coeff		Std. Err.
Female				0.16		0.18
Age				−0.03	**	0.01
Ethnicity (*Ref.*=European or other)						
Māori				−0.60	*	0.26
Asian				−1.15	*	0.45
Pacific				−1.34	*	0.64
Education (*Ref.*=post-school)						
School only				−0.05		0.24
University degree				0.65	*	0.23
Relative income				−0.11		0.10
Sector of employment (*Ref.*=private sector)						
Public sector				−0.23		0.22
Self-employed				0.45		0.27
Occupation (*Ref.*=non-manual)						
Manual				−0.35		0.25
Farmer				−0.95		0.55
No occupation				−0.37		0.54
Union household				0.29		0.22
Wealth/assets				0.01		0.08
On benefit				0.02		0.23
Left–right	−0.71	**	0.10	−0.66	**	0.10
Authoritarian	−0.37	**	0.09	−0.27	**	0.09
Left–right*authoritarian (interaction)	0.04	*	0.02	0.03		0.02
Constant	1.88	**	0.48	2.89	**	0.73
Pseudo R-squared	0.17			0.22		

Table 7.A2: Split voting, 2014 election (total percentages)

Party vote	ACT	Conserv-ative	Green	Internet-MANA	Labour	Māori	National	NZ First	United Future	Others	Independents & non-list parties	Candidate informals	Party vote only	Party vote
							Electorate vote							
ACT	0.18	0.03	0.02	0.00	0.09	0.00	0.32	0.01	0.00	0.00	0.00	0.02	0.01	0.69
Conservative	0.03	1.59	0.06	0.01	0.40	0.01	1.66	0.07	0.02	0.03	0.01	0.03	0.04	3.96
Green Party	0.03	0.09	3.69	0.18	5.05	0.15	0.91	0.13	0.02	0.08	0.03	0.08	0.21	10.65
Internet-MANA	0.01	0.02	0.16	0.60	0.39	0.05	0.05	0.02	0.00	0.03	0.01	0.01	0.07	1.41
Labour Party	0.04	0.20	1.31	0.40	20.58	0.32	0.79	0.36	0.04	0.10	0.03	0.22	0.64	25.02
Māori Party	0.00	0.01	0.06	0.09	0.26	0.66	0.14	0.02	0.00	0.01	0.00	0.02	0.05	1.32
National Party	0.80	1.04	0.89	0.06	2.79	0.28	39.00	0.47	0.47	0.18	0.05	0.33	0.49	46.83
NZ First	0.05	0.34	0.53	0.16	3.23	0.23	1.60	1.91	0.02	0.15	0.05	0.20	0.15	8.62
United Future	0.00	0.01	0.02	0.00	0.05	0.00	0.10	0.01	0.02	0.00	0.00	0.00	0.00	0.22
Others	0.01	0.03	0.12	0.03	0.21	0.03	0.15	0.04	0.00	0.15	0.01	0.02	0.03	0.84
Party Informals	0.00	0.01	0.01	0.01	0.12	0.01	0.05	0.01	0.00	0.00	0.00	0.21	0.01	0.45
Electorate vote	1.15	3.36	6.86	1.54	33.16	1.74	44.77	3.04	0.61	0.72	0.20	1.15	1.70	100.00

Note: Others are ACT New Zealand, Aotearoa Legalise Cannabis Party, Ban1080, Democrats for Social Credit, Focus New Zealand, NZ Independent Coalition, The Civilian Party.

Source: Electoral Commission 2017 (Recalculated from original source).

Chapter 8

Table 8.A1: Social groups and authoritarian–libertarianism: Ordinary least squares regression

	Coeff		r.s.e.
Female	−0.10	*	0.05
Age	0.00		0.00
(European)			
Māori	0.61	**	0.07
Pasifika	0.44	*	0.19
Asian	0.69	**	0.11
(Post-school qualification)			
School only	0.14	**	0.06
University	−0.38	**	0.07
Relative income	−0.07	*	0.03
(Private sector wage/salary)			
Public	−0.07		0.06
Self-employed	0.03		0.07
(Non-manual household)			
Manual	0.09		0.06
Farmer	−0.07		0.13
No occupation	−0.20		0.17
Union household	−0.17	*	0.07
Assets scale	−0.05	*	0.02
On benefit	−0.12		0.07
Church attendance	0.17	*	0.07
Urban	−0.12	*	0.05
Constant	0.35	*	0.15
R-squared	0.14		

Table 8.A2: Social groups and attitudes to immigration: Ordinary least squares regression

	Coeff		r.s.e.	Coeff		r.s.e.
Female	−0.080		0.052	−0.08		0.05
Age	0.004	*	0.002	0.00		0.00
(European)						
Māori	−0.335	**	0.094	−0.10		0.10
Pasifika	0.472	**	0.111	0.29		0.16
Asian	0.206		0.141	0.47	**	0.12

	Coeff		r.s.e.	Coeff		r.s.e.
(Post-school qualification)						
School only	−0.123	*	0.061	−0.07		0.06
University	0.179	*	0.071	0.09		0.07
Relative income	0.182	**	0.027	0.14	**	0.03
(Private sector wage/salary)						
Public	0.084		0.067	0.06		0.06
Self-employed	0.053		0.066	0.04		0.07
(Non-manual household)						
Manual	−0.025		0.064	0.00		0.06
Farmer	0.005		0.127	0.03		0.13
No occupation	0.131		0.140	0.14		0.15
Union household	−0.104		0.068	−0.11		0.07
Assets scale	0.014		0.025	0.00		0.02
On benefit	0.113		0.066	0.11		0.06
Married	−0.111		0.057	−0.10		0.06
Church attendance	0.160	*	0.071	0.19	*	0.07
New Zealand born				−0.27	**	0.07
Better in 10 years				−0.05	*	0.02
Can find job				0.07	**	0.02
Fear of income loss				0.00		0.02
Economy last year				0.16	**	0.03
Inequality				−0.03		0.11
Left–right				−0.08	**	0.01
Authoritarian–libertarian				−0.04	**	0.01
Constant	1.824	**	0.143	2.88	**	0.21
R-squared	0.10			0.16		
N	2,727			2,727		

Note: Those most in favour 5, those most against 1.

Table 8.A3: Social groups and attitudes to abortion: Ordinary least squares regression

	Coeff		r.s.e.	Coeff		r.s.e.
Female	−0.15	*	0.07	−0.13	*	0.06
Age	0.00	*	0.00	0.00	*	0.00
(European)						
Māori	0.50	**	0.13	0.39	**	0.12
Asian	0.66	**	0.16	0.56	**	0.16
Pasifika	0.58	*	0.25	0.52	*	0.25

	Coeff		r.s.e.	Coeff		r.s.e.
(Post-school qualification)						
School only	0.14		0.08	0.11		0.08
University	−0.26	**	0.08	−0.18	**	0.08
Relative income	−0.06		0.04	−0.06		0.04
(Private sector wage/salary)						
Public	0.01		0.09	0.03		0.09
Self-employed	0.09		0.10	0.08		0.10
(Non-manual household)						
Manual	0.11		0.08	0.10		0.08
Farmer	−0.06		0.15	−0.07		0.16
No occupation	0.14		0.17	0.15		0.17
Union household	−0.16		0.08	−0.11		0.08
Assets scale	0.01		0.03	0.02		0.03
On benefit	0.27	**	0.09	0.29	**	0.09
Married	0.04		0.07	0.02		0.07
Church attendance	1.98	**	0.10	1.95	**	0.10
Inequality				−0.14		0.13
Left–right				0.02		0.02
Authoritarian–libertarian				0.08	**	0.02
Constant	1.78	**	0.19	1.31	**	0.24
R-squared	0.29			0.30		

Table 8.A4: New Zealand First vote choice models

	Coeff		r.s.e.
Female	−0.473	*	0.215
Age	0.005		0.008
(European)			
Māori	−0.045		0.389
Asian	0.000		0.691
(Post-school qualification)			
School only	−0.146		0.230
University	0.056		0.308
Relative income	−0.039		0.123
(Private sector wage/salary)			
Public	0.054		0.249
Self-employed	−0.544		0.282
(Non-manual household)			
Manual	−0.141		0.245
Farmer	−0.416		0.599

	Coeff		r.s.e.
No occupation	0.868		0.555
Union household	0.031		0.312
Assets scale	0.174		0.101
On benefit	−0.299		0.314
Married	0.078		0.216
Church attendance	0.458		0.323
National parents	−0.284	**	0.087
Born in New Zealand	0.453		0.280
Better 10 years	−0.185	*	0.085
Could find job	−0.015		0.084
Fear income reduction	0.150	*	0.077
Economy last year	−0.206		0.116
Left–right	−0.034		0.046
Authoritarian–libertarian	0.104		0.055
Treaty not law	0.191	*	0.087
Targeted social	−0.038		0.715
Universal social	−0.112		0.503
For immigration	−0.295	*	0.116
Against inequality	0.300		0.484
Abortion wrong	0.005		0.072
Constant	−3.890	**	0.955
R-squared	0.121		
N	2,496		

Table 8.A5: Conservative Party vote choice models

	Coeff		r.s.e.	Coeff		r.s.e.
Female	−0.503		0.304	−0.421		0.285
Age	−0.006		0.012	−0.008		0.011
(European)						
Māori	−2.514	*	1.084	−2.106		1.139
Asian	−0.907		0.817	−0.853		0.849
(Post-school qualification)						
School only	0.545		0.373	0.364		0.370
University	0.151		0.373	0.305		0.399
Relative income	−0.403	*	0.163	−0.423	*	0.189
(Private sector wage/salary)						
Public	0.352		0.362	0.278		0.366
Self-employed	0.031		0.343	−0.054		0.357

	Coeff		r.s.e.	Coeff		r.s.e.
(Non-manual household)						
Manual	−0.383		0.387	−0.286		0.403
Farmer	−0.679		0.577	−0.527		0.555
No occupation	−1.715		1.109	−1.925		1.228
Union household	−0.243		0.435	−0.195		0.469
Assets scale	0.287		0.180	0.189		0.188
On benefit	−0.493		0.487	−0.551		0.473
Married	1.169	**	0.429	1.034	*	0.429
Church attendance	2.024	**	0.314	1.527	**	0.392
National parents	0.181		0.097	0.132		0.096
Born in New Zealand	0.140		0.370	0.189		0.386
Left–right				0.124		0.066
Authoritarian–libertarian				−0.133		0.079
Treaty not law				0.276		0.151
Targeted social				−1.744		1.321
Universal social				−0.419		0.810
For immigration				−0.172		0.175
Against inequality				−0.090		0.690
Abortion wrong				0.349	**	0.120
Constant	−4.068	**	0.855	−3.557	**	1.370
R-squared	0.143			0.19		
N	2,551			2,551		

Table 8.A6: Liking or disliking the ACT Party

	Coeff		r.s.e.	Coeff		r.s.e.
Female	0.28	*	0.12	0.43	**	0.11
Age	−0.01	*	0.00	−0.01		0.00
(European)						
Māori	0.32		0.19	0.35		0.19
Pasifika	1.03	**	0.34	0.74	*	0.31
Asian	1.34	**	0.36	0.96	**	0.32
(Post-school qualification)						
School only	0.10		0.14	0.01		0.13
University	−0.51	**	0.16	−0.24		0.15
Relative income	0.18	**	0.06	−0.01		0.06
(Private sector wage/salary)						
Public	−0.30	*	0.15	−0.25		0.13
Self-employed	−0.29		0.18	−0.33	*	0.17
(Non-manual household)						
Manual	−0.03		0.14	0.06		0.14

	Coeff		r.s.e.	Coeff		r.s.e.
Farmer	0.11		0.29	0.07		0.30
No occupation	0.47		0.43	0.39		0.35
Union household	−0.61	**	0.16	−0.32	*	0.15
Assets scale	0.17	**	0.06	0.10	*	0.05
On benefit	0.00		0.15	0.00		0.14
Married	−0.23		0.13	−0.33	**	0.12
Church attendance	0.41	**	0.15	0.17		0.17
National parents	0.20	**	0.04	0.07		0.04
NZ born	−0.24		0.14	−0.07		0.14
Urban–not urban	−0.08		0.12	0.02		0.11
Better 10 years				0.19	**	0.05
Could find job				0.00		0.05
Fears income loss				0.03		0.05
Economy last year				0.00		0.07
Left–right				0.17	**	0.03
Authoritarian–libertarian				0.05		0.03
Treaty				0.11	*	0.05
Universal social				−1.25	**	0.43
Targeted social				−0.30		0.34
Immigration				0.22	**	0.06
Inequality				−1.50	**	0.24
Abortion				0.14	**	0.05
Constant	3.11	**	0.39	2.91		0.62
R-squared	0.089			0.206		
N	2,672			2,672		

Chapter 10

The Māori Electorate NZES data

The 2014 NZES oversampled the Māori electorates, and within that young voters as well. The response rate for those freshly sampled (N=284) was 19.2 per cent. Another 263 Māori electorate respondents came from the 2011 panel that, overall, had a 61.7 per cent response rate from those responding in 2011. The full Māori electorate sample has an N of 547. Despite the low response rate, within expected margins of error it contained a good representation of the various groups of voters, although non-voters were under-represented. Findings are based on weighting to more accurately reflect the vote/non-vote distributions for the party and electorate votes.

Table 10.A1: Comparing candidate effects on the Labour vote: Māori electorate and the general electorate vote

	Coeff		r.s.e.
Age	−0.012	**	0.003
Female	−0.110		0.111
Parents Labour	0.396	**	0.071
Favours Labour candidate	2.930	**	0.151
Favours Māori Party candidate	−0.686	*	0.306
Labour MP incumbent	0.209		0.216
Favours MANA candidate	−0.785		0.433
Labour Party most favoured	2.303	**	0.191
Māori electorate	0.162		0.222
Labour candidate*Māori electorate (interaction)	−1.482	**	0.351
Constant	−1.754	**	0.222
/lnsig2u	−2.213		0.633
sigma_u	0.331		0.105
rho	0.032		0.020
N (Clusters)	2,805 (71)		

Note: This is a multilevel model with random effects, taking account of the clustering of the electorate-level data. The dependent variable is an electorate vote for Labour versus the rest. To make sure that the effects we identify are not due to deeper party preferences or to the advantages of incumbency, we control for the following: whether there is an incumbent Labour MP; whether or not people report that Labour is the party they most like; and preferences for other candidates. We also control for parental party preferences for Labour. By interacting a preference for the Labour candidate or not with Māori or general electorate, we therefore estimate the relative effects of candidate preferences in the two classes of electorate.

Table 10.A2: Baseline model of voting in the Māori electorates: The electorate vote (multinomial logistic regression)

	Non-vote			Green			Māori Party			MANA		
Age	-0.013		0.013	-0.007		0.021	0.013	**	0.012	0.018		0.014
Iwi connection	-0.770	*	0.444	0.195		0.647	0.260		0.454	0.642		0.589
Speaks te reo	0.239		0.737	-1.044		1.128	1.450	**	0.599	1.016		0.629
Low education	0.093		0.409	-0.421		0.568	-0.266	*	0.394	-0.248		0.418
Urban	-0.298		0.390	1.194	**	0.610	-0.478		0.426	-0.030		0.438
Manual Household	0.560		0.394	-0.295		0.673	0.238		0.411	1.078	**	0.426
Assets scale	0.082		0.167	-0.559	**	0.253	0.285	**	0.128	0.094		0.162
Parents Labour‡	0.017		0.213	-0.624	**	0.252	-0.145		0.224	-0.283		0.201
Constant	1.114	*	0.629	-0.731		1.090	-1.487	**	0.636	-2.411	***	0.697
R-squared	0.085											
N	448											

Notes: Labour vote is the missing or residual category in the multinomial logit model, all other behaviour is thus measured against a Labour vote. Not voting is indistinguishable from Labour voting, at least in terms of statistical significance.

‡ This variable measures parental partisanship and has a score of 2 when both parents voted Labour, one when one of the parents voted Labour, and zero when there is no knowledge about parental partisanship.

Significance: * p< 0.05; ** p< 0.01.

Table 10.A3: Baseline model of voting in the Māori electorates: The party vote (multinomial logistic regression)

	Non-vote			National			Green			NZ First			Māori Party			MANA		
Age	-0.015	*	0.012	0.013		0.015	-0.026	*	0.013	0.014	*	0.012	0.019		0.014	0.050	*	0.014
Iwi connection	-1.049	*	0.445	-0.788		0.662	0.307		0.555	-0.929		0.504	0.036		0.527	-0.098		0.730
Speaks te reo	-0.247		0.746	-1.551		1.118	0.591		0.703	-0.091		0.649	0.429		0.657	1.007		0.642
Low education	0.100		0.404	0.787		0.577	-0.432		0.486	0.632		0.446	-0.412		0.393	-0.782		0.493
Urban	0.079		0.382	-0.184		0.666	0.261		0.482	0.368		0.433	-0.321		0.427	0.761		0.484
Manual Household	0.215		0.400	-0.828		0.660	-0.229		0.490	-0.529		0.478	0.638		0.422	-0.045		0.441
Assets scale	0.329	*	0.168	0.652	**	0.218	0.428	*	0.167	0.461	*	0.184	0.478	**	0.146	0.110		0.244
Parents Labour‡	0.169		0.217	-0.436		0.275	0.056		0.255	0.110		0.248	-0.116		0.195	-0.147		0.260
Constant	0.816		0.612	-2.496	**	0.797	-1.007		0.619	-2.211	**	0.777	-2.654	**	0.757	-3.945	**	0.918
R-squared	0.100																	
N	511																	

Notes: Labour vote is the missing or residual category in the multinomial logit model, all other behaviour is thus measured against a Labour vote. Not voting is indistinguishable from Labour voting, at least in terms of statistical significance.

‡ This variable measures parental partisanship and has a score of 2 when both parents voted Labour, one when one of the parents voted Labour, and zero when there is no knowledge about parental partisanship.

Significance: * p< 0.05; ** p< 0.01.

Table 10.A4: Dimensional model of voting in the Māori electorates: The party vote

	Non-vote		National		Green		NZ First		Māori		MANA	
	B	SE	B	SE	B	SE	B	SE	B	SE	B	SE
Age	-0.023 *	0.013	0.010	0.018	-0.043 **	0.015	0.004	0.013	0.014	0.016	0.047 **	0.017
Iwi connection	-0.738	0.467	-0.389	0.701	0.627	0.628	-0.687	0.540	-0.211	0.606	-0.084	0.736
Speaks te reo	0.125	0.941	-1.186	1.316	0.044	0.761	0.257	0.699	0.483	0.846	0.146	0.786
Low education	0.173	0.426	0.826	0.609	-0.174	0.478	0.930	0.498	-0.276	0.452	-1.101	0.605
Urban	-0.061	0.406	-0.525	0.760	0.445	0.438	0.265	0.467	-0.142	0.455	0.786	0.606
Manual household	0.283	0.420	-0.820	0.738	-0.203	0.450	-0.661	0.499	0.945	0.495	-0.239	0.560
Assets scale	0.391 *	0.176	0.683 **	0.253	0.541 **	0.185	0.526 **	0.200	0.503 **	0.164	0.311	0.268
Parents Labour	0.150	0.222	-0.399	0.329	-0.045	0.242	0.068	0.249	-0.064	0.211	-0.496	0.334
Likes Labour c.†	-1.799 **	0.488	-1.301 **	0.642	-1.184 *	0.506	-2.124 **	0.550	-0.824	0.568	-2.231 *	1.007
Likes MANA c.	-0.292	0.754	-14.429 *	0.852	1.062	0.796	-1.042	0.843	-2.446 *	1.219	2.857 **	0.826
Likes Māori c.	-0.324	0.616	-0.593	0.792	-0.320	0.644	-0.634	0.620	1.447 **	0.476	-0.532	0.848
Incumb MRIMP	-1.401 *	0.560	-1.745 *	0.819	-0.020	0.660	-1.382 *	0.592	0.225	0.478	-1.237	0.770
Treaty	-0.579	0.627	-1.834 **	0.691	-0.487	0.717	-0.562	0.730	0.502	0.655	0.647	0.997
Inequality	-1.986 *	0.833	-2.351 *	0.954	1.599	1.169	0.343	0.928	0.110	0.895	-0.100	1.330
Constant	4.211 **	0.966	1.791	1.174	-0.232	1.436	-0.471	1.178	-2.676 *	1.144	-3.262	1.730
R-squared	.20											
N	511											

Significance: * p< 0.05; ** p< 0.01.

† c. = candidate.

Chapter 11

Regression Model, Figure 11.3

Data for the figure is estimated from a logistic regression of vote/not vote against age, female/male, Māori on Māori roll, Māori on general roll (with non-Māori on the general roll as a residual category). Gender and the two variables are also interacted with the age variable, which is continuous, using the mid-point within five-year bands.

Table 11.A1: Vote/not vote by age, gender, Māori and electorate

Voted or not	Coeff		Linear Std. Err
Female	0.530	**	0.079
Age	0.032	**	0.001
Māori electorate	−0.676	**	0.130
Māori on general roll	−0.366	*	0.148
Residual: non-Māori			
Interactions with age			
Female	−0.009	**	0.002
Māori electorate	−0.001		0.003
Māori on general roll	0.003		0.003
Constant	−0.352	**	0.059
Pseudo R-squared = 0.48			
N = 29,989			

Significance: * p< 0.05; ** p< 0.01.
Source: Vowles 2015b.

Table 11.A2: Non-voting and social structure, 2014 election

	Coeff		r.s.e.
Female	0.039		0.187
Age	−0.041	**	0.010
Assets scale	−0.479	*	0.208
Age*assets (interaction)	0.008	*	0.004
(European)			
Māori	0.548	*	0.238
Asian	0.933	*	0.379
Pasifika	0.340		0.449
(Post-school qualification)			
School only	−0.225		0.212
University	−0.859	**	0.294

	Coeff		r.s.e.
Relative income	0.062		0.090
Constant	1.003		0.575
Pseudo R-squared = 0.07			

Significance: * p< 0.05; ** p< 0.01.

Table 11.A3: How non-voters might have voted

	Social structure	Security	Values	Positional	Competence	Voters
Labour	27	27	29	25	25	26
National	42	37	38	40	37	47
Green	11	12	9	9	12	11
NZ First	8	11	10	10	10	9
Conservative	3	4	4	6	6	4
Maori	3	4	4	3	3	1
Internet-MANA	4	4	3	3	2	1
Other	3	3	4	4	4	1
	100	100	100	100	100	100

Notes: Social structure model: gender, age, ethnicity, education, relative income, employment sector, occupation, union household or not, assets scale, on benefit or not; Security model: adds difficulty of finding a job, economy over last year, aspirations over 10 years, likelihood of loss of income; Values: adds left–right scale and authoritarian–libertarian scale; Positional: adds inequality attitudes, environmental attitudes, universal welfare, targeted welfare, infrastructure and security expenditure scales; Competence: adds government performance and liking/disliking of John Key. The data was additionally weighted by the age structure of non-voting derived from the New Zealand Longitudinal Turnout Study (NZLTS). Figures in Table 11.A3 are the estimated frequencies among the non-voters, except for the column to the right which provides that among the voters.